W9-CLD-446

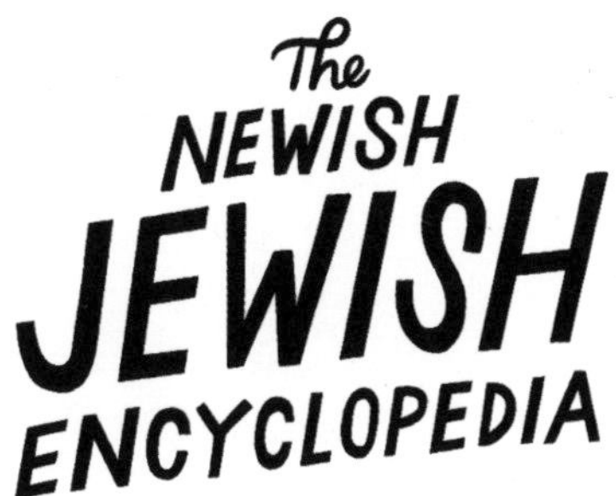
The
NEWISH
JEWISH
ENCYCLOPEDIA

The NEWISH JEWISH ENCYCLOPEDIA

From Abraham to Zabar's and Everything in Between

STEPHANIE BUTNICK, LIEL LEIBOVITZ, AND MARK OPPENHEIMER

Hosts of *Tablet* Magazine's *Unorthodox* Podcast

Artisan | New York

See page 319 for photo credits.

Tablet, formed in 2009, is the premier American Jewish magazine. It's a project of the not-for-profit Nextbook, Inc.

Library of Congress Cataloging-in-Publication Data is on file.

ISBN 978-1-57965-893-9

Design by Evi-O.Studio / Evi O & Susan Le
Cover and creative direction by Michelle Ishay-Cohen
Cover lettering by Kirby Salvador
Maps on pages 49, 86, 141, 146, 199, and 220 copyright © Roderick Mills

Font information: Ouroboros designed by Ariel Martín Pérez; Resistance Regular designed by A collective; Terminal Grotesque initiated by Raphaël Bastide, modified and contributed by Jérémy Landes; VTF Misterpixel Regular designed by Christophe Badani; Sporting Grotesque Bold and Regular initiated by Lucas Le Bihan, modified and contributed by George Triantafyllakos and Maciej Połczyński

Published by Artisan
A division of Workman Publishing Co., Inc.
225 Varick Street
New York, NY 10014-4381
artisanbooks.com

Artisan is a registered trademark of Workman Publishing Co., Inc.

Published simultaneously in Canada by Thomas Allen & Son, Limited

Printed in China

First printing, September 2019

10 9 8 7 6 5 4 3 2 1

To the *Unorthodox* listeners,
the J-Crew,
who have been with us since 5775

A Note About Your Guides

In the wee hours of June 9, 2009, a small group of writers and editors pressed "publish" on a new online magazine devoted to Jewish life and culture. We called it *Tablet*.

One of those present that very first morning was Liel Leibovitz. At the time, everyone who knew him (or knew of him) focused on his stridently left-wing politics, with which he would regularly set fire to various American Jewish spaces. I only cared that he wrote brilliantly, had a PhD in video games from Columbia, and had translated Proust into Hebrew.

A year and a half later, I received an internship application from a graduate student at New York University named Stephanie Butnick. All I knew when I hired her was that she had spent the summer studying at Auschwitz and (unrelatedly, I think) had profound and complex thoughts about Taylor Swift.

A few years after that, my friend Mark Oppenheimer—a newspaper editor, author, and Yale lecturer who was then writing the religion column for the *New York Times*—got me out of a bind when he came aboard temporarily to cover for me during my maternity leave.

Mark soon became so essential that not only did he stay at *Tablet*, but *I* eventually had to cover for *him* when he took paternity leave. At this point, Stephanie is effectively the boss of everyone, including me. Liel is now hated by all the people who used to love him, and loved by everyone else.

Most impressively, these three unlikely friends and colleagues—who can't find one thing on which they comprehensively agree—have become a massively influential font of wisdom and connection in American Jewish life. How?

After years of fierce but generative arguing in the privacy of our newsroom—about Israel, the Holocaust, the fetishization of food, and Gal Gadot—Mark and Stephanie and Liel decided to let people listen in, by creating a weekly podcast called *Unorthodox*.

It is decidedly not the booming, uncontestable voice from behind some pulpit that we've all been listening to (or avoiding) for decades. What seemed clear was that we were all starting to forget (if we ever knew) how real Jews talk to one another: forcefully, even angrily; with enough respect to come prepared with knowledge of some kind; delighted by the chance (however slim) to agree with another Jew; condescending yet somehow unashamed about their admiration for one another; with exasperation and excitement and even venom—but most of all, with a profound sense of human attachment.

You'll find all that here in this new encyclopedia. It is a feast of knowledge—that enviable table at the Jewish deli filled with people who look like they know a few important things about life, who are challenging one another, and who share, above all else, a deep bond. Pull up a chair; grab a pickle. Trust me: you're going to want to stay awhile.

Alana Newhouse
Founder and editor in chief of *Tablet*

Welcome!

You picked up this book, which means you must be a little curious about Jews, or Jewish life, or Judaism. Maybe you grew up Jewish but barely remember anything from Hebrew school. Maybe you know a lot about Jewish practice but not about Jews and popular culture, or you know a lot about our people's relationship to food but not enough about our engagement with politics. Maybe you love nothing more than being a member of the tribe, but have never felt truly connected to a Jewish community, or you live somewhere where there simply isn't one. Maybe you're dating a Jew, or thinking of becoming a Jew yourself. Maybe you finished binge-watching *Seinfeld* and are dying to know what's the deal with babka or shiksappeal.

Whoever you are, we have just one bit of rabbinic wisdom for you: the main way you can get Judaism wrong is by not asking any questions. We have a whole holiday meal devoted to asking questions, and it's delicious (see Passover, page 195).

We started our podcast *Unorthodox* in 2015 to offer a window into the kinds of conversations we were having as staffers at *Tablet*, the Jewish news and culture magazine. We wanted a place to discuss Israeli actress Gal Gadot as well as anti-Semitism, and Montreal bagel culture as well as Judaism's various fast days—from Yom Kippur to the more obscure Tzom Gedalia. We immediately started hearing from listeners who said they'd found something in our weekly episodes that they weren't getting at synagogue; or that listening to this podcast was the only Jewish thing they did; or that they had convinced their parents or children or grandparents to listen, too. In the past four years, we've heard from converts whose rabbis recommended our show as a supplement to Torah study, and from gentiles married to Jews, asking us to explain their in-laws' peculiarities.

After more than four million downloads, we've somehow become public explainers of Jewishness. From our bustling inbox to our active Facebook community, we are constantly being asked all sorts of questions. To the secular, we often find ourselves explaining religious concepts. To the religious, we offer a window into how secular Jews express our shared history and identity. And to anyone who has a question she is embarrassed to ask, we're there, never judging, explaining what Reconstructionism is, or why observant Jews don't mix meat and milk, or whether it's okay to use the acronym "JAP."

All of which is to say that people have *a lot* of questions—and we want to point you toward the answers. Since the publication of *The Jewish Catalog* in 1973, there has been no reference book that deals with Judaism, and Jewishness, in all its facets. Jews quarrel endlessly about whether we are a religion, an ethnicity, a tribe, a nation, a culture, a people, or a family. We're all of the above—but you'll look in vain for a book that reflects the diverse, indescribable Jewish people back at ourselves. So we decided to write one.

This is not a guide to Judaism, the religion, nor to Jewish "culture," if by that you mean bagels, kugel, Hanukkah presents, and *Seinfeld*. It's a guide to all that, and more. It's a guide to "being Jewish." For some, that means Jewish prayer, for others, Jewish hair—but for most of us, it's an eccentric mishmash. (Or is it mish*mosh*?)

And so, because this book is all about you, you can read it however you'd like. We've arranged the entries alphabetically, so you can read all the way from Aaron to Zyklon B (yikes), or hop around whimsically. Just remember that we are, in name and spirit, *Unorthodox*, which means that while we covered all the basics, we also had fun. We hope that you will, too, because there's not really a point to being Jewish—or anything else, for that matter—if it doesn't make you happy. Speaking of happy, see **latkes**.

Shalom, friends,
Stephanie, Liel, and Mark
Hosts of *Tablet's Unorthodox* podcast

FROM

Aaron

TO

Avinu Malkeinu

Aaron
Like a biblical Rodney Dangerfield, our first high priest couldn't get no respect. Sure, he was a prophet, and he wore the urim and thummim, the special breastplate through which God's Will could be divined. But his brother, Moses, was still way cooler.

"A-Ba-Ni-Bi"
The Eurovision song contest is to Europeans what the Super Bowl, the World Series, and the Oscars, combined, are to Americans. Which is why so many Israelis were shocked and elated when the Jewish state won for the very first time in 1978 with this perfect pop confection. The word *abanibi* means "*ani*," or "I," in Hebrew's version of pig latin, and the tune is as jaunty and sweet as the lyrics about a boy telling a girl he loves her in a language the grown-ups don't understand.

Abraham
The progenitor of the three great monotheistic, or "Abrahamic," faiths, is, quite literally, the Ur-Jew: he hailed from the city of Ur in what is today Iraq. His story, as related in Genesis, begins with God telling him to "go forth" from the land of his ancestors and into the land of Canaan, where God will make of him a *goy gadol*, a great nation. This covenant, or brit, lies at the heart of God's relationship with the Jewish people, and it was sealed by Abraham, and continues to be sealed to this day, with the ritual of circumcision. Abraham's greatest trial—the true test of his pact with God—comes later in Genesis when God commands him to take his son Isaac to the top of Mount Moriah and offer him as a sacrifice.

Abulafia Bakery
Legendary bakery on the border of Tel Aviv and Jaffa, open since 1879 and proof that Jews and Arabs can coexist if only they focus on dipping freshly baked sesame bagels in za'atar.

Abzug, Bella (1920–1998)
This civil rights lawyer, US congresswoman, and feminist leader was known for broad-brimmed hats and loud decibel levels. "They call me Battling Bella, Mother Courage, and a Jewish mother with more complaints than Portnoy," Abzug wrote of herself (see ***Portnoy's Complaint***). Norman Mailer said that her voice "could boil the fat off a taxicab driver's neck." She grew

up poor in the Bronx, became the student-body president at Hunter College, won a scholarship to Columbia Law School, and went to work representing the voiceless. During the McCarthy era, she came out swinging against the House Un-American Activities Committee. Later, she added opposition to nuclear testing and the Vietnam War to her causes. At fifty, she ran for a seat in the House of Representatives and won, as her fans cheered, "Give 'em hella, Bella!" Vice presidential candidate Geraldine Ferraro said of her, "She did not knock politely on the door. She took the hinges off of it."

Adam and Eve

The first man and woman. Eve ate a piece of fruit and offered Adam some because he looked hungry and why should fresh food go to waste? Innocent enough thought, but a lot of trouble ensued.

Adelson, Sheldon (b. 1933)
The son of a taxi driver, young Sheldon borrowed two hundred dollars from an uncle when he was twelve and purchased a license to sell newspapers in his native suburban Boston. It was his first business of many: a millionaire by the time he was thirty, he started and folded companies doing everything from selling toiletry kits to operating candy vending machines. When a company running computer trade shows made it big, Adelson sold his share for five million dollars and used his new fortune to buy hotels and casinos in Las Vegas, Macau, and Singapore. He and his wife, Miriam, are big donors to Republican candidates and major supporters of Israel's prime minister Benjamin Netanyahu. In 2007, Adelson launched *Israel Hayom*, a free daily publication that he quickly turned into Israel's most popular newspaper. He is also a major contributor to Jewish causes, most notably Birthright Israel.

Adolf
Nazis Hitler and Eichmann spelled it with an *f*. The lyricist Green and the *New York Times* publisher Ochs spelled it with a *ph*. It hardly matters: whatever the spelling, it's not a good baby name anymore.

Adon Olam
A Jewish liturgical hymn that has been part of the morning service, especially on Shabbat, since the fourteenth century. Adon Olam is especially beloved of children, both because it heralds the end of the ser-

vice and because, in its simple meter, it can be sung to almost any melody, from "Take Me Out to the Ballgame" to the "Cups" song from *Pitch Perfect* to Pharrell Williams's "Happy." Go to YouTube—you'll see.

AEPi (Alpha Epsilon Pi)

One of the leading Jewish fraternities, at this very moment hosting a game of beer pong in the sticky-floored basement of a campus frat house near you. It tells you all you need to know that on the "Notable Alumni" page of AEPi's website, Facebook founder Mark Zuckerberg is listed first. Casino magnate and Republican megadonor Sheldon Adelson is also a brother. So were both Simon and Garfunkel.

afikoman

A half piece of matzo that is hidden during the Passover Seder. The children at the table search for it, and then it is eaten as dessert. (If this is the only dessert you're offered, however, you need to find a better Seder.)

agunah

Meaning "anchored" or "chained" wife, an *agunah* is a woman who is unwillingly bound to a marriage. Because a Jewish marriage can be ended, religiously speaking, only by the death of either party or when a husband writes (and a woman accepts) a gett, a writ of divorce, women can become agunot (the plural) in a couple of different ways. In olden times, an agunah could be a woman whose husband did not return from battle or was lost at sea, but whose body was never found; in such a case, he was presumed to be alive, and the woman was not free to remarry. Today, such cases of wartime agunot are far rarer (though not unheard of). More typically, an agunah today is a woman who wants a divorce but whose husband won't give her a gett, which occurs almost exclusively in the Orthodox community, where the gett is still considered crucial. Some men use gett refusal to blackmail women into favorable divorce settlements, even outright cash payments. Technically, that kind of coercion is forbidden by Jewish law, but Jewish religious courts (see **beit din**) are often ineffective at enforcing that prohibition.

The legal pickle in which the agunah can find herself has over the centuries led agunot to go to extreme lengths to force their husbands' hands. In 2015, Rabbi Mendel Epstein of Brooklyn was convicted of conspiracy to commit kidnapping; he led a band of thugs for hire who used cattle prods and other torture methods to persuade recalcitrant husbands to liberate their wives. To really get the problem of the agunah, check out the 2014 Israeli film *Gett: The Trial of Viviane Amsalem.*

Ahasuerus

The jury's still out on just which of the ancient Persian kings Ahasuerus was—that is, if he even existed in the first place. But while the historicity of the king at the heart of the Purim story may be in dispute, his continued relevance is not. When the Clinton/Lewinsky scandal broke in January 1998, it was on the eve of what was expected to be a tense meeting between Bill Clinton and Benjamin Netanyahu, but when Monica knocked Bibi out of the headlines, Likudniks celebrated her as a latter-day Esther. The presidential parallels have continued into the Trump era, with a ruler who has Jews in his family, knows a thing or two about "Queens," and has a demonstrated taste for beauty pageants. It is unclear who the Haman figure is in these two scenarios, though an argument can be made, in both, for Newt Gingrich.

ahava

"Love" in Hebrew, or the Israeli cosmetics company whose products are made with mud from the Dead Sea.

AIDS activism

Jews have been active in the battle against AIDS since the beginning of the epidemic. Playwright Larry Kramer (*The Normal Heart*) cofounded the AIDS service organization Gay Men's Health Crisis and later the direct action group ACT UP. Medical researcher Mathilde Krim was the founding chair of amfAR (American Foundation for AIDS Reseach). Elizabeth Glaser, best remembered for her fiery speech about AIDS at the 1992 Democratic Convention, cofounded the Elizabeth Glaser Pediatric AIDS Foundation. Jewish artists—particularly LGBT Jews—created work in response to the epidemic (playwright Tony Kushner's Pulitzer-winning *Angels in America*, for instance) and took to the streets to protest governmental inaction and corporate greed in the pharmaceutical industry. Novelist David B. Feinberg protested with ACT UP and then wrote about it in his fearless essay collection *Queer and Loathing: Rants and Raves of a Raging AIDS Clone*, published shortly before his death in 1994; playwright and novelist Sarah Schulman, an ACT UP veteran who also cofounded Lesbian Avengers, helped create the ACT UP Oral History Project and coproduced the documentary *United in Anger: A History of ACT UP*. And that's just the tip of the activist iceberg.

ALEICHEM, SHOLEM

(1859–1916)

The pen name of Solomon Rabinovich, Sholem Aleichem was one of the most acclaimed Yiddish writers around the end of the nineteenth century. His short stories, depicting the lives of Eastern European Jews, captured something of the soul and ethos of a community that was vanishing. He is best remembered now for his series on Tevye the Dairyman, on which the musical *Fiddler on the Roof* is based.

SHOLEM'S SHTETL

Stempenyu
(1888)

Tevye's Daughters
(1894)

Motl the Cantor's Son
(1907; 1916)

Al Chet

A prayer of confession usually repeated ten times during the Yom Kippur services. Rather than confess to individual sins, the Al Chet (literally meaning "For the Sin") contains forty-four distinct categories of wrongdoing, from being hard-hearted to behaving haughtily. The prayer is worded in the plural, because sins, like triumphs, are ascribed not to individuals but to Klal Yisrael, the entirety of the Jewish people.

Al-Aqsa

The site in the holy city of Jerusalem on which this mosque is built, known to Jews as the Temple Mount and to Muslims as Haram al Sharif, is the third holiest place in Islam. According to tradition, the prophet Muhammad was transported from Mecca to the mosque's site during his Night Journey and, after leading a prayer there, was whisked up to heaven. Originally a small prayer house built by the prophet's companion, the caliph Umar, it was expanded by the caliph Abd-al Malik and his son al-Walid and inaugurated in 705 CE.

Alda, Alan (b. 1936)

Beloved actor you always thought was Jewish. He isn't.

Aleinu

Aleinu literally means "it's on us," it's our duty. It's the first word of the prayer also known as Aleinu, which is recited near the end of the three daily Jewish prayer services. When you hear the Aleinu, you know that in a matter of minutes the mourners will be saying the Mourner's Kaddish (see **Kaddish**)—so prepare to shut up, stand up, and show some respect.

aleph-bet

The Hebrew alphabet.

aliyah

Aliyah is Hebrew for "ascent" or "elevation" or "going up." In English-speaking contexts, you'll hear the word used in two ways: you can "have an aliyah" or "make aliyah." To "have an aliyah" (or "get an aliyah") is the honor of being called up to the *bimah*, or reading table, during a synagogue service to say a blessing before and after the Torah is read. To "make aliyah" is to move to Israel. By moving to Israel, the Holy Land, the Promised Land, the land flowing with milk and honey, you are figuratively ascending, going up, to a higher state of being. But note: The two forms of the word are pronounced differently. You get an "uh-LEE-yuh," but you make "ah-lee-YAH."

ALLEN, WOODY

(B. 1935)

THE ALLEN CANON

Bananas
(1971)

Manhattan
(1979)

Annie Hall
(1977)

Hannah and Her Sisters (1986)

Perhaps the most singular Jewish storyteller since Franz Kafka, Brooklyn's Woody Allen (Allan Stewart Konigsberg) started writing jokes for Sid Caesar as a teenager. He got into film directing when his first screenplay, *What's New Pussycat?*, was a huge box-office hit but a complete mess. His persona transformed in the 1970s from the nervous, klutzy schlemiel to the quintessential New York intellectual, and he won the Oscar for his masterpiece of modern romance, *Annie Hall*. (He didn't go to the ceremony, because one of the best jokes in the film mocks the pointlessness of Hollywood awards.) In the 1980s, he teamed up on- and off-screen with Mia Farrow, and from a strictly cinematic point of view, it was an incredible run. Allen's life later turned into something of a Greek tragedy when he married Farrow's adopted daughter Soon-Yi Previn and the family erupted in accusations—with daughter Dylan Farrow alleging that Woody had abused her, and son Moses identifying Mia as an abuser.

All in the Family

Television sitcom that ran from 1971 through 1979, mirroring the era's changing values and generational divide. Jewish producer Norman Lear set his version, adapted from an earlier British show, in a working-class section of Queens. Archie Bunker was a bigot with a heart of gold (somehow this worked back then) who had no love for blacks, Hispanics, homosexuals, commies, or "women's libbers." His main foil was his liberal longhaired son-in-law Michael "Meathead" Stivic who was Polish Catholic, but played by Jewish actor and eventual director Rob Reiner (son of Carl), and could easily be read as Jewish. (See *Seinfeld*'s George Costanza.) Bunker's attitude toward Jews was a smidge more enlightened than toward other ethnic groups. He once suggested that Jews would enter heaven without being baptized because "Moses got his feet wet crossing the Red Sea." He is annoyed when he suspects a neighbor is selling his house to a Jewish couple, only to have the bomb dropped that it's a black couple (George and Louise Jefferson). In a famous episode with Sammy Davis Jr. (don't ask), Bunker famously said, "You bein' colored, well, I know you had no choice in that, but whatever made you turn Jew?"

All-of-a-Kind Family

Sydney Taylor's classic stories of a Jewish family living in New York City at the turn of the twentieth century. The five-book series, originally published between 1951 and 1978, features five plucky sisters and vividly depicts Jewish and immigrant life on the Lower East Side. Four of the five books were reissued in 2014 by Lizzie Skurnick Books, an imprint dedicated to reissuing young adult literature.

alter cocker

Basically, an old fart. Literally, in Yiddish, an *alter cocker* is an "old pooper" or "old crapper" (from *alter,* "old," and the verb *tzu kokken*, "to defecate"), but as used today the term is gentler, even affectionate. The alter cocker is the old guy playing dominoes on the boardwalk, with little to do but lots to say. He's a curmudgeon, he's a fogey, but on good days he's lovable. Statler and Waldorf, who dwell in the box seats on *The Muppet Show*, are alter cockers. So is Uncle Leo on *Seinfeld*. So is your great-uncle who still refers to his wife's octogenarian friends as "the girls." No man wants to be called an alter cocker, but every man hopes to live long enough to be one.

Alter Rebbe (1745–1813)

The honorific given to Shneur Zalman of Liadi, the founder and first leader of the Hasidic sect known as Chabad-Lubavitch. When Shneur Zalman was twelve years old, his teachers informed his father that he was so brilliant and so knowledgeable that he no longer required tutelage. He was ordained as a rabbi and threw himself into developing a different approach to Hasidism (see Branches of Judaism, page 44), one that valued intellect and reflection over mindless obedience. He also wrote what is arguably the most influential work of Hasidic philosophy: called *Likkutei Amarim.* More commonly known as the Tanya, the book delivers a radically transformative account of the human soul and the origins of creation. It is still widely read by students of Jewish mysticism today.

Altneuland

Here's everything you need to know about Theodor Herzl, Zionism's founding father: he was the sort of chap who put all his best ideas in a utopian novel. Literally meaning "The Old New Land," the book was published in German in 1902 and became an instant bestseller. It tells the tale of a young Jewish intellectual from Vienna who visits the newly established Jewish state in the biblical land of Israel and finds it to be, well, paradise: most people speak German, everyone's industrious and kind, and the resident Arab minorities are thrilled at the opportunity to live in such a prosperous and peaceful nation. It's easy to mock the novel for its decidedly old-fashioned (and fanciful) feel, but it's impossible to remain unmoved by Herzl's famous dictum, appearing in its afterword: "If you will it, it is no dream." Nahum Sokolov, the famous Zionist leader, translated the book into Hebrew immediately after it was published, calling it *Tel Aviv*, or "The City of Spring"; seven years later, the new Hebrew city built on the shores of the Mediterranean adopted both the novel's title and its vision of thriving Jewish life.

Amidah

Judaism's central prayer. Composed in the time of the Second Temple, its central structure is a string of eighteen blessings in praise of God, which is why it's also sometimes known as Tefilat Shemonah-Esreh, or "The Prayer of the Eighteen." (There are actually nineteen blessings now, but that's a whole other story.) It's recited three times a day: once during *shachrit*, the morning prayer service; once during *mincha*, the afternoon prayer service; and once during *maariv*, the evening prayer service. On Shabbat and other special occasions, we say it more. It's customary to recite the words loud enough to hear yourself pray but not so loud as to disturb others. Because it's considered a personal communion with God, it's not to be interrupted, and it begins with taking three small steps forward, which is what you would do in ancient times before speaking to a mighty king.

analysis

See **therapy**.

Anielewicz, Mordecai (1919–1943)

See Warsaw Ghetto Uprising , page 284.

Ann Landers and Dear Abby

Advice columnists Esther Pauline Friedman Lederer ("Eppie") and Pauline Esther Friedman Phillips ("Popo") were born minutes apart on July 4, 1918. Their father was a Russian immigrant success story—he began life as a traveling chicken salesman and wound up the owner of a chain of movie theaters. The twins grew up in Sioux City, Iowa; they studied journalism and wrote a gossip column together for their college paper. Eppie took over an existing advice column called "Ann Landers" in 1955 (by 1993, it ran in 1,200 daily newspapers); three months later, Popo, who originally helped her sister answer letters, decided to hang out her advice shingle, too. "Dear Abby" immediately became Ann Landers's biggest competition, and the two feuded for nearly ten years. Eppie died in 2002, Popo in 2013. Here's a bit of genius, quoted in the *New York Times* obituary for Popo:

Dear Abby,

> *Two men who claim to be father and adopted son just bought an old mansion across the street and fixed it up. We notice a very suspicious mixture of company coming and going at all hours—blacks, whites, Orientals, women who look like men and men who look like women. This has always been considered one of the finest sections of San Francisco, and these weirdos are giving it a bad name. How can we improve the neighborhood?*
>
> *—Nob Hill Residents*

Dear Residents,

> *You could move.*

Ansky, S. (1863–1920)

Shloyme Zanvil Rappoport, a Russian Jew, was, in his early years as a writer, an internationalist and socialist. But in 1905 his work took a turn: he took on the pen name S. Ansky (often rendered "An-sky"), stopped writing in Russian, and turned to Yiddish instead, finding joy and meaning in Jewish folklore and Hasidic tales. Between 1912 and 1917, he composed his masterpiece, *The Dybbuk*, a play about a young woman possessed by the spirit of her dead lover. Konstantin Stanislavski, father of the world-renowned acting method and one of Russia's most famous directors, was an early champion, but Ansky died before the play was ever produced.

Anti-Defamation League (ADL)

The ADL was founded in 1913, in the wake of the lynching of Leo Frank, an Atlanta Jew convicted of murder in what many historians consider an anti-Semitic show trial, and who was subsequently killed by a mob after his death sentence was commuted. Today, it tracks anti-Semites, white supremacists, and other bad guys, while providing anti-bias training and educational materials to law enforcement and schools across America.

ANXIETY

anti-Semite, anti-Semitic, anti-Semitism

Anti-Semitism is not a social prejudice against Jews; it's a conspiracy theory. In fact, it's the oldest and most powerful conspiracy theory in the West. You can be an anti-Semite without being particularly prejudiced against Jews in your personal interactions with them, and you can hold prejudiced views about Jews without being an anti-Semite. The person who finds Jews to be loud and vulgar and doesn't want them in his country club is a bigot; if you asked him whether the reason he doesn't like Jews is because they nefariously control the government and all the banks and are bent on world domination, he'd probably look at you as if you were insane.

Conversely, there are people—including some Jews!—who happily watch *Seinfeld* and eat bagels and lox, but who also believe that a secret conspiracy of Likudniks dragged America into war in Iraq, or are responsible for the latest financial crisis, or the border crisis, which these Jews present in manipulative ways in the media, which (in their minds!) is secretly controlled by George Soros or Sheldon Adelson. To any normal person, whatever their prejudices, the core of anti-Semitic thinking is sheer insanity. To anti-Semites, it is revelatory—whatever their political affiliations.

Antiochus

History was graced with at least thirteen mighty kings named Antiochus, but the one we speak of is the notorious Antiochus IV Epiphanes, the Greek king of the Seleucid Empire who reigned from 175 to 164 BCE. Not a big fan of the Jews, he reversed the long-standing tradition of letting the Jews in the land of Israel manage their own religious affairs, and instead outlawed circumcision, observing the Sabbath, and other key commandments; he also made eating pork mandatory. Naturally, the Jews revolted, organizing themselves into a group called the Maccabees and waging war on Antiochus's well-armed phalanxes. If you're wondering how the fight ended, see Hanukkah, page 122.

anxiety

Jewish pastime that keeps therapists (and their therapists) in business (see **worrying**; **therapy**; **epigenetics**).

Apatow, Judd (b. 1967)

Producer, writer, and director whose work, which somehow simultaneously debunks and perpetuates male stereotypes, dominated comedy from the late 2000s through today. Bred in Long Island, Apatow grew obsessed with stand-up comedy, and later shared an apartment with a young Adam Sandler. In his feature films (*The 40-Year-Old Virgin*, *Knocked Up*, *Funny People*), the guys are a little bit gross, but not so gross that they aren't lovable. Many modern comedy stars cite an Apatow movie as their big break. The first wave of projects begat Jewish stars Seth Rogen, James Franco, and Jason Segel and rebranded Paul Rudd. He also helped break out some great gentiles like Emma Stone, Aziz Ansari, and Kumail Nanjiani.

appetizing

Appetizing stores are the fish-and-dairy answer to the Jewish delicatessen. Instead of pastrami sandwiches stacked high, you come here for the cured salmon (kippered, smoked, and pickled), herring in multiple preparations, golden-skinned whitefish and chubs, salads of the egg-tuna-coleslaw ilk, cream cheese and other schmears, and the breads that were made to accompany them. These shops, such as the exemplary Russ & Daughters, Zabar's, and Barney Greengrass in New York City, are magnets for demanding customers, who want the lox thinner and the bagels fresher.

apples and honey

Apples are traditionally dipped in honey and eaten on Rosh Hashanah to ensure a sweet new year. But since it's the Jewish New Year, nothing is simple: Talmudic-style arguments have been known to ensue over which type of apples are the best, and why my honey is better than yours.

arak

If you find yourself at an Israeli bar, forget the beer. Forgo the wine. And don't even think about ordering the whiskey. When in proximity to the Mediterranean, the only permissible libation is arak, a delightfully alcoholic beverage made of grapes and aniseed. The proper way to consume it is one-third arak, two-thirds water, and precisely two ice cubes. It also has the advantage of being about the cheapest liquor you can buy in Israel, as well as a potential bridge to peace: Israelis, Syrians, Jordanians, Palestinians, and Lebanese all adore it.

Arbeit Macht Frei

German phrase meaning "work sets you free" that appears on imposing signage at the entrance to various Nazi concentration camps, most notably at Auschwitz.

Arendt, Hannah (1906–1975)

One of the great political philosophers of the twentieth or any other century, Hannah Arendt was a German-born war refugee who settled in the United States and wrote, among other great works, *Eichmann in Jerusalem*, about the 1961 trial of Nazi war criminal Adolf Eichmann. The book, which began as a series of articles for the *New Yorker*, is famous for the phrase "the banality of evil," which she used to describe a man whom she found "terrifyingly normal," bureaucratic, and clueless rather than overtly monstrous. The book is widely misunderstood, usually by those who have never bothered to read it. Arendt was not excusing Eichmann, just as she was not—in the famous section on the *Judenräte*, the councils of Jews who, faced with no good choices, collaborated with the Nazis—blaming Jews for their fate. Arendt is one of those figures who endlessly fascinates: a woman in (at the time) a man's profession; an early Zionist who turned against the cause; the young, Jewish lover of philosopher Martin Heidegger, who was to join the Nazi Party; and a thinker of remarkable nuance and paradox. *Eichmann in Jerusalem* is not only an indispensable work of philosophy but an elegant, empathetic work of literature. Here's one great passage: "There are more than a few people, especially among the cultural élite, who still publicly regret the fact that Germany sent Einstein packing, without realizing that it was a much greater crime to kill little Hans Cohn from around the corner, even though he was no genius."

Argentina

Where many Jews went after the Holocaust. Also where many Nazis went after the Holocaust. It's complicated.

Armenian Genocide

On April 24, 1915, the police in Istanbul, displeased with the Armenian people's decades-long quest for national sovereignty, arrested and deported 235 of the community's leaders. Thus began the systematic genocide of as many as 1.5 million men, women, and children, who were marched to death, burnt, shot, beheaded, raped, and drowned by Turkish soldiers. This holocaust decimated as many as a third of all Armenians living at the time, and, more shamefully, is still brazenly denied by the Turkish government. Even more shamefully, many nations—including, as of 2019, the United States and Israel—still succumb to Turkey's diplomatic pressure and do not recognize the Armenian Genocide. One person who did recognize it, however, was Adolf Hitler.

Groucho Marx

Cigar enthusiast Groucho Marx is Karl Marx's second cousin once removed's wife's second husband's aunt's first cousin twice removed.

Karl Marx

Karl Marx is Lauren Bacall's husband's ex-wife's husband's aunt's great-great-uncle's fourth cousin once removed.

Zsa Zsa Gabor

Miss Hungary winner Zsa Zsa Gabor is Karl Marx's half sister-in-law's husband's nephew's wife's first husband's third great-grandson's wife.

Lauren Bacall

Zsa Zsa Gabor is actress Lauren Bacall's husband's ex-wife's husband's ex-wife's ex-husband's wife's uncle's great niece's husband's sister's husband's first cousin's wife.

Baruch Spinoza

Philosopher/telescope maker Baruch Spinoza is Karl Marx's second cousin twice removed's wife's uncle's fourth cousin.

Shimon Peres

Want to be really impressed? Lauren Bacall is second cousins with Shimon Peres.

Baal Shem Tov

Mysticism superstar the Baal Shem Tov is revolutionary thinker Karl Marx's fifth cousin twice removed.

Irving Berlin

Maggie Gyllenhaal is *also* Christmas-song composer Irving Berlin's wife's eighth cousin five times removed.

Sigmund Freud

The Baal Shem Tov is cigar enthusiast Sigmund Freud's third cousin eight times removed.

Maggie Gyllenhaal

The Deuce star Maggie Gyllenhaal is Lauren Bacall's husband's eighth cousin five times removed.

To paraphrase Sister Sledge, we are mishpocha. All of us. If you take a random Ashkenazi Jew, he or she is, on average, about fifth cousins with any other random Ashkenazi Jew. (Or seventh cousins, or eleventh cousins, depending on which geneticist you ask.)

The point is, our ancestors were a highly endogamous group—which is the polite way to say a lot of them married their first, second, or third cousins. An understandable situation, since they lived in small villages and didn't have the "anywhere on earth" setting on their dating apps.

"It's a matter of indifference to me what a weak western European civilization will say about me," he said when explaining his intent to unleash death and destruction on millions of people. "Who, after all, speaks today of the annihilation of the Armenians?"

Arthur, Bea (1922–2009)

One of the great stars of stage and small screen, Bea Arthur, born Bernice Frankel, did *Mame* and *Fiddler on the Roof* on Broadway, but she won her place in the world to come by creating the roles of Maude and Dorothy on television. Maude Findlay, the main character of Norman Lear's CBS sitcom *Maude* (1972–1978), was one of the first identifiably feminist characters in TV land. She was a liberal and an unabashed bigmouth, and she was on her fourth marriage. In the show's first season, Maude became pregnant at the age of forty-seven; her decision to have an abortion was a television milestone. From 1985 to 1992, Arthur returned to sitcom work as Dorothy Zbornak, one of the four *mature* Florida-dwelling roomies of NBC's *Golden Girls,* a show on which old women were depicted as having fun and, not unrelated, sex.

ArtScroll

One of the largest and most prominent Jewish publishers of traditional books in the United States, founded by two Orthodox rabbis in Brooklyn in 1976. Known especially for the ArtScroll siddur, a traditional Orthodox Jewish prayer book used by many congregations over the past forty years, the staff has produced the entire Babylonian and Jerusalem Talmuds in English translation, as well as translations of the medieval biblical commentaries of Rashi and Maimonides, plus other canonical texts of Jewish literature, including Susie Fishbein's Kosher by Design cookbook series.

Aryan

The Nazi ideal of beauty, all blue eyes and blond hair. You know, like Israeli supermodel Bar Refaeli.

As a Driven Leaf

"One of the few novels of literary quality written by a practicing rabbi," according to literary critic Josh Lambert, *As a Driven Leaf* was written in 1939 by Milton Steinberg, then the rabbi of Park Avenue Synagogue, in Manhattan. It offers a fictional version of the life of second-century rabbi Elisha ben Abuyah, who is mentioned in the Talmud but not given a very full biography. The story grapples with the tensions between religious observance and the modernizing forces of Hellenic intellectual life—a tension that feels relevant in every generation—and also includes a small portrait of Beruriah, who in the Talmud is the rare woman learned in Scripture.

Ashkenazi Jews, Ashkenazim

Jews with ancestors from Central and Eastern Europe. The word appears in the Hebrew Bible, but only in medieval times did it become the catchall phrase for a large and diverse group of people. Even though Jewish cultures across Europe varied—Lithuanian Jews and German Jews, for example, led very different lives—Ashkenazim, as they're known, retained much in common, including a shared language, Yiddish, and colorless culinary staples like kugel and gefilte fish.

Ashkenormative

Assuming that Jewish life and culture is limited primarily to the experiences and customs of Ashkenazi Jews. To some extent, most American Jews—even those who are not themselves Ashkenazi—fall prey to Ashkenormativity, as Ashkenazi Jews have, since the late nineteenth century, constituted the great majority of American Jewry and been most prominent in Jewish religious and cultural life. But with increased immigration from the Middle East, Iran, and other regions, and with overdue attention to the experiences of historically overlooked groups, we really hope the Ashkenormative tendency is weakening.

ass

The Bible's most celebrated animal, talking (see Numbers 22:28–22:33), dispensing wisdom, and making Hebrew school students laugh for six thousand years.

assimilation

Four generations ago, something newly arrived Jewish immigrants tried to do to look, sound, and feel as if they belonged. Three generations ago, something middle-class American Jews desperately hoped they had accomplished. Two generations ago, something countercultural Jews despised their parents for having done. One generation ago, the subject of many alarmist academic conferences. This generation, an entry in an encyclopedia of Jewish life.

Bar Refaeli: Ironically, a fair approximation of the **Aryan** beauty ideal

atheism

A belief system unusually common among Jews. Not only are many great Jews atheists, but many great atheists are Jews. How many humans have come to their disbelief in God through Sigmund Freud? Through Karl Marx? Through Trotsky? Nobody has an entirely convincing answer for why even observant Jews show relatively high rates of atheism. It's often suggested that because Jews value questioning, because our tradition has since Talmudic times honored argument and dissent, because we are allowed to be skeptical about most anything, we can be skeptical about God. Of course, among Orthodox Jews, belief in God is presumed. But even so, there's more room for atheism than in other observant communities. Unlike, say, evangelical Christians, Jews aren't expected to make ostentatious, public pronouncements of faith; a Jew who has lost faith but wants to retain his or her community can continue mouthing prayers, keeping the mitzvot, and acting like it's all good. In general, because Judaism can function in so many ways—as a religion, a system of rituals, a calendar of holidays, a home-based practice, an ethnic identity, a tribe, a family—there's ample room for an atheist Jew to still feel Jewish. By contrast, a Southern Baptist who has lost faith in God is adrift.

atonement

See **teshuva**.

aufruf

See Wedding, page 283.

Auschwitz

The most infamous Nazi concentration camp was actually a network of camps on the outskirts of the town of Oswiecim in Nazi-occupied Poland: Auschwitz I (the main camp), Auschwitz II (Birkenau, where the gas chambers were), Auschwitz III (Monowitz), and more than forty subcamps. Auschwitz was the German name for Oswiecim; in Yiddish the town was known as Oshpitzin. But today the word "Auschwitz" signifies pure atrocity, from the menacing "Arbeit Macht Frei" sign at the camp entrance to the horrific experiments performed on prisoners by Josef Mengele in Block 10. Upon arrival, prisoners were either sent directly to the gas chambers or registered for forced labor and tattooed with their identifying number (a practice that only occurred there). Also imprisoned were non-Jewish Poles, Roma, and Soviets, but of the 1.1 million people murdered at Auschwitz before the Soviet liberation in January 1945, almost 1 million were Jews. Today, the site is a museum and research facility, and it remains a popular tourist destination.

Avinu Malkeinu

Meaning "Our Father, Our King," Avinu Malkeinu is a prayer recited during worship on Rosh Hashanah, Yom Kippur, and the days in between, as well as on fast days (except for Tisha B'Av). If you haven't been to High Holiday services since you were a child, and you think you have forgotten it all, this is the part that, if you go back, you'll still remember. Its melody is like the smell of your elementary school hallway, safe and timeless. Barbra Streisand did an extraordinary recording of it.

FROM

Baal Shem Tov

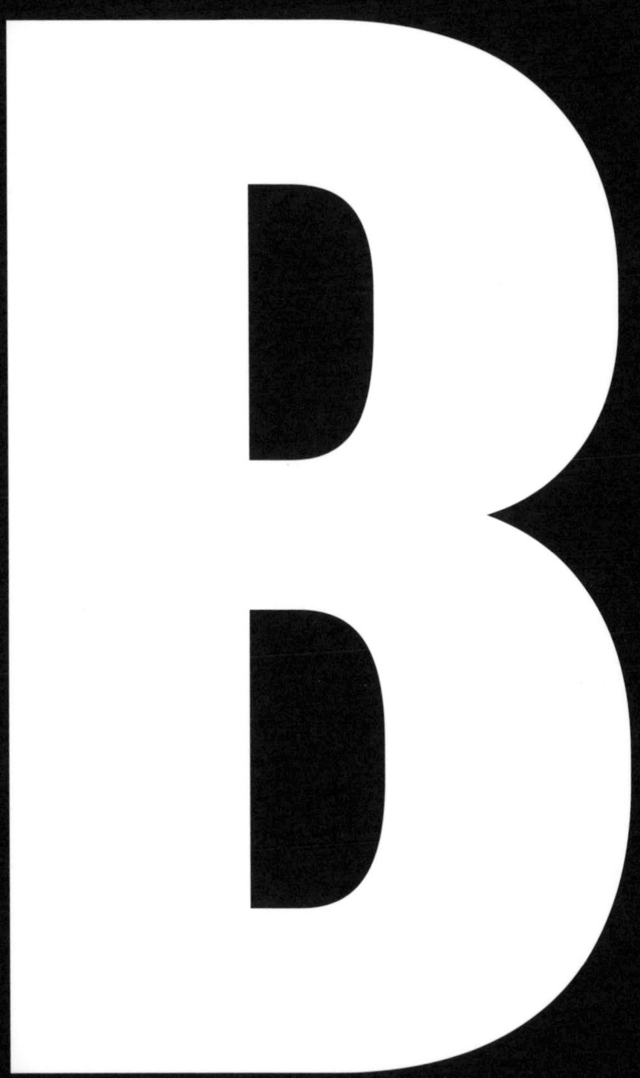

TO

“But is it good for the Jews?”

Baal Shem Tov (1698–1760)

Considered the founder of the modern Hasidic movement, the Baal Shem Tov, whose name means "Master of the Good Name," is sometimes referred to as the Besht. There is no shortage of stories and myths told about this holy rabbi and his followers, who emphasized prayer and a deep love of God over rote Talmud learning, and who inspired scores of disciples and Hasidic movements in his wake. Tales of the Baal Shem Tov range from the sweet to the profound to the strange and mystical.

baal teshuvah

The proper term for your friend who was super into Phish in college and now sports a long beard and a black hat. Literally meaning "a master of return," it describes a nonreligious Jewish person who has found his or her way back to traditional Judaism's fold, and the term may apply to as many as a quarter of all Israelis.

Babel, Isaac (1894–1940)

Babel was a Russian Jewish writer best known for his collection of short stories *Red Cavalry*, adapted from Babel's own recollections and diaries from his time as an army reporter. Many of the stories chronicled egregious acts of anti-Semitism by the army. Although at first Babel was able to elude the Soviet censors, his writing was eventually blacklisted. His other famous collection, *Odessa Tales,* explores life in a Jewish ghetto in Odessa, primarily through the character of a Jewish gangster named Benya Krik. Babel also wrote for the stage and the screen. In 1939, Babel was arrested on the false charge of espionage and forced to sign a confession. In early 1940, he was executed at the age of forty-five, a victim of Stalin's purges.

Babi Yar

On September 29, 1941, the Nazis rounded up nearly the entire Jewish community of Kiev, Ukraine; over the next two days, more than thirty-three thousand Jews were taken to a wooded ravine on the northern edges of the city and shot. Babi Yar is the site of what is thought to be the single deadliest massacre of the Holocaust. "No monument stands over Babi Yar. A drop sheer as a crude gravestone," the non-Jewish Russian poet Yevgeni Yevtushenko wrote in 1961, in a poem that bitterly protested the Soviet state's official manipulations of the country's history. "Wild grasses rustle over Babi Yar," he wrote. "The trees look ominous, like judges."

babka

A yeast cake stuffed with chocolate and topped with streusel. If you're Jerry Seinfeld, you make an episode about it. If you're Hungarian, you bake it flatter and without streusel and call it a *kokosh*. If you hate everything that's good, you make a mistake and fill it with cinnamon instead.

baby naming

By tradition, Jewish children in the diaspora get two names. Boys are given Hebrew names at their bris; by new tradition, baby girls may be honored, and their Hebrew names announced, at a *simchat bat*, or "celebration of the daughter." Then there are their vernacular names (in America, their English names): Ashkenazi Jews typically name sons after dead relatives (so no "Junior" or "IV"); Sephardi Jews may name after living or dead relatives. One hundred years ago, assimilating Jews in the United States named their sons Milton or Sidney, after great English poets, turning those names into the most Jewish names of all. Today, there are Jewish girls named Madison and Makayla, rebuking Jewish chauvinists who think we are somehow better than other people. (See **Hebrew names**.)

Bacall, Lauren (1924–2014)

Born Betty Joan Perske in the Bronx, this sultry siren made her Hollywood debut at the age of nineteen in *To Have and Have Not* (1944). She made an indelible impression on audiences, and on her costar, Humphrey Bogart; the two married shortly thereafter, forming one of the most storied on- and off-screen partnerships in Hollywood history, showcasing their chemistry in noir classics like *The Big Sleep* and *Key Largo*. In 1996, Bacall received her first and only Academy Award nomination for playing Barbra Streisand's exacting mother in *The Mirror Has Two Faces.*

bacon

The Great Forbidden, the Most Desired, the Ultimate Nemesis. Bacon defines Jewish food the way Voldemort defines Harry Potter: you can't think of one without the other.

bagel

America's least Jewish food. If you can get it at the airport in Des Moines (no offense, Iowa), you know it's no longer the authentic doughy treasure Jewish immigrants brought with them from Poland. Bagels belong to the world now.

bagel Jews

Know next to nothing about Judaism? Believe even less but still love a good bagel and lox? No worries: you're still a Member of the Tribe, and this delicious term is here to describe you and your casual commitment style. Maybe one day you'll upgrade your relationship to a bialy, but for now, enjoy your cultural schmear.

bageling

1. Using one's Jewdar; trying to figure out whether someone you're talking to is Jewish. You casually bring up things like summer camp, or drop a phrase like "mazel tov" just to gauge his or her reaction. 2. Discreetly letting your obviously Jewish conversation partner know that you are Jewish by dropping the name of your summer camp or a "mazel tov."

Bais Yaakov

A term referring to girls' schools affiliated with an Orthodox Jewish educational ideology, begun in 1917 by Orthodox female educator extraordinaire and divorced seamstress Sarah Schenirer. Schenirer argued that Jewish women, with increased access to secular education across Europe, would leave the faith unless Judaism provided them with religious education as well. Innovative in their time, today Bais Yaakov schools (officially known as Beth Jacob) are the domain of mostly Haredi Jewish communities. (See Branches of Judaism, page 44.)

balaboosta

An old-fashioned Yiddish phrase describing a crack homemaker, the sort of woman who can whip up a meal in twenty minutes, mend a coat, and keep the windows sparkling clean—all at once. It comes from the Hebrew phrase *ba'alat ha'bayit*, "mistress of the house." If you still don't understand what it means, ask your grandmother.

balagan

Hebrew word that when pronounced with an Israeli accent onomatopoetically captures its meaning perfectly—"mess"—and can be used to describe anything from the latest political scandal to the chaotic vibe on your Birthright trip.

Balfour Declaration

On November 2, 1917, Arthur Balfour, the United Kingdom's foreign secretary, wrote a letter to Lord Rothschild, a prominent British Jew, assuring him that "His Majesty's government view with favour the establishment in Palestine of a national home for the Jewish people, and will use their best endeavours to facilitate the achievement of this object." A month later, having defeated the Ottomans, the British general Allenby marched into Jerusalem, launching thirty years of British rule over Palestine and making the declaration a singularly influential document. Zionists worldwide were energized by it, while Arabs claimed it unfairly favored the Jews.

Bamba

You know who tend not to have nut allergies? Israelis. You know why? Because each of them eats about 712 pounds of this nut-based snack before they turn four. Kids crave it, soldiers dip it in chocolate spread, and stoned students melt it with noodles to make a poor man's pad thai. Sorry, falafel: this is Israel's true national food.

banking

See Banking and Jews, page 26.

banya

Forget the Finnish sauna or the Turkish hammam: the Russian banya is the sweaty, cleansing bliss you need. With temperatures reaching two hundred degrees Fahrenheit, bathers wear special felt hats to protect their heads from the heat and often massage themselves with bundles of eucalyptus leaves. Then they traditionally dip in a very cold pool to stimulate their circulation before enjoying a shot of vodka and some snacks. The banya, also known as the schvitz, was a tradition for Eastern European Jews and, thanks to Russian immigration, is flourishing in New York and elsewhere.

Bar Kochba (?–135 CE)

One of the most controversial figures in Jewish history, not much is known for certain about this warrior, who led a failed rebellion against the Roman emperor Hadrian. Despite waging successful guerilla warfare and wresting control over sizable chunks of land, he was eventually vanquished. The Talmud tells us that Bar Kochba was sentenced to death by his fellow Jews for the sin of declaring himself the messiah, a good reminder for us all never to presume that we can divine the will of God.

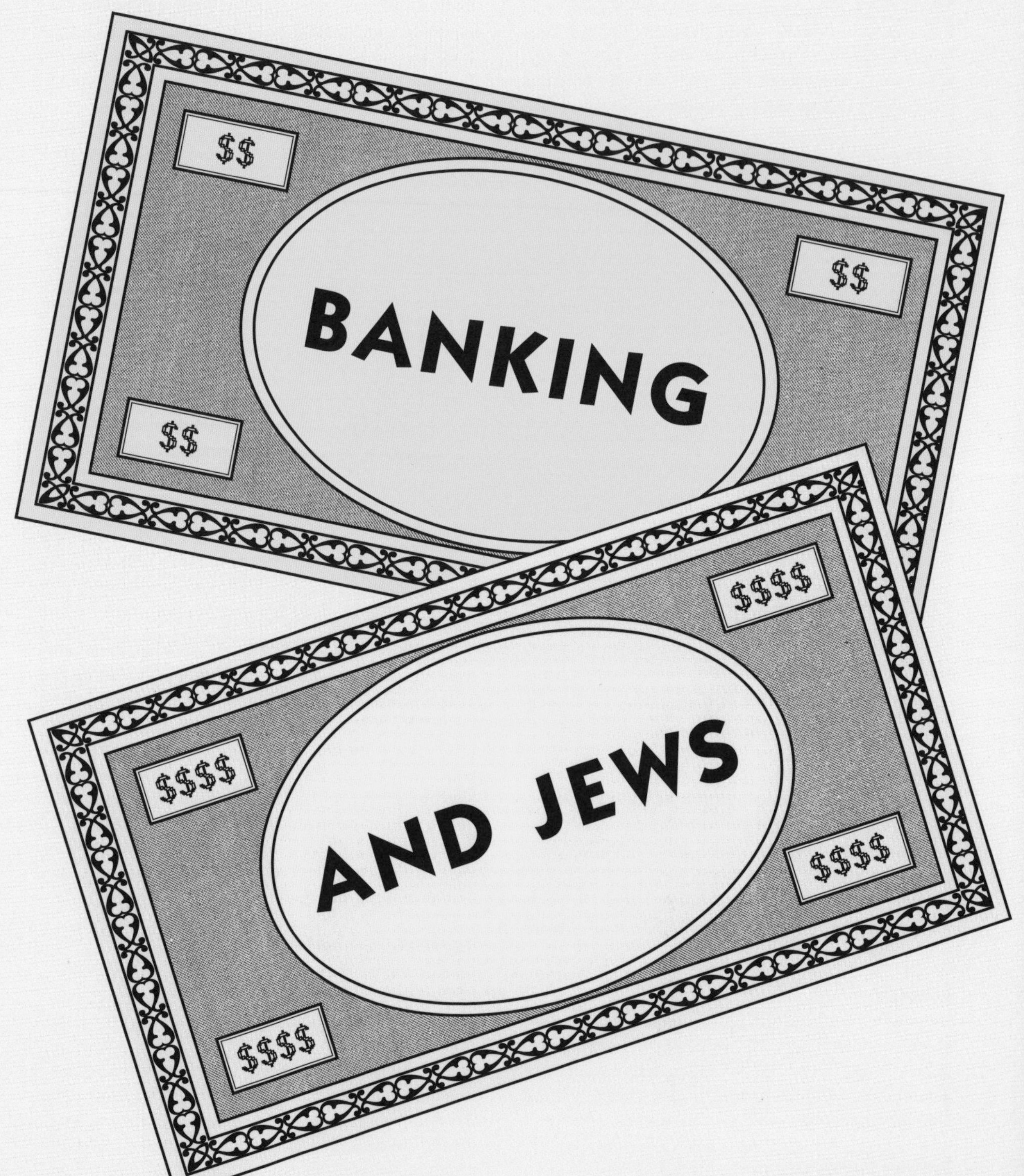
$$
$$
$$
BANKING
$$$$
$$$$
AND JEWS
$$$$
$$$$

The association between Jews and banking and money lending doesn't come from our genes—Kabbalistic numerology didn't give us a gift for figures, nor did centuries of Talmudic disputation give us a special aptitude for balance sheets and bank statements. Instead, it was a combination of negative Christian attitudes toward lending and the unique status of Jews in Europe after the destruction of the temple and the collapse of the Roman Empire.

As early as the beginning of the second millennium, Jews had established themselves as lenders throughout Europe. From the fourth century CE, Jewish scholars had permitted lending at interest, and even Deuteronomy makes a distinction between charging interest to foreigners and lending "unto thy brother." Christian thinkers, on the other hand, had long argued for and even instituted various bans and restrictions on usury—the charging of interest—starting with a ban on clergy engaging in usury in the Council of Nicaea in 325 CE.

This led to the establishment of networks between cities with thriving merchant activity united by a common language and a population that tended to be specialized in business activities like trade and crafts. Jews who migrated from the Middle East to Europe would sometimes be explicitly invited into European towns to work in financial and business occupations.

With the growing Jewish mercantile success and the religious mania of the Crusades, anti-Semitic sentiment was heightened. Despite official protection from the Crown, the Jewish community of York, England, was massacred in 1190 in a riot partially stoked by those who wanted to clear their debts.

But the dangers and pogroms didn't stop Jewish communities, especially large ones concentrated in urban areas, from continuing to specialize in trade and finance. The Jewish community in Amsterdam, founded in the sixteenth century, was full of Sephardi merchants and Ashkenazi bankers, and financiers of all types.

There is perhaps no better example of the connection between trade and finance than Nathan Rothschild, the German-born patriarch of the British branch of the (in)famous Jewish banking family. Rothschild was a textile merchant who branched out into the commodity trade, then into government finance and securities trading in London. He was the subject of a 1940 Nazi propaganda film alleging he was able to make massive profits by learning about the French defeat of Waterloo before any other traders. The myth of the Rothschilds' supposed control over banks, governments, and other institutions spawned centuries of conspiracy theories (see **dog whistles**), spouted to this day by everyone from white supremacists to Louis Farrakhan.

The association between Jews and finance has been particularly strong in the United States, where several of the largest and most influential financial institutions were founded by German Jewish merchants and financiers: Lehman Brothers, Bear Stearns, and Goldman Sachs. The firms have long since passed out of family control and have either gone bankrupt, gone public, merged, or all three.

LEHMAN BROTHERS

1850–2008

There really were three brothers: Henry (1822–1855), Emanuel (1827–1907), and Mayer (1830–1897), born in Germany. Henry came ashore in Montgomery, Alabama, as a dry goods merchant and then, with his two brothers, founded the family firm, which specialized in the cotton trade. The firm moved to New York after the Civil War and helped finance such iconic companies as Sears, Macy's, Woolworth's, Philip Morris, Campbell's, RKO, and 20th Century Fox. The Firm was purchased by American Express in 1984. In 2008, Lehman Brothers, hammered by its losses on mortgage securities, famously went bankrupt.

BEAR STEARNS

1923–2008

This brokerage was known as one of Wall Street's Jewish firms, a place where PSDs (people who were "Poor, Smart, with a deep Desire to become rich") could find a home in an industry dominated by WASPs and aristocratic German Jews. The firm, which went public in 1985, was overseen by a sucession of (Jewish) senior partners: Cy Lewis, who took over in the late 1940s, Ace Greenberg, from 1978 until 1993, and Jimmy Cayne, who ran the bank—which, at the time, was one of the most reckless players in mortgage securitization—until 2008. Bear Stearns was rescued by JPMorgan, with the assistance of the Federal Reserve and the US Treasury.

GOLDMAN SACHS

EST. 1869

Founded by German immigrant Marcus Goldman (1821–1904) in 1869, the firm became Goldman, Sachs & Co. when his son-in-law Samuel Sachs (1851–1935) joined in 1885. In the early twentieth century, alongside Lehman Brothers, Goldman was one of the premier brokerage houses. Under CEO Sidney Weinberg (1891–1969)—who, when he started at the firm, was literally wiping the partners' boots, and who would later be nicknamed "Mr. Wall Street"—the bank ascended again to the elite of American finance. In the lead-up to the 2008 housing crash, with former CEO Hank Paulson in the White House, CEO Lloyd Blankfein and the rest of the company executed a well-timed bet against the collapsing housing market, resulting in enormous profits, angry clients, and a tarnished public profile that follows the firm to this day.

BEN BERNANKE

B. 1953

Born Ben Shalom Bernanke, this grandchild of Polish and Lithuanian immigrants ran the Federal Reserve from 2006 to 2014. Bernanke lost the National Spelling Bee on the word *edelweiss*, got a near-perfect 1,590 on the SAT, and attended Harvard and then MIT. One of his era's great monetary economists and students of the Great Depression, Bernanke was put to the test during the 2008 financial crisis. After Lehman Brothers went bankrupt, he oversaw the rescue of the insurance giant AIG and the Fed's commitment of trillions of dollars' worth of loans and guarantees to the finance industry. He also set out on a multiyear process of bond buying known as "quantitative easing" in an effort to kick-start and maintain economic growth. Like many a central banker before him, he became the object of a populist backlash that often veered into anti-Semitism.

JANET YELLEN

B. 1946

The first woman to chair the Federal Reserve. Yellen worked as an economist at the Fed, and joined the Federal Reserve's Board of Governors in 1994 and the Clinton White House's Council of Economic Advisers in 1997. After a stint running the San Francisco Fed, she rejoined the Fed's Board of Governors, becoming Bernanke's number two before ultimately succeeding him as Fed chair in 2014. Not surprisingly for a glass-ceiling breaker, she had to deal with whispers from within the financial industry that Larry Summers deserved the job because he had more "gravitas" and sneers that she sometimes repeated outfits. Despite President Trump inheriting a growing economy with low unemployment, in 2017 Yellen became the first Fed chair in almost forty years to not be renominated.

ALAN GREENSPAN

B. 1926

As a young man, Alan Greenspan was in the thrall of a charismatic Jew on the way to founding what could be called a new religion: not a Lubavitcher or a Kabbalah-drenched mystic, but the business-friendly novelist and philosopher Ayn Rand. He took over as chair of the Federal Reserve in 1987 and was almost instantly greeted with one of the worst single-day stock downturns of all time: Black Monday, October 19, 1987. Reappointed by George H. W. Bush in 1991 *and* Bill Clinton in 1996, he oversaw one of the most sustained and fruitful periods of economic and stock market growth in US history. Greenspan left office in 2006 as one of the most admired central bankers in history. Since then, however, his libertarian take on financial regulation and relentless policies of low interest rates following 9/11 have been seen as helping fuel the subsequent financial crisis.

LLOYD BLANKFEIN

B. 1954

The man who led Goldman Sachs for more than a decade grew up in public housing in Brooklyn and sold hot dogs and sodas at Yankee Stadium as a kid. After briefly working for a law firm, he got a job in the commodities business in 1981 at J. Aron, a small firm that was acquired by Goldman Sachs in 1996. He succeeded Hank Paulson as Goldman CEO in 2006, overseeing years of huge profits, the 2008 financial crash, and more huge profits before the slow-grinding retrenchment, with sluggish growth and regulations crimping the once high-flying trading businesses he had overseen.

Ponzi scheme

Much like the Ivy League, the Ponzi scheme was the invention and province of the goyim before being taken over and driven to new heights of excellence by the Jews. The operators of these schemes promise big payouts to new investors, then use their money to pay the original investors—and got a name that stuck after the Italian Charles Ponzi executed a massive such scheme in Boston in the 1920s. But the original Ponzi scheme was nowhere on the scale of Bernard Madoff's fifty-billion-dollar fraud. Madoff built up a massive investing business with huge sums of money from high-profile Jewish nonprofits like Hadassah and the Elie Wiesel Foundation for Humanity and for wealthy clients (like Kevin Bacon). Following the financial crisis, when he couldn't meet his clients' demands for their money back, he confessed to his family that it was all a giant fraud and was sentenced to 150 years in prison (see Shonde, page 240).

bar mitzvah

A bar mitzvah is a "son of the commandment," as the ancient phrase goes. In Ashkenazi Jewish tradition, one becomes a bar mitzvah at the age of thirteen or so, and from then on is counted as a full adult Jew, expected to fast on fast days, give tzedakah, read Torah publicly, and be responsible for one's own actions. Historically, becoming a bar mitzvah marked the age when one's parents were no longer responsible for one's sins—before bar mitzvah, if you effed up, your dad took the fall. A bar mitzvah is also old enough to be counted in the minyan.

Becoming a bar mitzvah was always considered something to celebrate, but about five hundred years ago, the celebrations really began to take off, and later, in the United States, they *really* took off. Today, "a bar mitzvah" often means a party, not a person—a party complete with food stations, hired dancers, chocolate fountains, a live band, and the ever-present party "theme," which can be anything from board games to the Caribbean to golf. The over-the-top, materialistic bar mitzvah party has provoked a backlash, and today many rabbis and families work hard to "tone it down," suggesting there is more "bar" going on than "mitzvah." (As one gimlet-eyed mom put it when asked what the theme of her son's bar mitzvah would be, "The theme will be Judaism.")

A common misconception is that one "gets bar mitzvah'd," as if the rite is something *done to* a boy; rather, every Jew matures into adulthood, regardless of whether he or she has a ceremony. As one rabbi put it, bleakly but wisely, "Those kids who turned thirteen in Auschwitz? They're still Jewish adults, even if they didn't get the party."

Bara, Theda (1885–1955)

Theodosia Burr Goodman was born in Cincinnati, the oldest daughter of a wealthy tailor. She was named after the daughter of Aaron Burr, whom her parents admired. When she was in her twenties, she found her way to Fort Lee, New Jersey, which, before the birth of Hollywood, was where most movies were made. She was an instant sensation, becoming the Silent Screen's biggest star. Because the industry's mostly Jewish bosses thought a plain Jewish girl wasn't that sexy, she was given the moniker Theda Bara, an anagram for "Arab Death." The studio's publicists told the press that Bara was born under the shadow of the Sphinx, the daughter of a rogue Italian sculptor. Her outfits were revealing, earning her the nickname "the Vamp" and a place in history as the world's first film sex symbol. But even though she was famous and rich, she preferred a saner life, marrying the British film director Charles Brabin and returning home to Cincinnati for a life of domestic bliss.

Barbie

We have Ruth Mosko Handler, the daughter of Polish Jewish immigrants, to thank for the iconic blond doll. Handler, whose husband, Elliot, was the cofounder of Mattel, was inspired by a German doll she had bought for their daughter, Barbara. She made a few tweaks, named the doll after her daughter, and debuted Barbie in 1959. The male doll, Ken, named for their son, Kenneth, followed soon after, and the rest is Barbie Dream House history.

bark mitzvah

A party for a dog turning thirteen years old. More an urban legend than an actual practice. Yes, there have been bark mitzvahs, in which very committed dog owners of the Mosaic faith find, in their pooch's calendar, an excuse to have a party. But it's not exactly a Talmudically sanctioned practice. And if it were, wouldn't the dog get the party when it turned thirteen in dog years?

Barney Greengrass

See **appetizing**.

Baron Cohen, Sacha (b. 1971)

Enormously gifted British cringe-comic who was lucky enough to arrive just before the final nail of political correctness shut the coffin lid on this type of humor for good. He first hit it big as Ali G, a hodgepodge of Caribbean, Muslim, and black British stereotypes who would interview notable people and act like a complete nincompoop. "Is it because I is black?" the extremely not-black Ali G would ask when things went wrong. An even bigger hit was Borat, a news reporter from Kazakhstan whose malapropisms and catchy accent would delight frat boys for years to come. Those frat boys were some of the most savagely lampooned groups in the film *Borat: Cultural Learnings of America for Make Benefit Glorious Nation of Kazakhstan* (2006), and mocking prejudice, particularly anti-Semitism, is behind much of the comedy, if you can get past some of the more sophomoric jokes. Proof of its cultural staying power? There's a dubstep remix of "Throw the Jew Down the Well."

Barr, Roseanne (b. 1952)

Born in Salt Lake City, Utah, to a family that had lost many of its members in the Holocaust, Barr made her name as a stand-up comedian with a "domestic goddess" persona. Her situation comedy *Roseanne,* on ABC from 1988 to 1997, was a groundbreaking depiction of the joys, struggles, and sensibilities of a lower-middle-class American family in an Illinois suburb. As close to kitchen-sink realism as sitcoms ever got, it managed to be a funny and familiar portrait of everyday life. In her later years, she has become a humorous if often bizarre presence on Twitter, where she shares her Zionist and conservative views. A short-lived revival of the show, launched in 2018, was derailed by an offensive tweet by Roseanne herself.

baseball

Those who can, play (see **Koufax, Sandy**). Those who can't play but can follow numbers play fantasy baseball. Those who can't do either just talk about it all the time.

bashert

Meant to be, fated. Yiddish noun and adjective. Used to imply that you and that special someone were always destined to be together.

bat mitzvah

While its history has ancient roots, the bat mitzvah is a more recent creation. The first recorded coming-of-age ceremonies for girls were held in nineteenth-century Europe. America's first bat mitzvah, in 1922, came when the trailblazing Mordecai Kaplan, founder of Reconstructionism (see Branches of Judaism, page 44), held one for his daughter, Judith, at his own New York City synagogue. The bat mitzvah first became popular in the more egalitarian branches of Judaism in America, particularly in the mid-twentieth century. But by century's end, many Orthodox communities were also holding celebrations for twelve-year-old girls (the Mishnah says girls mature at twelve, a year before boys). Today most girls who become bat mitzvah get called to the Torah, with the exception of those in certain Orthodox communities. Recent decades have also seen the proliferation of late-life bat mitzvahs for women who didn't have the chance to "come of age" officially.

BDS

The Boycott, Divestment, and Sanctions movement against Israel seeks to mobilize international pressure against the Jewish state. To accomplish this, BDS advocates boycotts of Israeli products, artists, universities, and political officials. The movement's explicit aim is to compel Israel to both end its occupation of the Palestinian territories and to abrogate its Jewish character by admitting millions of Palestinian refugees and their descendants into Israel itself, rather than into a separate Palestinian state. While the movement's leaders oppose a two-state solution—instead supporting the replacement of the Jewish state with a non-Jewish one—its supporters are more diverse in their views, with some supporting boycotts of Israeli settlements but not of Israel proper. In the United States, the movement has had its greatest success winning supporters on college campuses, some of which have seen angry rifts between pro-BDS students and Zionist students.

BEASTIE BOYS

beards

What Orthodox Jewish men grow to comply with the dictates of halacha and hipster Jewish men grow to comply with the dictates of Brooklyn fashion.

Beastie Boys (1981–2012)

The trio of three Jewish MCs known as the Beastie Boys were the reigning geniuses of their time and place, New York City in the 1980s. They were hilarious and brilliantly talented. They were obnoxious and at the same time unpretentious. They made fun of themselves. They were the bridge between old-school jams and artists like Eminem, Kanye West, and Earl Sweatshirt. Ad-Rock, who grew up in the Village, was the most inventive and talented rapper of the three Beasties and could have been Eminem, like producer Rick Rubin wanted, but never had any interest in going solo. Instead, he wrote love notes to his girlfriends in his songs. Adam Yauch grew up in Brooklyn Heights and became a deeply sincere Buddhist who gave global publicity to the Tibetan Buddhist cause. Mike D. was everyone's favorite older brother, or younger brother, or weed dealer. They were the opposite of self-obsessed. They were humble, with giant inflatable onstage penises.

bedeken

The biblical Jacob worked for seven years to win Rachel's hand in marriage, but on their wedding night, his soon-to-be father-in-law, Laban, pulled a fast one on him and stuck Leah in her prettier sister's place. To keep modern grooms from suffering a similar fate, Jewish weddings contain a short ceremony known as the bedeken, in which the groom, after seeing the bride's face, lowers the veil.

BELLOW, SAUL

(1915–2005)

The sad truth is that his work is, at the moment, not in favor: young people who thrill to Jewish novelists like Nicole Krauss, Dara Horn, Gary Shteyngart, and David Bezmozgis may, if they have any interest in the old-timers, bone up on their Philip Roth or their Cynthia Ozick—but Bellow? He is curiously unread, despite being the first Jewish American novelist to really, *really* make it. His 1953 novel, *The Adventures of Augie March*, was compared to works by everyone from Cervantes to Joyce. Its famous opening lines announced Bellow's literary ambition, immediately forging his voice as an immigrant—he'd been born in Canada to Russian Lithuanian Jews, who moved the family to Chicago when Bellow was nine—who would claim his place in the millennia-old Western tradition:

> **I am an American, Chicago born—Chicago, that somber city—and go at things as I have taught myself, free-style, and will make the record in my own way: first to knock, first admitted; sometimes an innocent knock, sometimes a not so innocent. But a man's character is his fate, says Heraclitus, and in the end there isn't any way to disguise the nature of the knocks by acoustical work on the door or gloving the knuckles.**

He knocked, and the world opened: he won the National Book Award three times, a Pulitzer, and, in 1976, the Nobel Prize. The Nobel was like the capstone to the Jewish American literary efflorescence of the postwar years; it's as if he won it for Roth, Ozick, Bernard Malamud, and the rest. Today, people who want a difficult, long, stream-of-conscious novel about ethnic alienation just go to *Ulysses*, while those who want to read about second-generation Americanness have a wealth of Jewish, Indian, Nigerian, and Irish writers, among others, to choose from. But do read Bellow—start with *Herzog* (1964), which is funny, Bellow-vian in all the best ways, and won't take you six months.

BELLOW'S BEST

The Adventures of Augie March (1953)

Seize the Day (1956)

Henderson the Rain King (1959)

Herzog (1964)

Mr. Sammler's Planet (1970)

Humboldt's Gift (1975)

Begin, Menachem (1913–1992)

Few individuals had a greater impact on the founding and evolution of the State of Israel than Begin, a Polish survivor of the Soviet Gulag born in modern-day Belarus whose leadership of the hard-line Irgun militia made him one of the most wanted men in Palestine. The former close associate of the right-wing icon Ze'ev Jabotinsky ended nearly thirty years of Labor Party control and single-handedly changed the shape of Israeli politics when he became the country's sixth prime minister in 1977. During five consequential years in office, Begin made peace with Egypt, ordered the bombing of Saddam Hussein's nuclear reactor, and sent the IDF into Lebanon. Begin set the template for Israeli leaders who became convinced of the necessity of reaching a workable accommodation with the country's enemies, an example that Yitzhak Rabin and Ariel Sharon would later follow.

beit din

Rabbinical court consisting of at least three adjudicators entrusted to oversee divorces, conversions, monetary disputes, and other significant religious matters.

beit midrash

See **synagogue**.

Belzer, Richard (b. 1944)

You probably know him as Detective John Munch, a character appearing in ten series on five networks for more than two decades, most notably on *Homicide: Life on the Street* and *Law & Order: Special Victims Unit*. He's also a conspiracy theorist, a gifted stand-up comic, and Henry Winkler's cousin.

Ben & Jerry's

Socially conscious ice cream company founded in Vermont in 1978 by Ben Cohen and Jerry Greenfield (and now owned by international mega-über-conglomerate Unilever). Many flavors express the company's Deadhead gestalt (see **The Grateful Dead**) with names like Cherry Garcia, Phish Food, and Half Baked; Ben and Jerry's ice cream stores sometimes carry tie-dyed T-shirts.

Benes, Elaine

Fictional character on the television comedy *Seinfeld* (1989–1998). The only central female role on the series, she is played, and danced, to perfection by the half-Jewish actor Julia Louis-Dreyfus (Alfred Dreyfus is a distant relative!). Though she is famously a shiksa, Elaine's Jewishness is *so* apparent. Or perhaps that's just what people are like in New York.

Ben-Gurion, David (1886–1973)

Founding father of the State of Israel. Born in Plonsk, Poland, as David Grün, he became involved with Zionist politics early on and immigrated to Ottoman-ruled Palestine when he was twenty. Quickly emerging as the leader of the Zionist movement, he deftly navigated a host of thorny issues, from relations with the Arab community (he did his best to avoid conflict for as long as possible) to attitudes toward the British mandate (he collaborated with London during World War II, and resumed his drive for independence once it ended). Announcing Israel's independence on May 14, 1948—many of his colleagues had advised him to postpone the declaration until a diplomatic resolution with the neighboring Arab states could be negotiated—he became the nation's first prime minister, serving until 1953 and then again from 1955 to 1963. After retiring from politics, he moved to Kibbutz Sde Boker in the Negev, hoping to inspire more young Israelis to follow in his footsteps and make the desert bloom. Admiring his achievements, the creators of the Green Lantern comic books drew the Guardians of the Universe, an alien race of wise and powerful aliens, to look and sound just like Ben-Gurion.

Benjamin, Judah (1811–1884)

The Virgin Islands–born pro-slavery Louisiana lawyer was the first practicing Jew to serve in the US Senate and later became attorney general, secretary of war, and secretary of state for the Confederate States of America, which explains why he isn't better known today. For most of the Civil War, Benjamin—who overcame the rampant anti-Semitism of his time to become one of American history's leading agents of racism and disunity—was the second most important political figure in the Confederacy, maintaining critical trade ties with the cotton-hungry United Kingdom and generally struggling to keep control over the CSA's quarrelsome and underequipped army. He turned up in London after fleeing Richmond in 1865 and continued practicing law in Great Britain. He's buried in Paris, France.

bentscher

Yiddish for "blesser," a *bentscher* is a small booklet containing the grace after meals and other assorted prayers. In some corners of the Jewish world, a commemorative bentscher will be printed up for occasions like weddings and bar mitzvahs. For reasons known only to the elect, there was a period in the 1970s and '80s when they were produced with velvet covers.

Ben-Yehuda, Eliezer (1858–1922)

For millennia, following the Jewish expulsion from the Promised Land after the destruction of the Second Temple in 70 CE, Hebrew was considered a sacred language, to be used exclusively in prayer. Realizing that no national movement can survive for long without speaking its own native language, Eliezer Ben-Yehuda set out to change all that. A graduate of Paris's prestigious Sorbonne, he emigrated to Palestine in 1881 and dedicated his life to popularizing Hebrew. He spoke no other language with his son, Ben-Zion, and edited several Hebrew newspapers. Realizing that the ancient language had no words for many modern things, he set out

BERLIN, IRVING

(1888–1989)

A handful of song titles tell the tale: "Alexander's Ragtime Band." "Blue Skies." "Cheek to Cheek." "There's No Business Like Show Business." "Easter Parade." "God Bless America." "White Christmas." The greatest songwriter of the first half of the twentieth century, and perhaps the greatest pop songwriter ever, Irving Berlin embodied a peculiarly American idea: that crass commerce was not incompatible with enduring art, that a thirty-two-bar song could both pander to the mob and honor the muses. His life followed a Horatio Alger trajectory: childhood immigrant from Russia to the Lower East Side, propelled by pluck and luck to the summit of American success. He was an autodidactic genius, a self-taught musician who never learned to read or write music and played piano only on the black keys. He was also—unmistakably, audibly—a Jew. Early novelty song hits like "Yiddle on Your Fiddle, Play Some Ragtime" (1909) and "Cohen Owes Me 97 Dollars" (1915) lampooned the struggles of Jewish immigrants with "Yiddish dialect" lyrics and music borrowed from liturgical music. (Berlin's father was a cantor.) His biggest, most "goyish" songs were also Jewish songs. Philip Roth called "White Christmas" and "Easter Parade" "Jewish genius on a par with the Ten Commandments." Roth wrote: "The two holidays that celebrate the divinity of Christ—the divinity that's the very heart of the Jewish rejection of Christianity—and what does Irving Berlin brilliantly do? He de-Christs them both! Easter he turns into a fashion show and Christmas into a holiday about snow." Another great songwriter, Sammy Cahn, summed up Berlin's influence best: "Somebody once said you can't have a holiday without his permission."

I'M DREAMING OF A JEW ON CHRISTMAS: IRVING BERLIN'S GREATEST HITS

"God Bless America"
(1918; 1938 revised)

"Puttin' On the Ritz"
(1927)

"Easter Parade"
(1933)

"Cheek to Cheek"
(1935)

"White Christmas"
(1942)

"There's No Business Like Show Business"
(1946)

to revitalize it, inventing scores of words, including *glida* (ice cream), *ekdach* (gun), and *rakevet* (train). He was reviled by the Haredi community, who considered his daily use of the holy tongue a heresy, and not much better liked by the Zionists, many of whom found him an oddly obsessed pain in their sides. But his spirit overcame all objections, and today, largely thanks to him, there are six and a half million Jewish Israelis who speak Hebrew daily, still using many of the terms Ben-Yehuda coined.

Berg, Gertrude (1899–1966)

Born Gertrude (Tilly) Edelstein in Harlem, Berg is the powerhouse who created, wrote, and starred in *The Goldbergs*, which started as a radio show in 1929 and became a television show in 1949. The show depicted the struggles of a Jewish immigrant family adapting to life in America, and Berg played matriarch Molly Goldberg, with her trademark "Yoo-hoo," to perfection.

Berlin, Isaiah (1909–1997)

Latvian-born British immigrant who was admitted to Oxford as a young man and never quite left. As a preeminent university don and public intellectual, he wrote about a wide array of subjects. He's best known for his essay "Two Concepts of Liberty," which observed that freedom comes in two forms: freedom *from* external forces and freedom to do whatever we choose. The two concepts, he noted, are often in competition. His other philosophical treatise was "The Hedgehog and the Fox," which divided history's greatest thinkers into hedgehogs—philosophers like Plato, who viewed the world through one unified ideological lens—and foxes, like Shakespeare, who found meaning in a wide array of ideas and experiences.

Bernhardt, Sarah (1844–1923)

The grandest of all grandes dames of the stage. A legendary French actress whose talent was so fierce—she was, one critic gushed, "the queen of the pose and the princess of the gesture"—that she inspired, taught, intimidated, and motivated generations of thespians to shine. Even though her difficult life led her to a convent where she was baptized, she never forgot her mother's religion or stopped identifying as Jewish.

BERNSTEIN, LEONARD

(1918–1990)

Composer of *West Side Story*, *Candide*, and *On the Town*, conductor of the New York Philharmonic (from 1958 to 1969) and the summer festival at Tanglewood, internationally prominent pianist, and host of the Young People's Concerts on CBS (1958 to 1972), Leonard Bernstein was both a revolutionary Broadway creator and the most important American-born classical maestro ever.

BEST OF BERNSTEIN

On the Town (1944)

Candide (1956)

West Side Story (1957)

When a reporter asked her, at the height of her fame, if she was a Christian, she said, "No, I'm a Roman Catholic, and a member of the great Jewish race. I'm waiting until Christians become better."

Bialik, Chaim Nachman (1873–1934)

Arguably the most significant Hebrew writer in modern history, Bialik is considered Israel's national poet, a title he continues to enjoy even eight decades after his death. An orphan raised by his fervently Orthodox grandfather in Zhitomir, Ukraine, he distinguished himself early in life with his poems, capturing longing—spiritual, emotional, erotic—in all its complexity. In 1903, after the pogroms in Kishinev left dozens of Jews dead, he wrote a few of his most memorable works, including "In the City of Slaughter," a fiery indictment of God for letting so many innocents die. "And if there is justice," goes one famous passage from the poem, "let it show itself at once! But if justice show itself after I have been blotted out from beneath the skies, let its throne be hurled down forever!"

The Big Lebowski (1998)

Bible

Hebrew Bible. Don't call it the Old Testament.

The Big Lebowski (1998)

Cult film beloved of stoners, college students, and bowlers. While not exactly the most intellectual entry in the Coen brothers' oeuvre, it is endlessly quotable, and it has some hidden wisdom beneath the pot smoke and rattling White Russian ice cubes. Though the plot is impossible to follow until the third time you see it, Jeff Bridges's performance as a befuddled aging hippie ("the Dude") caught up in a web of conspiracy is hilarious. Among the more memorable characters is John Goodman's gun-toting, hot-headed Vietnam vet, Walter Sobchak, who converted to Judaism to marry. The wife didn't stick, but the religion did. Sobchak isn't just shomer Shabbos, he's "shomer *fucking* Shabbos" and is ready to pounce on the bowling-league organizer who scheduled a tournament game on a Saturday. As he explains to his doe-eyed pal Donny (Steve Buscemi), "I don't handle money, I don't turn on the oven, and I sure as shit *don't fucking roll! . . . Shomer Shabbos!*"

binding of Isaac

You know the basics: Abraham, called upon by God to sacrifice his only child, appears ready to do the deed, lifting his hand with the knife, only to be stopped at the eleventh hour. Is there a biblical story that has generated as much commentary? Is there one that continues to haunt us so viscerally? The idea that Abraham, that great ancestor all monotheistic religions share, was a moment away from slaughtering his own boy is disturbing, which is precisely why humanity's finest thinkers have, for millennia, treated this story as a philosophical chew toy on which to sharpen their teeth. Some have argued that it wasn't God who was testing Abraham but the other way around, the old man putting the Lord to the ultimate challenge. Others have claimed that neither God nor Abraham ever intended to go through with the slaughter, and that the whole thing was just a macabre dialogue between two guys who understood each other a bit too well. And Søren Kierkegaard, gloomy as ever, saw the whole thing as the perfect example of Man's ability to live inside the grotesque and absurd creation that is our world. This debate is not likely to die down anytime soon.

Birobidzhan

Administrative center of the Jewish Autonomous Oblast, Siberia, Russia. Also known as the Siberian Zion, the Promised Land at the confluence of the Bira and Bidzhan Rivers, the Soviet government's gift to the homeless and persecuted Jews of Russia. Established in the 1930s as the first modern official Jewish homeland for as many Jews as would settle there, the idea was to create a Jewish agricultural colony along the border with China, which was both a way of exiling Jews to the hinterland by calling it something else and serving Russian strategic interests. At its peak in the late 1940s, the region boasted thirty thousand settlers, mostly Russian Jews, but some from Eastern and Western Europe, South America, and the United States. Today, two thousand Jews remain in the city of seventy thousand.

birthright

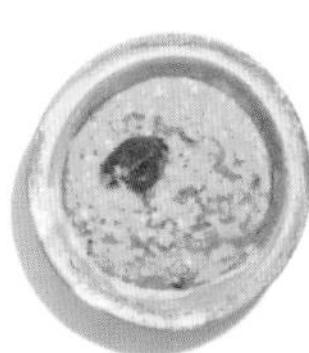

The Bible's great parable on the perils of instant gratification focuses on the twins Jacob and Esau. It's a really crazy story. Esau, who was minutes older than his brother and as such had the privileges of the firstborn, was a rugged hunter. Jacob was more of a mama's boy—and a bit of a conniver. One day, Esau came in from the fields as Jacob was cooking some lentil stew. Esau was literally starving. Jacob, ever on his toes, offered to give him some stew in exchange for his birthright. Esau, in one of history's more shortsighted deals, agreed.

Birthright Israel

Also known as Taglit-Birthright or simply Birthright. Since 1999, Birthright has provided diaspora Jews with free, ten-day (or so) tours of Israel, where they are encouraged to see the sights, fraternize with Israeli soldiers, and go home with a future spouse. Birthright isn't exactly brainwashing—it's more like a light brain cleanse. The quality of the cleanse varies widely, depending on what Birthright trip you take. Although the typical Birthright trip is run by a college Hillel, trips are also run by Chabad and numerous other organizations. There are themed trips for the enviro-conscious, for LGBT Jews, for those into "mindfulness," and much more. In other words, Birthright is now a franchise, and any trip that meets certain basic criteria for safety and educational curricula can get the Birthright imprimatur and open the money spigot. Some studies show that the trip promotes attachment both to Jewishness and to Israel. This being a Jewish trip, there are critics—of its Zionist agenda, of its refusal to take participants to the West Bank, and, above all, of the extraordinary expenditure on what amounts to a free, oft-drunken trip for teens and young adults. Might these hundreds of millions of dollars be better spent on day schools or other educational endeavors, or even on Jewish podcasts? You tell us.

Black Hebrew Israelite

A term describing several disparate groups of African Americans who believe themselves to be the descendants of a lost Tribe of Israel. Their exact beliefs and levels of observance vary.

black-and-white cookie

They look like cookies and they're eaten like cookies but they're actually round, flat cakes that have a slightly tangy quality, thanks to buttermilk (or sour cream) and a bit of lemon in the batter. The signature chocolate and vanilla glazes on top make this New York staple one extremely fashionable color-blocked cookie. It is a cousin to the monochromatic German Amerikaner and has made cameos in *Seinfeld*, a 2008 Obama campaign stop at a deli, and *The Marvelous Mrs. Maisel.*

blessing

See **bracha**.

blintzes

An uncharacteristically delicate Ashkenazi dish of sweetened pot cheese wrapped in a crêpe and griddled in butter until crisp. Or a not-so-delicate dish of what's basically cheesecake batter-wrapped in a pancake, then fried.

blood libel

In 1144, in the English town of Norwich, a little boy named William was found dead in the woods, stabbed all over. A local monk soon wrote a hagiography of the boy, arguing that William had been kidnapped and crucified by the Jews, who, he said, reenacted the killing of Christ every Easter for their perverse pleasure. Similar accusations were soon made throughout England, usually resulting in the murder of Jews and, in 1290, in the expulsion of all Jews from England for nearly four hundred years. The blood libel soon spread to the rest of the continent, the claim often being that a Christian child had to be sacrificed so that his blood might be used to bake matzo on Passover. Blood libels remain a depressingly popular conspiracy theory, particularly in the Arab world.

BLUME, JUDY

(B. 1938, MAY SHE LIVE FOREVER)

This prolific writer for children, teens, and adults became a star with her 1970 coming-of-age story *Are You There, God? It's Me, Margaret*, though many of us are fond of *Forever . . .* (1975), a first-love story featuring a penis named Ralph. It was illicitly passed around every bunk in every Jewish summer camp in the 1970s and '80s. Blume has sold more than eighty-five million books; her works have been translated into thirty-two languages. Her books are frequently banned by those who object to her depictions of teens' sexuality and—possibly worse—atheistic tendencies. Blume owns a bookstore in Key West where actual human fans have seen her in the actual flesh.

THE JUDY BLUME STARTER PACK

Are You There, God? It's Me, Margaret (1970)

Then Again, Maybe I Won't (1971)

Tales of a Fourth Grade Nothing (1972)

Deenie (1973)

Blubber (1974)

Starring Sally J. Freedman as Herself (1977)

Tiger Eyes (1981)

Booze and Jews

VODKA
& PICKLED HERRING

Sure, the traditional Russian pairing might be vodka and caviar, but for Jews nothing is more delicious than cold vodka and pickled herring. The sweet-and-sour flavor of the herring provides the perfect chaser for the cold vodka, making it ideal for any celebratory occasion.

LATKES & CHAMPAGNE

The Maccabees defeated the Greeks, and oil meant to last for one day lasted for eight, which is worth celebrating. And nothing says "Celebration!" like popping bottles of Champagne. But that's not the only reason for this pairing. Bubbly Champagne is the perfect accompaniment to fried foods, because the bubbles and acidity in the wine cut beautifully through the fat of the oil. It's a match made in heaven. It's bashert.

Perfect Pairings

SABLE (OR LOX) AND PILSNER

There is nothing like a crisp pilsner to balance the smoky saltiness of sable or lox. While Jews have a reputation for not drinking a lot of beer, this combination could change that. The pilsner is light, clean, and refreshing, cutting through the fat, smoke, and salt of the fish, refreshing your palate and causing you to want to eat more.

MANISCHEWITZ & BRISKET

If you've been to a Jewish holiday, it's likely you've had this classic combination. For festive meals it's essential. And the preparation of a traditional Ashkenazi brisket means there will be sweet and savory flavors in the meat that marry perfectly with the sugary wine. Your bubbe may have even used it to baste the brisket in the first place!

MOSCATO & BABKA

While Drake may drink Moscato any time of the day, the sweet (often kosher) wine is traditionally served as a dessert wine, making it the perfect match for a sweet chocolate babka. The honeyed notes of the wine pair beautifully with the sweet chocolate, creating a combination that is better together than apart.

Bloom, Harold (b. 1930)

American literary critic known for his scholarship on the Romantic poets, Shakespeare, and pretty much everything else. A prodigy at Bronx High School of Science, Cornell (class of 1951), then the doctoral program at Yale, where he was to spend his career as a professor, Bloom is known for his eccentricity and for his 1973 treatise, *The Anxiety of Influence.*

Bloomberg, Michael (b. 1942)

Former New York City mayor, founder of the data terminal and news organization that bear his name, philanthropist, and, depending on the day, the richest man in New York City.

Bloomsday

On June 16, we celebrate James Joyce, his novel *Ulysses*, and his country of Ireland. What does Bloomsday have to do with the Jews? Joyce saw the Irish as having been robbed of their distinct language and culture by English conquest. To Joyce, therefore, the hero of modern times was a person who—through the degradations of daily life and through the ravages of history, which Joyce's alter ego Stephen Dedalus calls "a nightmare from which I am trying to awake"—somehow ingeniously persevered. To Joyce, then, the hero of modern times had to be a Jew. And so he was: *Ulysses* is the modern-day epic of Leopold Bloom, a Dublin advertising salesman making his way through life on June 16, 1904. Halachically, Bloom fails to qualify: his mother was an Irish Catholic, and he himself has been baptized. But no matter. The novel leaves zero room for doubt as to where Bloom spiritually stands. The Jew abides.

blow jobs

According to one stereotype, something Jewish girls never give. According to another stereotype, something Jewish girls excel at.

Book of Life

According to Jewish tradition, this is the roster, written on Rosh Hashanah and sealed on Yom Kippur, that God keeps of all righteous people, indicating who will live and who will die. The ancient sages, however, advised us not to think of the book as a literal bound volume but rather as a metaphor for the lasting impression our good and bad deeds leave long after they're committed.

Boosler, Elayne (b. 1952)

Influential stand-up comedian for a generation of baby-boomer women. She was a hostess at the Improv in New York until the comedian Andy Kaufman convinced her to try her hand on the stage, and a star was born. Boosler, often a lone female voice in the club, told jokes about dating, disappointing her parents, and the differences between the sexes—jokes that would later be the fodder of a million sitcoms, although sadly, none in which she herself starred.

booze

See Booze and Jews, page 40.

Borscht Belt

See **Catskills**.

bracha

Blessings, we have them. If it starts "Baruch atah"—"Blessed are you"—then it's a blessing, or, in Hebrew, a bracha. We bless the bread with "the motzi"—*Baruch atah adonai, Eloheinu melech ha-Olam, ha'motzi lechem min ha'aretz*—and the wine with "the kiddush," which famously ends with "*borei pri ha'gafen.*" We have blessings for taking a trip, for seeing a rainbow, for seeing your son become a bar mitzvah, for smelling a nice smell, for being made a Jew, for waking up in the morning, and hundreds more good things. For Orthodox Jews, the day is punctuated by constant blessings. For the rest of us, the occasional bracha can serve as a reminder to be grateful, even for brown rice ("*Baruch atah adonai, Eloheinu melech ha-Olam, borei minei mizonot*").

Branches of Judaism

See page 44.

Brandeis, Louis D. (1856–1941)

Kentucky-born son of Bohemian immigrants who became the first Jewish justice on the Supreme Court.

Brandeis University

Despite the widespread misconception, Brandeis University is not a "Jewish school"—not officially, at least. Founded in 1948 in Waltham, Massachusetts, the school, named after Supreme Court justice Louis D. Brandeis, was "Jewish sponsored," and Jewish funded, but it was always secular and unaffiliated with any Jewish movement. At a time when many elite and Ivy League schools still had quotas keeping their Jewish populations low, Brandeis quickly became, along with City College of New York and the University of Chicago, known as an elite school where a young Jewish man or woman (it was coed from the start) could get a fair shake and a fine education. Alumni include Jewish

Louis Brandeis: The first Jewish justice on the Supreme Court, for whom Brandeis University is named

In the beginning, Judaism didn't have branches, or denominations—that's a Christian thing. In their early years, Christians were splitting into all sorts of camps, each calling the other heretical, and then they had their big split between the Roman and Eastern Churches in Catholicism, then the Reformation . . . you know the story. Jews weren't the same the world over, of course—there was a lot of regional variation in liturgy and practice, though not belief—but the idea that in one town there would be competing Jewish houses of worship, espousing competing theologies, would have seemed absurd until about 1800. Today, of course, the ideal of a unified am Yisrael, "people of Israel," seems to recede evermore into the distance. We splinter by theology, liturgy, and politics. To some, the existence of many flavors of Judaism is a strength, allowing the maximum number of Jews to find a religious path that feels right to them. To others, this pluralism is a goyish heresy, and we should long for a time when the atheist and the hasid could at least agree on the proper shul for the atheist to reject.

Reform

Coalescing in Germany in the early nineteenth century, Reform Judaism was a response to emancipation, which granted Jews full citizenship in their countries of residence. Honoring the demands of science and reason, as well as their gentile compatriots' expectations of what made a good citizen, they modernized: by abandoning the millennia-old yearning to return to Zion; by recasting many Hebrew prayers in the vernacular; by exchanging traditional garb for modern fashions. Migrating to America, the movement soared in the nineteenth century, boosted by the arrival of German Jews as well as by the conditions of American life, in which Saturday was often a day of commerce and keeping Shabbat was therefore impractical for hardworking, upwardly mobile Jews. American Classical Reform, as it is now called, rejected kosher laws, moved services to Sundays, and in many temples forbade men to wear kippot or yarmulkes. At the famous "Trefa [Treyf] Banquet" of 1883, ultra-assimilationist Reform Jews gathering in Cincinnati dined on a menu that featured shellfish—that's how eager they were to distance themselves from Orthodoxy. But Reform has gradually sought, in some ways, to return to tradition. Hebrew has reasserted herself in Reform prayer books, for example, and although Classical Reform was anti-Zionist, most Reform Jews came to support the State of Israel, especially after its imperilment in the Six-Day War. The movement remains progressive on key theological issues. In 1983, for example, the movement accepted patrilineal descent, and its rabbis are permitted to preside over marriage ceremonies between Jews and non-Jewish partners. Reform is the largest branch of Judaism in the United States.

Conservative

Conservative Judaism is an American wing of Judaism—with outposts in some other countries, which are often, as in Israel, called Masorti—that represents a middle path between the strictures of Orthodoxy and the religious liberalism of Reform. Rooted in the historical positivist tradition of the nineteenth century, Conservative Judaism appeared in the early twentieth century (its organization of synagogues, now called the United Synagogue of Conservative Judaism, was founded in 1913 by Solomon Schechter) as a movement of Jews who wanted to modernize their practice while keeping a decent measure of deference to *halacha*, Jewish law. So, for example, as the Reform movement jettisoned kosher eating as a requirement of Jewish observance, Conservative Jews continued to keep kosher—in theory. While Reform Jews decided it was okay to drive on Shabbat, Conservative Jews were supposed to refrain from driving—unless, according to one famous 1950s ruling, they were driving for the sole purpose of going to synagogue. And while Orthodox prayer books remained Hebrew dominated, and Reform prayer books were written mostly in English, the Conservative movement's books tried to maintain a balance; their worship services continued to be conducted nearly all in Hebrew, but their books contained a good deal of translation and transliteration.

By the end of the twentieth century, the reality was that Conservative Judaism struck many shrewd observers as hypocrisy in action: most Conservative-identifying Jews are no more observant than Reform Jews, but their rabbis are expected to behave, mostly, as if they are fairly Orthodox. The people in the pews eat what they want and pause only for High Holidays, Passover, and Hanukkah; the rabbis must obey the dictates of the movement—keep kosher, keep Shabbat, and fast on obscure occasions like Tzom Gedalia.

Once a large movement with about one million members or fellow travelers, now, in the twenty-first century, Conservative Judaism is in trouble, its numbers crashing. Is it a relic of the postwar transitional generations, who wanted the freedom of America but had nostalgia for the Old World? Perhaps. But it also may be the movement best suited for the growing minority of Jews who want to marry more traditional liturgy to a progressive, feminist, queer-friendly openness.

Orthodox

These days, if you say you are Orthodox, that doesn't tell people much. The next question is "What kind of Orthdox?"

Modern Orthodox

Just how modern? And how Orthodox? That depends on the community, on the shul, and on the person. But, generally, those who adhere to this philosophy believe in Torah u-Madda (Torah and worldly knowledge), meaning that you can and should observe Judaism's laws while still engaging fully with the world outside. These are the Joe Lieberman Jews, who daven every morning but make major moves in the secular world. They may attend Yeshiva University, which was founded for them, but they can also be spotted in the Ivy League and, in big numbers, at state schools like the University of Maryland and Binghamton. The differences between Modern Orthodox and Haredi Jews come down to the level of engagement with the secular world, as evidenced by attire; openness to secular education; willingness to live near gentiles; and—it's a biggie—the sex and gender stuff, like whether married women must cover their heads and whether women can take leadership roles in synagogue, which Modern Orthodoxy is more open to.

Haredi

When a journalist, or a Reform Jew, or a politician refers to Haredi Jews, or "the ultra-Orthodox," she means Jews who are both the most observant and most sectarian of all Jews. Whereas a Modern Orthodox Jewish man may dress just like any secular man, except for the yarmulke on his head (and perhaps the fringed undergarment under his shirt), a Haredi man is likely to be dressed in a black suit and white shirt. A Haredi woman, with her stricter definition of tznius (modesty), generally wears skirts, keeps her arms covered, and wears a wig or headscarf after marriage. Haredi elementary and high schools offer far less secular learning than other Jewish schools, and Haredi Jews either eschew higher education or attend professional schools. Haredi Jews place a premium on living, insofar as it is possible, only among other Jews like them.

But here's the tricky thing: Haredi Jews seldom call themselves "ultra-Orthodox," because they (rightly) believe that "ultra" has negative connotations and makes them sound like fringe extremists. They prefer either the Hebrew Haredim (literally, "trembling ones"), "Torah Jews," or "traditional Jews."

When in doubt, go with Haredi. It's a term with no negative connotations, and unlike "Hasidim," it embraces the whole community of stringently observant Jews.

Hasidic

Not all Haredim are Hasidic Jews, but all Hasidic Jews are Haredi. Starting in the early eighteenth century, the spread of Kabbalah and Jewish mysticism and declining trust in traditional communal structures led to Hasidism—in Yiddish, *hasidus*—whose believers were attracted to the courts of specific charismatic rabbis. While differences between Hasidic sects abound, most believe that God is omnipresent in the world, which means He should be worshipped not only by learning but also by experiencing His glory in nature and by revealing life's hidden, mystical layers. The movement's founding father was Yisrael Ben Eliezer, better known as the Baal Shem Tov, or Master of the Good Name. The rise of Hasidism evoked fierce condemnations from more traditional observant Jews, who claimed that the new movement, with its hero worship of rabbis, was teetering on heresy. Hasidism was nearly eradicated in the Holocaust, but it has seen a miraculous rebirth in Israel and in the United States (above all in certain Brooklyn neighborhoods), where one can find thousands of Hasidim, in their distinctive garb, still following rabbinic dynasties like Bobov, Ger, Satmar, Pupa, and Chabad-Lubavitch (which has really become its own thing).

Reconstructionism

Recently rebranded as Reconstructing Judaism, this branch of Judaism was conceived by Mordecai Kaplan (1881–1983), author of the unreadable but influential *Judaism as a Civilization* (1934). Kaplan was a Lithuanian-born Modern Orthodox rabbi in New York City whose conception of God took a naturalistic turn: he decided that, in light of science and reason, it was no longer tenable to think of God as anything like a personal, omnipotent Being. As his God became more abstract and metaphorical, Kaplan's view of Judaism changed from that of a particular people holding certain beliefs to a "civilization" in the ongoing process of evolution. After he lost his welcome in Orthodox circles, he founded his own congregation, the Society for the Advancement of Judaism. Today, Kaplan's view of Judaism as an evolving civilization is interpreted by Reconstructionists to mean that most forms of observance are optional, or chosen—and can be unchosen by subsequent generations. Reconstructionists tend to go further than even Reform Jews in rejecting *halacha*, Jewish law, as the basis for living. At the same time, because this tiny movement (which has a small seminary outside Philadelphia) is so radically open, it also includes some liturgical traditionalists, who pair old-fashioned observance (wearing yarmulkes, keeping kosher) with innovative theology.

Renewal

With the renewed interest in mysticism and spirituality in the counterculture movement of the late 1960s (see The Jewish Sixties, page 246), some young Jews banded together in *havurot* (see **havurah**), small egalitarian study and prayer gatherings designed to reject and replace the more traditional synagogue structure. One of the most prominent havurah leaders was Zalman Schachter-Shalomi, a lapsed Chabad rabbi interested in meditation and other mystical practices. His havurah eventually grew into a movement, whose founding generation of rabbis, which included Arthur Green and Arthur Waskow, incorporated neo-Hasidic elements like song and dance, Kabbalistic teachings, meditation, and other traditions like Sufism. Although relatively small, the movement that came to be known as Renewal Judaism has inspired numerous havurot and study groups around the world, as well as some enduring congregations and worship communities, like Romemu in New York City and Havurat Shalom in Cambridge, Massachusetts.

greats like Debra Messing and Mitch Albom, as well as notable gentiles like author Ha Jin.

BRCA

Ashkenazi Jews (and others with Eastern European ancestry) have a higher likelihood of inheriting BRCA1 and BRCA2 gene mutations, which indicate heightened risk for certain cancers. Both women and men can have and transmit BRCA gene mutations: for women with the mutation, there is an increased risk of breast and ovarian cancers; for men, breast and prostate cancers. There is also an increased risk of pancreatic cancer for both men and women with BRCA gene mutations. But a BRCA gene mutation does not mean you will get cancer, just that you may need to take preventive measures—anything from doctor check-ins to regular self-exams to more extreme prophylactic measures, depending on your family history and

BROOKS, MEL

(B. 1926)

THE BEST OF BROOKS

The Producers (1967)

History of the World: Part One (1981)

Blazing Saddles (1974)

Spaceballs (1987)

Young Frankenstein (1974)

If the clever novelists and lyricists represent the urbane Jewish wit of the mind, Brooklyn-born Mel Brooks (né Kaminsky) represents the rude, rules-averse comedy of the body. Every Hollywood western showed a bunch of cowboys sitting around the campfire eating beans. It wasn't until Brooks's 1974 masterpiece *Blazing Saddles* that we saw them ripping Manifest Destiny–sized farts. Brooks cut his teeth in the Catskills and early television (see Caesar, Sid). He and Carl Reiner would entertain friends at parties with a bit in which Reiner would "interview" Brooks, pretending to be a two-thousand-year-old man, who was basically just a cranky Jew. In 1967, Brooks decided that the world was ready to laugh at Hitler, so he wrote and directed *The Producers*, in which Zero Mostel and Gene Wilder play two shyster Broadway producers looking to intentionally make a flop. Unexpectedly, their *Springtime for Hitler* becomes a hit. Brooks's later films tweaked movie genres, not just westerns but historical epics (*History of the World, Part One*) and science fiction (*Spaceballs*). A Broadway musical version of *The Producers* in the early 2000s (with songs written by Brooks) broke box-office records.

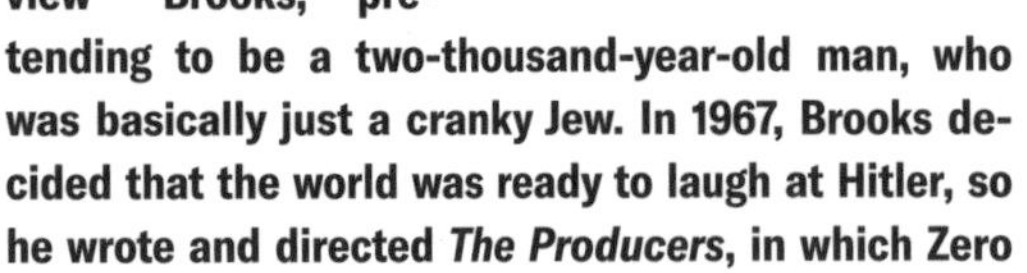

It wasn't just because the play, like all of Brooks's work, was funny; it was also because Brooks used comedy to point out larger, uncomfortable truths. It takes a good artist to deliver compelling films that explore racism, hypocrisy, greed, lust, and longing. It takes a great artist to do all that and weave in a few good fart jokes.

BROOKLYN

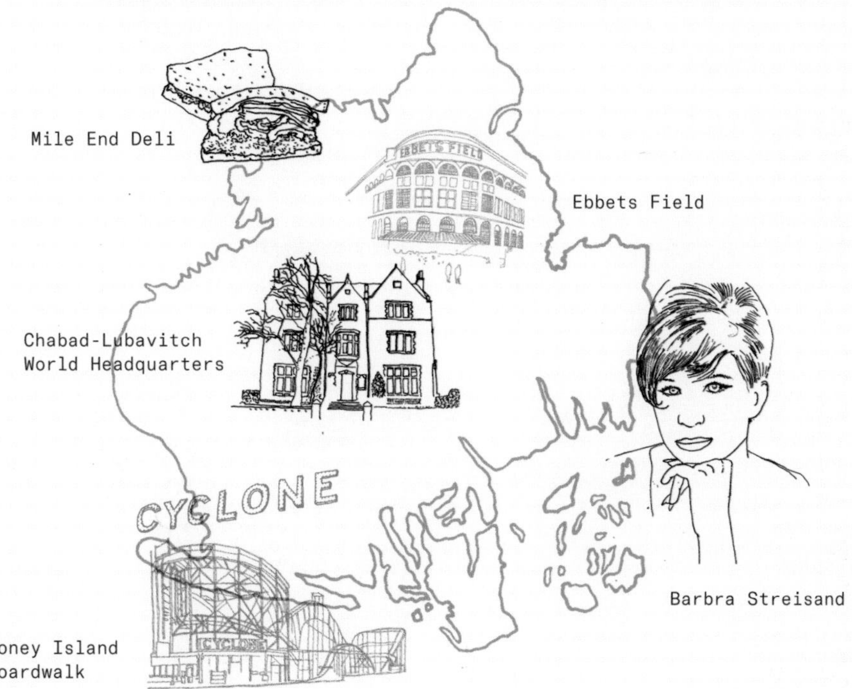

The most populous of New York City's boroughs, it runs in the north from the physical limits of Greenpoint and the spiritual heights of the Brooklyn Bridge to, at its southern tip, the Atlantic currents and Russian grandmas of Brighton Beach. Founded in the seventeenth century as a Dutch settlement named Breuckelen, after a town in the Netherlands, it remained an independent rural outpost through the early nineteenth century. That changed when urbanization driven by a thriving port transformed Brooklyn into a center of commerce and set in motion its eventual inclusion in New York City.

In 1898, the once thriving, independent borough of Brooklyn was incorporated into the unified city of New York by an act of Manhattan imperialism. In the twentieth century, Brooklyn distinguished itself by its contributions to World War II through the Brooklyn Navy Yard, and by the brief, exquisite reign of the Brooklyn Dodgers, whose second baseman, Jackie Robinson, broke baseball's color barrier, in 1947. The team went on to beat the Yankees and win the World Series in 1955.

In the postwar years, Brooklyn became a cultural mecca, giving birth to something like half of all people who would shape the second half of the twentieth century. Woody Allen, Barbra Streisand, Jay-Z, Henry Miller, Ruth Bader Ginsburg, Joseph Heller, the Beastie Boys, and Maurice Sendak—all from Brooklyn (and, most likely, so is your uncle Stu).

On the heels of falling crime rates in the 1990s and with the unstoppable onslaught of financialized real estate, modern Brooklyn has once again been transformed. The northern half of the borough, beginning with the experiment called Williamsburg, has increasingly become an adjunct of Manhattan—and Manhattan ain't what it used to be. The three great epochs in any personal history of Brooklyn include Old Brooklyn—before my time; Real Brooklyn—while I lived there; and New Brooklyn—when you moved in.

personal risk. BRCA made headlines in 2013 when Angelina Jolie (not Jewish, alas) underwent a preventive double mastectomy after discovering she had a BRCA1 mutation.

break-fast

The festive and frenzied meal that ends the Yom Kippur fast. See **bagel**; **lox**; **indigestion**.

Breitbart, Andrew (1969–2012)

See **Drudge, Matt, and Andrew Breitbart**.

Brice, Fanny (1891–1951)

Born Fania Borach, Brice was the singer and comic played by Barbra Streisand in the 1964 musical and 1968 movie *Funny Girl*. The daughter of immigrant saloon owners, Brice dropped out of school to work in a burlesque show called "The Girls from Happy Land." She became a Ziegfeld Follies headliner, then a radio star playing bratty toddler Baby Snooks. When Brice got a nose job, writer Dorothy Parker quipped that she'd "cut off her nose to spite her race."

Brin, Sergey (b. 1973)

Google it.

bris

Yiddish for *brit*, as in brit milah, the covenant of circumcision. Circumcision presents one of Jewish history's great mysteries. How is it that Judaism's most primitive and barbaric custom has also proved to be its most durable and lasting, still observed today even by assimilated Jews? Though the ritual has to an extent become eclipsed by the customary smoked fish and chocolate babka served afterward, lurking behind all the food is an uncomfortable ritual connecting baby boys to the patriarch Abraham, whose own circumcision was what sealed his covenant with God. See **mohel, mohelet**; **sandek**.

bris kit

Some gauze pads, some ointment, and a thimbleful of Manischewitz, just in case the mohel runs out.

brisket

One of the nine primal cuts of meat removed from the cow after butchering. Because the brisket is rich in muscle and takes a short eternity to cook, it's among the cheaper cuts of meat you can buy. Because it comes from the front of the cow, it's explicitly kosher (the back part is more complicated, as things often are when it comes to Jews and food). And because it's a really large cut, it's perfect for special occasions, like Shabbat dinner or a holiday meal. For all these reasons, the brisket has become the star of many a Jewish festive table, making appearances on Rosh Hashanah, Passover, and any other time when friends and family come together to celebrate and overeat. There are many ways of cooking a delicious brisket, but your grandmother's is probably the best.

brit milah

See **bris**.

Broflovski, Kyle

Fictional elementary school kid from the always-in-tumult town of South Park, Colorado, and voice of reason in the face of his clueless parents and the obnoxious Eric Cartman. Voiced by Jewish *South Park* cocreator Matt Stone, Kyle's Jewishness has been a significant plot point since the prurient show's debut in 1997. His loneliness on Christmas made for a memorable episode involving anthropomorphized excrement (of course) and Kyle singing a sad but catchy song with lyrics like "I'm a Jew, a lonely Jew . . . I'd be merry, but I'm Hebrew . . ."

Bronson, Action (b. 1983)

Chef turned rapper born Ariyan Arslani to an Albanian Muslim father and a Jewish mother in Queens. Responsible for the most Jewish rap lyric of all time: "I've been wilin' since the rabbi snipped it / then they laughed, and ate brisket."

Brooklyn

See page 49.

Bruce, Lenny (1926–1966)

Pioneering stand-up comic born Leonard Alfred Schneider on Long Island. His obscene bits, tame by today's standards, got him in trouble with the law. After he was arrested on obscenity charges following a Greenwich Village performance in 1964, nearly a hundred machers signed a letter in his defense, including the literary critic Lionel Trilling, the novelist Norman Mailer, the poet Robert Lowell, and the theologian Reinhold Niebuhr. The letter described him as a social satirist "in the tradition of Swift, Rabelais and Twain." It's not for nothing that he appears as a character on *The Marvelous Mrs. Maisel* fifty years after his death.

Fanny Brice: In character as Olga Chekaloff, the wacky maid, in the 1938 film *Everybody Sing*

His bit on Jewish versus goyish is just one of his works of genius that's still relevant, now and forever:

> Dig: I'm Jewish. Count Basie's Jewish. Ray Charles is Jewish. Eddie Cantor's goyish. B'nai Brith is goyish; Hadassah, Jewish. Marine corps—heavy goyim, dangerous. Kool-Aid is goyish. All Drake's Cakes are goyish. Pumpernickel is Jewish, and, as you know, white bread is very goyish. Instant potatoes—goyish. Black cherry soda's very Jewish. Macaroons are very Jewish—very Jewish cake. Fruit salad is Jewish. Lime Jell-O is goyish. Lime soda is very goyish. Trailer parks are so goyish that Jews won't go near them. *The Jack Paar Show* is very goyish. Underwear is definitely goyish. Balls are goyish. Titties are Jewish. Mouths are Jewish.

Well, his certainly was.

BUGS BUNNY

bubbe

Your grandmother. Would it kill you to call her?

Buber, Martin (1878–1965)

Austrian Israeli philosopher who wrote the Jewish existentialist classic *I and Thou* (*Ich und Du*, 1923). Over his long career as a public thinker, Buber also explored Jewish mysticism and penned a translation of the Hebrew Bible. After multiple run-ins with the Nazis, he fled Europe for Israel in 1938.

Buchdahl, Angela Warnick (b. 1972)

The first Asian American rabbi to lead a major syngogue, Buchdahl—who is also a noted cantor—was born in Seoul and raised in Tacoma, Washington, by her Ashkenazi Jewish father and Korean American mother. In 2014, she was installed as the senior rabbi of Manhattan's Central Synagogue, one of the largest congregations in the world. That year, she also got to do Hanukkah at the Obama White House.

Bugs Bunny

He was voiced by Mel Blanc and believed to be inspired by Groucho Marx (see **Marx Brothers**). He speaks with a heavy New York accent. His worst enemies are Elmer Fudd and Yosemite Sam, two murderous goyim with guns. This is one kosher rabbit.

burning bush

The form God takes when He first reveals himself to Moses. One of the key symbols in Jewish iconography, the bush is notable for being a paradox. It burns without getting burnt. "The bush burned with fire, and the bush was not consumed."

"But is it good for the Jews?"

The ultimate question about anything.

FROM

Caesar, Sid

TO

cultural Judaism

Caesar, Sid (1922–2014)

Television innovator known for wacky sketch comedy and for fostering a legendary writer's room that begat many tremendous careers. Isaac Sidney Caesar was born in Yonkers, New York, and worked in a luncheonette run by his immigrant parents. There he absorbed accents from all over, later incorporating them into the exaggerated gibberish of his memorable routines. Over a long career in television, he helped discover and foster many writing talents, including Mel Brooks, Carl Reiner, Neil Simon, Selma Diamond, and, later, Woody Allen.

Cahan, Abraham (1860–1951)

Founding editor of the *Jewish Daily Forward*, or *Forverts*, a Yiddish daily newspaper that launched in 1897. He helmed the influential, socialist-leaning paper for more than four decades, launching a widely read advice column called "A Bintel Brief" that helped Jewish immigrants navigate life in America. He was also a novelist, writing in English; he's best known for *The Rise of David Levinsky*, a semiautobiographical tale of a Jewish immigrant in New York City.

Cain and Abel

According to the Bible, the world's first siblings. Not coincidentally, the perpetrator and victim, respectively, of the world's first murder.

Cairo Geniza

A collection of three hundred thousand manuscript fragments independently discovered by several scholars in the late nineteenth century in the geniza, or storeroom, of the Ben Ezra Synagogue in Cairo. The documents spanned a head-spinning nearly fifteen-hundred-year period, from the fifth century to about 1880 CE, and consisted of both religious and secular writings. The trove provided an astonishingly detailed glimpse into centuries of Jewish life and thought, and has since been analyzed by generations of academics, writers, and rabbis.

camp

The place where Jewish kids spend the summer and learn how to play ga-ga. Or something entirely different that Susan Sontag wrote about.

Camp David Accords

On September 17, 1978, after twelve days of intense negotiations, Israeli prime minister Menachem Begin, Egyptian president Anwar Sadat, and US president

Jimmy Carter announced that the thirty-year war between the Middle Eastern neighbors had ended, thanks to a full peace agreement that few had dared to predict. Israel would withdraw its forces from occupied Sinai and dismantle several civilian communities in the peninsula. In return, Egypt would establish full diplomatic relations with its former enemy and commit to strict limits on its military deployments in Sinai. The deal became possible after Sadat made a historic gesture and traveled to Jerusalem to address the Knesset in November 1977.

The deal included a section where the parties promised to work toward a resolution of Israel's conflict with the Palestinians, but in practice the agreement ended an official policy of Arab unity in the struggle against the Jewish state. As punishment, Egypt was expelled from the Arab League until 1989. Camp David remains the single most important event in the often-troubled history of Israeli-Arab diplomacy. The fact that the deal came just five years after the Yom Kippur War, which Egypt launched on the holiest day on the Hebrew calendar and which involved the largest tank battles fought anywhere on earth since World War II, is proof that no conflict is truly intractable.

On the other hand, Sadat came to the negotiating table only after concluding that peace was Egypt's sole means of recovering the Sinai Peninsula, which the country had failed to reconquer during its 1973 sneak attack, despite its army's early success in dislodging the Israel Defense Force from the eastern bank of the Suez Canal. Whatever idealism clinched this history-moving accord only became possible after decades of wars in which Israel emerged victorious. Today, the peace between Egypt and Israel is one of the cornerstones of regional stability and has survived political upheavals on both sides of the border. It's also about as cold as peace can get—forty years after the agreement, there are almost no cultural, commercial, or academic exchanges between the two countries, and cooperation is almost entirely limited to the security realm.

Camp Kinderland

One of many progressive Jewish summer camps to dot western Massachusetts and upstate New York in the twentieth century, Camp Kinderland was founded in 1923 by the International Workers Order to infuse little Jews with secular, left-wing Yiddishkeit. Founded in New York but for most of its existence located in Tolland, Massachusetts, Camp Kinderland was a popular place for communists to send their red-diaper babies, who bunked for the summer in cabins with names like Joe Hill and Eugene Debs. Today, Camp Kinderland still draws the children of those members of New York City's secular Jewish professoriate and intelligentsia who like their Judaism lite, their politics heavy, and their food organic.

Camp Ramah

A network of Jewish summer camps affiliated with the Conservative movement, the first Ramah opened in Conover, Wisconsin, in 1947. Today, Ramah encompasses sleepaway camps, day camps, and teen tours and study programs in Israel. Its programs attract over 11,800 youngsters a year. In addition to the pioneering Wisconsin camp, there are sleepaway camps in the Berkshires; the Poconos; Palmer, Massachusetts (Camp Ramah in New England); Ojai, California; Ontario, Canada; Clayton, Georgia (Ramah Darom, Hebrew for "Ramah South"); plus a Ramah in the Rockies camp in Colorado, as well as camp programs around the country for children with special needs. Notable Ramah alumni include comic Jewess Debra Messing, former Federal Reserve chair Ben Bernanke (see Banking and Jews, page 26), Dell founder Michael Dell, US Rep. Jerrold Nadler, writer Chaim Potok, and CNN's Jake Tapper.

Ramah is clearly good at creating Jewishly identifying adults. A 2016 survey of 5,260 former Ramahniks found that over 80 percent feel that their Jewishness is very important in their lives; 80 percent belong to a synagogue, minyan, or havurah; and almost half report still having at least three close friends they originally met at Ramah. More than 40 percent (!) met their spouses through a Ramah connection.

Ramah is also surprisingly good at creating Broadway stars. Ben Platt (Ramah in California) won a Tony for *Dear Evan Hansen*; Caissie Levy (Ramah Canada) stars as Elsa in *Frozen*. (You can hear them duet on Hebrew Ramah songs if you search YouTube for "From Ramah to Broadway.") Other Ramahniks include Sharone Sayegh of *The Band's Visit* and Rachel Katzke, a child performer in *School of Rock* who wore her Ramah backpack to performances and took a week off during the summer to—yes—return to camp.

Canter's Deli

See Delicatessen, page 74.

cantor

In Hebrew a *hazzan*, a cantor is a ritual singer, the man or woman with a really good voice who leads the community in prayer. In Judaism, the person performing this role does not need any special ordination or investiture; if you can carry a tune, and the community accepts you, you can be their *shliach tsibbur*, or "emissary of the congregation," the head pray-er. In olden times, and still today in the most observant communities, the bar is a bit higher. For example, a sixteenth-century German set of guidelines for a hazzan insisted that he (and it was always a he) be humble, of pleasing voice, and agreeable in appearance, and not move his hands restlessly.

Cantor, Eddie (1892–1964)

His nicknames were apt: The Apostle of Pep. Banjo Eyes. Wacky and irrepressible, with large eyes that seemed permanently frozen in an expression of shock, Eddie Cantor brought the frantic energy of vaudeville into the age of mass media. A star of the variety stage, Broadway, motion pictures, radio, and television, Cantor was the consummate musical comedian, singing, dancing, and shticking with the virtuosity of a pro who had been working crowds since his days as a teenage singing waiter. Cantor's signature numbers include huge 1920s and '30s hits such as "If You Knew Susie," "Makin' Whoopee," "Ma! He's Makin' Eyes at Me"; he wrote "Merrily We Roll Along," the *Merrie Melodies* Warner Brothers cartoon theme song. Born Isidor Iskowitch in New York, he was the son of Russian Jewish immigrants, and Jewishness loomed large in his life and art. Millions tuned in to his radio shows to hear his gently comical stories about his wife, Ida, and their six daughters. Along with the hit radio show *The Goldbergs* (see **Berg, Gertrude**), Cantor's monologues gave many Americans their first taste of Jewish family life. In the 1930s, he used his bully pulpit to aggressively denounce anti-Semitism and the rise of the Nazis. He lived long enough to provide voiceover work in the 1953 biopic *The Eddie Cantor Story*.

carciofi alla giudia

Italian for "artichokes, Jewish-style." These artichokes fried in olive oil are the emblematic dish of the Roman Jewish kitchen and a remarkable crossover food that traveled from a medieval Jewish ghetto to bougie wine bars everywhere.

Cardozo, Benjamin (1870–1938)

The second Jew to sit on the Supreme Court (after Louis D. Brandeis) and a highly influential justice who wrote the majority opinions on a number of seminal cases, including the 1932 case that found an all-white Democratic Party primary in Texas unconstitutional. Namesake of Cardozo Law School of Yeshiva University in New York City.

Carlebach, Shlomo (1925–1994)

An Orthodox rabbi who was deeply influenced by the Greenwich Village folk music movement of the late 1950s and early 1960s, Carlebach introduced guitar to Jewish liturgy and services. He began setting Bible verses and other sacred texts to music, in an effort to make Judaism joyous and accessible. His melodies are still widely used in synagogues and prayer gatherings around the world, although his legacy has been diminished by posthumous allegations of sexual harassment.

Carnegie Deli

See Delicatessen, page 74.

OMRI CASSPI

Casspi, Omri (b. 1988)

The first Israeli player in the NBA, Casspi made his debut for the Sacramento Kings in 2009. His Omri Casspi Foundation takes players and assorted other celebrities to Israel every year (Jeremy Piven, have you sent your thank-you note yet?).

Catskills

A mountain range in New York State, familiarly known as the Jewish Alps or the Borscht Belt. The Catskills were a popular Jewish summer resort area in the mid-twentieth century. Accommodations ranged from fancy hotels with swimming pools, multicourse dinners, and live entertainment to more rustic and family-oriented bungalow colonies and *kuch-aleyns* (literally "cook-alones," bungalows or rooms with a kitchen). Musicians and other performers cut their teeth in front of the area's notoriously difficult audiences, but the Catskills became truly famous for comedy: generations of comedians got their start, or honed their acts, there, from Henny Youngman to Sid Caesar, Rodney Dangerfield to Joan Rivers, Billy Crystal to Jerry Seinfeld. (The 1987 film *Dirty Dancing* is set in the old Catskills, if you want to get a feel for the scene.) These days the big hotels—the Concord, Grossinger's, the Nevele, Kutsher's—are gone, and the kuch-aleyns have mostly been torn down. But recent decades have seen a different kind of Jewish revival in the Catskills, as Hasidim have moved to some of the small towns full-time, escaping the higher cost of living in New York City, and many more come up to the remaining bungalow colonies over the summer; kosher bakeries and Yiddish billboards abound. It's not the kind of scene that will nurture the next generation of comedians, but it ensures that you'll be able to find good rugelach in the Catskills for years to come.

Chabad-Lubavitch, Chabad

You know those people who stand on street corners in big cities and on college campuses and ask you if you're Jewish? They're Lubavitchers, members of the Hasidic sect known as Chabad. Following the teaching of their late Rebbe, Chabad is committed to inspiring all Jews to perform mitzvot, work they do out of "Chabad

Catskills: Jews, and maybe even a few gentiles, lounging poolside at Tony Leone's Resort in the Catskills in 1960

Chabad-Lubavitch Mitzvah Tank: Among the more visible manifestations of the Chabad-Lubavitch outreach effort, these repurposed RVs blare Hebrew music and transport emissaries brandishing seasonally appropriate Jewish ritual items.

Houses"—they're ubiquitous, from Boston to Bangkok—where you can always get a warm meal, learn how to put on tefillin or light Shabbat candles, and see an oil painting of the Rebbe on the wall. Chabad is probably the most visible form of Judaism, with its members out there on the front lines, cheerfully engaging anyone around them in anything Jewish.

chai

The Hebrew letters *chet* and *yud* spell *chai*, which means "alive," making it a very auspicious term. It's why you sometimes see people—including Elvis! And Drake! And Hall of Famer Rod Carew!—wearing chai necklaces. Also, because of gematria, the word's numeric value, eighteen, is considered a lucky number as well, which explains why so many of us give gifts or make donations for $18, $180, $360, or other numbers related to our magical number.

challah

Everyone's favorite part of the Shabbat meal. When done right, this fluffy braided bread is just a little bit sweet and perfect for soaking up anything delicious on your plate. We traditionally tear it rather than cut it with a knife, and say a special blessing, Hamotzi, thanking God for this delicious gluten delivery system. The word *challah* originally referred to the portion of dough one was required to donate to the priests, or kohanim, when making large amounts of dough in Temple times. Now it just means the bread we love. Excellent for French toast, terrible when called "challah bread" by gentiles.

Chaney, Goodman, and Schwerner murders

Andrew Goodman (b. 1943), Michael Schwerner (b. 1939), and James Chaney (b. 1943) had traveled to Mississippi with the Freedom Summer campaign in 1964 to register African Americans to vote. Goodman and Schwerner were Jewish, Chaney was black. After visiting a church that had been burned down by white supremacists, they were arrested outside Philadelphia, Mississippi, for speeding and held for a few hours. They were released, but as they drove out of town, they were abducted and executed. After an extensive search, their bodies were discovered, and it was revealed that members of the Ku Klux Klan, along with several law enforcement officials, were involved in their murders. Forty-one years later, a single man, Edgar Ray Killen, was convicted of the murders and

CHAGALL, MARC

(1887–1985)

Born Movsha (Moyshe) Shagal in Vitebsk, a small and heavily Jewish Belarussian town made mostly of wood, Chagall showed an immense artistic talent from a very young age. His mother didn't like it, arguing that painting was impractical. But the boy insisted, and before too long he moved to St. Petersburg and then to Paris, becoming one of the masters of modernism. He frequently painted Jewish themes, capturing, in bright colors and dreamlike settings, the traditional community in which he grew up. His windows adorning the synagogue of the Hadassah Medical Center in Jerusalem are among his best-known works. "Chagall reads the Bible," one critic said of the famous stained-glass masterpieces, "and suddenly the passages become light."

CUBIST CHAGALL

I and the Village (1911)

sentenced to sixty years in prison; he died, incarcerated, in January 2018. The murders did much to galvanize public opinion and contributed to the passage of the Civil Rights Act of 1964. A popular movie, *Mississippi Burning* (1988), was loosely based on the case, and Schwerner and Goodman's sacrifice is often mentioned as an example of the considerable role Jews played in the civil rights movement.

Chaplin, Charlie (1889–1977)

British-born comedian, silent-film star, director, composer, and gentile who was frequently thought to be Jewish. "I do not have that good fortune," said Chaplin when asked the question directly in 1915. The Nazis banned his films anyway. He showed what he thought of them in his important 1940 anti-Nazi film, *The Great Dictator*. In his first talkie, Chaplin tweaked his iconic persona to become a persecuted Jewish barber. He also played Adenoid Hynkel, an obvious parody of Hitler. He was inspired to make the movie after finding great absurdity in Leni Riefenstahl's Nazi propaganda film *Triumph of the Will*; he later said he would not have gone forward had he been aware of the full depth of the Third Reich's barbarism. We're glad he did go forward.

CHARLIE CHAPLIN

cheeseburger

Second only to bacon on the list of forbidden things we crave, although in recent years vegan products have given hungry, kosher-keeping Jews a few pretty good substitutes.

chevra kadisha

Literally "the holy society," this group of men and women, lay volunteers whose identities are usually not known to their community, are trained in the Jewish rites of preparing a body for burial. The work is considered of particular merit and is carried out along gender lines (women prepare female bodies, men prepare male bodies; this strict division is changing now to include all Jews and all types of gender expression, though often slowly and not quite across all communities). Children are forbidden from preparing the bodies of their parents, and all the work is carried out with an air of solemnity and deep respect. Because the dead cannot return the favor, there are few mitzvahs that are considered more sacred, which is why the duty is sometimes referred to as *chesed shel emet*, or a true kindness.

Broadly, the body undergoes what is known as *tahara*, or purification, in which it is cleansed, washed all over, and dressed in a plain white garment known as a kittel. The body is wrapped in shrouds and only uncovered partially as needed, while each area is washed, then covered again, as the society members recite prayers and ask forgiveness for the intrusion on the privacy of the corpse. Members of the chevra kadisha traditionally fast on the seventh day of the Hebrew month of Adar, the day of Moses's death—as the Bible tells us, it was Moses who not only took Joseph's bones from Egypt and ensured he would be reburied in Israel, but who is buried by God himself—to atone for any acts of disrespect they might have shown the dead (see **death**).

chicken soup

Jewish penicillin. Chicken-infused water was singled out by Maimonides as the fix for what ails you, and unlike vitamin C, echinacea, Saint-John's-wort, yoga, homeopathy, or positive thinking, it actually cures colds. Just ask your mother!

Chinese food

See Chinese Food and Jews: A Christmas Love Story, page 63.

cholent

Observing Shabbat but still want a hot meal? Then cholent, a slow-cooking meat-and-potato stew, is your best bet. The genius of cholent is how it simmers for hours or days in the oven without losing any of its flavor. There are many variations on cholent, and each community insists that its take is the best, but the basics usually involve beef, potatoes, barley, and beans. Sephardi Jews call this dish hamin, a key feature of which is haminados, eggs left to cook all night until they turn a pleasing brown. In Ashkenazi cholent, on the other hand, the pièce de résistance is the kishke, an intestine stuffed with meat and grains, which, trust us, is much more delicious than it sounds.

Chomsky, Noam (b. 1928)

Prominent American linguist. Raised in a Zionist family in Philadelphia and doing some of his early scholarly work on Hebrew, Chomsky rose to prominence for suggesting that humans' shared biological structure enabled them to understand language in the same way, irrespective of cultural differences. He rose to even greater prominence for his lifelong pursuit of radical leftist ideas, some mainstream (he opposed the war in Vietnam and is a critic of Israeli policies) and others (such as downplaying communist-led Cambodia's genocide of 1.5 to 2 million of its own citizens) more controversial. He remains one of America's most prominent and best-recognized public intellectuals.

chopped liver

A member of the extended family of Jewish foods (see Food and Jews, page 100) that takes a less-than-desirable part of the chicken and spins it into gold (by cooking it with plenty of onions and chicken fat, then mashing it into a spreadable paste, maybe with hard-boiled eggs thrown in). Other members of the genre include schmaltz (chicken fat), gribenes (chicken skin), helzel (chicken skin stuffed with grains and chicken innards), and the tuchus (chicken butt). Chopped liver was also popularized in the guilt-tripping vernacular, "What am I, chopped liver?" which comes from the idea that the spread was always an appetizer or a side dish, but never the main course—erasing any doubt for anyone that it is, indeed, a Jewish food.

CLUELESS

chosenness

The foundational tenet of Jewish theology. At the height of the biblical drama, God speaks to the Israelites and tells them, "Unto Me you shall be a kingdom of priests and a holy nation." Standing at the foothills of the mountain, the baffled Israelites probably had a few questions: "Why us?" "What exactly is our job as God's chosen people—what exactly were we chosen for?" "Are our children automatically chosen, too?" "Is this a good thing?" And "Is there a way to get unchosen?" These are logical questions, but God never says another word on the subject. Which is precisely the magic of chosenness: to have been chosen means spending millennia wondering what exactly it means to have been chosen, a divine brainteaser that, arguably, has inspired Jews through the centuries to ask really good questions and come up with really good arguments, even or especially in the absence of concrete answers (see **lawyer**).

Chrismukkah

A true American holiday. Chrismukkah was invented by *The O.C.* protagonist Seth Cohen, the son of Jewish lawyer Sandy Cohen and "Waspy McWasp" Kirsten Nichol, to distill the very best of Christianity and Judaism. Proper observance includes Chinese takeout, holiday movies, eight days of presents followed by one day of many presents, the ceremonial wearing of Yamaclauses, and love triangles involving teenagers. A source of miracles.

Christian Zionists

Devout Protestants have been praying for the return of Jews to their Promised Land since at least the seventeenth century, and many continue to cheer for Jewish sovereignty in Israel today, decades after said return resulted in the establishment of a Jewish state. While the reasons for this support are frequently theological—the return of the Jews to Zion, and, often, their conversion to Christianity, is a herald of the Second Coming of Jesus—political calculations have frequently fueled Christian Zionism as well. For the past few decades, the fiercest Christian Zionists have emerged from the evangelical community, often pairing their religious beliefs with partisan support for the Republican Party and right-wing Israeli politicians.

Christmas

A Jewish boy's birthday (see Jews and Christmas, page 62).

chuppah

Jewish wedding canopy (see Wedding, page 283).

chutzpah

What it takes to think you can write an encyclopedia of Jewish life.

circumcision

See **bris**.

JEWS AND CHRISTMAS

For Christians, Christmas is the holiday that celebrates the birth of Jesus Christ, whom they consider to be the son of God and their savior. For Jews, it's often seen as an occasion to go to a movie and eat Chinese food.

CHINESE FOOD & JEWS

"Over the years," write scholars Gaye Tuchman and Harry G. Levine in their 1992 scholarly paper "New York Jews and Chinese Food: The Social Construction of an Ethnic Pattern," "New York Jews have found in Chinese restaurant food a flexible open symbol, a kind of blank screen on which they have projected a series of themes relating to their identity as modern Jews and as New Yorkers." Put another way: American Jews have a thing for Chinese food. The question is why. Tuchman and Levine posit three answers. First, although Chinese food is not kosher, it appeared to many Jews—like the immigrants on the Lower East Side who lived minutes from New York's Chinatown—to be, among other cuisines, *relatively* okay, or, as the expression goes, "safe treyf." It used familiar ingredients, like chicken, beef, and noodles, and above all, it didn't mix meat and dairy, because Chinese food contains no dairy. Second, "Jews construed Chinese restaurant food as cosmopolitan. For Jews in New York, eating in Chinese restaurants signified that one was not a provincial or parochial Eastern European Jew, not a 'greenhorn' or hick." Finally, within a generation, Jews saw Chinese restaurant food as a Jewish thing: Jews did it because it was the kind of things Jews did. But there's another reason: Chinese restaurants are open on Christmas Eve (and Christmas). It's a truth not lost on Supreme Court justice Elena Kagan, who famously told Senator Lindsey Graham, when he asked during her Senate confirmation hearing what she'd been doing one Christmas, "Like all Jews, I was probably at a Chinese restaurant."

A Christmas Love Story

IS "RUDOLPH THE RED-NOSED REINDEER" A JEWISH SONG ?

The question may seem absurd—but cue up the Gene Autry recording that topped the US hit parade in Christmas 1949, and listen close. What you will hear is a Jewish American wish-fulfillment fantasy. The song tells the story of a social outcast with a funny schnoz who bootstraps his way to success, saving Christmas and earning the love of the goyim and a place in the history books.

Now consider the song's provenance. "Rudolph the Red-Nosed Reindeer" was composed in 1949, by the Jewish songwriter Johnny Marks. Marks's brother-in-law, a Jewish advertising copywriter named Robert May, had created the character Rudolph the Red-Nosed Reindeer a decade earlier as a promotion for the Chicago department store Montgomery Ward. The Rudolph song, the Rudolph myth, Rudolph himself, is the product of Jewish commercial culture. For Johnny Marks, "Rudolph" was just the beginning: he named his song publishing company St. Nicholas Music and made his fortune specializing in Christmas music. His hits included "Rockin' Around the Christmas Tree," "A Holly Jolly Christmas," and, of course, "Run Rudolph Run."

Marks was not unique. For most of history, the Christmas song canon consisted of hymns and wassails that can be traced back as far as the early Middle Ages; the nineteenth century brought more sacred songs—"Hark! the Herald Angels Sing," "Good King Wenceslas"—as well as secular carols like "Jingle Bells" and "Deck the Halls." But the body of Christmas songs that are most widely heard and sung today were created in the mid-twentieth century, and Jews had a hand in most of them. "Santa Claus Is Comin' to Town" debuted on Eddie Cantor's radio show. "Let It Snow! Let It Snow! Let It Snow!," "The Christmas Song (Chestnuts Roasting on an Open Fire)," "Winter Wonderland," "I'll Be Home for Christmas," "Silver Bells"—all were written, or cowritten, by Jewish songwriters. To the extent that we regard Christmas as a civic-secular celebration involving reindeer, Santa Claus, falling snow, tree trimming, gift giving, and good cheer, we have Jewish Tin Pan Alley to thank.

The ne plus ultra of Christmas anthems is "White Christmas" (1942), Irving Berlin's evocation of a pastoral yuletide "where the treetops glisten / And children listen / To hear sleigh bells in the snow." For decades, "White Christmas" stood as the top-selling song of all time. Philip Roth extolled the "Jewish genius" of the song, which, Roth wrote, "de-Christs" Christmas, turning it into a "holiday about snow." But Berlin's song does something cleverer still. The song is a nostalgia trip, an ode to Christmas past: "I'm dreaming of a White Christmas / Just like the ones I used to know," croons Bing Crosby on the recording that made the song famous. Berlin captured the longing that defines Christmas for millions: that hope that the season will bring back yesteryear's joy, enchantment, innocence. That same vague yearning, it turns out, keeps Christmas music on airwaves and charts year after year. A Christmas song, Irving Berlin and Johnny Marks and the other yuletide Jews discovered, a hit that comes back each December.

RUDOLPH THE RED-NOSED REINDEER, YOU'LL GO DOWN IN HISTORY!

City College of New York

Since its founding in 1847, this public school has provided accessible higher education to the poor and the just-off-the-boat, a huge number of them Jews. In the first half of the twentieth century, City College educated future political thinkers—Irving Howe and Irving Kristol attended together, along with Daniel Bell and Nathan Glazer; the school's cafeteria was a famous site of Trotsky versus Stalin debates—as well as the finest young minds in math and science. Ten CCNY graduates from the years 1933 to 1963 went on to win Nobel Prizes, in physics, chemistry, medicine, and economics. Artists went there, too: Alfred Stieglitz was a City College boy, as were Zero Mostel and Ira Gershwin and Henry Roth and Bernard Malamud. Was City College the Harvard of the Jews? No, Harvard was at best the City College of the gentiles. Today, there are way fewer Jews at City College, but no fewer ambitious, striving young Americans.

Clueless

Classic 1995 comedy directed by Jewess Amy Heckerling. It is deservedly beloved for its deft updating of the plot of Jane Austen's *Emma*, for its sumptuous outfits, for its simultaneously loving and snarky take on Beverly Hills rich-kid teen culture, and for its unabashedly Jewish heroine, Cher Horowitz, who simultaneously confirms and transcends the stereotype of the JAP, played by the perfectly blond and generally perfect Jewess Alicia Silverstone.

cohen

See **kohanim**.

COEN BROTHERS

Actual brothers Joel and Ethan hail from the Minneapolis suburbs and have made some of the craftiest movies of all time. Their work ranges from screwball comedy (*Raising Arizona*, *The Hudsucker Proxy*, *Burn After Reading*) to crime capers (*Fargo*, *The Big Lebowski*, *The Ladykillers*) to bleak, existential howls (*Blood Simple*, *Barton Fink*, *No Country for Old Men*). They are also responsible for the closest thing we'll ever get to a big-screen adaptation of the Book of Job, *A Serious Man*, arguably the most Jewish movie ever made. Set in the Jewish Midwest of their youth, the movie opens with a prologue in Yiddish about a dybbuk, then cuts to a man who yearns for a righteous life, but is hit with (ridiculous, hilarious) obstacles at every turn. He seeks wisdom from his rabbis, who baffle him with seeming non sequiturs, and is cuckolded by Sy Ableman, an aggressively empathetic, husky Jew with a deep voice who likes to give hugs. And this is all *before* it gets bad! One can find Jewish subtext in a lot of the Coens' work—is the Dude a Jew? Llewyn Davis? Certainly Bernie Bernbaum from *Miller's Crossing* and Barton Fink were, even if played by Italian American John Turturro. And lest we forget, *The Big Lebowski's* Walter Sobchak doesn't roll on Shabbos.

GOIN' COEN

Barton Fink (1991)

The Big Lebowski (1998)

Fargo (1996)

A Serious Man (2009)

COHEN, LEONARD

(1934–2016)

A singer and songwriter best known for his unavoidable hymn, "Hallelujah," too frequently covered but still perennially gorgeous. A modern-day prophet who, like his biblical predecessors, saw just one more layer of truth and beauty in life than most of us ever notice. And if you think that's taking it too far, put on a pair of headphones, turn off the lights, and listen to "If It Be Your Will."

THE GOSPEL OF ST. LEONARD

- "Suzanne" (1967)
- "Sisters of Mercy" (1967)
- "So Long, Marianne" (1968)
- "Bird on the Wire" (1969)
- "Famous Blue Raincoat" (1971)
- "Chelsea Hotel No. 2" (1974)
- "Hallelujah" (1984)
- "If It Be Your Will" (1984)
- "Who By Fire" (1984)
- "Anthem" (1992)
- "You Want It Darker" (2016)

Cohen, Andy (b. 1968)

Unrivaled impresario of reality television. The St. Louis native almost single-handedly turned the Bravo network from a place viewers could go to watch taped broadcasts of opera performances into a candy-colored parallel reality of programming as intricate and overlapping as any comic book universe thanks to the Real Housewives franchises (and their three-part reunion specials), which he executive produces. With his deft commodification of female rage and his love of dishy gossip about his famous friends, ably displayed in his late-night talk show, *Watch What Happens Live*, Cohen is the Florenz Ziegfeld of yentas. In 2019, he welcomed a son, Benjamin Allen Cohen, via surrogate.

Cohen, Lyor (b. 1959)

Born in New York to Israeli parents, Cohen started out as Run-DMC's road manager. Within three years, however, his talent and drive had propelled him to partner with Russell Simmons and become a talent manager, signing up artists like Eric B. & Rakim and A Tribe Called Quest. He became a record label boss before moving to serve as YouTube's global head of music. Not everyone in hip-hop is a fan, though: in 2004, Mos Def recorded a track in which he rapped that "some tall Israeli is runnin' this rap shit," not exactly meaning it as a compliment.

comic books

Next to Scripture, it's the second greatest literary gift Jews have given the world. It was the Jewish entrepreneurs Max Gaines and Harry L. Wildenberg who helped turn comic books into a truly massive commercial phenomenon in the early 1930s, but by the end of the decade, the potential for illustrated stories that could fit in a few strips seemed exhausted. Enter Jerry Siegel and Joe Shuster, who, in 1938, gave us *Action Comics #1*. It was published by DC Comics' Jewish boss, Harry Donenfeld, and featured a crypto-Jewish protagonist, an immigrant from a foreign and

decimated culture who had to hide his true identity. His name was Superman. Thus began the golden age of comics, which was almost entirely influenced by Jews: Joe Simon and Jack Kirby created a hero who started out as a scrawny kid from Brooklyn and soon morphed into a supersoldier named Captain America, and shipped him overseas to fight the Nazis; Bob Kane went darker, giving us Batman, the orphaned and moody Caped Crusader; Will Eisner's hero, the Spirit, was also a vigilante in a mask, albeit one who could tell (and take) a joke; Bill Finger went magical with a super ring that turned whoever possessed it into the Green Lantern; and Mort Weisinger dove underwater for inspiration, reemerging with Aquaman.

That all these works were created and published by Jews is no coincidence: just like the movies, comic books were another unguarded, low-brow territory where smart and creative outsiders could gather to tell fantastic stories that helped them overcome their sense that American culture wasn't exactly meant for folks like them. Harvey Kurtzman and Al Feldstein took this energy to its logical conclusion with *MAD* magazine, which more or less single-handedly shaped American humor for decades to come. And in the 1960s, as the counterculture was going mainstream, Stan Lee was there with Marvel Comics to deliver Ben Grimm, the Lower East Side Jewish thug who became the Thing, founding member of the Fantastic Four; Max Eisenhardt, the Auschwitz survivor who discovered his mutant powers and, as Magneto, unleashed them on humanity; the Silver Surfer, who, like Abraham, was commanded by an angry deity to leave his home, roam the earth, and sacrifice people; and a long string of others, from Spider-Man and the Hulk to Doctor Strange and Iron Man. Everywhere you look these days—from your PlayStation to the multiplex to Netflix—you see the work of a few ink-stained Jews who, half a century ago, dreamed big and bold.

commandment

See **mitzvah**.

concentration camp

The Nazis weren't the first to intern a large number of people without cause or trial—the Spanish military did so in Cuba in the 1860s—but they were, by orders of magnitude, the most efficient. First built in Germany in 1933, immediately after Hitler's rise to power, concentration camps spread across Europe with the Nazis' advance and numbered, according to some estimates, fifteen thousand by the war's end. While some camps, like Auschwitz-Birkenau, were death camps, designed to systematically murder people, mainly Jews, others, like Dachau and Bergen-Belsen, were designed to hold large groups of slave laborers, prisoners of war, and potential threats to the regime. Still, the inhumane conditions and the Nazis' cruelty meant that millions perished in these concentration camps, too.

Congregation Beit Simchat Torah

This Manhattan congregation is the world's biggest and best-known queer shul. It was founded in 1973 by Jacob Gubbay, a gay Jewish immigrant from India. Although in its early years it attracted mainly gay men, CBST now also draws lesbians, bisexuals, trans people—all manner of LGBT Jews—and a substantial number of straight congregants, too. Its Yom Kippur services are so popular, drawing over three thousand worshippers, that they are held at the massive Jacob K. Javits Convention Center.

Conservative Judaism

See Branches of Judaism, page 44.

conversion

There have always been converts to Judaism. If we follow Torah and say that Abraham was the first Jew, then his wife, Sarah, was the first convert. And the second would have been their daughter-in-law, Rebecca. These women converted just by marrying in. So did Moses's wife Zipporah. But the most famous convert in Torah, and a hero to all Jews by choice, is Ruth, who after being widowed chose to stay with the Israelites, her late husband's people. As we learn in the Book of Ruth, which is read on Shavuot, she said to her mother-in-law, Naomi, "Do not entreat me to forsake you, to turn back from after you. For whither you go, shall I go; where you lie down, shall I lie down; your people are my people; and your God is my God" (Ruth 1:16).

In Talmudic times, the rabbis made conversion more complicated, requiring study, approval by a beit din, and immersion in a mikveh. There are many who believe that this heightened legalism was a wrong turn; indeed, most synagogues today, including Orthodox ones, have in their communities gentile spouses, children, or other fellow travelers who, while not technically Jewish, live as Jews and may be more knowledgeable, and more committed, than many halachic Jews. Should they need to be quizzed to be accepted, when Ruth was not? On the other hand, Judaism has always been a family—or nation, or tribe—as much as a religion, and it's not surprising that Jews developed certain rituals of belonging. In any event, right now, there is a process, a hoop (made up of Stars of David) that you have to jump through, as many thousands willingly do every year.

converso

Much of Spain's preexpulsion Jewish population converted to Catholicism as a hedge against the pogroms and official persecutions it frequently faced. King Ferdinand and Queen Isabella were not so easily fooled. The Spanish Inquisition began in 1481 to root out secret Jewish practice and other heresies among Spanish subjects who had been threatened and coerced into conversion; when that proved inadequate, the monarchs simply expelled their country's Jews in 1492 (the Inquisition would continue in some form until 1834). The sheer number of conversos ensured that some form of Jewish practice and identification survived the 1492 purge: *marranos*, a derogatory term possibly taken from the Arabic for "hypocrite" or the Spanish word for "swine," were conversos who secretly continued practicing Judaism. The notion that conversos were inherently suspect or deceitful meant that they couldn't hold certain public offices and were generally looked upon with suspicion. The number of conversos, like the number of pre-1492 Jews, was fairly significant: a 2008 study in the *American Journal of Human Genetics* found that at least 20 percent of the current Iberian population was descended from Jews, which hints at the mind-boggling scope of the persecution.

Copland, Aaron (1900–1990)

With Leonard Bernstein, Aaron Copland was one of the two foremost Jewish American composers of classical music. In some ways, he was nothing like Bernstein: where Bernstein was flamboyant and self-promoting, Copland was retiring and private. But the two men shared an interest in populist forms and had a knack for accessible melodies. While Bernstein spoke to the masses through musical theater, Copland had a strong interest in ballets, and his score for *Appalachian Spring* (1944), commissioned by Martha Graham, is one of three Copland pieces—with *Billy the Kid* and *Fanfare for the Common Man*—that will forever signify, musically, the American frontier and its pioneer spirit.

Cosell, Howard

See Sports and Jews, page 251.

Cossacks

The Russian horsemen who raped your great-grandmother.

covenant

An agreement between God and Man. The first to receive the divine offer-you-can't-refuse was Noah: God promises never again to amuse himself with a flood, and in return gives the ark builder a set of rules for ethical conduct that apply to all of humanity. Later, the Almighty, in a more specific mood, strikes another covenant with Abraham; this time, the contract is only between God and Abraham's descendants—us, the Jews—and is marked by circumcision, setting us apart from all other nations. Other covenants followed, with Isaac, Jacob, Aaron, and King David, as well as, most notably, with Moses, to whom God delivers the Torah and anoints the Jews His chosen people. That last covenant is one to which we are all still beholden, whether we like it or not.

Crossing Delancey (1988)

Starring Amy Irving of *Yentl* fame, the most Jewish New York City movie between 1977's *Annie Hall* and 2001's *Kissing Jessica Stein*.

Crusades

In 1095, Pope Urban II called on Christians to march on Jerusalem and redeem it from the Muslim infidels. Almost immediately, armies of believers set out, hoping to be whisked to heaven once they achieved their goal. En route to the Holy Land, however, many holy warriors seized local Jewish communities and demanded that they convert or die. Thousands of Jews were slaughtered as a result, a grim tradition that was upheld in future Crusades. Needless to say, the Crusades didn't exactly improve the Church's relations with Muslims, either.

HOW TO CURSE IN JEWISH

#@$%&!!?

Our favorite maledictions in Ladino, Esperanto, Yiddish, and Hebrew.

LADINO

The Sephardi language has a flowery and potent way of telling someone off.

"ORARE LAS DI KORACH A UNO."

"Shower Korach's curses on someone."

This expression is used to wish someone the same fate that befell Korach, the figure who revolted against Moses, fell from grace, figuratively, and was swallowed by the earth, literally.

"DE MI KULO."

"It is like my ass."

This expression is used to describe something or someone who is not what he pretends to be.

ESPERANTO

Esperanto has both *fivortoj*—literally, "shameful words" (often vulgar terms for body parts)—and *sakroj*, which are swear words or expletives. Here are a couple of the latter:

"DIABLE."

"Devilish" or "deviltry"

"MERDULO!"

"Shithead!"

"SEP DIABLOJ KAJ UNU DIABLINO!"

"Seven devils and one female devil!"

"PALAVRO DE KADAVRO!"

Literally, "Cadaver palaver," meaning "Bullshit!"

YIDDISH

Yiddish is renowned for its deeply literal and deeply literary curses.

"GAY KAKEN OFN YAHM!"

Literally, "Go shit in the ocean," used more like the expression "Go jump in a lake!"

"VAKSN ZOLSTU VI A TSIBELE MITN KOP IN DR'ERD."

"May you grow like an onion, with your head in the ground."

HEBREW

Short, sweet, and to the point.

"BEN ZONA."

A very popular phrase suggesting that your mother might've supported your family by practicing the world's oldest profession.

"KIBINIMAT."

Borrowed from the Russian, this staple of modern Hebrew cursing suggests that you go visit your mother, who, apparently, had just concluded enjoying sexual intercourse.

Crystal, Billy (b. 1948)

If he had only played Jodie Dallas, one of the first gay characters in prime time (on ABC's *Soap*, 1977–1981), *dayenu*, it would have been enough. If he had only, as a cast member of *Saturday Night Live*, given us the catchphrase "You look *mahhvelous*," *dayenu*. If he had only incarnated Harry Burns, the haimish bachelor who eventually settles down with Meg Ryan's character in the unimprovable rom-com *When Harry Met Sally* (1989), *dayenu*. If he had only hosted the Oscars nine times, *dayenu*. Few entertainers have been as present, reliable, and intermittently inspired as Billy Crystal, born to a Long Island jazz promoter and record store owner.

cultural Judaism

To its adherents, it's a way of being Jewish even without believing or knowing much about the faith, primarily by means of keeping some traditions alive and indulging in Jewish cultural offerings, from babka to Barbra Streisand. To its critics, it's a cop-out, a way to claim Jewish identity without bothering to learn or do much. To us, it's just another way to be Jewish.

FROM

Daf Yomi

TO

Dylan, Bob

Daf Yomi

The seven-and-a-half-year cycle of reading all 2,711 pages of the Talmud at the rate of one a day. Begun in August 1923 in Vienna by a rabbi named Meir Shapiro as a method for uniting the Jewish people through common daily study, Daf Yomi also ensures that Jews will have at least one new thing to argue about every day.

dairy restaurants

Kosher eateries that serve anything that's not fleishig (meat)—including vegetarian fare and fish dishes, everything from borscht to kasha varnishkes to smoked whitefish—these institutions are best known for their dairy-based Ashkenazi options, like pierogies smothered in sour cream, or cheese blintzes smothered in sour cream, or potato pancakes smothered in (wait for it) sour cream. Some of these diners—like New York City's Ratner's (which closed in 2002) and B&H (still open)—became legends, key alternatives to the delicatessen for people looking for kosher restaurants that wouldn't break the bank.

Daniel Deronda

Sure, *Middlemarch* is all right, but *Deronda* is George Eliot's real masterpiece. It would have been a great book even if it didn't prefigure Zionism, but, astonishingly, it did: decades before Theodor Herzl had strange ideas about returning to the Promised Land, Eliot's Jewish protagonist completes his journey by abandoning the life of a British gentleman of leisure and instead traveling eastward, determined to establish a Jewish state in the Land of Israel.

daven

Yiddish for "pray." Jewish law dictates that we do it three times a day: the morning service is called *shachrit*, the afternoon *mincha*, and the evening *maariv*. The central part of each service is the Amidah. On special occasions, like Shabbat or a holiday, we add a fourth prayer called a musaf.

David, Larry (b. 1947)

Olympic gold medalist in kvetching, Larry David is the black hole of tsuris at the center of *Curb Your Enthusiasm*, a half-hour TV comedy exaggerating (we hope) Larry's problems with day-to-day modern living. It began in 2000 and, despite a hiatus or two, doesn't appear to be going away. Prior to *Curb* (and very relevant to the program's narrative), David cocreated *Seinfeld*, arguably the most important Jewish television sitcom. (See TV and Jews, page 264.) David's stand-in on the show was Jason Alexander's George Costanza, whose bad luck and eternal rage offered the character also named Jerry Seinfeld, and fictional friends Elaine Benes and Cosmo Kramer, opportunities to riff in their own styles. Before *Seinfeld*, David was a writer and performer, most notably on an ill-fated challenger to *Saturday Night Live* called *Fridays*. He also has a great small scene in Woody Allen's 1987 masterpiece *Radio Days* as the communist neighbor who refuses to fast on Yom Kippur.

Davis Jr., Sammy (1925–1990)

An irrepressible singer, dancer, and shticker, child-vaudeville-star-turned-Rat-Pack-fixture Sammy Davis Jr. was a showbiz force from nearly the day he was born until his death from throat cancer. Davis formally converted to Judaism in 1961. The conversion was prompted, Davis wrote in his autobiography, by his admiration for Jewish history and teachings, and his realization of "the affinity between the Jew and the Negro." In a radio interview shortly after his conversion, Davis was asked if it was true that he wanted to become "a Jew because all your friends are Jewish." Davis answered: "Frank Sinatra is my closest friend, and I never yet saw him wear a yarmulke. I'll admit he eats a bagel every now and then."

day school

Instead of saying "private Jewish day school," in some Jewish circles you can shorten it to "day school." (As in, "I'd love to stay with the public-interest law, but day-school tuition being what it is, I had to go work for a firm.") Really, you'll only hear this spoken in Conservative and Modern Orthodox circles. Very few Jews from the most liberal branches (Reform, Reconstructionist, Renewal, secular) send their children to Jewish schools, and Haredi Jews, the most religious, are likely to just say "school."

Dayan, Moshe (1915–1981)

Born on Israel's first kibbutz, Degania Alef, Moshe Dayan was one of the young State of Israel's leading soldiers and statesmen. He played a key role in all the state's defining conflicts: as commander of the Jerusalem front in 1948, as army chief of staff during the Suez Crisis of 1956, and as defense minister during the Six-Day War of 1967. He was initially close with David Ben-Gurion but, always more an independent actor than a party man, he later joined Menachem Begin's Likud-led government as foreign minister. He played a central role in negotiating Begin's 1978 peace treaty with Egypt. But for all his many accomplishments, Dayan is perhaps best known for his trademark eyepatch, which he began wearing in 1941 after a bullet flew through his binoculars when he was fighting the Vichy French in Syria. Tough though he was, the eyepatch, early on at least, caused him considerable psychological strain. "The attention it drew was intolerable to me," he wrote in his 1976 autobiography, *Story of My Life*. "I preferred to shut myself up at home, doing anything, rather than encounter the reactions of people wherever I went."

dayenu

If the Passover Haggadah gave us only one phrase to give thanks when things were going really, really well, it would have been enough.

Days of Awe

Traditionally, the ten days from Rosh Hashanah to Yom Kippur. We actually begin our spiritual accounting forty days before Rosh Hashanah, commemorating the forty days that Moses spent on Mount Sinai. Then, as we enter the Days of Awe, we get one more chance to repent before the Book of Life is sealed. That's why many religious Jewish men go to shul on Yom Kippur wearing a kittel, the same white robe in which they'll eventually be buried: even as we pray for a year of life and joy, we fully prepare for the eventuality of death. There's much comfort in that, and some very real awe.

Dead Sea

The lowest place on Earth, so stuffed with salt you can float on your back and read a newspaper: the water is too dense for you to sink. Its mud is really good for your skin, to say nothing of the Instagram potential.

Dead Sea Scrolls

Tending to his flock in the winter of 1947 in Wadi Qumran, near the Dead Sea, a Bedouin shepherd stumbled upon one of the most astonishing discoveries of modern archaeology: there, in clay jars, were thousands of scroll fragments, from as early as the eighth century BCE. Most of them are believed to have been written by the Essenes, a zealous Jewish sect that lived in egalitarian communes in the area. About half the scrolls contain passages from the Hebrew Bible, and a quarter contain nonbiblical texts, like the Book of Enoch, that aren't considered canonical. The rest, and arguably most fascinating, of the scrolls detail the Essenes' lives, rules, and beliefs. The scrolls are a thousand years older than the previously available written versions of the Hebrew Bible, and provide proof of the remarkable accuracy with which the traditional texts have been passed on from generation to generation for millennia.

Dear Abby

See **Ann Landers and Dear Abby**.

death

Jews, as you might've noticed, think a lot about death, which is why Judaism, in its infinite wisdom, prescribed several stages of mourning (known in Hebrew as *avelut*). First comes *aninut*, the initial shock of losing a loved one, which lasts until burial. (Jews try to arrange for the funeral and burial to take place within twenty-four hours of the death, barring extenuating circumstances.) During this stage of aninut, Jewish law forbids the mourner from fulfilling any positive commandments, such as praying or even participating in a minyan or reciting blessings on food. Then comes the funeral and burial, where eulogies are offered, psalms are recited, and the departed is remembered. Family members typically shovel a bit of dirt into the grave to begin the burial process. The mourner is then commanded to have a meal, typically one in which eggs are served, symbolizing the circle of life. Immediately following it is the shiva: Literally meaning "seven," this is a period of seven days during which one mourns for an immediate relative by sitting on low stools (hence the phrase "sitting shiva") and accepting visitors who come by to pay their condolences, often comforting the bereaved with unreasonable amounts of food. Any garment worn by mourners is ceremoniously ripped. After the shiva concludes, the final two stages are the *sheloshim*, which lasts for thirty days after the burial, and the twelve-month period during which some activities, like going to concerts, are avoided and the Mourner's Kaddish is recited (until the start of the twelfth month). Once the year is up, the mourner commemorates with the yahrzeit, the anniversary of the person's passing, when the headstone is unveiled. Jews may then remember the dearly departed every subsequent year on the yahrzeit by lighting candles and saying the Mourner's Kaddish, and also with the family gathering to remember their loved one.

Pastrami and pickle lovers agree: paradise is a Jewish delicatessen. These sacred temples of corned beef and salami, knishes and kasha, have become, for many, a home away from home—a place where memories are served on seeded rye bread, with a schmear of mustard.

The Jewish delicatessen as we recognize it today is a product of immigration. The German immigrants (both Jewish and not) who arrived en masse in New York City starting in the mid-nineteenth century brought with them a deep devotion to sausages and salami. They opened pushcarts and small butcher shops to sell these meaty treats to their homesick neighbors. After an influx of Eastern European Jews (including Jews from Romania, who brought their technique for making pastrami) arrived in the late nineteenth and early twentieth centuries, these small establishments quickly grew and set down permanent roots in the Lower East Side and beyond. By the early 1930s, New York City's five boroughs boasted a stunning 1,550 kosher delicatessens, according to *Save the Deli* by David Sax.

Over the decades, the Jewish deli spread to other American cities. Delis also expanded their menus, becoming reputable places to find Ashkenazi classics like pillowy knishes, crispy potato latkes, gravy-drenched brisket, steaming bowls of matzo ball soup, and velvety chopped liver. And to wash it down, there was Dr. Brown's root beer, cream soda, and the curiously vegetal Cel-Ray soda. Of course, any deli worth its salt also offered diners a gratis bowl of half- and full-sour pickles and coleslaw.

The delicatessen became a fixture of New York City culinary lore and, for many Jews, a gastronomic second home. But in the second half of the twentieth century, thanks both to a desire on the part of American Jews to move beyond their roots and to a massively successful public–health campaign against cholesterol and saturated fat, the delicatessen began its decline. Many turned to mass-produced pickled meats, pasteurized sauerkraut, and other subpar ingredients. Their food simply wasn't what it used to be. Stalwarts like Katz's Deli and the 2nd Avenue Deli in New York, and Langer's and Canter's in Los Angeles, kept chugging along. But hundreds of others across the country—some iconic, some neighborhood establishments—shuttered.

But in recent years, a new crop of diners have shown a resurgence of interest in the delicatessen, particularly artisanal delis that go back to their roots, curing meat in-house, baking sturdy rye breads, and fermenting vegetables the traditional way. Today, places like Mile End Deli in New York (with outposts in Nashville and Birmingham), Wexler's Deli in Los Angeles, Wise Sons in San Francisco, Kenny & Zuke's in Portland, Oregon, Rye Society in Denver, Zingerman's Delicatessen in Ann Arbor, and Larder Delicatessen in Cleveland, among others, are breathing new life into this Jewish culinary establishment. With a little luck, and a lot of pastrami, the Jewish deli will be alive and kicking for generations to come.

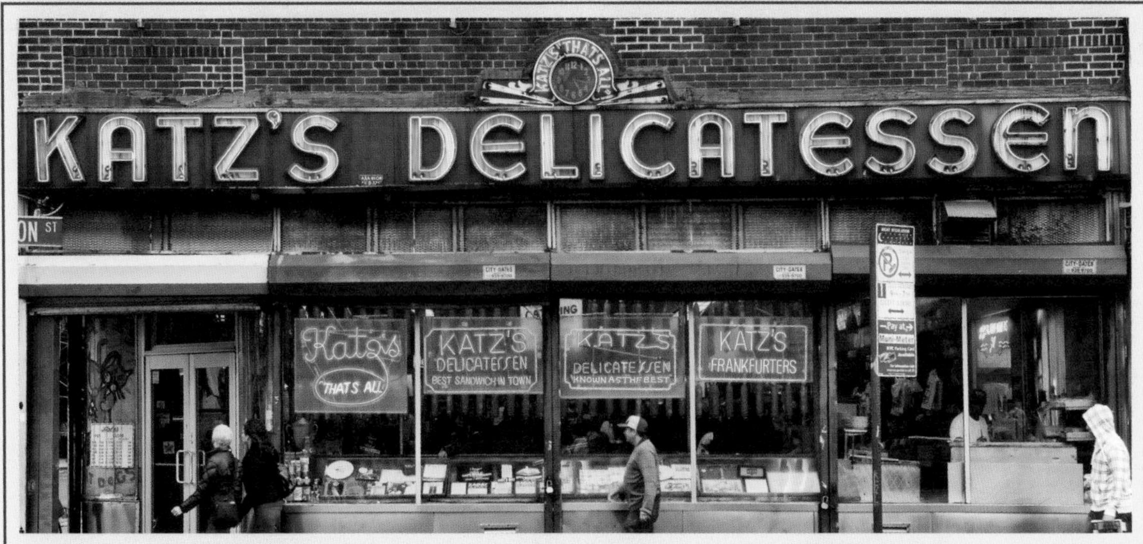

Department store: Selfridges department store in London, 1966

delicatessen

See page 74.

department stores

B. Altman, Bergdorf Goodman, Bloomingdale's, Filene's, Gimbels, Macy's: Jews were a driving force behind the birth and development of department stores in Europe and in the United States. You're welcome.

Der Stürmer

Der Stürmer

Die Antwort

The old joke had it right: if you were feeling down on your luck, all you had to do was leaf through this infamous Nazi weekly to learn that our people were all-powerful captains of industry who ran the entire world. In a grim twist of irony, *Der Stürmer* was a victim of its own success: as millions of Jews were murdered in the Holocaust, the weekly became irrelevant, because the only people it ever wrote about disappeared from public view. Its publisher, Julius Streicher, was tried and hanged at Nuremberg in 1946.

Dershowitz, Alan (b. 1938)

A retired Harvard law professor, an appellate lawyer, and a famously pushy Jew. Who says he's pushy? He does, in his 1991 book *Chutzpah*, in which he argues that American Jews in particular aren't assertive enough. Dershowitz is never afraid to assert, whether on behalf of his clients (including, famously, O. J. Simpson), the State of Israel, which he ardently supports, or himself.

desert

According to Google Maps, walking from Cairo, Egypt, to Jericho takes 145 hours. Somehow it took Moses and the gang forty years.

Diamond District

You'll find one in Antwerp, Tel Aviv, Manhattan, and elsewhere. And when you do, chances are it'll be run mostly by Jews. Prohibited from pursuing traditional occupations, in the sixteenth century Jews entered the diamond trade, which was both portable—if you were expelled or harassed, you could escape with your belongings—and profitable (see Banking and Jews, page 26). Charmingly, much of the business in most diamond districts is still predicated on trust, with handshakes sealing million-dollar deals and credit extended based on reputation. Sometimes it helps to live in a small shtetl where everybody knows your name.

Diamond, Neil (b. 1941)

Successful Jewish singer-songwriter and performer whom grandparents love and grandchildren recognize that, yes, there definitely is some inherent cool here. Born in Brooklyn, Diamond attended Erasmus Hall High School at the same time as Barbra Streisand (just *what* was in the water fountains there?). His career began as a Brill Building songwriter, penning tunes for Jay and the Americans and the Monkees (see Pop Music and Jews, page 182). He began recording his own tunes with the country-ish "Solitary Man" and poppy "Cherry Cherry." In 1969, he released "Sweet Caroline" and, well, we've all been impersonating his deep voice ever since. He had a string of hits in the 1970s, some with small combos and others with big orchestrations—and even a duet with Barbra! He was also a massive concert draw. This led to his questionable decision to star in a remake of *The Jazz Singer* in 1980. On one hand, this flick led to the release of "America," a remarkable anthem about the immigrant experience. On the other hand, oy, have you seen Neil Diamond try to act? It was all worth it, though, to see him sing Kol Nidre at the end and make amends with his rabbi father, played by Laurence Olivier (atoning for his *Marathon Man* Nazi?). Diamond continued the Jewish tradition of making a mint off Christmas music (see Jews and Christmas, page 62); his 1992 album of Yuletide tunes went double platinum.

NEIL DIAMOND

diaspora

After the destruction of the Second Temple in Jerusalem in 70 CE, Jews were expelled from their ancestral homeland and dispersed all around the world. Because we never stopped believing in our eventual return to Zion, we began referring to life anywhere else as life in the diaspora. We still do, although now that there is an independent Jewish state that will accept anyone with at least one Jewish grandparent, the term is more academic, less tragic.

Dirty Dancing

Surprise hit film from 1987 with lasting cultural impact, most notably in answering the eternal question, "Who puts Baby in a corner?" (Answer: nobody.) The film stars Jennifer Grey as a nice Jewish girl who joins her parents (her father the doctor is played by Jerry Orbach) at a bungalow colony in the Catskills and falls in love with a leather jacket-wearing dance-instructor sheygetz named Johnny Castle (really) played by dreamy dreamboat Patrick Swayze. They pair up to dance, with that famous lift at the end of their routine. The film is based on screenwriter Eleanor Bergstein's memories from the early 1960s, and while period music is heard (the Ronettes, the Drifters, Otis Redding), new songs were written—including radio hits "Hungry Eyes" by Eric Carmen, "She's Like the Wind" by Swayze and Wendy Fraser, and, of course, "(I've Had) The Time of My Life" by Bill Medley and Jennifer Warnes—making the *Dirty Dancing* soundtrack a tremendous success, selling over eleven million copies. For a brief moment, the whole world identified with a righteous, lithe Jewess with a big schnoz, a sense of social justice (Baby planned to join the Peace Corps), and a "no duh" affection for the very handsome Patrick Swayze.

DRAKE

Disraeli, Benjamin (1804–1881)

The first British Jew to serve as prime minister of the United Kingdom. All right: the only British Jew to serve as prime minister. Fine: he was born Jewish but became Anglican at twelve, after his family got into a scuffle with their shul. But Disraeli always saw himself as an outsider, telling Queen Victoria that he was "the blank page between the Old Testament and the New." He was a brilliant politician who solidified the Tories' appeal to the working classes, as well as an accomplished writer, a poet, and an enthusiastic cheerleader of the British commitment to its empire.

dog whistles

Few bigots these days proudly parade themselves as such. Instead, they use code words and insinuations to spread their hatred while maintaining plausible deniability and social respectability. For example, rather than openly state that Jews are disloyal to their countries, manipulate the media, and exploit their fellow citizens, today's fashionable anti-Semites instead say that "globalists" or "Zionists" or "George Soros" or "Rothschilds" do those things. As the terms themselves have nonracist meanings, the bigot can always feign ignorance. Meanwhile, the bigot's intended audience knows exactly what is meant.

Dome of the Rock

An Islamic shrine—it's not a mosque and does not hold regular prayers—located on the Temple Mount in Jerusalem known to Muslims as Haram al Sharif. Completed in 691 CE, it is one of the world's most ancient Islamic structures that remains intact and largely unchanged. With its golden dome, it is also one of the world's most instantly recognizable landmarks.

Douglas, Kirk (b. 1916)

Classic Hollywood leading man who played tough guys and historical righteous men. Douglas was born Issur Danielovitch Demsky, which makes him tied with Michael Landon of *Bonanza* and *Little House on the Prairie* for most egregious name change—that is to say, the wildest swing from super-Jewish to super-goyish. Landon was born—wait for it—Eugene Orowitz. Also: Kirk Douglas begat Michael Douglas (or as we like to think of him, Moshe ben Issur).

Drake (b. 1986)

Canadian American rapper Aubrey Drake Graham, the son of a Canadian Ashkenazi Jewish mother and an African American father, is the most successful and influential Jewish musician to emerge in the twenty-first century. Drake, who attended a Toronto Jewish day school as a child, began his career as an actor on the Canadian teen drama *Degrassi: The Next*

Dirty Dancing: Frances "Baby" Houseman and Johnny Castle fell in love in this 1987 Catskills classic, and we had the time of our lives.

Generation. On his debut album, *Thank Me Later* (2010), and the string of smash releases that followed, Drake redefined pop. His music combines deft rhymes and big hooks, while mixing typical hip-hop braggadocio with, well, humble braggadocio: lyrics that express ambivalence and angst about fame, success, and a sex life Drake depicts as prodigious but emotionally alienating. It's a style that critics have identified as "millennial," but Drake can also be seen as classically Jewish: sharp-witted and dyspeptic, swinging wildly between self-regard and self-loathing, he is a textbook Jewish neurotic, a character out of Philip Roth or Woody Allen. Drake has often spoken about his Jewishness in interviews and has referenced it in his lyrics. The video for the 2012 single "HYFR (Hell Ya Fucking Right)" is a kind of Jewish burlesque: Drake reenacts his bar mitzvah, with scenes showing the rapper in a kippah and tallit on the synagogue bimah, dancing the hora, and eating a cake shaped like a Torah scroll.

drasha

See **d'var Torah**.

dreidel

Four-sided top popular with kids—okay, with everyone—at Hanukkah parties. The four Hebrew letters on the top's sides (nun, gimel, hei, shin) stand for the Hebrew expression "A great miracle happened there." (In Israel, the shin is replaced by a pei, for in the Promised Land the proper expression is "A great miracle happened *here*.") There is a game associated with the dreidel, and it involves coins or chocolate gelt, but nobody ever remembers how to play. It's just fun to spin the dreidel while eating latkes, sufganiyot (jelly doughnuts), and chocolate. The holiday song beginning "Dreidel, dreidel, dreidel, I made it out of clay . . ." is, while insipid, quite catchy.

Drescher, Fran (b. 1957)

Brilliant comedian and actress with an unrivaled nasal voice and bleating, sheeplike laugh. Drescher was born in Queens and first gained attention with the small but important scene in '70s disco classic *Saturday Night Fever* in which she asks John Travolta's Tony Manero if he is as good in bed as he was on the dance floor. Drescher became a household name with *The Nanny*, a throwback screwball sitcom that ran from 1993 to 1999. As Fran Fine, a down-on-her-luck but streetwise cosmetics saleswoman from Queens, she ends up looking after the three children of one very Waspy Manhattanite named Maxwell Sheffield. Lainie Kazan often dropped by as Fran's Aunt Freida and Renée Taylor played her mother, Sylvia. There was also a Grandma Yetta. They all liked to talk about Barbra Streisand, and from time to time Fran taught the goyish kids some Yiddish. Drescher wrote the bestselling 1996 book *Enter Whining* and later, after surviving uterine cancer, began the Cancer Schmancer movement, promoting earlier screenings for female cancers.

FRAN DRESCHER

The Dreyfus Affair

Alfred Dreyfus (1859–1935) was a French Jew and a captain in the French Army who was falsely accused of spying for Germany in 1894. Despite a lack of evidence, the French Army and government leaders moved to have him convicted at trial, then again at a second trial once the first was challenged. Known as the Dreyfus Affair, his trial revealed the ongoing pervasive anti-Semitism in French society and had deep ramifications for the Jewish people. Most significant, one of the people present at his ceremony of dishonor, where Dreyfus was stripped of his medals and had his sword broken before being exiled to Devil's Island, was Theodor Herzl, the founder of modern Zionism. A young journalist and secular Jew, Herzl was struck by how the angry mob not only called Dreyfus a traitor but chanted "Death to the Jews!" Herzl concluded that Jews in any society would always become the scapegoats, and here began his dream for a modern return to the Promised Land. The proceedings also so outraged public intellectual and novelist Émile Zola that he published a fiery defense of Dreyfus, "J'accuse," which accused France of sullying its honor with the false conviction. For this, Zola was convicted of libel and forced to flee to England. Dreyfus himself was eventually exonerated, although his trial remains a flash point in the history of Jews and modern Europe.

DYLAN, BOB

(B. 1941)

YET ANOTHER SIDE OF BOB DYLAN

The Freewheelin' Bob Dylan (1963)	*Blood on the Tracks* (1975)
Bringing It All Back Home (1965)	*Desire* (1976)
Highway 61 Revisited (1965)	*Time Out of Mind* (1997)
Blonde on Blonde (1966)	*Modern Times* (2006)

There's little doubt that the man born Robert Allen Zimmerman in Duluth, Minnesota, will be remembered as an incomparable American bard. Dylan expanded the poetic possibilities of popular music in the 1960s, wrote and recorded hundreds of revelatory songs, and won the Nobel Prize for Literature in 2016. He is one of history's greatest Jewish artists, and one of its most mischievous. He converted to Christianity in the late 1970s but some years later popped up on a Chabad telethon (1989); a few years earlier, he was spotted in tefillin at the Western Wall (1983). Dylan's definitive statement on his own Jewishness may be "Talkin' Hava Negeilah Blues" (1963), a comically halting performance of a great niggun that Dylan introduces with a deadpan quip: "Here's a foreign song I learned in Utah."

Drudge, Matt (b. 1966), and Andrew Breitbart (1969–2012)

Matt Drudge and Andrew Breitbart first collaborated on a right-wing political gossip sheet that they e-mailed out to subscribers from Drudge's one-bedroom apartment in Los Angeles. Drudge had barely made it through high school. Breitbart had drunk his way through Tulane. But they knew that the world was changing and that the Internet was their generation's equivalent of Woodstock. The Drudge Report soon became a website, an agglomeration of headlines from other people's newspapers that read like a Dada-ist ransom note from the basement of the American id. Proper journalists were appalled.

Twenty years later, the proper journalists are dying off. The newspapers whose headlines Drudge and Breitbart rewrote in wise-guy Walter Winchell prose have largely collapsed. The Drudge Report outlived them all.

After Breitbart's death in 2012, his politically contrarian newswire, Breitbart, became the property of an egomaniac named Steve Bannon, who used it to publish race-baiting crap, then took credit for putting Donald Trump in the White House. Which is to say, we inhabit the world that Drudge and Breitbart made.

DRY GOODS

dry goods

Fabrics, toiletries, and other knickknacks your newly arrived immigrant great-great-grandfather sold for a living, starting off with a pushcart and soon, if he was lucky, setting up shop.

dual loyalty

When Jews are accused of "dual loyalty," the term is actually a misnomer. When an anti-Semite says that a Jewish politician has "dual loyalty" to Israel and his home country, what he means is that the Jew is *more* loyal to Israel, not equally loyal to both. Because plainly saying that you hate Jews is kind of crass, anti-Semites and other shady types have often couched their bias in the rational-sounding accusation that Jews couldn't be trusted because, well, they had other masters to serve.

During the Dreyfus Affair, for example, many on the French right argued that the Jewish officer accused of espionage was guilty because Jews were more loyal to Germany, and during the recent debate on the nuclear deal with Iran some American lawmakers hinted that those Jews who opposed the deal only did so because they were more loyal to Israel than to the United States.

Duke, David (b. 1950)

The former grand wizard of the Ku Klux Klan and the only person more obsessed with Jews than we are.

d'var Torah

The Mishnah tells us that eating at a table around which no Torah is taught is like engaging in idol worship. Therefore, it's customary among religious Jews to offer a brief teaching at mealtime, a short speech that introduces a single point from Scripture or elsewhere, usually complete with some moral instruction. In at least one kosher restaurant in New York, you can deliver a nice d'var Torah and win yourself free dessert. Also called a drasha.

dybbuk

Not to be confused with the equally eerie golem, a dybbuk in Jewish lore is a demon, the wandering soul of a dead person. Dybbuks are not nice; they can take possession of your body, requiring an exorcism—not the Catholic, horror-movie kind, but no picnic either.

FROM

Eban, Abba

TO

Exodus

Eban, Abba (1915–2002)

Legendary Israeli diplomat and long-serving foreign minister known for his razor-sharp wit. The Palestinians, he once quipped, never miss an opportunity to miss an opportunity. As a liaison officer to the United Nations in 1947, he was instrumental in successfully promoting Resolution 181, which called for a partition of Palestine into an Arab and a Jewish state and paved the way for the birth of the State of Israel.

Edelman, Marek

See Warsaw Ghetto Uprising, page 284.

Efrat

A town in the Judean mountains, roughly eight miles south of Jerusalem. One of the largest and most thriving of the West Bank settlements. It was established in 1983 and populated by, among others, followers of Shlomo Riskin, a charismatic Manhattan rabbi who left his New York City pulpit to found Efrat and become its chief rabbi. "So many Americans moved here with Riskin," according to a 1995 dispatch in the *Washington Post,* "and they brought so much of American suburbia with them, that Efrat became known in some circles as 'Occupied Scarsdale.'" The biblical matriarch Rachel is said to be buried nearby.

egg cream

A soda fountain drink that contains no eggs and no cream. Instead, it's got milk, seltzer, and syrup (ideally, Fox's U-Bet chocolate syrup).

Egypt

See page 86.

Eichmann, Adolf (1906–1962)

Known as the architect of the Final Solution, Adolf Eichmann was a Nazi lieutenant colonel who orchestrated the logistics of sending millions of Jews to their deaths in ghettos, concentration camps, and death camps. After the war, he escaped to Argentina, living there under a false name. On May 20, 1960, Mossad agents successfully apprehended him near his home in Buenos Aires, held him in a safe house, and, drugging him and disguising him as an inebriated airline crew member, transported him to Israel. News of his abduction sparked an international discussion, with some cheering on Israel's courage in bringing the fugitive Nazi to justice and others arguing that Israel had no right to try Eichmann for crimes that were committed neither against its citizens nor in its jurisdiction.

His trial began on April 11, 1961. Widely covered around the world, it marked one of the first times in history that Holocaust survivors had a chance to tell their stories publicly. The trial concluded after four months, and the verdict was delivered in December: Eichmann was found guilty of fifteen counts of crimes against humanity, war crimes, and crimes against the Jewish people. He was hanged the following June, his body cremated and the ashes scattered over the Mediterranean, outside Israel's territorial waters.

Einstein, Albert (1879–1955)

Scientist who believed God does not play dice with the universe.

Einstein Bros. Bagels

Fast-casual chain that at one point in the mid-'90s sported a hip industrial vibe and offered hope for those middle-America suburban kids craving a taste of the Big Apple, right down to a deliciously cakey black-and-white cookie. However, today, after decades of all-too-rapid expansion (and a merger with Caribou Coffee), calling their soulless circle-shaped bread rolls "bagels" is about as accurate as calling a Pamplemousse LaCroix "grapefruit juice."

El Al

Israel's national airline. In addition to very good in-flight movies, each flight also features a bit of live theater starring some religious dude refusing to sit next to women and delaying takeoff by an hour.

Elbaz, Alber (b. 1961)

Moroccan-born, Israeli-bred fashion designer. Helmed the luxury brand Lanvin from 2001 to 2015 and designed all the costumes Natalie Portman wore in her 2015 film adaptation of Amos Oz's *A Tale of Love and Darkness.*

Elijah

Everyone's favorite Jewish grandfatherly figure, Elijah is the prophet from the biblical book of I Kings who,

$E=MC^2$, BABY

EGYPT

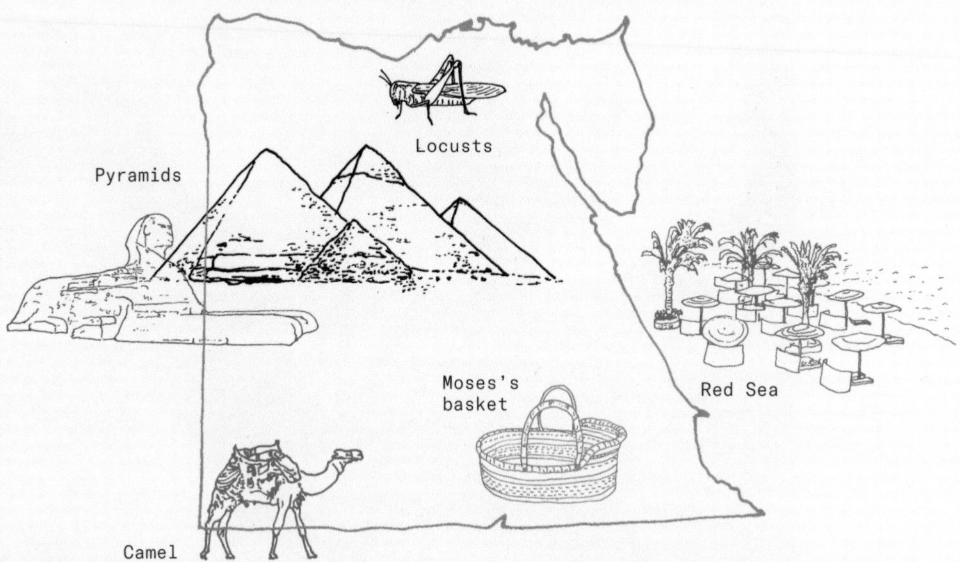

North African country of ninety-nine million, with Cairo as its capital. The Jewish people and the Nilotic civilizations have been fatefully entangled with one another for the better part of three thousand years, and Mitzraim (Egypt) is one of Judaism's various bywords for exile, slavery, spiritual disquiet, and every other national or existential ill. Egypt has been one of the Jewish people's metaphysical bogeymen from the very beginning—as well as one of the Jews' real-world, political bogeymen. Thutmose III went to war in Canaan in the fifteenth century BCE, while the book of Kings (and Chronicles) describes multiple pharaonic expeditions into Israelite lands. Passover, the entire book of Exodus, the Yom Kippur War, etc., notwithstanding, the Jewish relationship with Egypt isn't entirely negative. Yes, the pharaoh Mernepteh apparently laid waste to the Israelites in the thirteenth century BCE—but the stele recording this feat, which sits in Cairo's Egyptian Museum, is the oldest existing reference to "Israel" and crucial corroboration that such a people existed at this early point in history.

"Egypt" and "Jewish" were never opposites. The Egyptian Jewish community produced a murderers' row of notables, including the influential first-century Platonist philosopher Philo of Alexandria, along with Maimonides, who settled in Egypt for the last thirty years of his life and wrote his Guide for the Perplexed there. But in the twentieth century, Egypt stripped the country's Jews of their citizenship after the founding of the State of Israel, and between 1948 and 1973, under Gamal Abdel Nasser and Anwar Sadat, Egypt made a number of unsuccessful attempts at conquering their northern neighbor.

Yet even this story has a happy-ish ending: with the 1978 Camp David Accords, Egypt became the first Arab country to recognize Israel's right to exist. The agreement, a turning point in the history of the Middle East, has held throughout decades of turmoil in the region, even if the countries have never been on especially warm terms. Visitors to Egypt can still see the ancient Ben Ezra synagogue, where the famed Cairo Geniza documents were uncovered, and there are a few shuls and rabbinic tombs scattered throughout the country. They won't find many Jews, though: there aren't more than one hundred left in a country that had a community of nearly eighty thousand in 1948.

according to later tradition, appears at every Passover Seder and every bris. He also pops up throughout the Talmud, offering sage advice to the rabbis or bringing messages from heaven, and Hasidic stories even today often attribute miraculous events to his mysterious hand. While not a very warm and fuzzy guy in the Bible, he is also credited as the prophet who will announce the coming of the Messiah. Until then, we fill a glass of wine and open the door for him every year at the Passover Seder.

emancipation

The hundred-year process of granting Europe's Jews full civic rights. It began in 1782, with the Edict of Tolerance, a letter from Habsburg emperor Joseph II declaring that Jews were now allowed to attend any school of their choosing and seek employment in a growing list of professions. One by one, Europe's nations granted their Jewish citizens previously unimagined privileges, with some, like France and Holland, enthusiastically embracing emancipation and others, like England, doing so slowly and gradually. Now free to study what they wanted, work wherever they wanted, and live wherever they wanted, many Jews responded by shedding their traditional language, Yiddish, and their traditional clothes and seeking to assimilate in their communities.

Emanuel brothers

Ezekiel (b. 1957), Rahm (b. 1959), and Ariel (b. 1961). Quite simply, the wonder boys. These Jewish brothers were born in Chicago; their dad was an Israeli immigrant who had served in the Irgun, the paramilitary organization in pre-Israel Palestine. Ari grew up to be a Hollywood super-agent, the co-CEO of William Morris Endeavor, Zeke a top oncologist and bioethicist, and Rahm a congressman, then chief of staff to President Obama, and later mayor of Chicago. In 1997, journalist Elisabeth Bumiller wrote, "Of the three brothers, Rahm is the most famous, Ari is the richest, and Zeke, over time, will probably be the most important." Their existence poses the question to every underachieving Jewish son: "Why can't you be more like the Emanuel boys?"

EPHRON, NORA

(1941–2012)

I'LL HAVE WHAT SHE'S HAVING

Heartburn **(1986)**

Sleepless in Seattle **(1993)**

When Harry Met Sally **(1989)**

You've Got Mail **(1998)**

She might not have invented the romantic comedy, but she sure did perfect it. The Beverly Hills–bred, Wellesley-educated writer, producer, and director is best known for *When Harry Met Sally* (1989), which she wrote, and *Sleepless in Seattle* (1993) and *You've Got Mail* (1998), which she wrote and directed. She was married to Watergate journalist Carl Bernstein, and the story of her discovery that he was cheating on her with a friend of hers became the basis of her 1983 novel *Heartburn*, which subsequently became a Mike Nichols film starring Meryl Streep as Rachel, a food writer, and Jack Nicholson as her philandering newspaper-columnist husband. She later chronicled the tribulations of aging in *I Feel Bad About My Neck*, her brilliant and hilarious 2006 essay collection. Ephron was candid and fabulous and wise: "You can never have too much butter—that is my belief," she once told NPR. "If I have a religion, that's it."

Entebbe: Photographer David Rubinger captures the scene of the successful rescue mission on July 4, 1976.

Entebbe

The Israeli commando operation that inspired a hundred action films. On June 27, 1976, an Air France plane took off from Tel Aviv for Paris, with a stopover in Athens. There, the flight was boarded by four terrorists: two Palestinians and two Germans. Soon after takeoff, the terrorists hijacked the plane, diverting it first to Libya and then to Entebbe, Uganda. They demanded five million dollars and the release of fifty-three Palestinian terrorists, and threatened to execute their hostages if their demands weren't met. In the airport in Entebbe, the hostages were separated into two groups, the Jews and Israelis kept apart from the rest of the passengers. Determined to rescue the hostages rather than succumb to the terrorists' demands, Israeli commandos took off for Entebbe on July 3, flying low to avoid being detected by radar. Landing in Uganda, they drove to the terminal in a convoy that included a black Mercedes meant to mimic the car used by the country's despot, Idi Amin, and stormed the terminal. The operation was a success, even though three of the hostages were killed in the crossfire and one was later murdered in a Ugandan hospital, and the force's commander, Lt. Colonel Yoni Netanyahu, the future prime minister's brother, was shot and killed as well. The operation inspired armies around the world to emulate the IDF's incomparable operational prowess, and was an enormous moral victory for the Jewish State.

epigenetics

The emerging field of study that examines alterations to genes (rather than changes to the genetic code itself) that change the way those genes function. Put plainly: Among other things, epigenetic research seeks to identify how traumatic stress may permanently alter the survivors' physiology in ways that can be passed on to their descendants. Which, as you can imagine, is of deep interest to the Jewish community.

Eretz Yisrael

In Hebrew, "the land of Israel." You'll find this expression in the Torah and in prayers, but you'll also find it in conversation: "I won't make the Mets game tomorrow—I'm really jetlagged, just got back from Eretz Yisrael."

erev

"Eve of," in Hebrew, but also "the day before." So "Erev Rosh Hashanah" refers to both the day before Rosh Hashanah and the evening that begins the holiday. Shabbat is Saturday, so "Erev Shabbat" is all day Friday, but more colloquially it's Friday night, which is when Shabbat starts (since Jewish holidays go from sundown to nightfall). Get it?

eruv

The ultimate Jewish life hack. Observant Jews are prohibited from carrying objects outside their homes on Shabbat. Which makes, say, leaving the house with your keys or your baby stroller somewhat of a challenge. Enter the eruv: a thin wire that runs all around certain blocks, neighborhoods, and even towns, the eruv turns everything into one big symbolic private domain, allowing you to carry stuff as if you've never left your living room. The eruv is checked regularly to make sure the boundaries are intact, so next time you see a couple of rabbis walking around and looking upward, know that they may be observing the ritualistic enclosure—and rabbinic workaround—that makes life much easier for religious Jews.

Esperanto

Ah, Jews, ever the utopians! Maybe because our Messiah is so slow to come, we like to pass the time dreaming up plans for a better world. How else could one small people have given the world Jesus, Marx, Herzl, and Freud? Or, for that matter, Ludovik Lazarus Zamenhof (1859–1917), the Polish Jewish ophthalmologist who in 1887 invented Esperanto, the most successful constructed, "universal" language ever. In a 1905 letter, Zamenhof, who lived in Warsaw, explained the roots of his plan for world peace through a new common language: "My Jewishness has been the main reason why, from earliest childhood, I have given my all for a single great idea, a single dream—the dream of the unity of humankind." Like many young, emancipated Jews of his time, Zamenhof was torn between two vocations: a nationalist calling to build a Jewish homeland in Palestine, and a universalist calling to promote harmony among all peoples. By 1887, Zamenhof had decisively left Zionism behind for universalism. But the Nazis never forgot the Jewish roots, or spirit, of Esperanto; Hitler worried in *Mein Kampf* that Jews could use the language to plot world domination, and his ministry of education forbade its teaching. Today, alas, nobody has to forbid Esperanto: despite a recent revival of interest, there are at most a few thousand "native" speakers of the language. It was not the Nazis, through, who thwarted Esperanto. More likely, it was that the first half of the twentieth century had another, more compelling linguistic project, in a land more promising than Zamenhof's Poland. For more on that, see **Ben-Yehuda, Eliezer**. (And *ne dankinde*, as they say in Esperanto. You're welcome.)

Esther

Purim heroine. No other woman in the Hebrew Bible gets so much attention, and for good reason. She is entered into a mandatory beauty pageant (Miss Universe has nothing on Miss Persia) and wins the dubious honor of marrying the drunken tyrant King Ahasuerus. At the insistence of her cranky uncle Mordechai, she summons her bravery and her brilliance to save herself and her people from evil Haman's plot to destroy the Jews. The Talmud's rabbis extolled her beauty and praised her soul, saying there's a thread of grace hanging over her head that sets her apart from all others. Hallelujah.

Ethiopian Jews

Also known as the Beta Israel, or the House of Israel, this group of as many as 150,000 Jews (accounts differ) believes itself to be the descendants of one of the original twelve tribes of Israel, which migrated to Ethiopia millennia ago. Most of the community was airlifted to Israel in Operation Moses in 1984 and Operation Solomon in 1991. Some Israeli rabbis called into question the Jewish status of some of the newcomers, but most of the community became part of Israeli society.

etrog

The etrog—or *Citrus medica*, if you're nasty—is a lemonlike fruit that hails from Southeast Asia (though today is more likely to come from Greece, Italy, or Morocco) and plays a central part in the holiday of Sukkot, where it is one of Arbat Ha'Minim, the four species we bless daily. Observant Jews are known to scrupulously examine their etrog before making a purchase, as any small blemish makes the fruit not kosher for the ritual. Entire schools of thought have emerged to parse every quality of the fruit, with some caring for yellow etrogs over green, some preferring smooth skin and others bumpy, and many obsessing over the shape of the pitom, the protruding nipple-shaped bit up top. The Greeks have provided a good answer to the question of what might be done with your etrog once Sukkot is over, using it to brew a limoncello-like liqueur called kitron.

Exodus

The mass departure of the Israelites from the house of bondage in Egypt to the Promised Land, Canaan. We tell this story every year at the Passover Seder.

Also: The second book of the Torah. Like a classic sequel, this one, too, has many more special effects, a higher body count, and a charismatic hero, Moses, with plenty of catchphrases ("Let my people go!").

Exodus

The 1958 novel by Leon Uris (1924–2003) depicting the birth of the State of Israel. It became a massive hit, staying on top of the *New York Times* bestseller list for nineteen weeks and introducing many Americans, Jewish and non-, to Israel and to Zionism. In 1960, director Otto Preminger turned the book into a movie, starring Paul Newman as the fearless Israeli Ari Ben Canaan. While the film may suffer from a few hoary clichés, the sight of a young Paul Newman climbing out of the Mediterranean, a Star of David glinting in the moonlight against his bare chest, was the best advertisement any young country could ask for.

EXODUS

FROM

fantasy baseball

TO

frum

fantasy baseball

Invented by magazine writer and editor Daniel Okrent, it originally was a game played by mail, applying the Rotisserie scoring system, named after the Manhattan French restaurant where it was conceived. Today computerized, it remains an obsession for nerdy Jewish boys who could never quite throw a changeup but who could do some math and figure out who's on top.

farbrengen

If you're a Lubavitcher Hasid and it's your birthday, or Shabbat, or a holiday, or some other meaningful date, you may celebrate by throwing or attending a farbrengen, a gathering where hard liquor is consumed, Torah is taught and discussed, hard liquor is consumed, Hasidic stories are told, hard liquor is consumed, soulful songs are sung, and hard liquor is consumed. Menachem Mendel Schneerson, the late Lubavitcher Rebbe, believed a farbrengen was a terrific way to inspire spiritual growth, which is why he threw them often. Other Hasidic courts have a very similar tradition called a tish, which takes place only on Friday nights, at which the court's Rebbe distributes leftovers of his dinner to all in attendance.

TOVAH FELDSHUH

Farrakhan, Louis (b. 1933)

Boston-bred leader of the Nation of Islam, a black supremacist group that at its best promotes self-improvement and racial uplift for black people but at its worst—and its worst is always there—hates whites, Jews, and gays (and promulgates deeply bad ideas about female subservience). The bow-tied Farrakhan has dedicated decades to pursuing his anti-Semitic convictions, from arguing that it was God who put Jews in Hitler's ovens to accusing Jews of orchestrating the attacks on 9/11. Despite his vile bigotry, he continues to be welcomed by allegedly liberal and progressive activists.

fast days

See page 94.

Feldshuh, Tovah (b. 1952)

American actress, singer, and playwright. Born Terri Sue Feldshuh, she played Golda Meir in *Golda's Balcony*, the longest-running one-woman show in Broadway history. Having a taste for the undead, she also joined the cast of the hit series *The Walking Dead*, playing the role of a congresswoman turned zombie. She based the role on Hillary Clinton.

feminism

See Feminism and Jews, page 96.

Fiddler on the Roof

Tony Award-winning 1964 Broadway musical that became an Oscar-winning 1971 movie musical. It also became an unlikely hit on stages from Berlin to Tokyo, and a perennial staple of dinner theater and high school productions. It's based on the short stories of Yiddish author Sholem Aleichem, with music by Jerry Bock, lyrics by Sheldon Harnick, and a book by Joseph Stein. In the show, a milkman named Tevye is raising five daughters in a shtetl called Anatevka, just as the old world is crashing up against the new. Life is tough for Tevye, who has to scramble to make ends meet while trying to find suitable husbands for his daughters—who have their own ideas about what makes an ideal mate. Meanwhile, revolution is in the air, pogroms are on the rise, and Anatevka's Jews are wondering if they should look for a new home—and if so, where? The show is crammed with songs that have become standards, for Jews and for gentiles, too: "Tradition," "Matchmaker, Matchmaker," "Sunrise, Sunset," "To Life," and "If I Were a Rich Man." It's fortunate to see a production of this show—but if your good fortune never comes, here's to whatever comes.

Fischer, Bobby (1943–2008)

Possibly the greatest chess talent who ever lived, Bobby Fischer would become better known for the slow, public deterioration of his mental health. Raised in New York City, Fischer was a child chess prodigy, then United States chess champion, then world champion: his 1972 victory over Boris Spassky in a match held in Reykjavik, Iceland, got the attention one would expect for a young American dethroning an older Russian during the Cold War. But his talent was soon derailed by his madness, which led both to a series of diplomatic incidents—he played in wartime Sveti Stevan, Yugoslavia, in 1992, breaking a United Nations embargo and generating a warrant for his arrest—as well as increasingly

Fiddler on the Roof: Keeping tradition alive in the 1971 film version, starring Israeli acting legend Chaim Topol

FAST DAYS

Food is central to many important days in the Jewish calendar—latkes on Hanukkah, apples and honey on Rosh Hashanah, hamantaschen on Purim—so it stands to reason that the absence of food can be just as significant (see Food and Jews, page 100). There are several days in the Jewish calendar designated for fasting. Fasting allows for reflection, atonement, or mourning. There are two “major” fast days—Yom Kippur and Tisha B’av—which last from sunset to sunset, and five “minor” fast days, which last from sunrise to sunset. (In Judaism, all fast days include a complete restriction on consuming any food or drink, even water.) And you don’t need a holiday to fast! Brides and grooms may fast on their wedding day, in acknowledgment of its holiness, and fast days can be convened in times of great crisis. Occasionally, people undertake a fast in response to tragedy, to atone for a personal wrongdoing, or as an extra measure of piety.

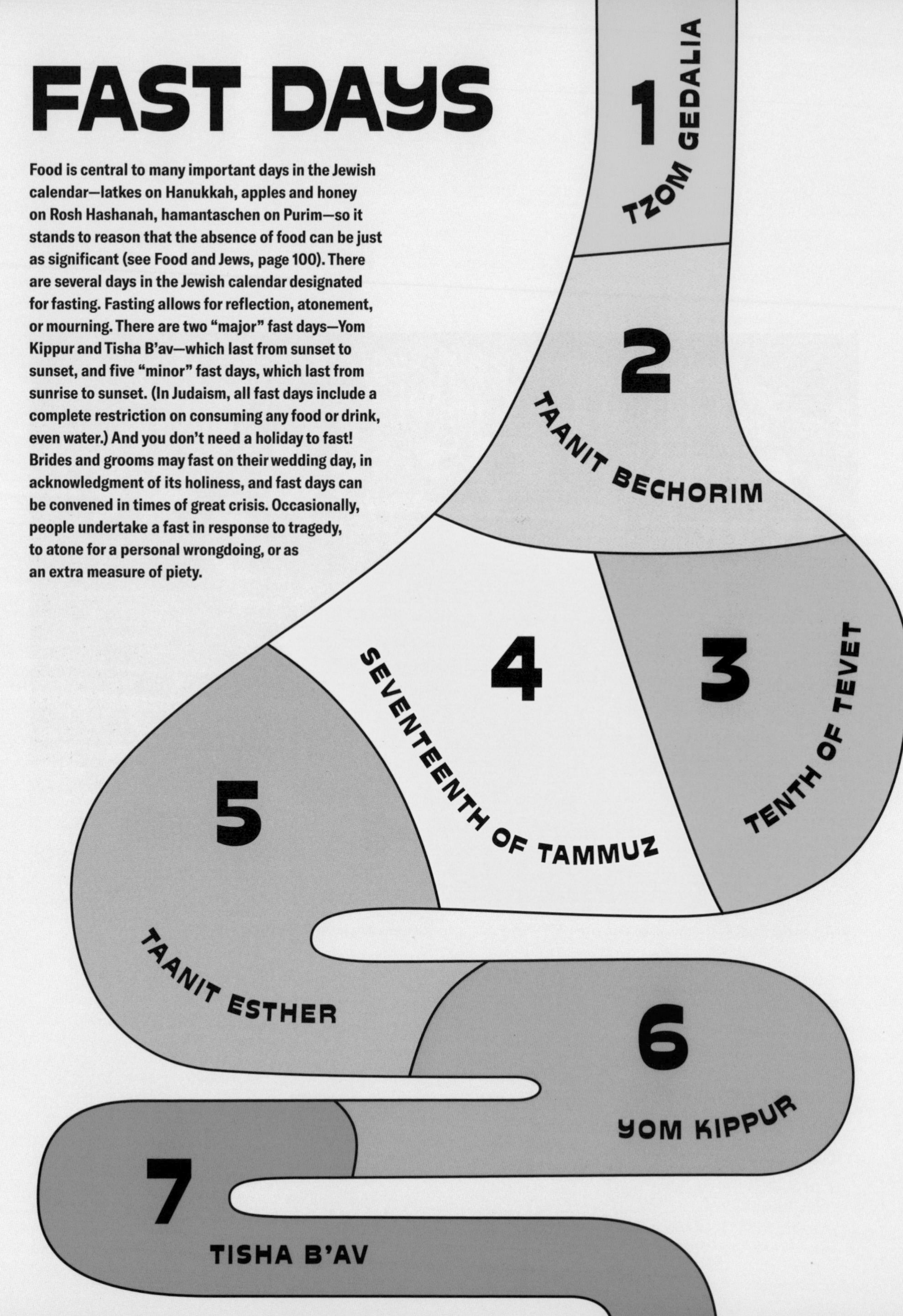

1
TZOM GEDALIA

Peckish

A fast day ("tzom") in memory of Gedalia, a governor of Judah and an early victim of Jew-on-Jew violence, and whose assassination is recounted in 2 Kings. Tzom Gedalia falls the day after Rosh Hashanah and lasts only from sunrise to sunset. Think of it as a post–Rosh Hashanah cleanse.

2
TAANIT BECHORIM

Ready for a snack

Only observed by firstborn sons the day before Passover, this fast day commemorates the miracle that kept Jewish firstborn sons safe during the final plague in Egypt, which killed off the Egyptian firstborns. Today, firstborns can opt out of the fast by simply attending a siyyum, a celebration for completing a unit of Torah learning.

3
TENTH OF TEVET

How soon til lunch?

A minor fast day commemorating the beginning of the siege of Jerusalem in 69 CE, which ended, catastrophically, on Tisha B'Av. In observance of this historical tragedy, we refrain from eating from dawn to nightfall. In keeping with the day's somber tone, Israel's Chief Rabbinate has designated it a general Kaddish day, allowing the relatives of Holocaust victims whose date of death is unknown to mourn for their loved ones by saying the mourner's prayer on this day.

4
SEVENTEENTH OF TAMMUZ

That sound? My stomach growling

This fast day, which marks when the walls of Jerusalem were breached, kicks off the period of mourning known as the Three Weeks, which conclude with Tisha B'Av. The Three Weeks are a somber time: no attending events with live music, no cutting your hair, no shaving, no celebrating weddings or other parties (circumcisions and engagement parties are permitted).

5
TAANIT ESTHER

Hunger pains

The day before the joyous holiday of Purim is a minor fast day that acknowledges the three days of fasting by the Jewish people in the Book of Esther. This was undertaken as spiritual support before Esther went to plea before King Ahasuerus to save the Jewish people from Haman's mass murder plot. This fast is typically broken after the evening reading of the Book of Esther.

6
YOM KIPPUR

Starving here

We're so concerned with the fate of our souls, the story goes, that we simply can't eat, drink, have sex, adorn our bodies with lotions, or even wear comfortable, sturdy leather shoes. Yom Kippur gets the prize for most hard-core fast day because it's the only one that supersedes Shabbat, meaning that if Yom Kippur falls on a Saturday, we go ahead with it. The 25-hour fast lasts from sundown to sundown, and all restrictions apply, including all the traditional Shabbat and holiday prohibitions, as this day is known in Torah as the "Sabbath of Sabbaths."

7
TISHA B'AV

Famished and banished

The Temple in Jerusalem was destroyed not once but twice, and with that second, final destruction in 70 CE, we lost a permanent home for God on earth, and a unifying central worship tradition for the Jewish people. We mourn the loss of both temples every year on Tisha B'Av, the ninth day of the Hebrew month of Av, by not eating, drinking, or engaging in intimacy, and by sitting on the floor like a mourner, at least until halfway through the day. It doesn't help much that this day falls smack in the middle of summer, making for a memorable, if depressing, day of summer camp.

Jewish women have a long history of being rabble-rousers. In many Jewish communities during the Middle Ages and beyond, they supported their scholar husbands and ran businesses. The diary of Glückel of Hameln, a seventeenth-century mother of fourteen, depicts a woman fretting and kvelling about her kids while negotiating deals like a boss. In Victorian England, Grace Aguilar wrote books about women's intellectual, educational, and spiritual enlightenment, while in America, Ernestine Rose fought for suffrage and the abolition of slavery. (She also sold perfume and invented a new kind of room deodorizer.) In the early twentieth century, Jewish women like Clara Lemlich, Rose Schneiderman, and Emma Goldman led socialist and labor movements, working as organizers and giving fiery speeches.

Jewish texts and tradition have always stressed education and intellectual achievement, fighting injustice, and advocating for others. And Jewish women, who were never perceived as dainty or retiring, have always stepped up. Powerhouses like Rose were active in the feminist First Wave of the mid-nineteenth century, but the Second Wave, starting in the 1960s, was when Jewish leadership truly came to the fore. Writers Betty Friedan, Gloria Steinem, Susan Brownmiller, Alix Kates Shulman, Andrea Dworkin, and Shulamith Firestone, as well as birth control activists Barbara Seaman and Alice Wolfson, pioneering women's historian Gerda Lerner, poet Adrienne Rich, artist Judy Chicago, and many others, fought for women's rights: rights to our own bodies, to economic opportunities, to equal protection under the law, to a place at the table. They fought for women's health and women's spiritual and artistic pursuits to be taken as seriously as those of men.

→ Gloria Steinem

→ Susan Brownmiller

Many of these women were uninterested in, or even hostile to, Judaism. So perhaps we should make a distinction between "Jewish feminists" and "feminist Jews." The latter—including women like Paula Hyman, Blu Greenberg, Arlene Agus, Laura Geller, Evelyn Beck, Judith Plaskow, Elizabeth Koltun, Sally Priesand, Amy Eilberg, Ellen Umansky, Marcia Falk, Rachel Cowan, Debbie Friedman, Anne Lapidus Lerner, Susannah Heschel, and Judith Hauptman, among others—have focused their efforts on creating a less patriarchal, more egalitarian Judaism.

Today, most Jewish denominations have accepted women as rabbis and cantors. And the creativity and fierceness of feminist Jews led to new rituals like baby-naming ceremonies for girls, new mikveh traditions that celebrate the complex realities of women's lives, feminist Passover Seders, and ceremonies linking rosh chodesh (the new moon) to women's spirituality. Feminist Jews have fought for new interpretations of ancient texts, advocated for women's greater participation in Jewish communal institutions, and increasingly made "feminist Jewish" concerns simply, you know, *Jewish* concerns.

→ Andrea Dworkin

disturbing statements. Although his mother was Jewish, Fischer refused to identify as Jewish and eventually took to denying the Holocaust. The United States, he declared, was "a farce controlled by dirty, hook-nosed, circumcised Jew bastards." Hours after the attacks of September 11, 2001, he told a reporter that he applauded the attack, which he saw as fair retribution for American and Israeli aggression. Later in life, he was arrested in Japan for traveling on an invalid passport, found refuge in Iceland, and died there of renal failure.

CARRIE FISHER

Fisher, Carrie (1956–2016)

Princess Leia in *Star Wars*—but that's the least interesting thing about her. She was once married to singer-songwriter Paul Simon, and when he sings about "one and one-half wandering Jews," Fisher is the "one-half." Watch her Emmy-nominated appearances on TV's *30 Rock* or *Catastrophe* to get a sense of her comic range, or read her semiautobiographical novel *Postcards from the Edge* (or see the film adaptation starring Meryl Streep) to understand her struggle with addiction and an extremely challenging mother (played in the movie by Shirley MacLaine). Her father was actor-singer Eddie Fisher (who was Jewish). Her (real-life) mother was actor-singer Debbie Reynolds (who was not); the two were as close as a mother and daughter can be—they even lived next door to each other. Fisher died on December 27, 2016; Reynolds died the very next day.

fleishig

Yiddish for "meaty," indicating that a meal contains meat, which matters because Jews who keep kosher don't mix milk and meat. So after eating anything fleishig, they wait for a period of time before eating anything dairy again.

Florida

Where aging Jews and hurricanes go for one last furious spin.

food

See Food and Jews, page 100.

foreskin

How would we know?

Fortunoff Video Archive

An archive of recorded interviews with Holocaust survivors, housed at Yale University. Beginning its collection in 1979, it pioneered the use of video testimonies.

Four Questions

A portion of the Passover Seder chanted, according to tradition, by the youngest person present. It's designed to call attention to all the ways in which the festive Passover meal is like no other dinner we have all year, as if the four mandatory cups of wine weren't enough of a giveaway.

How is this night different from all other nights?

On all other nights, we eat chametz [leavened bread] and matzo—why, on this night, only matzo?

On all other nights, we eat all vegetables—why, on this night, only maror [bitter herbs]?

On all other nights, we don't dip [our greens] even once. Why, on this night, do we dip twice?

On all other nights, we eat either sitting upright or reclining. Why, on this night, do we all recline?

Frank, Anne (1929–1945)

Iconic Jewish teenage diarist, murdered in Bergen-Belsen. Her account of her two years hiding in an attic in her native Holland was published by her father after her death and became one of the most frequently translated and widely read books of the twentieth century.

Freud, Sigmund (1856–1939)

The father of psychoanalysis, and, by extension, all therapy. Every time we walk into the shrink's office, every time Woody Allen's characters refer to their analysts, we're in a tradition established almost single-handedly by Freud. We talk Freud all the time: "the Oedipus Complex," "repression," dreams as reflections of desire, even the mere idea that belonging to a society with rules takes an enormous toll. He is one of the few humans who has changed the way the world thinks during his own lifetime.

Florida: The Sunshine State welcomes Jewish retirees with open arms and early-bird dinners.

FOOD AND JEWS

"In the beginning, there was an apple."

Look, we can argue about who/Who laid the foundation of the story of the Jews—and when, and how, and let's not even get into why—but for incontrovertible proof that there was genius at work, one need look no further than the recurring role granted to food. The very origins of human life and consciousness were rooted in a drama about a piece of fruit, and things only got more culinarily spectacular from there: a birthright is stolen over lentil soup; a Jewish son, sold by his own brothers into slavery, rises to power by taking care of all Pharaoh's needs outside of what he eats; many men are brought to sin, and some to death, by a love of wine; a slavery is ended, and a nation made, as dough baked into crackers.

Throughout the Bible, stories are animated and lessons driven home with the help of almonds, dates, pistachio nuts, pomegranates, figs, melons, grapes, cucumbers, leeks, onions, garlic, grains of all kind, cheeses (especially salty ones), fish, fowl, meats—and that's a very partial list. In the covenant between God and this people, the ultimate gift given in exchange for devotion is described not as a place of high mountains or abundant water or some other geographic advantage but, simply and majestically, as a land of milk and honey.

But the truly inspired move was the elevation of food—what one eats, and particularly what one must not eat—as a marker not simply of piety but of belonging. Yes, it can feel irrational. And yes, it was and is about separating ourselves from others, and there can be and has been isolation and shame and danger as a result. But the decision to adhere to a set of possibly random rules that determine how you move through the world on a daily basis connects one, in ways that are hard to describe, with others who've made the same choice—in the present, in the past, and in the future. It's no accident that when Paul the Apostle set out to annul the separation between Jews and gentiles, he knew exactly what cord to cut first: the dietary laws.

Throughout history, the Jews who accepted that they were not like

everyone else—and could not be, and maybe didn't even want to be—were ultimately the Jews who maintained and improved upon Jewishness for the ages. And on the list of things these folks managed to enhance, food is at, or close to, the top.

Religious observance to the vagaries of agricultural seasons, dietary laws, and Sabbath observance generated a variety of slow-cooked dishes from around the globe—based and seasoned differently, depending on the country and its native offerings—and flavors for meats and poultry were sought outside of dairy. Fields have been left untended every seven years. Holidays and life-cycle events were glorified by foods that held narrative and religious symbolism: apples and honey to put us on track for sweetness in a coming year; fried latkes and doughnuts to celebrate Hanukkah's miracle of oil; charoset to represent Egyptian mortar on Passover; and more. Polish Jews gave us schmaltz and bialys and the chicken soup you believe your grandmother invented. Jews in Yemen made at least three kinds of Sabbath breads, Moroccan Jews ended Passover with mufleta, and on auspicious occasions—births and brises, engagements, graduations, recovery from sickness, housewarming parties—Jews in India gather together to pray and offer platters of malida to the prophet Elijah.

And then, of course, there are the days even a child can tell are grave and solemn—because they are the days where there is no food at all (see Fast Days, page 94). Indeed, deprivation is vital and it too demands attention—our most profound.

In our immediate era, the lack of food took on additional meaning, as millions of Jews were starved—many to death—in the Holocaust, a legacy of emptiness seared into the contemporary Jewish psyche. Think twice before you joke about why there always seems to be far too much food at any Jewish gathering, why many of our elders fear the sight of a clean plate and others seem capable of turning a single meal into a week of leftovers.

We can't seem to escape food, or the lack thereof. We're just wired that way (see **epigenetics**). Jews and food. It's a tale of Darkness, and Love.

Freundel, Barry (b. 1951)
See Shonde, page 240.

Friedan, Betty (1921–2006)

Betty Friedan's 1963 classic *The Feminine Mystique* is often credited with sparking Second Wave feminism. She described "the problem that has no name" as "a strange stirring, a sense of dissatisfaction, a yearning . . . Each suburban wife struggled with it alone. As she made the beds, shopped for groceries . . . she was afraid to ask even of herself the silent question—'Is this all?'" In 1966, Friedan cofounded the National Organization for Women (NOW), which battled workplace discrimination and lobbied for paid maternity leave, decent child care, and legal abortion. Friedan wasn't easy to get along with (she and Gloria Steinem were, shall we say, not close). She fought with her fellow feminists about battling for the rights of nonwhite women, lesbians, and sex workers, and she's frequently criticized today for highlighting her own middle-class, white concerns. But there's no denying that she earned the right to brag, as she once did: "The truth is that I've always been a bad-tempered bitch."

Friedman, Kinky (b. 1944)
With his band, the Texas Jewboys, this writer, crooner, and philosopher-king spent decades dispensing bits of wisdom like "They ain't makin' Jews like Jesus anymore / They ain't makin' carpenters that know what nails are for."

Frozen Chosen
Cutesy name for the Jews of Alaska, although the brothers and sisters in Minnesota have a pretty good case to make as well.

frum
Yiddish for "devout" or "pious," the term is often used to describe particularly observant Orthodox Jews. (See Branches of Judaism, page 44.)

FROM

Gadot, Gal

TO

Gut Shabbes

Gadot, Gal (b. 1985)

Israeli actress cast as Wonder Woman in the 2017 blockbuster, and the most kickass Israeli woman since Golda Meir.

GAL GADOT

ga-ga

A dodge ball–like game popular at Jewish summer camps. Theories of its origins vary; some say it was created in the IDF, others say it was created stateside. In the end, where it came from matters less than where it went: to every Jewish summer camp worth its salt.

Garden of Eden

Is it a real place, where God created Adam and Eve, as described in Genesis? Some say yes, locating it somewhere in modern-day Iraq. Is it an allegory for utopia? Many believe so, although Jewish theology doesn't, for the most part, believe in a concrete heaven to which the righteous go after they die. Still, Eden remains the scene of the greatest human drama in history, and any time we struggle with lust, defiance, faith, or hunger, we're reliving the Garden's ancient vexations.

Garfunkel, Art (b. 1941)

Key figure in folk revivalism and 1960s pop whose enormous voice was matched only by his enormous Jewfro. Born in Queens, Garfunkel took to singing early in life. He sang cantorial songs at his bar mitzvah at around the time he met his future partner and eventual frenemy, Paul Simon. The pair sang close harmony in imitation of the Everly Brothers. The first song they recorded with their own names, "The Sound of Silence," was not a success, and they split up (Garfunkel returning to Columbia University). Then producer Tom Wilson reworked it with an orchestra, and it went to number one on the charts. They recorded songs for the movie *The Graduate*, and the hits kept coming, including "Mrs. Robinson" and "Bridge Over Troubled Water." After they broke up, Simon's solo career took off, but Garfunkel's did not. The pair did reunite for some key concerts over the years, most famously a gig in Central Park in 1981.

garment industry

See page 110.

gebrokts, gebrochts

Yiddish, literally meaning "broken," *gebrokts* refers to matzo that has come into contact with liquid, generally for cooking purposes. Matzo balls or matzo brei, for example, are gebrokts, because their recipes include both matzo and liquid. Many Hasidic Jews do not eat gebrokts on Passover, and their matzo is fastidiously kept separate from liquids, not to be used in any cooking, except on the eighth day of Passover, when wetting matzo is permitted. The belief is that wetting matzo may further leaven it, which halacha prohibits. Some are so passionately anti-gebrokts that matzo is eaten into a bag, so that all crumbs are contained and there's absolutely no risk of even a fleck of matzo falling into someone's water glass.

gefilte fish

According to some, the ultimate Ashkenazi food: an appetizer made from ground carp, whitefish, or pike, often served (with horseradish) at Shabbat dinner. According to others, the prime reason they don't like Ashkenazi food—especially as most people's idea of gefilte fish involves the giant store-bought jars of gray balls floating in a jelly of unpleasant odor. A new wave of artisanal gefilte fish makers are trying to split the difference—more convenient than making it yourself, less repulsive than opening that jar—for a new generation who might previously have turned up their noses at the very notion of eating such a thing.

gelt

In seventeenth-century Poland, parents celebrated Hanukkah by giving money to their children to give to their teachers as a token of gratitude. Those children being Jewish, they soon wised up and argued that they, too, deserved a little something to sweeten the pot. In the 1920s, an enterprising American candy maker made a bet that the only thing kids would appreciate more than cold, hard cash was cold, hard cash that's actually chocolate. He was correct, and generations of

Jewish children still honor his spirit by using the chocolaty coins as currency for gambling on high-stakes dreidel games.

Gemara

Between roughly 230 CE and 500 CE, a second wave of rabbis, called Amoraim ("those who speak"), emerged to continue the work of explaining and annotating Jewish law. Whereas their predecessors, the Tannaim who composed the Mishnah, saw their work as delivering the oral tradition as it stood, the Amoraim, generally, saw theirs as expounding upon, expanding upon, and clarifying difficult questions. And whereas the Mishnah delivered rulings, the Gemara delivers dialectical questions riffing on the Mishnah; these questions are called sugyot, or sugya in the singular. These commentaries on the Mishnah make up the main body of the Talmud.

gematria

We see your Da Vinci Code, and raise you this ancient Jewish system of assigning numeric values to words or sentences based on their letters. If you've ever wondered why Judaism considers the numeral 18 to be lucky, it's because the letters chet (numeric value of eight) and yud (numeric value of ten) spell *chai*, or "alive." "Bagel," in case you were looking for a new lucky number, equals 55 in gematria. In gematria, as in life, it's okay to be off by a little.

Genesis

Even in a book like the Bible, thick with wondrous moments and miraculous characters, Genesis stands alone. Like season one of your favorite TV show, it starts with a big bang and picks up the pace as it moves along, giving us everything from a deluge to near child sacrifice to next-level sibling rivalry. If you wanted to

GERSHWIN, GEORGE

(1898–1937)

"I like New York in June, how about you? / I like a Gershwin tune, how about you?" So went the refrain of a pop hit in 1941, four years after George Gershwin's death from a malignant brain tumor at age thirty-eight. Arguably the supreme musical talent of the Great American Songbook era, Gershwin composed dozens of enduring songs with his brother, lyricist Ira. "I Got Rhythm" is the bedrock upon which literally thousands of jazz songs have been formed; "Someone to Watch Over Me," "Embraceable You," "They Can't Take That Away from Me," "Summertime," and dozens of other hits embody Gershwin's melodic and harmonic genius.

Gershwin grew up in Brooklyn and on the Lower East Side, the child of Russian Jewish immigrants. His heritage is audible in his music: you can detect the influence of both black blues and cantorial music in the groundbreaking "contemporary opera" *Porgy and Bess* (1935), and the famous opening clarinet strain in *Rhapsody in Blue* turns the keening sound of klezmer into a twentieth-century American soul cry. **(See Pop Music and Jews, page 182.)**

GERSHWIN'S GOT IT

Rhapsody in Blue
(orchestral work, 1924)

"Someone to Watch Over Me"
(1926)

"I Got Rhythm"
(1930)

"Embraceable You"
(1930)

"Summertime"
(1935)

Porgy and Bess
(opera, 1935)

"They Can't Take That Away From Me"
(1937)

JEWISH GANGSTERS

n 1919, the United States adopted the Eighteenth Amendment to th onstitution, which beginning the following year made it illegal to manufacture ell, or transport "intoxicating liquors . . . for beverage purposes." As soon a ne law passed, it seemed as if every American over the age of twelve had t ave a drink. In response to this great American thirst, two hundred thousan nlicensed saloons soon sprang up across the United States. These bars an estaurants were euphemistically called "speakeasies" and "blind pigs." Larg ootlegging organizations led by tough, ruthless lawbreaking sons of Irish alian, and yes, Jewish immigrants arose to service them.

Jewish mobsters were generally men who never finished high school and refused to work in a shop or factory. Yet they wanted the good life, the money and beautiful women and fancy cars and homes. During Prohibition, 50 percent of the nation's leading bootleggers were Jews. And Jews and Jewish gangs bossed the rackets in some of America's largest cities.

DAILY NEWS FINAL

SCHULTZ DEAD

Police Jail Gangster's Widow

The End!

But the man who masterminded New York's underworld was no mere gangster. Best known as the man who allegedly "fixed" the 1919 World Series, Arnold Rothstein is recognized as a pioneer of organized crime in the United States, transforming American crime from petty larceny into big business. During the 1920s, Rothstein put together the largest gambling and bookmaking empire in the country, masterminded a million-dollar stolen-bond business, and controlled most of New York's gangs, as well as the city's traffic in narcotics, bootlegging, and gambling.

Rothstein moved freely in all circles, from politicians and statesmen to bankers and bums. In the 1920s, he had on his payroll many future machers of the underworld, including Italians such as Charles "Lucky" Luciano and Frank Costello, and young Jewish hoodlums, including Meyer Lansky, Benjamin "Bugsy" Siegel, Louis "Lepke" Buchalter, and Arthur Flegenheimer, better known as Dutch Schultz. Rothstein taught them that the dollar had one nationality and one religion: profit. After Prohibition, Siegel would turn Las Vegas into the nation's gambling mecca, while Buchalter would muscle into New York's labor unions. In 1944, Buchalter became the only national crime boss to be put to death in the electric chair.

DAILY NEWS EXTRA EDITION

ARNOLD ROTHSTEIN SHOT

PETTING KILLER PRIMPS IN COURT

During Prohibition, Abner "Longy" Zwillman reigned as king of the rackets in Newark. Bootlegging in Philadelphia was directed by Max "Boo Boo" Hoff, who headed a powerful gang of young Jewish toughs. In Minneapolis, there was Isidore "Kid Cann" Blumenfeld. In Cleveland, bootlegging and gambling were bossed by the "Cleveland Four": Morris "Moe" Dalitz, Morris Kleinman, Sam Tucker, and Louis Rothkopf. Detroit's all-Jewish purple gang was led by a transplanted New Yorker, Ray Bernstein. The gang, which at its peak had fifty members, dominated the city's bootlegging and narcotics traffic throughout Prohibition.

← Benjamin "Bugsy" Siegel's mug shot, 1928

These men did everything. They dealt in bootlegging, narcotics, extortion, prostitution, and contract killing. But they reigned for one generation only. They had no Jewish successors. Unlike the Italians, they kept their families out of the business. Jews moved to the suburbs, sent their children to universities, and became part of America's economic, educational, and occupational elite. The era of the Jewish gangster became part of history, something for their grandchildren to read about.

ponder all of human morality, you would need look no further: the jealous Cain slaying Abel, the righteous Abraham bargaining with God on behalf of Sodom and Gomorrah, the soulful Joseph forgiving his brothers—it's all there, urging you again and again to just start from the beginning.

gentile

Everyone but us.

Germany

A country in Central Europe, with Berlin as its capital. Jews have lived in Germany since about 850 CE and enjoyed eras of prosperity and peace there, producing great thinkers like Hannah Arendt; great engineers like Ralph Baer, who invented the video game; great psychologists like Erich Fromm; great composers like Felix Mendelssohn; great directors like Ernst Lubitsch; great writers like Walter Benjamin; and the great Dr. Ruth Westheimer. This German Jewish renaissance went more or less uninterrupted, with a few exceptions, for hundreds of years. Like the pogroms in 1096. And the thousands of Jews massacred between 1298 and 1337. And the Black Plague panic (1348–50), which blamed Jews for the epidemic and led to the wholesale destruction of three hundred Jewish communities. Oh, and some troubles between 1933 and 1945.

gett

The writ of divorce required to dissolve a Jewish marriage. By tradition, a divorce only occurs when a groom, or an emissary of the groom, hands a gett, usually written by a *sofer*, or scribe, to the wife. If the husband refuses to give his wife a gett, she cannot get divorced. Today, most secular and liberal Jews do not insist on a gett, taking a civil divorce as confirmation of the end of a marriage. But in Orthodox and even some Conservative circles, the gett is essential; without one, a Jew cannot remarry, and any children born of a woman's remarriage are considered *mamzerim*, or bastards, and carry that stigma their whole lives. When a wife wants to leave the marriage and her husband does not wish to grant her a divorce, he can refuse to offer the gett, and the wife becomes an *agunah*, or "chained wife."

ghetto

On March 29, 1516, the Republic of Venice decreed that all its Jewish citizens must live in a specifically designated area. It was called the Ghetto, most likely due to its proximity to a nearby foundry, or *ghetto* in Italian. Other European governments adopted both the name and the idea, creating Jewish ghettos across the continent. The Nazis gave the term a ghoulish twist when they forced vast numbers of Jews to relocate to ghettos across Europe, condemning them to starvation and disease before they were deported to concentration camps (see **Holocaust**).

Gidget

Fictional character developed by Frederick Kohner, based on his teenage daughter Kathy (b. 1941), for his 1957 novel subtitled *The Little Girl with Big Ideas*. The prototypical beach-bunny surfer-girl persona would feature in a handful of novels, a pair of novelizations, a series of films starring Sandra Dee, a sitcom with Sally Field, three TV movies, and one "Ambassador of Aloha" posting at Duke's, a Hawaiian-themed restaurant in Malibu. All of which is to say that the embodiment of postwar American female surferdom is the daughter of a Czech Jew.

Ginsberg, Allen (1926–1997)

Beat poet who wrote "Howl" and "Kaddish." Only a truly great Jewish bard could capture the human condition so succinctly by writing about a man lounging through town "seeking jazz or sex or soup."

Ginsburg, Ruth Bader (b. 1933)

Only the second woman ever—and the first Jewish woman—to sit on the Supreme Court. But first, earlier in her career, she helped create sex-discrimination jurisprudence. Now in her mid-eighties, she is still working out. She is smarter than you, and tougher than you, too. "The Notorious RBG" has become a pop culture icon and is one of the few justices ever to be portrayed in their very own biopic.

glatt kosher

And you thought just keeping kosher was hard enough. There's a debate about whether we're allowed to eat a kosher animal who underwent a kosher slaughtering if it turns out that one of its internal organs was blemished. Those who say no, mainly Ashkenazi Jews, insist on their meat being glatt kosher, the first word meaning "smooth" in Yiddish and guaranteeing that the animal they're about to enjoy was perfect both inside and out. This arms race for who can be more kosher than thou has meant that many restaurants and food purveyors have had to up their level of kashrut certification—many observant Jews whose parents ate in any "kosher" restaurant now walk right by establishments that don't post "glatt kosher" in their windows.

Glazer, Ilana (b. 1987)

See **Jacobson, Abbi, and Ilana Glazer.**

Glückel of Hameln (c. 1646–1724)

Best known for the diaries she kept, an invaluable glimpse into German Jewish life in the early modern period. She is considered the first female memoirist to have written in Yiddish. Her great-granddaughter Bertha Pappenheim (1859–1936), who translated the diaries into German, shared Glückel's talent for confession: one of the best-documented psychological case studies of the nineteenth century, she was Freud's "Anna O."

God, aka G-d

What's He/She/It like? Judaism is pretty honest on this point: we have no way of knowing. But what we do know is that all of us, even those who aren't really believers, are in a relationship with God. What kind of relationship? It's complicated: we summon God to a little chat three times a day, when we pray, and God, by giving us Judaism and its commandments, summons us, too, to behave and think and feel a certain way. Most important, however, God is just another way for us to be with each other: unlike many other religions, Judaism can't be practiced in private. It was designed to be impossible without the company of other Jews, which is why we daven together, celebrate holidays together, kvetch together, and argue together about difficult questions, like the true nature of God.

Gold, Ari

The unrepentant asshole in the HBO show *Entourage* (2004–2011). The character, inspired by super-agent Ari Emanuel (see **Emanuel brothers**) and played by Jeremy Piven, is crude, crass, and craven, but he's also fun and funny and throws a hell of a bar mitzvah. Plus, he gifted to the world a vital new concept in conflict resolution: "hugging it out."

Goldberg, Rube (1883–1970)

Contrary to popular belief, a Rube Goldberg was not just a device but a man—a cartoonist whose most famous works were his depictions of extremely complex machines that ended up doing very simple things. Some

of the devices depicted in his cartoons did things like remove olives from a jar, or empty ashtrays. But Goldberg also won a Pulitzer in 1948 for his political cartoons.

Goldberg, Whoopi (b. 1955)

Born Caryn Johnson, Whoopi Goldberg did the reverse of what so many Jews in Hollywood did: the African American gentile chose the most Jewish last name she could think of. She figured it could only help her career. Director Mike Nichols (Mikhail Peschkowsky) saw her perform a collection of monologues and helped her bring it to Broadway. From there she won a part in Steven Spielberg's 1985 adaptation of *The Color Purple*, one of his first "mature" films, and the rest is history.

Goldblum, Jeff (b. 1952)

Actor and Internet daddy. A performer with unusual speech patterns and a blazing, indescribable sexuality, Goldblum, who grew up attending an Orthodox shul, has appeared in major moneymaking Hollywood hits like Steven Spielberg's *Jurassic Park* (and its sequels) and *Independence Day*. His first notable film appearance was in Woody Allen's *Annie Hall*, as a Los Angeles partygoer calling his guru on the phone because he has forgotten his mantra. Three years after doing the aging-hippie flick *The Big Chill* (1983), Goldblum took off his shirt, crouched down in a pod, and transformed into a monstrous insect in Jewish director David Cronenberg's strange horror-drama *The Fly*. In the 2010s, he popped up in the work of Wes Anderson and some of the spacier Marvel movies. He's also taken to wearing intentionally dorky sweaters and embracing his role as a silver fox. For a real thrill, find early footage of him and Ben Vereen in their quickly canceled cop/buddy TV comedy from 1980, *Tenspeed and Brown Shoe.*

THE GARMENT INDUSTRY

Well before Jews were associated with Wall Street, Tin Pan Alley, Broadway, or Hollywood, they were known for Chatham Street. This was once the center of the shmatte business: the place where New Yorkers would come to buy secondhand clothing, before ready-made garments were affordable. The Jewish proprietors of these dingy storefronts gained national notoriety for their ability to ensnare passing pedestrians. Few in the 1820s and '30s—at the height of this trade—would have imagined these merchants were pioneering the relationship between Jews and garments, which has lasted, and been transformed, in the two centuries since.

Until the Civil War, there were few signs that this relationship would culminate in Ralph Lauren. Jews were not well represented among the innovators, like Brooks Brothers, who worked out how to mass-produce ready-made clothing in the 1830s and '40s. Instead, Jews were initially much more likely to sell this clothing than to produce it. In the mid-nineteenth century, peddling became a rite of passage for tens of thousands of Central European Jewish immigrants. The ones who ventured from metropolises like New York traipsed from farm to farm, footsore salesmen filling their packs and bundles with clothing and fabric, items that offered a healthy weight-to-worth ratio. Peddling dispersed Jews across the American hinterland and, by accident rather than design, created a ready-made distribution network, as they later settled down and opened stores in the towns and villages dotting the countryside.

Yet the shmatte business would not have become a Jewish industry but for the Civil War. The sputtering of the American economy in the months before the war toppled many of the leading players within the garment industry. But because Jewish wholesalers and manufacturers were less exposed to the Southern market, they were better placed to weather the crisis. Drought was soon replaced by deluge. In the desperate rush to outfit the Union Army, the government threw money at any firm that could plausibly claim to be able to stitch uniforms. Wartime opportunity catapulted Jews from the foothills of the clothing industry into its upper reaches.

The long-term effects were monumental. Some of those who profited from the wartime boom and its long afterglow chose to leave the retailing business behind; the Seligman and Lehman brothers, for example, classed up their act and went into banking (see Banking and Jews, page 26). Others took advantage of the dramatic expansion of the American marketplace. By the end of the century, firms once started by peddlers and their enterprising children were landmark emporia on main streets across America. Jewish-owned stores became bright stars in American retailing: Rich's in Atlanta, Filene's in Boston, Macy's in New York, Gimbels in Milwaukee, Kaufmann's in Pittsburgh, and Neiman Marcus in Dallas.

And at the messier end of the business—the cutting, stitching, and pressing of garments—Jewish moguls who made their fortunes during and after the Civil War threw the gates open wide to a new generation of Jewish garment workers. These wholesalers and manufacturers were in need of ever more workers to feed the insatiable desire of American consumers for cheap clothing. The flood of Jews fleeing Eastern Europe more than satisfied their needs. Jewish needle workers now sewed clothing in workshops operated by Jewish contractors, who competed for orders placed by Jewish wholesalers for goods that would be sold by Jewish retailers. By 1910 Jews accounted for at least 39 percent of the total workforce in the garment industry in New York City—and a quarter of the workforce nationwide.

For the most part, this was difficult, unpleasant, and poorly paid work, done in sweatshops and workshops. It was sometimes dangerous, too. The infamous Triangle Shirtwaist Factory fire in 1911 still ranks as one of New York City's worst industrial disasters. Paradoxically, miserable working conditions produced two important outcomes. Some workers were at the forefront of labor activism. Others sought relief by leaving the sweatshops behind. And since other sectors were loath to hire Jews, many former garment industry workers flocked to new consumer-oriented industries—like film and music. Several Hollywood moguls and sheet-music publishers started as salesmen in the clothing trade. (Morris Brill is better remembered for the music produced in the building that bore his name than for the clothing store he ran on the ground floor.)

And the Jews left behind in the garment industry? These entrepreneurs, like their cousins in showbiz, sought glamour and prestige. They became designers like Ralph Lauren, haberdashers like Jacobi Press of J.Press, and tastemakers like Barney Pressman and his son, Fred, whose Barneys store stocks the brands sought by Jews and gentiles whose affluence meant they never had to give a thought to Chatham Street.

Goldman, Emma (1869–1940)

Anarchist, activist, socialist, writer, nurse, midwife, and ice cream store proprietress falsely credited with coining the phrase "If I can't dance, I don't want to be part of your revolution." Goldman immigrated to the United States from Lithuania in 1885 and soon became a hugely popular rabble-rouser. In 1892, she and her lifelong friend/fellow anarchist/sometimes lover Alexander Berkman plotted the murder of industrialist Henry Clay Frick. Frick had crushed a strike in the Pennsylvania steel plant he managed; the resulting violence led to multiple deaths and injuries. Police couldn't tie Goldman to the crime, but she was later jailed for "inciting to riot" and for illegally distributing information about birth control. Upon her release from prison, Goldman was deported to Russia, where she soured on communism.

Goldring/Woldenberg Institute of Southern Jewish Life

Organization devoted to preserving Southern Jewish life in America and recording its history. It operates the Encyclopedia of Southern Jewish Communities, a free, searchable online archive featuring the history of every congregation and notable Jewish community in the South, offering proof that American Jewish life can exist outside New York City.

Goldstein, Al (1936–2013)

American pornographer and publisher of the magazines *Screw, Bitch*, *Smut*, and the short-lived *Death.* A fearless, irreverent, openly unapologetic vice-peddler, Goldstein was also a transformative First Amendment warrior, sued and arrested dozens of times for obscenity and other assaults on American decency. In its obituary of Goldstein, the *New York Times* said he "took the romance out of sex." But his review of the otherwise obscure low-budget film *Deep Throat* ("I was never so moved by any theatrical performance since stuttering through my own bar mitzvah") indirectly led to the rise of the modern porn industry.

golem

In Jewish folklore, a golem is a zombielike thing made of mud or clay, conjured into being by prayer or mystical incantation. In one story in the Talmud, the first human, Adam, is created as a golem. There is the Golem of Prague, famous even though there is no historial evidence he existed, but who, according to Jewish legend, was conjured by Rabbi Judah Loew ben Bezalel in the sixteenth century to protect the city's Jews in times of crisis. There is also a golem in Cynthia Ozick's *The Puttermesser Papers*, from 1997, and in the opening pages of Michael Chabon's 2000 novel *The Amazing Adventures of Kavalier & Clay.* In 2006, the Golem of Prague appeared in an episode of *The Simpsons* (d'oh!). Golems everywhere.

Goodman, Benny (1909–1986)

Influential jazz performer and bandleader of the swing era. Born poor in Chicago, Goodman first started clarinet lessons through his synagogue at age ten. His ear led him to the music emerging from New Orleans, and by fourteen he was sitting in with renowned cornetist (and one of the principal architects of jazz) Bix Beiderbecke. He moved to New York and played with notable bandleaders Tommy Dorsey, Glenn Miller, and others. Columbia Records producer John Hammond (who would discover Bob Dylan and Bruce Springsteen) recorded him in 1933. He later formed a band that was heard on NBC radio, and began working with African American arranger Fletcher Henderson. Goodman's orchestra, which included some members of Henderson's band, is considered the first substantial integrated musical group in American history. Goodman's recording of Louis Prima's "Sing, Sing, Sing" (with Gene Krupa on drums) is among the most famous instrumental tracks of all time. Even if you think you don't know it, you know it.

Gornick, Vivian (b. 1935)

Essayist, critic, journalist, memoirist, New Yorker, feminist. In the great Jewish literary tradition, she attended City College. Begin with her 1987 memoir *Fierce Attachments*, a portrait of her complex (to say the least) relationship with her mother. Then double back to her classic *The Romance of American Communism* (1977). Then read everything else she wrote. She is one of the Jewesses—along with Susan Sontag and Janet Malcolm, all of them born between 1933 and 1935—who set a new standard for literary nonfiction in America.

goy, goyim

Meaning, literally, "a nation," it's become a term to describe all *other* nations, meaning anyone but the Jews.

goyish

"Goyish" means of or relating to the goyim, the non-Jews. You know, like sipping gin on your sailboat with your pal Muffy. At its best, "goyish" is used humorously, one Jew to another, as a wink and a nod to some-

Goyish: Muffy and Tripp plan their weekend getaway to the Cape to sail on Tripp's granddad's schooner.

JEWISH GREETINGS

WHAT TO SAY AND WHEN

GENERAL

Hebrew	English	When to use
"Shabbat shalom"	**Literally, "a peaceful Shabbat"**	A standard Shabbat greeting, it is typically used from about Friday midday through Saturday evening. (The Yiddish-inflected "Gut Shabbes" is also common.)
"Shavuah tov"	**"Good week"**	Good for greeting people on Saturday night, once Shabbat has ended. Acceptable through the weekend; iffy by Monday night.
"Chag sameach"	**"Happy holiday"**	Good for any Jewish holiday. Some people use the Yiddish version, "Gut yontef."

LIFE EVENTS

Hebrew	English	When to use
"Mazel tov"	**"Congratulations"**	All-purpose phrase for a celebratory moment. Good for baby namings, graduations, bar mitzvahs, your boyfriend's third cousin's uncle's wedding.
"Baruch Dayan Ha-Emet"	**"Blessed be the True Judge"**	Traditional response to news that someone has died. This phrase evokes the idea that ultimately only God can judge when it is our time to go. When speaking to a mourner at a shiva or funeral, the traditional phrase is *Hamakom Yenachem et'chem b'toch avlei tzion v'yerushalayim*, which means "May God comfort you among the mourners of Zion and Jerusalem." You can also say "Hamakom Yenachem."
"Besha'ah tovah"	**"All in good time"**	What to say upon hearing the news that someone is pregnant. (For superstitious Jews, saying "Mazel tov!" before the baby is born is considered bad luck.)

LIFE EVENTS
(CONTINUED)

Hebrew	English	When to use
"Refuah sheleimah"	**"A complete healing"**	Compassionate response to news that someone is sick, along the lines of "Get well soon." Equally appropriate for serious illness, like when bedside at a hospital, or simply when parting with a friend who has a bad cold. Applicable to both physical and mental illnesses.
"Oyf simchas"	**"Of happy occasions"**	When Jews part ways after a shiva, funeral, or other somber occasion, they may use this send-off, expressing hope that they meet again under happier circumstances.

SPECIFIC HOLIDAY GREETINGS

Hebrew	English	When to use
"Shanah tovah (u'Metukah)"	**"Good (and sweet) New Year"**	Good for the lead-up to Rosh Hashanah through Yom Kippur.
"Gmar chatimah tovah"	**Literally, "a good final sealing"**	Used between Rosh Hashanah and Yom Kippur, this is an expression of the hope that the year to come is a good one. It's a weightier phrase, more in line with the reflective mood of Yom Kippur than the celebratory vibe of Rosh Hashanah. Often shortened to "Gmar tov."
"Moadim l'simcha"	**"Happy holiday"**	This phase is used during the intermediate days of Passover and Sukkot—the days that aren't the holy days at the start and end. A standard "Chag sameach!" in response will do the trick, but if you want to get real fancy you can reply, "Chagim u'zemanim l'sason." (An acceptable response: "To you too!")
"Chag kasher v'sameach"	**"Happy and kosher holiday"**	Passover phrase that you can start using during the lead-up to the holiday. People like to throw in the "kosher" bit, possibly because of the holiday's demanding food restrictions. (An acceptable response: "To you too!")
"Chag Purim sameach"	**"Happy Purim holiday"**	Common greeting on Purim, the holiday of festivities and joy. You can also use the Yiddish *freilichein Purim*, which means "Happy Purim."

thing—or someone—fundamentally not *us*. Goyish doesn't necessarily mean bad—it can just mean out of place in a Jewish setting. Christmas is goyish even though many Jews secretly love it. "Goyish" can sound derisive to non-Jews and thus must be wielded delicately. See **Bruce, Lenny**, one of the great scholars of goyishness versus Jewishness.

grape juice

The gateway drug to Manischewitz.

The Grateful Dead

Only one of the band's core members, Mickey Hart, is Jewish, but there's a reason why so many Members of the Tribe took so strongly to the Dead. The Dead's infinite catalog of bootleg concerts feels like an endless Talmudic disputation, with true believers parsing the meaning of each note. If you believe that little in life is definitive, and that your time is best spent finding new meaning in very old songs, you're probably both a Jew and a Deadhead.

Green Line

Israel's pre-1967 borders, before it acquired Judea and Samaria in the Six-Day War. It's called the Green Line because of the green ink used to draw the line on maps during negotiations.

greetings

See Jewish Greetings, page 114.

Grossman, Chayka

See Warsaw Ghetto Uprising, page 284.

guilt

Something unique to Jews. And Italians. And the Irish. And people with parents.

Gut Shabbes

See Jewish Greetings, page 114.

FROM

Hadassah

TO

Hydrox

Hadassah

Founded in 1912 by Henrietta Szold, this Jewish women's volunteer organization—its helpful subtitle is "the Women's Zionist Organization of America"—focuses on health, education, and welfare in Israel, where it does everything from run hospitals to help underprivileged children get a better education. It has also been a pioneer in working for amity between Jewish and Arab Israelis. More than three hundred thousand Americans are members.

Haganah

A Jewish paramilitary organization in British-occupied Palestine. Initially, the Haganah was formed in 1920 to defend Jewish communities against Arab attacks, and it was largely composed of small platoons lacking structure or leadership. Throughout the 1930s, the Haganah grew more organized, with a central command overseeing training and missions. During World War II, it helped the British prepare for the possibility of a Nazi invasion of Palestine, as well as recruit Jewish men to the British Army. Once the war was over, however, the Haganah joined forces with two other Jewish groups, the Etzel and the Lehi, in an effort to bring the British Mandate for Palestine to an end and declare independence. This collaboration, however, was short lived, and by 1947 the Haganah, sensing that independence was imminent, focused on preparing for the transition into statehood. Among its key activities in that period was dispatching armed convoys to the Jews of Jerusalem, besieged by the Jordanian army. On May 31, 1948, as Israel was fighting its War of Independence, the Haganah was officially disbanded and all its members appointed to the newly formed army, the IDF (Israel Defense Forces). Dr. Ruth Westheimer remains its most famous alumna.

Hagar

She appears in Genesis, first as Sarah's (at this point, Sarai's) Egyptian handmaid. When Sarah is unable to produce an heir for Abraham, Hagar becomes his concubine. Hagar quickly conceives, and Sarah begins to despise her. Hagar gives birth to Ishmael, who, at thirteen, is circumcised by Abraham. When Sarah finally does have a baby, at ninety-nine, she becomes certain that her own son, Isaac, not Hagar's, will father the Jewish people, and she commands her husband to send Hagar and Ishmael away. With this cruel act, Sarah fiercely protects her territory and future legacy. Hagar roams the desert with her son, but when they grow weak and run out of water, she weeps and abandons him under a tree, lest she see him die. An angel of God appears, guides her to an oasis, and promises her that a great nation will come from her son, too. They survive, and from Ishmael came the Ishmaelites, and the Islamic faith venerates Ishmael as a patriarch. Hagar is a revered character in Islam and the Baha'i faith, somewhat detested in the Judeo-Christian tradition, and yet another reminder that polygamy is, well, not great.

Haggadah

A Jewish text that will still be read hundreds of years from now and is best enjoyed with four cups of wine. (See Passover, page 195; **Seder**.)

haimish

The Danish hygge has nothing on this Yiddish word meaning homey, cozy, comfortable, familiar. A haimish home is one that will always let you raid the fridge, crash on the couch, and drop by unannounced. Sometimes, Orthodox Jews will use the word to describe a fellow observant Jew: "My car broke down on the highway, but fortunately a van full of haimish *bocherim*"—yeshiva students—"passed by, and they picked me up." It's a word that is nuanced and descriptive and almost always positive.

hair

What some Jewish girls and women spend a ton of time blow-drying, flat-ironing, and keratin-treating—or thinking about blow-drying, flat-ironing, and keratin-treating. (Guys, too: see **Jewfro**.) A complicated ethnic marker that reveals our feelings about belonging and isolation, pride and shame, beauty and sex and money.

halacha

Jewish law. There's a lot of it, millions of words, and there is no set of rules that can definitively say what is halacha and what's not. Halacha includes the commandments in Torah, their elaborations in the Mishnah and the Talmud, and refinements by later sages down to the present day. You would typically only hear talk of "halacha" from an Orthodox Jew, but every time a Conservative Jew wonders what's kosher and what's not, she is asking a halachic question; when a Reform or secular Jew inquires about what makes a proper Jewish wedding, or how one converts, those, too, are questions of halacha. Halacha is everywhere.

Hadassah: Members of Hadassah, the Women's Zionist Organization of America, in 1951

Haganah: Jewish paramilitary organization in British-occupied Palestine

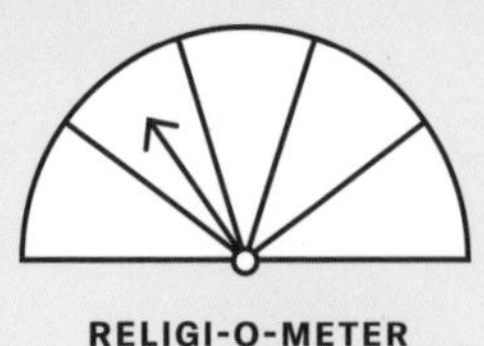

HANUKKAH

Hanukkah, the Festival of Lights, is an eight-day celebration commemorating the rededication of the Second Temple in the second century BCE and the Maccabees' uprising against the Greeks.

WHAT DO WE DO?

There's the tradition of playing with a dreidel, the Hebrew letters on which stand for "a great miracle happened there" (or, in Israel, "a great miracle happened here"). There is also the habit of giving gelt to children.

ANYTHING GOOD TO EAT?

It's traditional on Hanukkah to eat fried foods like latkes and sufganiyot (jelly doughnuts)—a natural choice for an oil-themed holiday.

ANY BAD GUYS?

Absolutely: Antiochus IV, one of the best villains in all of Jewish history. As his nicknames—"the Illustrious" and "Bearer of Victory"—suggest, the ruler of the Hellenistic Seleucid Empire was fond of waging war. He was engaging in that pastime in Egypt when a rumor that he'd been killed circulated in the region. Meanwhile, Jason, a Hellenized Jew who'd been deposed as the Temple's high priest, heard of Antiochus's death and saw an opportunity to reclaim his position, so he marched on Jerusalem with a thousand men. Antiochus interpreted the clash in the holy city as a full-fledged Jewish revolt against the foreign rulers, and in 167 BCE, he attacked Judea and punished its population by outlawing all Jewish rites and practices and mandating the worship of Zeus.

By so doing, most modern scholars agree, the king was simply intervening in an existing civil war between those Hebrews who called for a strict adherence to tradition and those, like Jason, who preached assimilation to Hellenism. Antiochus's involvement, however, aggravated the internecine struggle and prompted the traditionalists to launch a genuine anti-Greek revolt, led by an aged priest, Mattathias the Hasmonean, and his five sons—Jochanan, Simeon, Eleazar, Jonathan, and Judah—the latter nicknamed HaMakabi, or "the Hammer," for his combat skills. Followers of the fighting family eventually became known as Maccabees. Two years later, led by Judah, the Maccabees succeeded in defeating Antiochus's troops, recaptured the Temple, and set out to purge it of idols.

According to the Talmud, the Maccabees wished to light the Temple's menorah, a traditional candelabrum that customarily burned through the night in Judaism's holiest place, but they discovered just enough oil to last for one day. Miraculously, however, the oil burned for eight days, a wonder we commemorate by lighting candles for eight nights.

Haman
Jewish history's ultimate villain. It's hard to read the Book of Esther, which tells the story of Purim, in which Haman tries to get all the Jews murdered, without feeling a little bit sorry for this genocidal maniac: far from being a one-dimensional asshole, he's a complex knot of pride, prejudice, and envy, coveting everything and fearing everyone. In part, that's why some Hasids believe that we all have our own inner Haman, causing us to succumb to vanity or despair or other unruly emotions.

hamantaschen
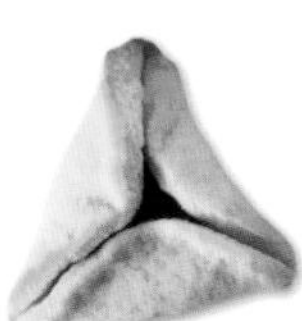

Do these triangular Purim cookies symbolize Haman's ears or Haman's hat? And does it matter, when it's really the filling that counts? The old-school trifecta is apricot jam, prune butter, and poppy seed fillings—newfangled flavors like cookie dough, funfetti, and brownie, plus bougie savory renditions like goat cheese and beet, are a whole other megillah.

Hamilton, Alexander (c. 1755–1804)
A musical, a ten-dollar bill, and a founding father some people think might have been secretly Jewish. The theory is that his mother converted in 1745, which explains why he went to Hebrew school. We'll take him.

Hanukkah
See opposite page.

"The Hanukkah Song"
The original version of Adam Sandler's continuously updated musical saga of celebrated Semites debuted on December 3, 1994, on *Saturday Night Live*. It's a holiday gift that keeps on giving, making Christmastime radio a tiny bit friendlier: we see your Frosty and your Rudolph and raise you Captain Kirk and Mr. Spock (both Jewish!).

hanukkiah
Don't call it a menorah! A typical menorah, or Jewish candelabra, has seven branches, all of equal height, and is an ancient symbol of Jewish faith and nationhood, probably because it evokes the burning bush. The Temples in Jerusalem had a majestic golden menorah, stolen by the Romans—you can see it depicted on the Arch of Titus in Rome. A hanukkiah, on the other hand, is a special menorah, featuring nine branches,

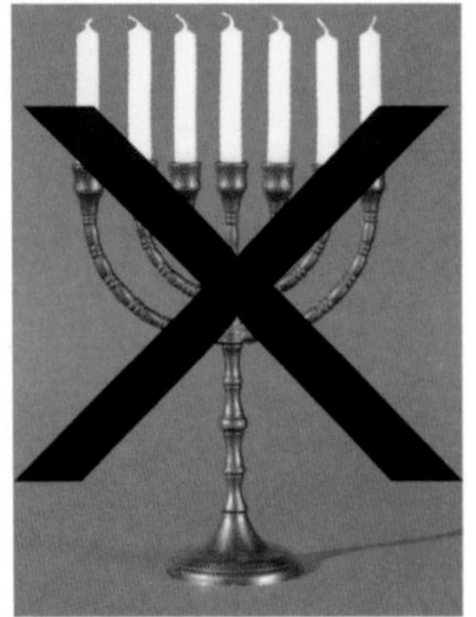

with one—called the Shamash—elevated above the rest and used to light up all the others.

Haredi, Haredim
See Branches of Judaism, page 44.

Hasid, Hasidic, Hasidism
See Branches of Judaism, page 44.

Haskalah
As the Enlightenment swept Europe in the eighteenth century, Jews launched their own version, called the Haskalah, Hebrew for "erudition." For many, it meant embracing freedom of thought and favoring rationalism over anything that smacked of superstition. Members of the movement, known as Maskilim, advocated far-reaching changes to daily Jewish life, from speaking in the vernacular to swapping traditional garb for modern dress. Most notably, the movement gave us Reform Judaism, the religion's first major departure from the orthodox norms that had guided it for millennia.

Hasmoneans
See Hanukkah, opposite page.

"Hatikvah"
Literally "The Hope," "Hatikvah" is the Israeli national anthem. The lyrics are taken from a poem by Naftali Herz Imber, a nineteenth-century Polish Jewish writer, and the music, based on a folk melody, was added in 1888 by Samuel Cohen. "Hatikvah" presents a bit of a problem for anti-Semites, anti-Zionists, and even anyone who is just skeptical of jingoism, patriotism, or nationalistic symbols—because it is really, really good.

"Hava Nagila"
See **hora**.

MODERN HEBREW 101

Want to learn a little Hebrew but don't have time to enroll in a language course? Here are ten words or phrases that will make you sound like you're straight outta Tel Aviv.

"Sababa"

In Arabic, it means "passionate love." In Hebrew, it was adopted as a catchall word suggesting that everything is groovy, peachy, and cool. Whenever anyone asks you how it's going, you can't go wrong with a good old-fashioned "sababa."

"Ma HaMatzav?"

Literally, "What's the situation?" It's a common way to ask someone how they are doing. The answer, obviously, is "sababa."

"Khai BeSeret"

If someone says this about you, they mean you're "living in a movie," which means you're a bit delusional about your life and should get a grip.

"Tov yalla bye"

A complete ethnography of Israeli society in three words, combining Hebrew, Arabic, and English. It's what many Israelis say when they leave a room, a short and charming admission that language is a wonderfully dynamic thing that knows no boundaries.

"Khaval al hazman"

If someone said to you, "It's a pity about the time," what would you think they meant? If they were speaking Hebrew, they meant that whatever they were talking about was most excellent.

"Chukumuku"

Nothing is more fun to say than this portmanteau, which came to Hebrew from Ladino. *Chuka* means "penis," and *moko* means "snot," so a *chukumuku* is literally a runny-nosed schmuck, or figuratively someone or something that is just too third-rate for words.

"Dugri"

Adapted from the Turkish word *dugru*, which means "straight ahead," it means being honest, candid, and no-nonsense, the ultimate compliment among Israelis.

"Kodkod"

A vertex is the point where two or more lines meet in geometry. The Hebrew term for it is *kodkod*, and intelligence officers in the IDF thought it was sufficiently obscure to use it as code when discussing high-ranking officers on their walkie-talkies. Any time you want to speak of someone very high-ranking, you can call her or him the kodkod of the bunch.

"Jora"

Arabic for "cesspool." A bit too fond of four-letter words? You have a *peh jora*, or "cesspool mouth." Didn't really like the movie? Say it was jora.

"Shushuist"

Charming bit of army slang. If you serve in some top-secret role, you probably have to shush it up, which makes you a shushuist. The term also applies to anyone who is not too fond of sharing personal information, stories, or feelings.

Havdalah

The Hebrew word for "separation," Havdalah is the weekly ceremony that ends Shabbat at nightfall on Saturday. The brief, moving service, beloved of anyone who has ever been to Jewish summer camp, involves smelling spices and inspecting one's fingernails in the glow of a braided candle, which is then extinguished in a cup of wine.

havurah

Hebrew for a fellowship or community of friends. In religious life, the term refers to a small group that comes together for worship, Shabbat dinners, study, holidays, or other Jewish practice. A havurah may be a group of families' primary Jewish community, in effect replacing the synagogue, but some synagogues organize their members into havurot (the plural), giving them a more intimate community within the larger congregation. The "havurah movement" was started in the late 1960s by countercultural, progressive Jews; the first havurot, like Havurat Shalom outside Boston, the New York Havurah, and Farbrengen, in Washington, DC, incubated Jewish feminism, antiwar activism, and innovative, nontraditional styles of prayer. Today, the National Havurah Committee sponsors a summer institute where havurahniks learn and share new melodies, prayers, and ideas for forward-looking Judaism.

hazzan

See **cantor**.

Hebrew

Our sacred, ancient language. After millennia of being relegated solely to prayer books and shul services, it was resurrected by Eliezer Ben-Yehuda, who made sure we speak today more or less in the same exact way our ancestors did as early as the sixth century BCE. But while biblical Hebrew featured slightly fewer than nine thousand words, modern-day Hebrew boasts a vocabulary of sixty thousand, including *botzer*, the correct Hebrew term for "brunch" (it combines *boker*, or morning, and *tzeharaim*, or noon).

Hebrew calendar

Unlike our gentilic brothers and sisters, who count the time from the Birth of Christ, we're old school: the Hebrew calendar begins with the very creation of the world. There are twelve months: Tishrei, Cheshvan, Kislev, Tevet, Shevat, Adar, Nisan, Iyar, Sivan, Tammuz, Av, and Elul. (Some years there are two Adars, but that's for another time.) Like the traditional Chinese calendar, it is lunisolar, which means it takes into account both the phases of the moon and the time of the solar year. This is why it seems to American children that Hanukkah can fall any time from Halloween to Valentine's Day. Cheshvan is the only month that doesn't have a Jewish holiday, which is why it is sometimes referred to as Mar Cheshvan, or "bitter Cheshvan."

Hebrew Immigrant Aid Society (HIAS)

Founded in 1881 to help Jews who fled Russia and immigrated to America, this nonprofit organization spent roughly the first century of its existence focusing on aiding Jews facing persecution, from helping rescue Jews from Europe during the Holocaust to advocating on behalf of Soviet Jewry in the 1960s, '70s, and '80s. These days, the organization is largely dedicated to helping people living in conflict areas, from Chad to Venezuela, relocate.

Hebrew names

Like a bar mitzvah, a Hebrew name isn't required for someone to be a Jew. Nevertheless, it is common practice for many Jews to have, in addition to their birth certificate name, a Hebrew name, which takes the form of so-and-so, daughter-or-son of so-and-so. The name is conferred at a boy's bris, or at a girl's baby-naming, or it's just kind of decided upon by the parents (it can also be chosen after three Gold Star beers on Birthright Israel). It's used when the person is called to the Torah in synagogue, at his or her wedding, and when being buried.

Hebrew National

Hebrew National was founded on the Lower East Side in the first decade of the twentieth century by a shochet from Russia. What started as a way for the Manhattan pig-averse to get their street-meat fix (at a time before halal rice-and-lamb carts) became, eventually, a large company, today a subsidiary of international conglomerate Conagra. Hebrew National's

It Should Be a Holiday!

Days That Didn't Make It on the Official Calendar

Yom HaGolda

Honoring the day in 1898 that Golda Meir was born.

Shavua Sally

Begins a weeklong festival honoring the day in 1972 that Sally Priesand became the first woman ordained a rabbi in the United States.

5
JULY

Shemini Seinfeld

Recollecting the day in 1989 when *The Seinfeld Chronicles*, soon to have its name changed to *Seinfeld*, debuted on NBC.

24
MAY

Zichron l'Shlomo

Honoring the day in 1991 when the two-day Operation Solomon began, airlifting over fourteen thousand Ethiopian Jews to their new home in Israel.

18
OCTOBER

Tzom Jackie

A fast day honoring the painful memory of the day in 1964 when comedian Jackie Mason allegedly gave Ed Sullivan the middle finger on Sullivan's prime-time show. Mason denied making the obscene gesture, but Sullivan banned him from future appearances on the show, harming Mason's career but inspiring his legendary Sullivan impersonation.

25
DECEMBER

Laila Lo Mein

The Night of the Chinese Food.

28
SEPTEMBER

Simchat Durocher

So that we never forget the day in 1941 when the Brooklyn Dodgers, beloved of that borough's immigrant community, defeated the Philadelphia Phillies 5–1 to conclude their first pennant-winning season.

We are a people of many holidays—not as many as those crazy Catholics, who honor hundreds of saints with their own days, but still, a shortage of holy days we don't have. We've got your Tu B'Av, your Shemini Atzeret, your Tzom Gedalia. We could go on, but we won't, because the real shonde is that the days above never got their own spot on the Jewish calendar. (We give here the dates according to the gentile calendar; they would, obviously, move around according to the Jewish lunar calendar.)

famous slogan offered its customers a luxuriously self-serving narrative: "We Answer to a Higher Authority." The sentiment is immaculately American, and, as a bonus, great with delicatessen mustard.

Hebrew school

What began as the after-school heder, supplementing little Jews' public school education with a daily smidgen of Torah or Hebrew, declined in postwar America into the two- or even one-day-a-week "Hebrew school" in which children typically learn enough Hebrew to forget right after their bar or bat mitzvah. That said, Hebrew school is undergoing a quiet revolution, as thoughtful educators, mindful of the bad rap several generations of alumni have given Hebrew school, are importing better pedagogy, song, dance, art, and philosophy; they have replaced the proverbial ruler or slap with a whole lotta love. It's not unusual today for a Hebrew school student to school his parents in a little aleph-bet (alphabet) and bal tashchit (the prohibition, as in environmentalism, against wastefulness).

hell

"A dungeon horrible," according to the poet John Milton, as well as a place "where peace and rest can never dwell, hope never comes," where one can look forward to "torture without end." Jeez. Anyway, Jews don't really believe in this sort of thing, and our hells (Los Angeles, dairy products, standing in any kind of line for any reason) tend to be earthier affairs. We do have Gehennom, a vaguely formulated idea that is as close as the Hebrew Bible and the Talmud come to elucidating some supernatural penalty box, which is named after a valley in Jerusalem that runs just south of the Old City and is now home to a very lovely park. In Pirkei Avot, the students of Bilam, men who engage in frivolous conversation with women, and the "stubborn-faced" (literally: goat-faced) are said to "inherit Gehennom." Still, the rabbis make clear that Gehennom is a place of temporary rather than eternal punishment, and they decline to go into lurid or explicit detail about the awful things a sinner will experience there.

One could posit any number of possible explanations as to why Jews never developed any real concept of a punitive afterlife: by one view of things, rejecting the mitzvot and eschewing the Jewish people's unique relationship with God is a punishment unto itself. Another hunch: For centuries, hell was something Jews were threatened with as payback for their rejection of Christianity, meaning that believing in a "Jewish hell" would internalize the claims of a different and hostile faith. It's also possible that Jewish guilt, which we know to be the absolute most powerful force in all existence, makes the whole thing rather unnecessary.

Hellenic, Hellenism

With Alexander the Great spreading Greek culture across the vast area he had begun conquering around 334 BCE, many Jews, particularly wealthy elites, chose to live a Hellenistic lifestyle, which meant anything from taking on Greek names to adopting Greek pastimes, like wrestling. More traditional Jews did not look kindly on their Hellenized brothers and sisters, and when the Hasmoneans declared war on Antiochus around 167 BCE, a rebellion that gives us the miracle of Hanukkah, they found themselves engaged in a civil war with the Hellenized Jews who supported the Greek king. It was absolutely, positively the very last time in Jewish history anyone argued about tradition and assimilation.

Herod

Stop me if you've heard this one before: the ambitious and narcissistic son of a rich man shocks the world by somehow ascending to power, mainly by colluding with a large empire, but he's still a real estate guy at heart so he spends most of his energy building huge structures that are very, very fancy, lives an exorbitantly flashy lifestyle, and is hated by pretty much everybody. We're talking, of course, about Herod, the puppet king the Romans installed in 40 BCE to govern Judea. We owe him Masada, the port in Caesarea, and, most important, the Second Temple.

Herzl, Theodor (1860–1904)

Born in Budapest, the future father of modern political Zionism moved to Vienna at eighteen, where he became a writer for the *Neue Freie Presse*. As Paris correspondent, he was spooked by the anti-Semitism unleashed by the Dreyfus Affair, which led him to the conclusion that Jewish assimilation wasn't possible and that the only solution to the "Jewish question" was a Jewish state. He launched the First Zionist Congress in Basel in 1897 and made his first visit to the Holy Land the next year. With books like *Der Judenstaat* and *Altneuland*, he mapped out a vision for what a Jewish state might look like. "If you will it, it is not a dream," he wrote. The phrase became a rallying cry for the Zionist movement. He didn't live to see that dream become a reality. He died of cardiac sclerosis at forty-four. His remains were moved to Jerusalem in 1949, where the cemetery at which he was interred, and the mountain on which it sits, were named in his honor.

Heschel, Abraham Joshua (1907–1972)

Famous Polish-born American rabbi who stressed the centrality of Judaism's prophetic vision and argued for social action. He is best known for marching with Dr. Martin Luther King Jr. "When I marched in Selma," he famously wrote, "my feet were praying."

High Holiday tickets

What a person should pay to attend a High Holiday service: whatever they can. What a person can pay to attend a High Holiday service at a fancy shul in New York City: approximately $1,800 (for the cheap seats!).

High Holidays

Judaism's holiest time of the year. Strictly speaking, the term applies only to Rosh Hashanah and Yom Kippur. But, as is the case with all big events, preparation begins well before we break out the apples and honey: the month of Elul, leading up to Rosh Hashanah, is dedicated to reflection, meditation, and preparation, including saying Selichot, or penitential prayers. After Rosh Hashanah, we dive into the Ten Days of Repentance, our last chance to atone for our sins before the Book of Life is sealed on Yom Kippur. The High Holidays conclude with Ne'ilah, the emotional prayer in which the entire community loudly proclaims God as the Lord before rushing home to break the fast with some bagels and lox.

Hillel International

The preeminent address for Jewish life on campus. With student centers on more than five hundred campuses, from the United States to South America to the former Soviet Union, Hillel provides pluralistic Jewish programming for thousands of Jewish students throughout the academic year. In addition to educational, cultural, and religious programming, many campus Hillel houses offer kosher food.

Hillel the Elder

With Shammai, one of the famous pairs of sparring rabbis in the early compendium of rabbinic teaching known as the Mishnah. He was alive when Jesus was born, although nobody knows his exact dates. He is as quotable as Churchill or Lincoln, and he said things like "What is hateful to you, do not do to your fellow: this is the whole Torah; the rest is the explanation; go and learn," and "If I am not for myself, who is for me? And if I am only for myself, what am I? And if not now, when?" In 2016, Ivanka Trump posted on her Instagram account, "If not me, who? If not now, when? — Emma Watson." Watson had used the phrase in a 2014 speech at the United Nations—although, like Ronald Reagan and former Michigan governor George Romney, who had also used it, she was not the originator. Historians have not been able to discern how these goyim came across a quotation from the Mishnah.

Hinjew

A Jew, often a semi-Semite, whose non-Jewish parent or ancestors are Hindu. Most Hinjews are American, and Hinjews are a growing proportion of American Jews, as Jews and Indian Americans have multiple opportunities to meet and fall in love: at prefrosh weekends on Ivy League campuses, in bar exam study groups, and at mixers for newly minted medical residents.

Hirschfeld, Al (1903–2003)

Whether or not you know it, you've seen the work of Al Hirschfeld. His line drawings appeared mainly in the *New York Times*' arts pages, for which he sketched everybody: Sinatra, Minnelli, Chaplin, and more. He was famous for hiding his daughter's name, Nina, in his drawings, and he had an excellent beard.

Hitler, Adolf (1889–1945)

Jewish history, sadly, hardly lacks for homicidal villains—Antiochus, Haman, et al.—who set out to humiliate, crush, and exterminate the Jews. Yet even among this gallery of rogues, Hitler stands alone. By tethering his maniacal hatred to the instruments of modernity, from pseudoscience to mass-mediated propaganda to industrialized murder, he succeeded not only in killing more Jews than anyone before him in history but also in reminding us in the starkest of terms that ancient bigotry, like all other forms of energy, never dissipates but is simply recycled into more potent and frightening forms. This is why we continue to obsess about him even today, more than seven decades after his demise: the man himself may be dead, but the dark potential he unleashed lies dormant, awaiting its next and terrifying reincarnation. See **anti-Semitism**; **Holocaust**.

Hoffman, Abbie (1936–1989)

Raised in a middle-class Jewish home in suburban Massachusetts, Hoffman was ready to rumble by

Abraham Joshua Heschel: The impeccably coiffed rabbi, along with George Maislen of the United Synagogue of America, presents the Reverend Dr. Martin Luther King Jr. with the Solomon Schechter Award in 1963.

Al Hirschfeld: The artist, famed for hiding his daughter's name, Nina, in his work, at home in New York City in 1974

the time the 1960s swung by. He became an anarchist and an activist with a flair for theatrics, including nominating a 145-pound pig named Pigasus for president and throwing out fake dollar bills on the floor of the New York Stock Exchange. For his role in the protests outside the Democratic National Convention in Chicago in 1968, he was arrested and brought to trial as one of the Chicago Seven. At one point, he famously accused the judge, Julius Hoffman, of being a "shonde for the goyim," and argued that the judge would've served Hitler had he been born in Germany. He was sentenced to five years in prison and a fine, but the conviction was later overturned. Regardless, Hoffman went underground, where he wrote his most famous work, *Steal This Book*. In 1989, suffering from bipolar disorder, he washed down 150 tablets of phenobarbital with booze, killing himself. He and the group he had founded, the Yippies, remain iconic examples of media-savvy radicalism.

hole in the sheet

The preposterous, bizarre, and crazily offensive urban legend that Orthodox Jews are so antipleasure that they will only enjoy marital relations through, well, a hole in the sheet. Don't bother walking through Crown Heights looking at the laundry: the scurrilous rumor isn't true.

Hollywood

See Hollywood and Jews, page 132.

Holocaust

In addition to the murders of six million Jews, nearly a third of whom were children, through gassing, mass shootings, starvation, beatings, and every other form of physical torture of Jewish bodies that a gang of nihilistic sociopaths could devise, the Holocaust was also, and perhaps more importantly, a systematic attempt to uproot and destroy Judaism, which the Nazis understood to be their grand rival for global domination. At that they did not succeed.

See also **Anielewicz, Mordecai**; **anti-Semitism**; **Arbeit Macht Frei**; **Arendt, Hannah**; **Aryan**; **Babi Yar**; **concentration camp**; **Edelman, Marek**; **Eichmann, Adolf**; **epigenetics**; **Frank, Anne**; **Germany**; **ghetto**; **Grossman, Chayka**; **Hitler, Adolf**; Holocaust Movies: A Guide, page 137; **Karski, Jan**; **Kindertransport**; **Kristallnacht**; **Lanzmann, Claude**; **Lemkin, Raphael**; **Lipstadt, Deborah**; **March of the Living**; ***Maus***; **Nazis**; **neo-Nazis**; **Nuremberg**; ***The Producers***; **Ringelblum Archive**; **Rumkowski, Chaim**; **Shoah**; **Shoah**; **Spiegelman, Art**; **survivor**; **swastika**; **tattoos**; **United States Holocaust Memorial Museum**; Warsaw Ghetto Uprising, page 284; **Wiesel, Elie**; **Wiesenthal, Simon**; **Yad Vashem**; **Yom Hashoah**; **Zyklon B**.

Holy Land

See **Promised Land**.

hora

A Romanian circle dance, with varieties across Eastern Europe and the Balkans, that got big in Israel among the folk dancers and kibbutzniks of prestate Palestine. It later spread to the United States, where it became popular wherever klezmer was played, or wherever two or more Jews gathered with a band and an open bar at a country club. You have seen degraded, but undeniably joyous, versions of this dance at many a wedding or bar or bat mitzvah, whether in real life or in the movies. In the middle of the concentric circles of dancers, honorees may be hoisted on chairs. "Hava Nagila" is not the required soundtrack, but just try picturing a hora and not hearing it in your head.

horns

Why do so many anti-Semitic cartoons depict Jews with horns? The popular explanation blames the Satanic stereotype on Saint Jerome, who, in the fourth century CE, translated the Bible into Latin. Reading a line in Exodus about Moses's face radiating with light, the scholarly Jerome, goes one theory, mistook the Hebrew verb *karan*, or "radiated," for the word *keren*, or "horn." Reading Jerome's translation, Michelangelo and others gave us one horned Moses after

HOLLYWO

"THE JEWS CONTROL HOLLYWOOD!"

A HATE-SPEWING ANTI-SEMITE MIGHT SAY.

The facts are undeniable. Nearly every major movie studio has Jewish roots. Harry and Jack Cohn (Columbia Pictures), Carl Laemmle (Universal), Adolf Zukor (Paramount), Jesse Lasky (Paramount), Louis B. Mayer (MGM), Marcus Loew (Loew's Theaters and MGM), Samuel Goldwyn (MGM), William Fox (Fox Film Corporation), Irving Thalberg (Universal and MGM), B. P. Schulberg (independent), and the four Warner brothers (Warner Bros.), among others, can be safely called the foundational pillars of motion pictures. All were immigrants with little formal education who essentially created a new form of

How did this happen? First, consider that, in the beginning, the production and distribution of recreational distractions that flickered on a wall was déclassé. Who but immigrants with few options would want to dirty their fingers with such low-class work? As with Jews in European banking, the industry fell to those who didn't have many opportunities elsewhere.

But this industry birthed by a working-class minority produced scant material that represented that minority. With few notable exceptions, American movies were essentially *Judenrein* during the industry's first few decades. *The Jazz Singer* (1927), widely promoted as the first talkie, climaxes with the singing of Kol Nidre on Yom Kippur, but it is very much an assimilationist tale. *Gentleman's Agreement* (1947), about lurking, unspoken anti-Semitism, was produced by Darryl F. Zanuck at 20th Century Fox, at the time the only gentile studio chief. The "don't make waves" mentality did not really begin dissi-

OD AND JEWS

"THE JEWS INVENTED HOLLYWOOD!"

A PROUD JEW MIGHT SHOUT BACK.

The next generation of Jews in Hollywood, born in America or refugees from Nazism, not pogroms, were less afraid to call attention to their Jewishness. Director-producers like Billy Wilder and Stanley Kubrick represented the vanguard of auteurs who imbued their work with much Jewish wit and weltschmerz. And when television came, Jews were prominent both on air (what would early TV have been without Milton Berle or Sid Caesar?) and in the boardroom, with William S. Paley at CBS, David Sarnoff at RCA/NBC, and Leonard Goldenson at ABC.

As time passed, diversity came to Hollywood. You didn't have to be Jewish to work there, or take meetings at Canter's Deli—though it didn't hurt. The New Hollywood of the 1960s and 1970s saw the first out-and-proud Jews as leading men and sex symbols. No one gasped to learn that Dustin Hoffman, Elliott Gould, and Barbra Streisand celebrated Hanukkah, not the way they had upon learning that Kirk Douglas grew up as Izzy Demsky.

Over time, the industry grew more comfortable with its Jewishness. There's even the old joke about non-Jewish agents and producers going to Yom Kippur services because they wanted to be seen.

Like all industries, Hollywood has been slow to accept women in top roles, but the noticeable exceptions have often been Jewish women. Sherry Lansing was the first female president of 20th Century Fox in 1980, then became chairperson of the Paramount Pictures Motion Picture Group in 1992, where she led the studio to tremendous profits. In 1999, Stacey Snider became chairperson of Universal Pictures. From 2006 through 2014, she was cochair of Dreamworks, and in 2017 she took over 20th Century Fox. The late Laura Ziskin was an independent producer, then ran the Fox 2000 shingle, until producing the first *Spider-Man* trilogy at Columbia Pictures—ushering in the superhero craze that totally changed the entertainment industry. Amy Pascal ran Sony Pictures Entertainment's Motion Picture Group (and cochaired all of Sony Pictures Entertainment) from 2006 through 2015.

By the time of Larry David and *Curb Your Enthusiasm*, a debate about whether saying "the Jews run Hollywood" was anti-Semitic rhetoric or complimentary could be, it turned out, the plot of an entire half-hour episode.

JEWISH STARS

Jewish achievement in Hollywood hasn't only been in the boardroom or behind the camera. Over the years, there have been different types of Jewish stars.

THE EARLY, SECRET JEWS

The first class of Hollywood legends is lousy with Hebrews who, for a variety of reasons, felt the need to anglicize their names. They include Theda Bara (Theodosia Goodman), Douglas Fairbanks (Douglas Ullman), Al Jolson (Asa Yoelson), the Marx Brothers (okay, not too secret), Edward G. Robinson (Emanuel Goldenberg), Paul Muni (Meshilem Meier Weisenfreund), Eddie Cantor (Isidor Iskowitch), Jack Benny (Benjamin Kubelsky), George Burns (Nathan Birnbaum), Fanny Brice (Fania Borach), Peter Lorre (László Löwenstein), Danny Kaye (David Daniel Kaminsky), Hedy Lamarr (Hedwig Kiesler), Paulette Goddard (Pauline Marion Levy), Kirk Douglas (Izzy Demsky), Red Buttons (Aaron Chwatt), Shelly Winters (Shirley Schrift), Tony Randall (Aryeh Leonard Rosenberg), Jerry Lewis (Joseph Levitch, but, again, not too secret), Rodney Dangerfield (Jacob Cohen—why change your name with this material?), Tony Curtis (Bernard Schwartz), and Lauren Bacall (Betty Joan Perske).

THE "NEW HOLLYWOOD" JEW

By the 1960s, the Jews who had founded the movie studios were gone, and with them went the self-censoring attitude of not admitting to the world that the entertainment industry had a disproportionate number of Members of the Tribe. Urbane Jewishness was very in, taking its lead from the worlds of literature (Bernard Malamud, Saul Bellow, and Philip Roth), modern art (Mark Rothko, Marc Chagall, Barnett Newman), and folk music (Bob Dylan, Simon and Garfunkel, Leonard Cohen, every single promoter on the scene). Faces unafraid to be Jewish and sexy included Dustin Hoffman, Barbra Streisand, Elliott Gould, Leonard Nimoy, Harvey Keitel, Judd Hirsch, Alan Arkin, Linda Lavin, Tina Louise, Jill St. John, Peter Riegert, Bette Midler, Barbara Hershey, Albert Brooks (Albert Einstein!), and Goldie Hawn.

MODERN JEWESSES

Today's Jewish actresses aren't just beautiful. They're talented and funny and smart. Think Rachel Weisz, Scarlett Johansson, Natalie Portman (Hershlag), Mila Kunis, Evan Rachel Wood, Gal Gadot, Michelle Trachtenberg, Emmy Rossum, Maggie Gyllenhaal, Kat Dennings, Alison Brie, Zosia Mamet, Lizzy Caplan, Emmanuelle Chriqui, Selma Blair, Mélanie Laurent, and many, many (many) more.

THE '90S-AND-AFTER NICE-GUY JEWS

Funny, handsome (but not threatening), and good providers: the Jews of the '90s and after presented us with stars to bring home to bubbe. Among them: Jerry Seinfeld, Jon Stewart (Leibowitz, but he regrets taking the stage name), Adam Sandler, David Schwimmer, Paul Rudd, Andy Samberg, Daniel Radcliffe, Sacha Baron Cohen, Justin Bartha, Seth Rogen, Seth Green, Jake Gyllenhaal, Michael Ian Black, Jason Segel, Jonah Hill (Feldstein), Joseph Gordon-Levitt, Josh Gad, Jesse Eisenberg, Jay Baruchel, Zac Efron, Andrew Garfield, Ansel Elgort, Alden Ehrenreich, Timothée Chalamet, and more.

MODERN JEWS YOU DON'T REALIZE ARE JEWS

They aren't denying it, but they aren't going out of their way to tell you, either. Check the records and you'll say "oh, really?" on James Caan, Harrison Ford (on his mother's side), Peter Coyote (Robert Cohon), Winona Ryder (Winona Laura Horowitz), Andrew Dice Clay (Andrew Clay Silverstein), Danny McBride, Yaphet Kotto, Henry Winkler, Paula Abdul, Joaquin Phoenix (technically), and others that would no doubt surprise us.

THE JEWS WHO AREN'T ACTUALLY JEWS

You better sit down for this: these actors, who have perfected the art of portraying Semitic and otherwise ethnically ambiguous characters, are as goyish as ham on white bread: Alan Alda, Jason Biggs, Tony Shalhoub, Ben Kingsley, F. Murray Abraham, Rachel Brosnahan, Charlie Chaplin, and both Garry and Penny Marshall.

another, leading generations to believe that there was something demonic about the Chosen People. It's a good theory, but it's not without its flaws. First, Jerome was no novice translator and seems to have resolved similarly confusing passages without damning the Jews to centuries of persecution. And second, humanity had been obsessed with horns long before even Moses arrived on the scene, seeing them as a symbol of virility, which is why prehistoric graves found in France, for example, featured the skulls of horned beasts, believed to bring the deceased good fortune in the afterlife. Jerome, then, may have believed that Moses, like some of the regional divinities in the Middle East, was himself some sort of superhuman horned deity. Still, his legacy is as indisputable as it is tragic: In 1267, an ecclesiastical synod meeting in Vienna, eager to prevent the town's Jews from interacting with good Christians, ordered them to wear horned hats. Others followed suit, and by the time the Nazis reached for an instantly recognizable visual stereotype, the horns were there to shame and humiliate the Jews. Even today, upon meeting a Jew for the first time, some people earnestly ask about their horns.

HARRY HOUDINI

Horovitz, Adam (b. 1966)

A-D-R-O-C-K (see **Beastie Boys**).

Horowitz, Vladimir (1903–1989)

Born in Kiev to an assimilated Jewish family, Horowitz was a child prodigy on the piano and was paid for his early performances in bread, the most valuable currency at the time of the Russian Revolution. In 1925, he escaped to the West, playing and recording in Berlin, Paris, and New York. He was to piano what Jascha Heifetz (1901–1987), another immigrant boychick, was to violin: the best ever.

Houdini, Harry (1874–1926)

Houdini, the Budapest-born son of a rabbi, came to the United States as an infant and grew up to become the most famous stage magician of all time. Although he began with card tricks, he won fame as an escape artist. No handcuffs, straitjacket, or chains could hold him. Like many magicians, he despised fraudulent "spiritualists" and "mediums," like those who said they could help you speak with dead relatives. Houdini believed there was a crucial difference between entertaining people and preying on their grief, and he had a sideline as an investigator of those who claimed supernatural or paranormal abilities.

Howe, Irving (1920–1993)

Writer and famous "New York intellectual," known for his literary criticism and his political activism. After he died, one editor said of Howe, "He lived in three worlds, literary, political and Jewish." As one of the founding editors of *Dissent*, he fueled the magazine's perennial rivalry with the more conservative *Commentary.* He won the National Book Award for *The World of Our Fathers* and taught English literature at the City University of New York for many years.

Humanistic Judaism

Want all the fun of Judaism without any of that pesky believing-in-God and following-ancient-traditions business? Want to chant a version of the Shema or the Kaddish that accords with all your rationalist beliefs? Founded in Michigan in 1963 by Sherwin Wine, Humanistic Judaism has just the thing for you! Their Shabbat services don't mention "God," and their rituals—bar and bat mitzvahs, weddings, funerals—are conducted from an entirely nontheistic point of view. The cynic would say that it's religion for Jews uncomfortable with Judaism; the booster would say that Humanistic Jews are the only Jews honest about the skepticism and atheism that so many Jews admit privately. Whether they are hopelessly conflicted or radically candid, one thing about Humanistic Jews is certain: numbering several thousand (at most), there aren't that many of them in the world.

hummus

Archaeological evidence suggests that hummus was already popular in ancient Egypt, and it is mentioned in the Bible as Boaz offers Ruth a dish of the delicious chickpea spread. Frequently consumed using a pita—the term of art is "wiping," after the correct motion of getting the maximal amount of spread on the bread—it comes in many varieties, depending on the region and

Holocaust Movies: A Guide

The Holocaust on film has been a source of education, a font of discussion, and, perhaps, an opportunity for some healing. The first use of concentration camp footage in a fiction film came quickly, with Orson Welles's 1946 film *The Stranger*, concerning a Nazi fugitive hiding in small-town America. Kirk Douglas starred in 1953's *The Juggler* as a camp survivor trying to adjust to life in Israel. 1960's *Exodus*, Otto Preminger's epic about the founding of the State of Israel starring Paul Newman, featured many displaced persons, including Sal Mineo. All these Hollywood productions, however, were tame, avoided dwelling on the atrocities, and didn't highlight the specificity of Jewish persecution. That changed with Stanley Kramer's 1961 production *Judgement at Nuremberg*, in which Spencer Tracy oversaw the proceedings that put Nazism on trial. Footage of the naked, stacked corpses from the camps is shown, and Judy Garland gives testimony of anti-Semitic abuse.

Here are five different types of Holocaust films.

The Gateway Film

Steven Spielberg's 1993 film *Schindler's List* is a one-stop shop to understand the enormity of the Holocaust, how the camps worked, and what conditions were like. Some have noted, correctly, that this movie is so pleasing to the masses in part because it's a tale we all know well: that of the gentile savior. But it's also an entertaining film: its character development is fascinating, the drama is gripping, the camerawork is exemplary, and the original score is magnificent.

The Exhaustive Film

If *Schindler's List*'s poetic red coats and lush violin music feel a little too Hollywood for so grave a topic, Claude Lanzmann's blunt-force documentary *Shoah* may be for you. It is a relentless collection of interviews from witnesses, survivors, and perpetrators. Most famous is the barber who tells the story of a fellow barber who saw his sister and wife entering the gas chambers.

The Abyss Film

Some critics of *Schindler's List* point out that only Steven Spielberg could make a movie about the Holocaust with a happy ending. But László Nemes's *Son of Saul* (2015) is darkness put to film. It follows the Sonderkommando, the Jews who worked inside the machinery of death at Auschwitz.

The Psychological Film

Some of the best movies about the Holocaust are set *after* the Holocaust. Notable stories of people dealing with their trauma are found in *The Night Porter* (1974), *Sophie's Choice* (1982), *Enemies: A Love Story* (1989), and *Ida* (2013). But to pick just one, go with Sidney Lumet's groundbreaking 1964 drama *The Pawnbroker*, in which Rod Steiger deals with survivor's guilt, PTSD, and internalized anti-Semitism. Steiger's character witnessed the death of his children and the brutal rape of his wife in the camps, and now he runs a pawn shop in a dicey New York neighborhood.

The Fantasy Film

What if we could turn back time and get revenge? That's what writer-director Quentin Tarantino did in his philo-Semitic *Inglourious Basterds* (2009). This weird movie has many threads, including a young Jewish woman (Mélanie Laurent) on the run from a Nazi tracker, and a special ops team of mostly Jewish soldiers led by Brad Pitt. It all comes together with Laurent burning down a theater full of Nazis while a character called "the Bear Jew" machine guns Hitler into hamburger meat. There are a lot of movies where you get to see Nazis get killed, but none quite so satisfying as this one.

the mood. Frequently accompanied by tahini, olive oil, and cumin, it is served warm, and it is eaten, traditionally, either early in the morning or late at night. It is exceedingly popular in Israel, with dedicated hummusiyot serving loyal clienteles. It's also taking America by storm, with the hummus company Sabra winning a bid to become the official dip of the NFL.

Hydrox

Back in the day, Oreos were not kosher. Pig involvement! Lard! Kids from kosher homes were stuck with Hydrox, regarded as a sad imitation of the real thing. Little did the Jewish youth of late-twentieth-century America know, Hydrox were actually the original—they hit the market in 1908—and Oreos, first made in 1912, were the copycat cookie. But who cared? Oreos were more popular, the forbidden fruit, the unholy wafer. When Oreo went kosher in 1997—each of Nabisco's 300-foot ovens had to be manually blowtorched on superhigh heat to meet the standards of the Orthodox Union—Jewish children celebrated, but Hydrox became your bubbe's cookie. The company went belly-up in 1999, but returned in 2015 with cool new midcentury-retro packaging, no artificial flavors, and a crunchier cookie.

FROM

IDF

TO

IDF (Israel Defense Forces)

Military service is mandatory for all Israelis. Men serve slightly less than three years, women slightly more than two. Most men also serve on reserve duty a month or so each year until they turn forty, giving the IDF an easy-to-mobilize force of another half million or so soldiers, should the need arise—as, alas, it often does.

indigenous people

What Jews are in their ancestral homeland of Israel, from which they were expelled and to which they miraculously returned. No other indigenous people in the modern era have pulled off a similar feat.

indigestion

What you're probably feeling right about now.

Inquisition

According to Monty Python, a thing no one expects. According to King Ferdinand II of Aragon and Queen Isabella I of Castille, a necessary enterprise that began in 1478 and was designed to guarantee a purely Christian kingdom by ridding their empire of Muslims and Jews. By 1492, all Jews who did not convert were expelled, with most settling in North Africa. They called themselves Sephardim, after Sepharad, the biblical name for Spain (see **converso**).

intermarriage

We've come a long way since *Bridget Loves Bernie*, the 1972–1973 TV comedy that scandalized American Jewry by showing a happy, functional marriage between a Jew and a non-Jew. The show was a hit, but protests from rabbis and pressure on advertisers led to its cancellation after one season. Today, the majority of Reform Jews marry non-Jews, as do a growing percentage of all other Jews. Just ask Marc Mezvinsky (Chelsea Clinton); Mark Zuckerberg (Priscilla Chan); and Rachel Weisz (Daniel Craig). The Reform movement now permits its rabbis to officiate at interfaith weddings, and some Conservative rabbis have gone rogue to do the same. Some say that intermarriage hastens the end for the Jewish people, but some rabbis say that only welcoming interfaith couples will allow us to survive. Now, if we could just work on that low birth rate . . .

interrupting

According to research done on American Jews, presumably of Ashkenazi ancestry, interrupting is something we do more often than most other people. To describe this phenomenon, the linguist Deborah Tannen uses the term *cooperative overlapping*, which sounds nicer than, say, "brashly interjecting while someone is in the middle of saying something they should probably be allowed to finish." "Jewish New Yorkers, many New Yorkers who are not Jewish, and many Jews who are not from New York have high-involvement [conversational] styles," Tannen writes in her 1990 book *You Just Don't Understand: Women and Men in Conversation*, "and are often perceived as interrupting in conversations with speakers from different backgrounds." This tendency to interrupt, or to leave only the tiniest of pauses between speakers, is certainly one cause of the stereotype that Jews are "pushy." But it's more complicated than just seeing interrupting as "Jewish." Tannen's research shows that Californians expect shorter conversational pauses than Midwesterners and New Englanders, so Minnesotans and Mainers perceive Californians as the big interrupters. And it gets better! Linguists have found that Midwesterners are the aggressive interrupters when in conversation with Athabaskan Indians, who take *really* long pauses between sentences. And, Tannen writes, "Swedes and Norwegians are perceived as interrupting by the longer-pausing Finns"—but Finns from certain regions take longer pauses than Finns from other regions, whom they in turn perceive as . . . pushy. Sounds familiar.

Intifada

The term refers to two distinct violent Palestinian uprisings against Israel, one in 1987 and the other in 2000. If you understand perfectly why they started, how they ended, and what to do to make sure they never happen again, please get in touch: there's a century-old conflict we'd like your help resolving.

ISRAEL

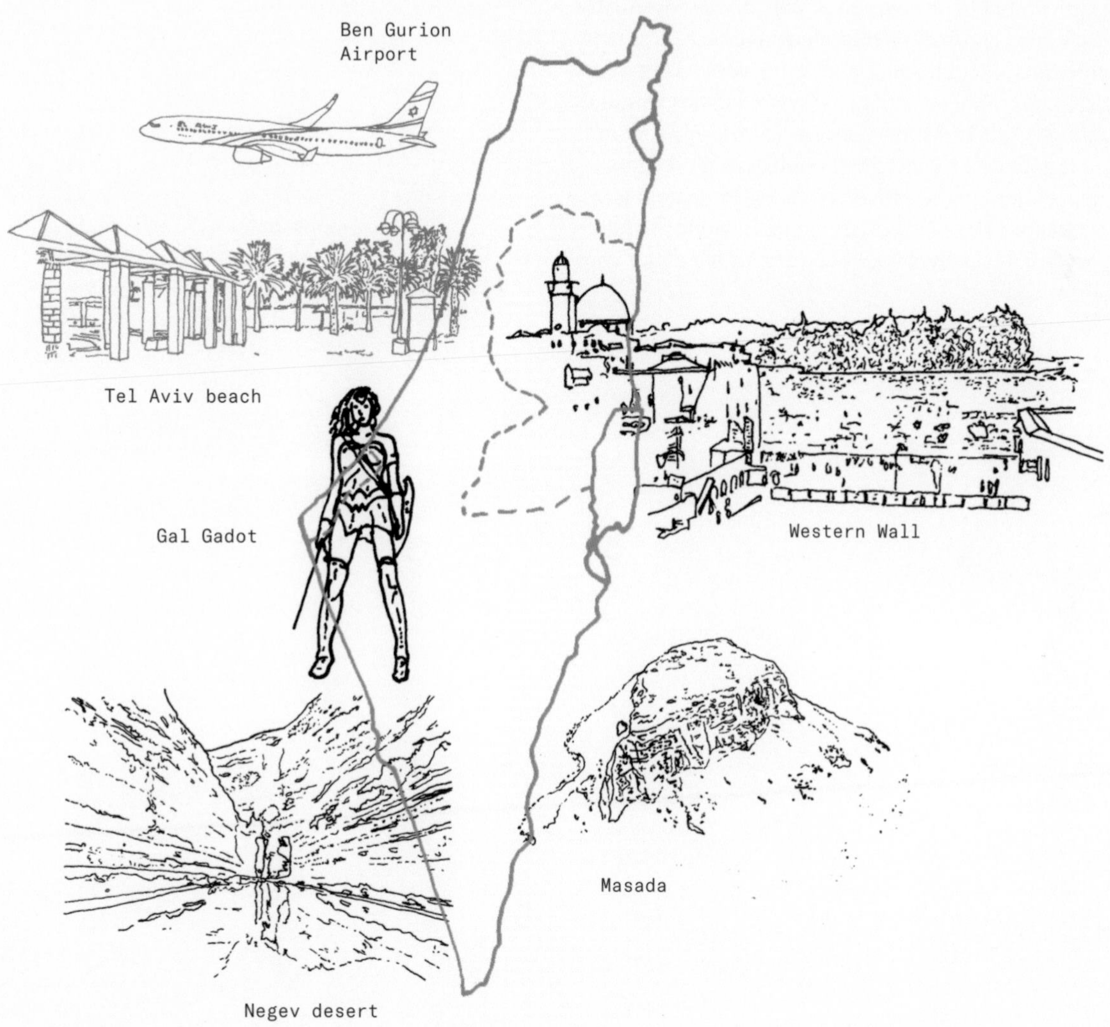

The world's only Jewish state, established in 1948 in the historic homeland of the Jewish people—where more than a million Arabs also lived—has absorbed waves of immigrants and refugees, from Holocaust survivors and their descendants to airlifted Ethiopian Jews to millions fleeing persecution from the former Soviet Union and the Middle East and North Africa. The country is currently home to just less than half of the world's Jewish population, with some 6.5 million Jews living alongside approximately 1.7 million Arab citizens as of July 2017.

Iran Deal

The commonly used moniker for the Joint Comprehensive Plan of Action, a 2015 agreement between Iran, the United States, the European Union, Russia, China, France, Germany, and the United Kingdom. Its goal was to slow Iran's path to obtaining nuclear weapons, in return for easing international sanctions on the Islamic republic. It was one of the Obama administration's most controversial foreign policy achievements, with most Republicans and even some Democrats opposing it. These opponents argued that it would do little to curb Iran's nuclear ambitions while rewarding it with one hundred billion dollars it could use to support military initiatives, particularly against Israel. In October 2017, President Donald Trump withdrew from the deal, which had been one of his major campaign promises.

Isaac

See Matriarchs and Patriarchs, page 176; **binding of Isaac**.

Israel

See page 141.

FROM

Jabotinsky, Ze'ev

TO

Judea and Samaria

Jabotinsky, Ze'ev (1880–1940)

Statesman, politician, and founding father of Revisionist Zionism. He started out as a poet, and was so good that Maxim Gorky, fearing that the czarist police might ban one of Jabotinsky's early books, bought all the copies and distributed them himself. But Theodor Herzl soon captured Jabotinsky's imagination, and he decided to dedicate his life to the Zionist cause. When World War I broke out, Jabotinsky volunteered in the British Army, encouraging other Jews to do the same. If His Majesty's government ended up liberating Palestine from the Ottomans, he argued, Jewish soldiers ought to take part. After the war ended, however, he grew deeply critical of the British Mandate for Palestine and advocated armed struggle against the Brits that would end with the establishment of the Jewish state. That was too much for most of Zionism's leaders, who resented both Jabotinsky's ideas and his cultlike status among his believers. David Ben-Gurion routinely compared him to Hitler. Finally, in 1923, Jabotinsky and his supporters resigned from the World Zionist Organization and soon after started their own movement, Revisionist Zionism, as well as a youth movement, Betar. He believed in traditional liberal values but thought that there could be no peace with the Arabs unless the Jews in Palestine forcefully demonstrated their indisputable military might. His followers, including Menachem Begin, were the founding fathers of the Israeli right, and Likud, the party they eventually established, remains heavily indebted to his ideas. He died of a sudden heart attack at age sixty while visiting a Betar summer camp in New York. His funeral, the press reported at the time, was one of the most heavily attended in the city's history. His death, however, did little to lessen the fury of his political enemies: Ben-Gurion refused to allow Jabotinsky's remains to be buried in Jerusalem; Jabotinsky was only so honored in 1964, when Ben-Gurion was temporarily out of power.

Jacob

See Matriarchs and Patriarchs, page 176.

Jacobson, Abbi (b. 1984), and Ilana Glazer (b. 1987)

What Laverne and Shirley were to the 1970s, Cagney and Lacey to the '80s, and Salt-N-Pepa to the '90s, this dynamic duo are to their generation. Proudly Jewish, sexually adventurous, and cannabis-friendly, Abbi and Ilana weren't only the stars of the TV show *Broad City*, which ran on Comedy Central from 2014 to 2019, but also its creators, teaching a new generation of young women that the only thing cooler than being on a TV show is owning it. Yas, queens.

Jaffee, Al (b. 1921)

Iconic American cartoonist best known for his work in *MAD* magazine. He was responsible for the *MAD* "fold-in," which, when the pages of the magazine are folded in, obscures the original image and reveals a new one; he also created the long-running Snappy Answers to Stupid Questions. He helped invent *MAD*, and *MAD* helped make the sensibility of *National Lampoon* and Hollywood comedy as we know it. Without Jaffee, it's safe to say, no *Animal House*, no *Saturday Night Live*, no Judd Apatow. Or maybe they'd exist, but just be much worse.

AL JAFFEE

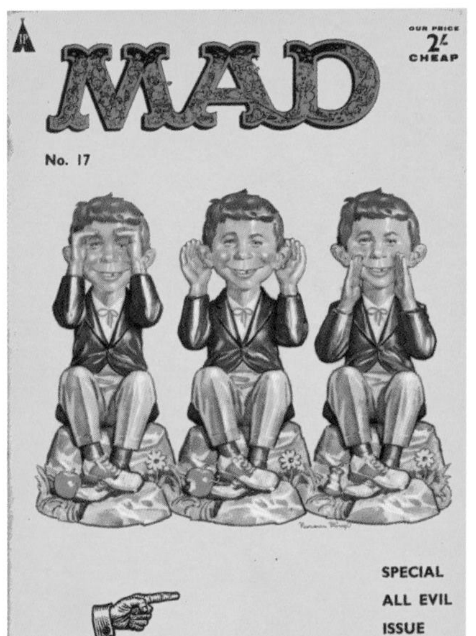

JAP (Jewish American Princess)

Somehow both an anti-Jewish *and* anti-woman slur, the JAP has its roots in the "Ghetto Girl" stereotype of the 1920s and '30s, which was aimed at stylish Jewish working women, seen by the community as a symbol of assimilation, materialism, and women's wildness. Popularized in its midcentury incarnation by Herman Wouk's *Marjorie Morningstar* and Philip Roth's *Goodbye, Columbus*, the JAP morphed into a spoiled woman interested only in a good marriage and a good blowout. Not incidentally, this stereotype was perpetuated mainly by Jewish men, who transformed the phrase from an intracommunity tsk-tsk-ing to an archetype familiar to the wider American community. In recent years, however, some Jewish women have embraced the term, finding empowerment in taking back what was once used against them.

jazz

Benny Goodman. Artie Shaw. George Gershwin. While jazz is an African American art form, these and other Jewish musicians, composers, producers, and club owners played a seminal role in its evolution and popularization. Often, the affinity between Jews and blacks stemmed from the persecution and exclusion both peoples have experienced, although the relationship was, at times, fraught. If you want to hear this collaboration at its best, listen to Ella Fitzgerald and Louis Armstrong's version of George Gershwin's "Summertime."

JCC (Jewish Community Center)

Where gentiles play racquetball.

JDate, JSwipe

The two most popular Jewish dating apps didn't exactly have a Hollywood meet-cute. They were once locked in a legal dispute: JDate sued JSwipe for co-opting its "J" branding. But this Jewish love story has a happy ending. JDate's parent company ended up acquiring JSwipe, and they all lived happily ever after.

Jerusalem

See page 146.

Jesus Christ

They don't make Jews like him anymore.

Jew

To an Orthodox Jew, anybody whose mother is Jewish; to a Reform Jew, anybody whose mother or father is Jewish; to the Nazis, anybody with one Jewish grandparent; to 23andMe or Ancestry.com, any one of millions of people who never had an inkling until now. And to anyone thinking sensibly about it, a Jew could be you, me, or the person next to you on the public bus, no matter what she looks like. Many Jews—those who have converted—have no Jewish ancestry. Many Jews don't "look Jewish," whatever that means. As Bernard Malamud wrote in "Angel Levine," "Believe me, there are Jews everywhere."

Jewdar

"Are you Jewish?"

"Yes! How did you know?"

If you have no good answer to the latter question—if you *just knew*—then your Jewdar is probably pretty spot-on. That bearded fellow studying Masechet Sanhedrin on the subway? Probably Jewish, and obviously so. But what about Arizona Cardinals quarterback Josh Rosen? NFL quarterbacking isn't traditionally a Jewish profession, although his name certainly *sounds* Jewish, doesn't it? Too slow, my non-Jewdar-having friend! I'm writing in this book—maybe I'm Jewish? And you're reading it—so maybe you are, too? Go through the ways one could spot a Jew—physiognomy, dress, speech, the books she happens to be reading at a given moment, some ineffable sense of the presence of another neshama—and one realizes that not all of these criteria are logically rigorous, and that many of them can't be politely said aloud, and that the whole enterprise of sight-reading someone's Jewish identity (of "bageling" someone, to use the delicious slang) has an unsavory historical resonance or ten. Better just to say you have good Jewdar than probe the truth of the matter too deeply. Incidentally, yes, Rosen is Jewish and even had a bar mitzvah. Go Cardinals!

Jewess

Outmoded term for a Jewish woman. Used ironically, self-knowingly, and proudly, "Jewess" has seen something of a renaissance in the twenty-first century. For instance, in the 2014 debut episode of the half-hour comedy *Broad City*, the lead characters—two horny, pot-smoking Shebrews—end up cleaning an apartment in their underwear after one writes in a Craigslist ad, "We're just 2 Jewesses tryin' to make a buck." There's an online magazine called *Jewess*, and for a time the Jewish Women's Archive hosted a blog called *Jewesses with Attitude*. There was once a print magazine called *The American Jewess*, but it folded in 1899, a reminder that, to most people's ears, the word sounds about as modern as "aviatrix" or "poetess."

Jewess Jeans

An imaginary brand of designer jeans (with Stars of David on the back pockets) that were the subject of a legendary fake TV ad on *Saturday Night Live* in 1980. Gilda Radner starred in the spot as "the Jewess in Jewess Jeans," a stereotypical JAP dancing around in a tube top and gold chains as a jingle described the brand's ideal customer: "She shops the sales for designer clothes, she's got designer nails and a designer nose . . . she's the Jewess in Jewess Jeans!" Riffing off a popular series of print ads for Levy's Jewish rye bread from the 1960s and '70s, captioned "You don't have to be Jewish to love Levy's," the Jewess Jeans ad concludes with a male announcer saying, "You don't have to be Jewish." A gum-chomping Radner gets the famous last words,

JERUSALEM

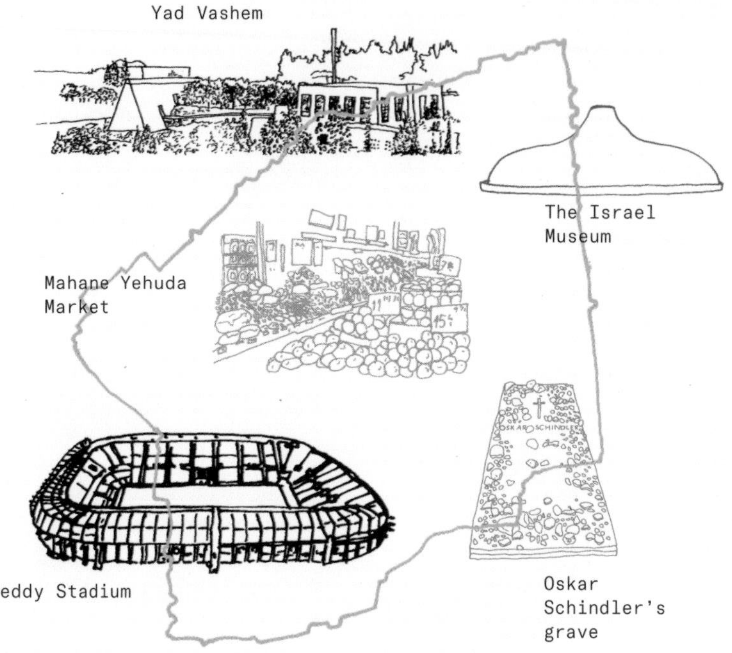

Israel's capital and its largest city. Holy to all three monotheistic religions. According to recent archaeological findings, there was a permanent dwelling where the modern city now stands as early as the nineteenth century BCE. At its heart is the Temple Mount, or Mount Moriah, which, according to Jewish tradition, provided God with the dust to create Adam and was later chosen as the site of Abraham's aborted binding of Isaac.

The city was controlled by the Jebusites until King David conquered it and declared it his capital. His son, King Solomon, built the First Temple, giving the sacred mount its name. After the destruction of the Second Temple in 70 CE, Hadrian renamed the city Aelia Capitolina, and it thrived as a Roman town for three centuries. Constantine, determined to turn the empire Christian, recognized Jerusalem's centrality to his newfound faith and built several churches, including one on the site of Jesus's reported crucifixion and burial. From the seventh to the sixteenth centuries, Jerusalem was a holy hot potato, drawing legions of true believers who wanted to claim it for their own faith, including the Arabs, the Crusaders, and the Mamluks. The Ottomans, upon taking over in 1517, rebuilt many of the city's holy sites, including the ancient Tower of David. Under their reign, the Jewish community grew rapidly; in the nineteenth century, bolstered by a new wave of Western interest and investment, Jews left the walls of the Old City, building new neighborhoods.

The city was divided shortly after Israel's Declaration of Independence, with Jordan holding on to its eastern part, including the Temple Mount and the Kotel. In the Six-Day War of 1967, Israeli soldiers reunited Jerusalem, once again declaring it the undivided capital of the Jewish state. Still, rabbis debating whether to omit a prayer said specifically for the city's redemption decided that a military victory was not reason enough to declare Jerusalem redeemed: there was, they said, an earthly Jerusalem and a heavenly one, and Jews should continue to pray until the city unlocks its true spiritual mysteries with the coming of the Messiah.

however, looking directly into the camera through her oversize tinted glasses: "But it wouldn't hurt."

Jewfro

What happens to many of us when we just let our hair do whatever it wants for a few months.

Jewish

The adjective that somehow sounds softer, and more palatable, than the noun *Jew*. It's true: say that someone is "a real Christian," and that's a compliment, but say that she is "a real Jew," and it sounds insulting. So people will say that Joe Lieberman or Ivanka Trump or Gal Gadot is "Jewish," when what they mean is that they are Jews. Sigh. It's not going anywhere, but maybe it could if when asked what our religion or ethnicity is, we all start saying, "I'm a Jew."

The Jewish Catalog

The epic 1973 DIY guide to Judaism, offering sensible peer-to-peer advice, just enough halachic wisdom (you'll find no better synopsis of the laws of kashrut), and the best diagram for wrapping tefillin that was ever rendered by your friend in Hebrew school who was always sketching things under his desk. It tells you how to build a sukkah, how to affix a mezuzah, which blessings to say over what, and how to get by when hitchhiking around Israel ("Get a haircut; Israelis are wary of foreign 'hippies'"). It offers instructions for sitting shiva, and it tells you where in all the major American cities you can rent Jewish movies. It's a panoramic view of a young idealist's American Judaism, circa *Laugh-In* and *Portnoy's Complaint* and Nixon. And it's the kind of handbook that the Internet was supposed to render useless, but which, in fact, the morass of the Web has made more desirable than ever.

While there were a lot of books being written about American Judaism—aren't there always?—there was nothing like this, with practical skills like cooking alongside tefillah, or prayer, treating them all as components of an integrated Jewish life. "It was a catalog—if you want to tie tzitzit, here's how to do it," coauthor Michael Strassfeld has said. And yet it wasn't prescriptive, at least not obnoxiously so. "It didn't imply that to be a Jew you had to keep kosher, observe Shabbat, etc., etc. What the catalog really was about was sharing our Jewish lives with people, saying, 'We are doing this, we enjoy this, we think you might.'" According to Strassfeld, if you include the second and third editions (1976 and 1980), the catalog has sold about half a million copies. Approximately half of them are available used online, so get yourself a copy, or three, today.

Jewish Defense League

See **Kahane, Meir**.

Jewish gangsters

See page 106.

Jewish geography

That thing where you meet someone at a party and within minutes realize that he went to college with your camp friend and camp with your home friend.

Jewish mother

Q. How many Jewish mothers does it take to change a lightbulb?

A. Never mind, I'll just sit here in the dark.

Jewish mothers are awesome and got a raw deal in misogynist midcentury comedy.

Jewish New Year

See Rosh Hashanah, page 218.

Jewish nose

An ethnic stereotype and, as such, a lucrative business idea for anti-Semites and plastic surgeons.

Jewish Orthodox Feminist Alliance

JOFA, as it is known, was founded in 1997 by a group of women, including Orthodox feminist writer Blu Greenberg. Its members are mostly Modern Orthodox, and they advocate for increased participation for women in Orthodox life, within the bounds—they are always careful to stress—of halacha. They walk a tightrope: to more orthodox Orthodox Jews, JOFA is seen as impertinently liberal and disrespectful of tradition, while to some more liberal Jewish feminists, they are seen as hopelessly deferential to outmoded, sexist rules. Some of the big issues for its members include giving Orthodox women opportunities to study religious texts and encouraging women to take leadership roles in synagogues, as clergy (see **Yeshivat Maharat**), as prayer leaders, or otherwise.

BILLY JOEL

Jewish time

When a Jew arrives late somewhere, he may offer up the excuse that he was "running on Jewish time." We disagree. This is just an internalized stereotype, as if we were incapable of observing social niceties. We're no less capable of reading an invitation properly than any other ethnic group.

But there's a kernel of truth in "Jewish time": our simchas—weddings and bar mitzvahs and even funerals—don't start *precisely on time*, the way some cultures' celebrations do. When an Irish family says their church wedding begins at eleven a.m., you'd better not show up at ten past, or you'll be following the bride down the aisle. They're running on Mass time, which is prompt. If a Jewish wedding is called for seven p.m., and you're still parking the car at 7:05, don't sweat it—there'll be a seat for you.

And there's another meaning of "Jewish time." Rabbis and other Jewish teachers sometimes say "Jewish time" to refer to time marked by our special calendar, according to which days run sundown to sundown, and months are keyed to lunar cycles. When a Jew gets more observant, or even just moves to a Jewish neighborhood, she may find that time moves differently—she begins to think of her weeks as ending with Shabbat, for example, and she develops a sense in early springtime that Passover is coming. She is living in Jewish time.

Jews for Jesus

A particularly well-known sect of Messianic Jews founded in the early 1970s.

Jews of color

A newish American term referring to Jews whose families originally hail from Africa, Asia, or Latin America. Jews of color may also identify as, for example, black, Latino, or Asian American. They may (or may not) be Mizrahi or Sephardi. The term is useful, because Jews of color have unique experiences, such as facing racism from "white" Jews and from society at large, and because many share family legacies and similar narratives.

It's also, as many evocative terms can be, tricky. Consider the hypothetical case of a son of Mexican American Jewish immigrants. In the United States, he may be treated as a Latino, feel solidarity with other "people of color," and thus identify as a Jew of color. But back in Mexico, and throughout Latin America, most Jews are of the upper, "white" classes—and thus his parents would likely find the term "Jew of color" absurd when applied to their son. Descendants of the Portuguese and Spanish Jews who arrived in the United States in the 1600s are unlikely to call themselves "Jews of color," even if their ancestry makes them Latino. Unlike "Ashkenazi" or "Sephardi," "Jew of color" is deployed contingently and pragmatically; it's a self-description more than a description.

Job

The Bible's most put-upon man. He is subjected to one of God's cruelest tests: he is stripped of his wealth, his children, and his servants, then has his body covered in boils, all to see if his faith can be shaken. (Spoiler alert: It can't be.) The story is an exploration of the problem of theodicy or, in more contemporary terms, why bad things happen to good people. Job's ordeal has been rendered in countless modern tellings, inspiring everything from Kafka's *The Trial* to the Coen brothers' *A Serious Man*.

Joel, Billy (b. 1949)

Look, you either get Billy Joel or you don't. If you get him, then this Bronx-born, Long Island–raised rocker has helped author a sizable chunk of the great American songbook. Without Billy Joel, no "Piano Man," no "New York State of Mind," no "Uptown Girl," no "Movin' Out (Anthony's Song)," no Brenda, no Eddie, no multiple "final farewell tours" with multi-night stands at Madison Square Garden. If you get Billy Joel, he is no less essential to the FM dial than, say, the far more critically beloved Bruce Springsteen. To those who don't get him, he is a musical crime, a schmaltzmeister par excellence, nothing but sonic Cheez Whiz. Jewishly speaking, Joel has always been less "out," somehow, than Neil Diamond, Paul Simon, and other peers. His most Jewish moment probably came in 2017, when he wore a yellow star onstage at Madison Square Garden to protest Donald Trump's claim that "both sides" were to blame for the violence at the white supremacist rally in Charlottesville, Virginia. But generally he can be found off to the side laughing with the sinners, in a New York state of mind, leaving a tender moment alone.

Johansson, Scarlett (b. 1984)

Husky-voiced Hollywood Jewess. She's best known for quirky, indie faves like *Lost in Translation* and overblown superhero fare like *The Avengers*. In 2014, she was the paid spokesperson for SodaStream, the handy carbonation appliance manufactured, at the time, in a plant in the West Bank. This gig of hers gave much tsuris to BDS rabble-rousers. As a result of the controversy, Johansson stepped down from her ambassador role at Oxfam, which opposes trade with Israeli settlements. Johansson did not back down, and she criticized the protests that led to the plant's dissolution, which ultimately put many Palestinians out of work.

Jolson, Al (1886–1950)

Before Frank Sinatra, before Elvis Presley, before Michael Jackson, there was Al Jolson, the twentieth century's first pan-media "rock star." With his cyclonic stage act and rafter-rattling voice, he was for millions of fans the embodiment of pop modernity—the poster boy for ragtime, which was unmooring America from its Victorian past one raucous song at a time. But Jolson was not just a New American; he was vividly, unapologetically a Jewish American, with a fearless devotion to schmaltz and a "tear in a voice," his birthright as a cantor's son. Born Asa Yoelson in a Lithuanian shtetl, he immigrated to the United States as a child, and by his late teens was performing in vaudeville. Jolson's biography closely mirrors the plot line of his most famous film role, Jakie Rabinowitz in *The Jazz Singer* (1927), the epochal first talkie. Posterity has not been kind to Jolson. He was famous for performing in blackface; today, it is impossible to ignore the coarse racism of signature songs like "My Mammy." But if Jolson embodied the ugliness of that bygone age, he also transcended it: his raw talent, his huge voice, and his live-wire charisma have been matched by few performers of any era.

Jonah

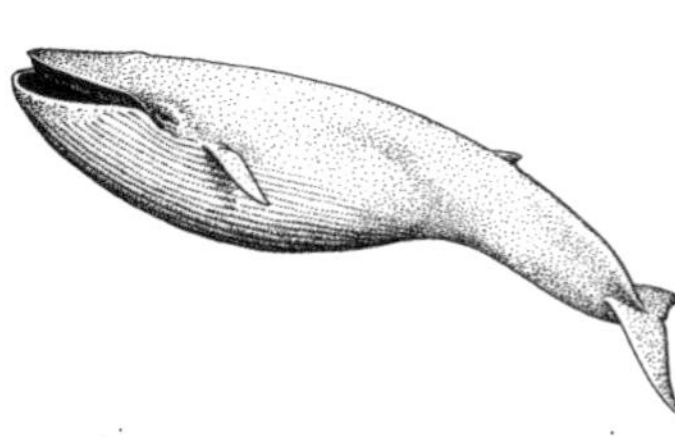

The most reluctant of all Hebrew prophets. When God tasks him with a mission, he tries to run, boarding a boat headed far away. When God troubles the boat with a terrible storm, he goes to sleep. Only after he's tossed overboard and swallowed whole by a large fish does he finally come to his senses, repenting in earnest and inspiring us to read his tale each year on Yom Kippur.

Joseph

Anyone who has ever had an annoying sibling will fully understand why Joseph's brothers threw the little braggart into a ditch and told their father he was dead. But let that be a lesson to us all: the little braggart grew up, according to Genesis, to be a fine man who, when the moment came, forgave his brothers and helped save them all, not to mention the entire kingdom of Egypt. And if that doesn't merit an Andrew Lloyd Webber musical, we don't know what does.

Jubu

Jews who practice some form of Buddhism, often alongside, or mixed with, Jewish practice. Most Jews are not Buddhist, but a sizable number of American Buddhists—white American Buddhists, that is—were raised Jewish. This is especially true of the generation of Jewish teachers in the 1970s and '80s whose books, retreats, and Buddhist communities helped take Buddhism mainstream, often through meditation practices or "mindfulness." Jon Kabat-Zinn, Jack

Kornfield, Sharon Salzberg—all Jews. Same goes for many of the most famous Buddhism-influenced celebrities, like Allen Ginsberg and Leonard Cohen. Go to a Buddhist retreat at Insight Meditation Society, in the Berkshires, for example, and there will be enough Jews for a minyan or ten. It is an enduring source of pique for some rabbis that so many Jews who crave intense spirituality turn to Buddhism rather than looking to their own tradition. In response, some rabbis have worked to import Buddhist practices into Judaism—for a famous, and successful, example, check out *This Is Real and You Are Completely Unprepared* (2003), by the late San Francisco rabbi Alan Lew.

Judea and Samaria

Rather inconveniently for some today, the only parts of Israel that the Bible explicitly mentions as the site of the ancient Jewish homeland. The contested heartland of the Israeli-Palestinian conflict, this narrow piece of land on the West Bank of the Jordan River was captured by Israel from Jordan in the 1967 Six-Day War and has been the locus of controversy ever since. Palestinians, many of whom have lived in the region for centuries under an array of rulers, claim the land as part of their future state. Israelis see the area as their historic home, where the ancient Kingdoms of Judah (Judea) and Southern Israel (Samaria) once stood. Israel's security hawks view the territory as essential for the country's strategic defense against border incursions, while its doves are willing to vacate much of the land in exchange for a peace agreement. Meanwhile, religious nationalist settlers drawn to the land for its theological significance have dotted some 2 percent of the region with Jewish settlements, hoping to thwart a two-state solution.

FROM

Kabbalah, Kabbalist

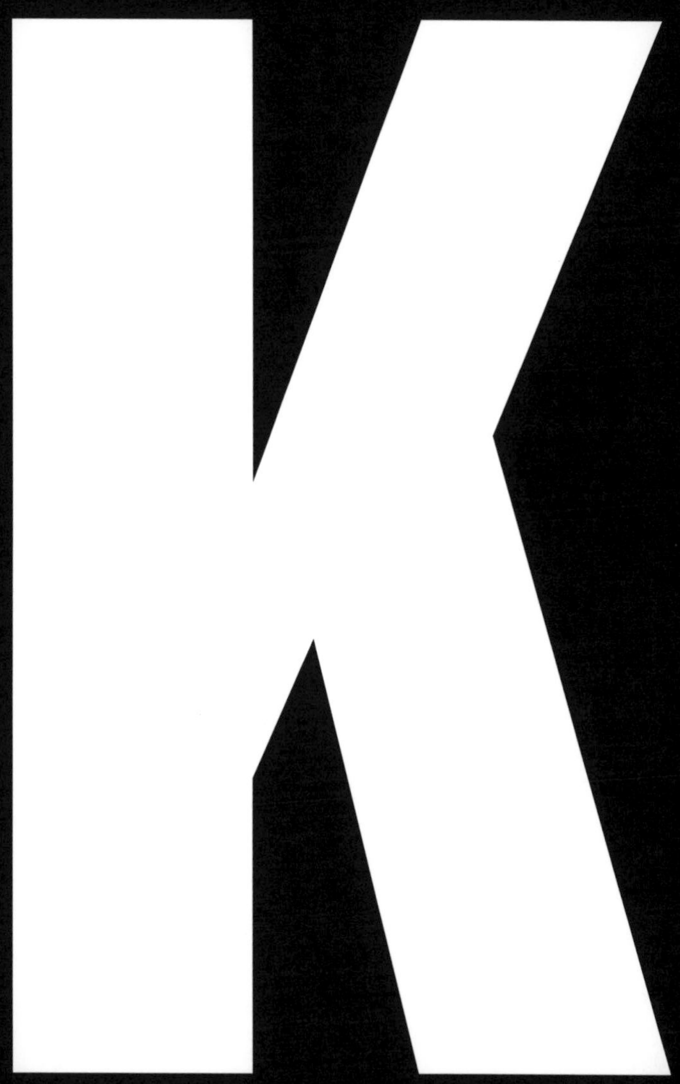

TO

kvetch

KAFKA, FRANZ

(1883–1924)

German-speaking, Bohemian Czech Jewish novelist and short-story writer, son of a merchant, grandson of a *shochet*, or kosher butcher. The bizarre, fantastical plots of works like *The Metamorphosis* (1915) and *The Trial* (written in 1914–1915, published posthumously) helped define our modern concepts of alienation and guilt. Kafka's terrifying absurdities keep giving, informing the imaginations even of people who have never read the actual works: any educated Westerner knows that in *The Metamorphosis*, the protagonist, Gregor Samsa, awakens to discover that he has been transformed into a large insect. To this day, anything nightmarishly incomprehensible can be called "Kafkaesque"—and what other author, besides Orwell, had a really good adjective made from his name? Before he died of tuberculosis at the age of forty, Kafka left instructions that his unpublished writing be destroyed. Fortunately, his friend and literary executor, Max Brod, didn't heed this request.

A KAFKAESQUE READING LIST

The Metamorphosis (1915)

In the Penal Colony (1919)

The Trial (1925)

Kabbalah, Kabbalist

OLD SCHOOL Back in the day, people weren't even allowed to study this strand of Jewish mysticism until they were middle-aged and well educated in all other facets of Talmud and Torah. So proceed with caution, because the Kabbalah's wisdom—about the creation of the world, the nature of God, and the condition of the human soul—may blow your mind. But if you want to jump in anyway, begin with the Zohar, Kabbalah's foundational text, ascribed to the second-century rabbi Shimon Bar Yochai. Open it, and the world will never look the same again.

NEW SCHOOL If studying ancient texts isn't your thing, you can take advantage of the newfound popularizations of this complex and demanding philosophy. From Kabbalah-inspired yoga to Kabbalah-branded "holy water," there's a lot of Kabbalistic krap out there, and a lot of gullible folks vying to buy into Kabbalah as a lifestyle. (Surprise, surprise: Many of them are celebrities. Madonna, Demi and Ashton, Lucy Liu, Britney Spears, and James Van Der Beek—yes, *Dawson himself*—all dabbled.) But look, the New Agers, most notably the founders of the Kabbalah Centre in Los Angeles, deserve credit for bringing these difficult ideas to the masses. Just don't buy any books that spell the word "Qabbalah"—the *q* is your sign that it's beyond New Age and into total froot-loopiness.

Kabbalat Shabbat

The Friday-evening service that ushers in Shabbat. If you went to Jewish summer camp, you may remember some of the key KabShab *piyyutim*, or liturgical songs, like "Yedid Nefesh" and "L'kha Dodi." Kabbalat Shabbat is hard to screw up: a good service leader has dozens of beautiful melodies to choose from; the service is fairly short, well under an hour; it comes at a time when children are still awake and not yet falling apart; and there's dinner afterward. Many Reform congregations, especially, come together as a community principally on Friday night, rather than Saturday morning, and for them Kabbalat Shabbat is the main service of the week.

Kaddish

A major prayer, repeated at least once in every Jewish prayer service, that despite being associated with death—its last recitation in every service is given over to those in mourning—never mentions death at all. It's just about the awesomeness of God's creation.

Kahane, Meir (1932–1990)

A Brooklyn-born Orthodox rabbi who gained notoriety in 1968, when he and his group, the Jewish Defense League, attacked Soviet targets stateside to protest the Kremlin's abuse of Jewish refuseniks. A powerful writer and orator, he moved to Israel in 1971 and soon gained a loyal enough following that it inspired him to run for office. In 1984, he was finally elected to the Knesset and shocked many with his extreme views, which included advocating a transfer of Israel's Arab population and outlawing marriages and sexual relations between Jews and gentiles. Responding to Kahane, the Knesset amended the nation's Basic Law, barring a party determined to be racist from participating in elections, a stipulation that prevented Kahane from seeking reelection. In 1990, after speaking in a Manhattan hotel, he was assassinated by an Egyptian-born American named El Sayyid Nosair. Nosair's mentor, Sheikh Omar Abdul-Rahman, rose to infamy three years later for his part in conspiring to blow up the World Trade Center.

Kaplan, Roberta (b. 1966)

American lawyer who argued on behalf of Edith Windsor in *United States v. Windsor* (2013), the landmark Supreme Court decision that recognized same-sex marriages.

kapo

In history, a Jewish concentration-camp prisoner tasked by the Nazis with keeping his fellow prisoners in order. On Twitter, anyone you don't agree with.

Karan, Donna (b. 1948)

Iconic New York designer. Raised on Long Island in the Five Towns, she was born into a fashion family, albeit one not as glamorous as the world she would soon occupy: her mother worked as a fit model (helping designers see how their garments fit on a person, versus on a mannequin) and her father, who died when she was three years old, was a tailor and haberdasher. Karan attended the Parsons School of Design and began working at Anne Klein in the 1960s, ultimately becoming Klein's number two. She took over the company when Anne Klein died in 1974, then in 1984 started her own company, Donna Karan New York, which became famed for the simple mix-and-match outfits of her Seven Easy Pieces line. Her attention to real women's bodies, rather than the supermodel aesthetic, made her designs staples of many women's wardrobes and helped change the conventions of the fashion world.

Karski, Jan (1914–2000)

Fought in the Polish resistance against the Nazis and was a key figure in alerting the Western Powers to the atrocities being committed on Polish soil. He traveled widely and met with numerous heads of state—including President Roosevelt—to give eyewitness testimony about the unfolding extermination of European Jewry. Karski's story stands as a firm rebuke to those in the West who later claimed that they knew nothing of the Holocaust until it was over. After the war, Karski earned a PhD from Georgetown University and proceeded to teach there for forty years. In the 1960s, he had Bill Clinton as a student.

kashrut

Jewish dietary laws. You may remember the basics from Torah: To be kosher, animals must have cloven hooves and chew their own cud (sorry, piggie), fish must have fins and scales (adios, shrimp), and birds must not be scavengers or birds of prey. Kosher animals—cows, chickens, etc.—must be slaughtered by a shochet, a certified professional who cuts their jugular vein, their carotid artery, their esophagus, and their trachea in one smooth motion. There's no mixing of milk and meat. The rest is commentary, the sort of commentary that continues to keep rabbis busy. There are different organizations certifying products as kosher, different classifications for products like dairy, bread, and wine, and different traditions among different communities. At last count, there are some two thousand kosher certification organizations.

Katz's Deli

See Delicatessen, page 74.

Kaufman, Andy (1949–1984 . . . if, that is, you believe he's really dead)

Comedian Andy Kaufman didn't influence anybody. That's because his act was impossible to follow. It involved, early on, pretending to be a meek immigrant from the small nation of Caspiar, and doing terrible "impersonations" that went something like, "Hello! I am Meester Carter, de president of de United States. Tank you veddy much." Then, just as the act was getting too tedious to take, he'd break into a pitch-perfect Elvis. Performance artist, prankster, and TV star—he took his Foreign Man act to the sitcom *Taxi*, on which his character was named Latka—he died at thirty-five of a rare form of lung cancer. So great was his reputation for pulling off weird and wild stunts that many still believe it was all a hoax, and that Andy will return someday soon. (Like Tupac.)

Kazin, Alfred (1915–1998)

More than any other work of criticism, Alfred Kazin's *On Native Grounds* (1942), a study of American fiction from William Dean Howells through Faulkner, showed the

KING, CAROLE

(B. 1942)

Brooklyn-bred composer of some of the great songs of the Brill Building era (many cowritten with first husband Gerry Goffin), who reinvented herself as a performer in the early '70s. King's songbook is indomitable: "Will You Love Me Tomorrow?," "The Loco-Motion," "Up on the Roof," "One Fine Day," "Pleasant Valley Sunday," "(You Make Me Feel Like) A Natural Woman," etc. King relocated from New York to LA's Laurel Canyon in the late '60s; in 1971, she released the chart-topping album *Tapestry*, which added new classics to her canon ("It's Too Late," "You've Got a Friend," "I Feel the Earth Move," "So Far Away"), establishing her as a star recording artist and a leader of the post-hippie singer-songwriter movement.

THE (CAROLE) KING OF POP

"Pleasant Valley Sunday" (1967)

"Up On the Roof" (1970)

"(You Make Me Feel Like) A Natural Woman" (1971)

"It's Too Late" (1971)

"You've Got a Friend" (1971)

"I Feel the Earth Move" (1971)

"So Far Away" (1971)

"Will You Love Me Tomorrow?" (1971)

"One Fine Day" (1980)

"The Loco-Motion" (1980)

absurdity of the anti-Semitic lie that Jews would never be at home in American high culture. The Brooklyn-bred, City College–educated Kazin was not only a magisterial critic and essayist but a fine memoirist, whose *A Walker in the City* (1951) is a beloved portrait of a young man making it across the bridge, from the Brooklyn of his childhood to the Manhattan of his dreams.

ketubah

See Wedding, page 283.

kibbitz

Yiddish word, firmly imported into English, meaning to stand around and chat or wisecrack; it can have implications of offering unsolicited advice or being inconsiderate of those trying to focus on their business. Kibbitzers should keep their voices down but never do.

kibbutz

A kibbutz is a communal farm or settlement in Israel. Different kibbutzim (the plural) specialize in different industries or products, and in the earlier, more utopian days of the State of Israel, it was very much the thing for a pioneering young American Jew to take some time abroad to work on a kibbutz: "After I didn't get into the Peace Corps, I went and worked on a kibbutz for six months. We made olive oil." The early kibbutzniks were usually socialist in their outlook; children were often raised communally, and on some kibbutzim all property was held in common. Today, the kibbutz is past its prime—there are fewer kibbutzim, and those that persist have often become partially privatized—but as of 2010, they still accounted for almost 10 percent of Israeli industrial output. For a terrific portrait of a kibbutz in contemporary Israeli society, check out Jessamyn Hope's novel *Safekeeping.*

Kiddush

The Kiddush ("holiness") is the prayer sanctifying a cup of wine; to recite the prayer before a meal begins is to "make Kiddush." A lowercase *kiddush* is, perhaps confusingly, a communal luncheon, particularly at synagogue after morning services (or in some Orthodox communities, during the rabbi's sermon). As in: "Who wants to make Kiddush at the start of the kiddush?"

Kindertransport

Effort to rescue Jewish children from the advancing Nazi threat. Children were taken by train and resettled in the United Kingdom. There were also Kindertransports to Switzerland, France, Sweden, Belgium, and the Netherlands. The initiative saved some ten thousand children, many of whom never saw their parents again. Dr. Ruth Westheimer was saved by the kindertransport.

Kibbutz: Making the desert bloom at Kibbutz Givat Brenner in Israel, circa 1950

King David

The Bible's most famous king began his wild ride with what some conclude was a gay love affair with Jonathan and was certainly a passionate friendship. He then coveted the married Bat Sheva, had his way with her while her husband was away at war, and, when he found out that she was pregnant, had her husband killed. His eldest son, Amnon, raped his eldest daughter, Tamar, leaving his other son, Avshalom, to murder Amnon, which must've been tiresome because, to blow off steam, Avshalom then had sex with his father's mistresses on top of the king's palace, with all of Jerusalem watching. Oy. So next time you read the Psalms, David's great literary masterpiece, remember that the author is a dude who knew a thing or two about unbridled passion.

King Solomon

Builder of the First Temple, lover of seven hundred wives and three hundred mistresses, a wise and poetic king who could write beautiful poems and talk to animals in his spare time.

kippah

Raised on Yiddish, your grandfather called this a "yahmulke" and spelled it *yarmulke*. The kippah (as they say in Hebrew) is a skullcap that offers too little coverage to really stay put, thus necessitating clips or bobby pins—although some real daredevils wear a tiny circular disc that miraculously perches at the peak of the skull, while still others wear a fuller hat that offers nearly ski-hat levels of coverage. The kippah fulfills Maimonides's dictum that a Jewish man at prayer must cover his head, as well as the Orthodox tradition that a man cover his head during all waking hours. Although, as Joe Lieberman knows, head coverage is not a halachic requirement, and many Modern Orthodox Jews leave the kippah at home when they go to the office. Nobody over the age of bar mitzvah should wear a yarmulke with sports-logo embroidery—same goes for a post-bat mitzvah girl, now that some of them, inspired by Jewish-feminist egalitarianism, have taken to wearing kippot (the plural). Keen scholars of such matters can tell an Orthodox Jew's particular community by inspecting his kippah: a knit kippah is Modern Orthodox, a black-velvet kippah is Haredi—and it gets more complicated still.

Kissinger, Henry (b. 1923)

Through his influence on American presidents from Richard Nixon to Donald Trump, he played a decisive role in opening American relations with China, reframing US relations with Russia, ending America's involvement in Vietnam, destroying large parts of Laos and Cambodia, and resupplying Israel with ammunition during the most critical hours of the Yom Kippur War. For better or worse—which will depend on your own views—no single individual in the history of the Jewish people had a greater impact on global politics.

kitniyot

For most of the year, this Hebrew term, meaning "legumes," is useless. On Passover, however, it marks the boundary line of a great divide: Sephardi Jews eat them during the holiday, which means that rice, corn, lentils, and peas are all on the menu, while Orthodox Ashkenazi Jews consider them just as verboten as bread. Why? The reason is still largely unclear but most likely had to do with these grains being stored in sacks that looked a lot like flour, driving the rabbis to declare them out-of-bounds simply to avoid confusion. These days, however, more and more people seem to gravitate toward eating kitniyot on Pesach, making the Seder (and the week that follows) that much more delicious.

kittel

Unadorned lab coat–like garment that some Jewish men wear on august occasions, such as their wedding day, Yom Kippur, the Passover Seder, and their burial.

Klal Yisrael

All of Israel, which means every Jew, anywhere, ever, regardless of nationality, sexual preference, skin color, or dietary restrictions. We may all disagree, but we are all one.

klezmer

Ashkenazi musical style. Klezmer takes its name from a combination of the Hebrew words *kley* (tool) and *zemer* (song). Beginning around the eighteenth century, the term shifted away from musical instruments and toward the klezmorim who entertained the guests at weddings. Much as the music of the klezmorim absorbed elements from the Romanians and Lithuanians who surrounded them in Europe, the music continued to metamorphose when the genre's practitioners made their way to the New World. And the cross-fertilization was not just one-way. The sound of Benny Goodman's clarinet became as American as apple pie. In the 1970s, as "roots" music came into vogue, Jewish musicians came to look more deeply at the sounds of the shtetls their ancestors had fled. This "klezmer revival" continues to bloom, and, in one of the ironies of history, among the places where klezmer is most alive today—Berlin, Krakow, Budapest—are parts of the world from where it was once stamped out.

ABRAHAM ISAAC KOOK

Knesset

Literally "gathering," the Knesset is the Israeli parliament.

kohanim

Priests. Judaism's priests are descendants of Moses's brother, Aaron. In the days when there was still a Temple in Jerusalem, the priests were in charge of overseeing ritual sacrifices. Though less important in the post-Temple period, kohanim still have certain privileges: They receive the first aliyah whenever the Torah is read, and they perform the ritual known as "duchening," in which they offer blessings over the community. (They do so while making the letter *shin* with their hands—a symbol that can be found on the tombstones of many kohanim and was the inspiration for Leonard Nimoy's "Live Long and Prosper" salute on *Star Trek*; see **Spock**.) Kohanim are also subject to certain restrictions. In Orthodox Judaism, the kohen (singular) is forbidden from marrying a divorcée or coming into contact with a dead body, and as a result, he often will not enter cemeteries. Because nothing can be simple with us, not all kohanim are named Cohen and not all Cohens are kohanim—though there is a good deal of overlap between the two.

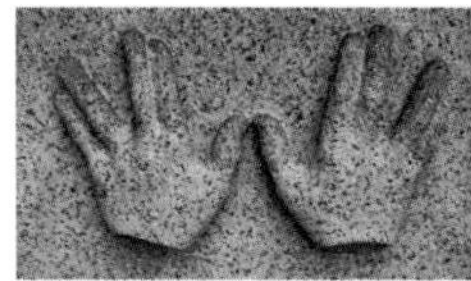

Kol Nidre

One of Judaism's most important prayers. Largely in Aramaic, it is recited early on the eve of Yom Kippur. Originally, the prayer absolved those who said it of all the sins they'd committed in the past year, but the rabbis disliked the idea of a sweeping absolution and changed the prayer to grant us forgiveness for all the sins we're *about* to commit in the coming year. This way, we enter the new year on a note of mercy, moved to do and be better. Throughout the centuries, the prayer was often brought up by anti-Semites who claimed that it was proof that Jews are not to be trusted, which is why early Reform Jews omitted it from their prayer books. Thankfully, it persisted, with its words and melodies remaining among the best known in Jewish liturgy.

Kominsky-Crumb, Aline (b. 1948)

Artist who makes deeply personal and subversive comics that blend introspection and lewdness while conveying an unapologetically feminist point of view. She is known for her character "the Bunch" and for her early work on the all-female anthology *Twisted Sisters*. Kominsky-Crumb is married to Robert Crumb, known as R. Crumb, with whom she has collaborated on the series *Dirty Laundry*, an autobiographical work about their family.

Kook, Abraham Isaac (1865–1935)

The first Ashkenazi chief rabbi of Mandatory Palestine, he was one of his generation's leading rabbinic lights. Unlike many Orthodox Jews at the time, who were wary of modernity, Kook embraced it, arguing that "that which is old shall be renewed, and that which is new shall be sanctified." Most important, he differed from most other Orthodox rabbis in embracing the budding Zionist movement. While traditional Judaism argued that only the coming of the Messiah can lead to the return of Jews to Zion, Kook believed that the secular pioneers resettling the land were moved by a messianic spirit, and that, whether they realized it or not, they were instruments of the divine plan.

Kook, Zvi Yehuda (1891–1982)

With a mighty father like Rav Abraham Isaac Kook, what could Junior do for an encore? As it turns out, a lot: after the Six-Day War, with Israel now controlling

Sandy Koufax: The Dodgers pitcher led his team to victory in the 1965 World Series, despite sitting out Game 1 because it conflicted with Yom Kippur.

Judea and Samaria and the Gaza Strip, Zvi Yehuda Kook was a highly influential advocate of building new Jewish communities on the biblical hilltops, making him the father of the settlement movement.

kosher

Food that aligns with Jewish dietary laws (see **kashrut**). Also an adjective for anything that is aboveboard, meets requirements, or is all good.

kosher for Passover

Food that is "kosher for Passover," or *kasher l'pesach*, is not just kosher in the usual sense (no pork, no shellfish, produced under rabbinic supervision, etc.), but also meets the specific dietary requirements of Passover. It must contain no wheat, barley, rye, oats, or spelt that is leavened or fermented. So, you know, skip the croutons on your salad, no chicken rolled in cornflake crumbs. Mass-produced ingredients must say "Kosher for Passover" on their packaging. Wine is a special case: for wine to be kosher at all—and thus kosher for Passover—it needs to be handled from crush to bottling not just by Jews but by observant Jews.

kosher-style

Although "kosher-style" sounds like a designation for clothing trends coming out of Orthodox neighborhoods, it refers to food that is not actually kosher according to the strictest rules, but which is largely in the spirit of kashrut. Let's say your caterer is serving corned beef and pastrami and is avoiding dairy, pork and shellfish, but there is no official kosher supervision on-site, and not all the products the caterer is using have an official kosher seal: the food there is kosher-style. The feel is Jewish, your guests aren't committing any of the big no-nos, like popping shrimp cocktail, but you can't call the food kosher, because somebody really observant would object. That's kosher-style.

Kotel

See **Western Wall**.

Koufax, Sandy (b. 1935)

The greatest left-handed pitcher ever to take the mound. But never, of course, on Yom Kippur. See Sports and Jews, page 251.

krav maga

Literally, "contact combat." A martial art developed by Hungarian-born badass Imrich "Imi" Lichtenfeld so Israelis can kick some motherlovin' ass. In the face. Or balls. Or the solar plexus. For some unknown reason, the technique assumes your attacker is trying to kill you. Later, for a time in the early 1990s, a fashionable fitness class for Manhattanites that was too hard for most people to stick with. See also the common Jewish lie: "I know krav maga."

Kristallnacht

The "Night of Broken Glass," and a major turning point in the Nazi assault on Europe's Jews. On November 9 and 10, 1938, German mobs stormed and set fire to thousands of synagogues and vandalized Jewish-owned businesses throughout Germany and Austria. Amid the chaos, thirty thousand Jews were arrested and sent to concentration camps. For German and Austrian Jews, this signified that the situation was really, *really* bad, and many attempted to flee the country.

Krusty the Clown

"A Jewish entertainer?" wonders Homer. "Get out of here." Herschel Shmoikel Pinchas Yerucham Krustofski is *The Simpsons'* Al Jolson, or at least he's Al Jolson's character in *The Jazz Singer*: an entertainer who has betrayed his father—"my father was a rabbi," sighs Krusty, "his father was a rabbi, his father's father was a—well, you get the idea." In a way, he's also the comedian Jackie Mason, who, too, comes from a long line of rabbis but who clearly does not feel so weighted by that burden that he couldn't guest-star as the voice of Krusty's father, Rabbi Hyman Krustofski.

kugel

Think potato kugel at Passover or, for all other occasions, cornflake-topped lokshen kugel made with egg noodles, sour cream, cottage cheese, raisins, and canned fruit. There's also Yerushalmi kugel, made from thinner noodles that are caramelized and doused in black pepper. But there it is, at every holiday, year after year—at least fifty shades of kugel.

Kushner family

From the fields of Belarus to the White House in three acts: Partisan fighters Joseph and Rae Kushner bravely stymie the Nazis, then move to America in 1949, rebuilding their lives and establishing a New Jersey real estate empire, which their children inherit. In a sibling feud straight out of the Bible, their son Charles Kushner, under investigation by the US Attorney's office, blackmails his brother-in-law by hiring a prostitute to seduce him, taping the encounter, and then *mailing it to his sister*, Esther. Charles goes to jail, leaving his son Jared to look for fatherly figures wherever he can find them, which was most often in media mogul types. Jared meets Ivanka Trump and courts her; then, after an intervention by Rupert Murdoch and his then wife, Wendy Deng, Ivanka agrees to convert to Judaism and marry Jared. Donald Trump wins the 2016 presidency, and installs his son-in-law Jared as his White House innovations director. *Fin.*

Kushner, Tony (b. 1956)

An American playwright best known for the Tony- and Pulitzer-winning *Angels in America*, which opened on Broadway in 1993. But he's written much more that's worth your time, including *Homebody/Kabul*, the musical *Caroline, or Change*, and *The Intelligent Homosexual's Guide to Capitalism and Socialism with a Key to the Scriptures*—a title that may clue you in to the fact that Kushner is gay, left-wing politically, and verbose. He frequently deals with Jewish themes: he wrote the Oscar-nominated screenplay for Steven Spielberg's movie *Munich*, adapted S. Ansky's Yiddish play *The Dybbuk*, and coedited (with Alisa Solomon) the book *Wrestling with Zion: Progressive Jewish-American Responses to the Israeli-Palestinian Conflict*. At times, Kushner sports an admirably full Jewfro.

kvell

What you do when your kid aces the Torah portion, gets into Harvard, finds a perfect soul mate, becomes a person you actually like and admire, etc.

kvetch

From the Yiddish (naturally), it's a verb meaning "to complain": "Stop your kvetching already, or I'll give you something to really kvetch about." As a noun, it can be the complaint itself: "You have a sour look on your punim—what's your kvetch?" Or, better still, it's a person given to much kvetching: "I used to do krav maga with him at the JCC, but he's such a kvetch, so I dropped him totally." Look in any Yiddish dictionary and you'll find kvetching associated with squeezing, pressing, forcing, or straining—whether for a high note or, as is delicately noted in some dictionaries, at stool. Some will indicate that *kvetshn zikh* (reflexive) can mean to equivocate or beat around the bush. You have to go to the Bible of Yiddish in English, Leo Rosten's *The Joys of Yiddish*, to find fretting or complaining among the multitude shades of kvetch. Make no mistake, though—that whiny, straining key of complaint is integral to Yiddish; it's what led Michael Wex to call his bestselling exploration of Yiddish culture *Born to Kvetch*. As Wex so eloquently writes, "The connection with complaint lies, of course, in the tone of voice: someone who's kvetching sounds like someone who's paying the price for not having taken his castor oil—and he has just as eager an audience."

FROM

Labor

TO

lulav

Labor

For the first twenty-nine years of Israel's existence, it was dominated by a single party: Labor, the mighty political machine built by David Ben-Gurion. During that period, elections were held not so much to determine who would be prime minister—that part was obvious—but rather to find out what other tiny parties got to fight over scraps from Labor's big table. The party pursued its policies uninterrupted, balancing its socialist worldview with Israel's national security needs. When Likud shocked the nation and won its first election in 1977, one Labor grandee famously said that if that's the outcome, it's time to vote out the people. Labor made a big comeback in the 1990s, led by Yitzhak Rabin and cheered on for its role in engineering the Oslo Accords. But once Rabin was assassinated and the peace process faltered, so did Labor's political fortunes. It enjoyed a short bout of success under the leadership of Ehud Barak, then went into a tailspin from which it has yet to recover.

Ladino

Also known as Judeo-Spanish or Judezmo, Ladino is the language of Sephardi Jews; it originated in Spain in the fifteenth century. After their expulsion from Spain in 1492, the majority dispersed throughout the Mediterranean toward the Ottoman Empire. The exiled Jews carried their Castilian dialect with them, adding bits of languages from the countries they traversed and settled in along the way. Grounded in Spanish and Hebrew, Ladino also includes traces of Portuguese, Italian, French, Arabic, Greek, Turkish, and more. For five centuries, Ladino grew into a vibrant language that represented the rich multicultural history of Sephardi life in the Eastern Mediterranean. It was traditionally written with Hebrew characters as well as Solitreo, but is now written with Latin letters. Ladino is still spoken in pockets around the globe, though since World War II, the language has been in steep decline.

Lamarr, Hedy (1914–2000)

The future movie star and genius inventor was born in Vienna and named Hedwig Eva Maria Kiesler. When Lamarr was eighteen, the director of one of her earliest films used a special telephoto lens to film her in the nude and to capture her face in what publicity for the film leeringly touted as "the precise moment of rapture," driving critics to view the movie as sheer pornography. On the boat to New York, fleeing Europe after Hitler's rise, she met Louis B. Mayer, who was moved by her beauty and not much else, casting her in roles that required very few speaking lines. When World War II broke out, Lamarr volunteered to help, saying that she was an inventor and had a few ideas that might be of use; instead, she was sent on a fundraising tour with a sailor named Eddie, who took the stage every evening asking for a kiss and prompting the audience to donate generously and put Lamarr in a giving mood. None of it, however, deterred the brilliant actress, who was just as brilliant an engineer: although she never received any formal scientific training, she soon learned that radio-controlled torpedoes could be easily jammed by the enemy, so she took to a makeshift lab that she created in her Los Angeles home and developed a frequency-hopping signal that turned out to be an extremely useful development, then and now. If you enjoy, say, Wi-Fi, GPS, or cellular phones, you have Lamarr to thank.

landsman

Yiddish word meaning someone from where you're from; basically, a homeboy. It's a warm term, always used positively, and the farther from home you both are, the more exciting it is to meet a landsman. In Queens, a fellow Lutowisker is a real landsman. By contrast, in Boca, a resident of West Palm Beach is just somebody to hitch a ride home with.

Lansky, Meyer

See Jewish Gangsters, page 106.

Lanzmann, Claude (1925–2018)

French intellectual and filmmaker. After spending his early life hiding from the Nazis, he joined the French Resistance at eighteen. After the war, he edited *Les Temps Modernes*, the intellectual journal founded by Jean-Paul Sartre and Simone de Beauvoir. But his most towering accomplishment was *Shoah*, his epic nine-hour masterpiece documentary about the Holocaust.

latkes

An absolute pain to grate, drain, and fry, but what you get for your troubles is a scrumptious Hanukkah hash brown.

Lauder, Estée (~1908–2004)

Born in Queens as Josephine Esther Mentzer, she became Estee, then became Estée after she started selling face creams made by her chemist uncle. She married Joseph Lauter in 1930, and they later changed their surname to Lauder. She died at ninety-five, still

Hedy Lamarr: The bombshell actress was also an engineer—she created a frequency-hopping signal that paved the way for Wi-Fi technology.

LEE, STAN

(1922–2018)

Growing up during the Great Depression, young Stanley Lieber escaped the hardship by reading books and watching Errol Flynn movies. When Lieber was seventeen, a relative got him a job as an assistant at Timely Comics, where he fetched coffee and filled inkwells while Timely's artists, men like Jack Kirby and Joe Simon, churned out popular series like *Captain America*. Less than two years later, after Timely's editor left, Lieber was asked if he wanted to temporarily take over. He said yes, but because he harbored hopes of one day writing the Great American Novel, he began writing comics under the name Stan Lee. Timely soon changed its name to Marvel, and Lee eventually proved himself as an editor and storyteller of genius. Among the characters he helped create are Spider-Man, Thor, the Incredible Hulk, the X-Men, the Fantastic Four, Iron Man, Doctor Strange, and other dudes you just can't avoid at the multiplex these days. (See comic books.)

THE INCREDIBLE STAN

The Fantastic Four (1961)	**Doctor Strange** (1963)
The Incredible Hulk (1962)	**The Avengers** (1963)
Thor (1962)	**Iron Man** (1963)
Spider-Man (1962)	**X-Men** (1963)
Ant-Man (1962)	**Black Panther** (1966)

the picture of glamour. Her son Ronald is a former US ambassador to Austria and is president of the World Jewish Congress. He runs the Ronald S. Lauder Foundation, which supports Jewish life in Europe.

Lauren, Ralph (b. 1939)

When he was born in the Bronx, he was Ralph Lifshitz. When he started Polo in 1968, after stints in the army and at Brooks Brothers, he was Ralph Lauren. Except perhaps for Jacobi Press, of the Ivy League haberdasher J. Press, no Jew was as responsible for the uniform that we associate with Waspy prep-dom.

lawyer

If you're not smart enough to be a doctor, this will do.

Lazarus, Emma (1849–1887)

Best known as the author of the poem "The New Colossus" on the base of the Statue of Liberty ("Give me your tired, your poor / Your huddled masses yearning to breathe free"), Lazarus grew up near Manhattan's Union Square, part of a wealthy, assimilated Sephardi family. Emma wrote like she was running out of time: by 1882 she'd published dozens of poems and other works and had translated the work of German Jewish poet Heinrich Heine. Ralph Waldo Emerson was her mentor (her poems have aged about as well as his), and she traveled widely, hobnobbing in Europe with Robert Browning, William Morris, and Henry James, who said of her, "You appear to have done more in three weeks than any lightfooted woman before; when you ate or slept I have not yet made definite." An activist who worked with Russian refugees detained in terrible conditions on Ward's Island in New York Harbor and volunteered with the Hebrew Immigrant Aid Society, the country's first refugee resettlement agency, it is fitting that her tribute to immigrants is immortalized on a universal symbol of freedom and democracy.

l'chaim

L'chaim means "to life" in Hebrew, and it's the standard Hebrew toast: raise a glass of schnapps or whiskey or slivovitz, say "L'chaim!" then down the hatch it goes. The phrase has moved from interjection to noun, so you can now "do a l'chaim" or "make a l'chaim." But please note: a l'chaim is properly a shot of hard liquor—don't try to make one with a glass of wine or a mug of beer.

l'dor vador

Literally, "from generation to generation." Taken from the Amidah's Kedushah prayer, it's shorthand for Jewish continuity and the Jews' obligation to maintain it.

Leah
See Matriarchs and Patriarchs, page 176.

Lear, Norman (b. 1922)
Superstar sitcom producer of the 1970s and '80s, Lear created such shows as *All in the Family*, *The Jeffersons*, *Maude*, *Sanford and Son*, and *Good Times*. His lead characters were often irascible kvetches like Sanford, the junk dealer portrayed by Redd Foxx, and the inimitable Archie Bunker, played by Carroll O'Connor.

leftovers
"The most remarkable thing about my mother is that for 30 years she served the family nothing but leftovers," the humorist Calvin Trillin famously wrote. "The original meal has never been found." Surely leftovers are a by-product of Jews' tendency to prepare way too much, which, in turn, is itself a by-product of our history of not having nearly enough (see Food and Jews, page 100).

Lemkin, Raphael (1900–1959)
Polish-born lawyer and scholar who fled World War II, in which he lost dozens of relatives, for the United States, where he taught law and coined the term *genocide*. He was instrumental in crafting the legal basis for the prosecution of Nazi war criminals at Nuremberg.

"Let my people go"
In the early chapters of Exodus, as God begins visiting the Ten Plagues upon the Egyptians, Moses repeatedly asks Pharaoh to "Let my people go," a request Pharaoh consistently denies. The phrase is a key line in the spiritual "Go Down, Moses," a song made popular by Paul Robeson, Louis Armstrong, and innumerable choirs. In more recent decades, the phrase was used on the posters of the movement to liberate Soviet Jewry.

Levi, Primo (1919–1987)

Italian Jewish chemist who in 1947 wrote *Survival in Auschwitz*, one of the first, and best, memoirs of the Holocaust. He later killed himself by jumping down the stairwell of the Turin apartment where he had lived as a child and to which he had returned after liberation.

Levine, Adam (b. 1979)
Proof that Jewish boys can grow up to become tatted, ripped, supermodel-marrying rock stars.

Lévy, Bernard-Henri (b. 1948)

This prominent Algerian-born French public intellectual, colloquially known as BHL, thinks Yiddish, dresses French, and smoulders in all languages. In the 1970s, he rose to prominence as a television-friendly swaggering lefty journalist-philosopher, which is to say that he lived in France. He writes books, directs movies, supports Israel, defends the Kurds, advocates for assorted military interventions, and marries and divorces *de temps en temps*.

Lewinsky, Monica
American activist, television personality, fashion designer, and prominent antibullying activist. Think something's missing? Fight us.

LGBT Jews

Lesbian, gay, bisexual, and trans Jews have come up in the Jewish community in recent years. They've established their own synagogues while also fighting for greater inclusion in all congregations. Rabbis in the Reconstructionist, Reform, and Conservative movements can now perform same-sex weddings, and openly LGBT members of those movements can be ordained. Community-based organizations and online communities offer queer Jews of every stripe—including the Orthodox—everything from religious programs to support groups to social events. Queer Jews have also gained tremendous visibility among the wider public: think of politicians like slain San Francisco supervisor Harvey Milk or Colorado governor Jared Polis, or performers like actor/comedian Sandra Bernhard or pop singer Troye Sivan, or writers from playwright/screenwriter Paul Rudnick (*Addams Family Values*, *In & Out*) to poet Joy Ladin, the first openly trans professor at an Orthodox institution (Yeshiva University). You can see queer Jewish life portrayed on television (*Transparent*, *Andi Mack*), film (*Call Me by Your Name*, or the documentary *Trembling Before G-d*), and stage

Lower East Side: A Jewish Festival on Essex Street in 1986

S ARTICLES
MIRADOR' PASAJE
TRAV
PHONE. 533-6660 • PASAJES
BOOKS
TALAISIM
TFILIN
MEZUZAHS
SIFREI
TORAH
Silverware
PLASTIC
TABLE CLOTHS
CANDLESTICKS
YARMULKES
PASAJES
TRAVEL
MIRADOR
PASAJ
3 HR CL
45 S&W MANUFACTURERS OF SKULL CAPS 45
SKULL CAPS & BENTCHERS
PRINTED FOR ALL OCCASIONS
APRENDA A MANEJAR
3 HORAS DE CLASE Y PELICULA
LEARN TO
REQUIRED
TAPE C

(Paula Vogel's *Indecent*, Tony Kushner's *Angels in America*). You can read about queer Jewish life in dozens of books, from *Wrestling with God and Men* by openly gay Orthodox rabbi Steven Greenberg, to editor Noach Dzmura's trans anthology *Balancing on the Mechitza*, to historian Lillian Faderman's memoir *Naked in the Promised Land*, to Lev Raphael's short-story collection *Dancing on Tisha B'Av*. Twenty-five years ago, you could have fit all the books ever published about LGBT Jews in a knapsack; today, you need a whole section of the library.

Lieberman, Joe (b. 1942)

Elected to the US Senate in 1988, Joe Lieberman became the first Jew to appear on a major party presidential ticket when he served as Al Gore's running mate in 2000. A Democrat from Connecticut who is Modern Orthodox and thus unwilling to drive on Shabbat, he famously walked through frosty Washington winters to Congress for major votes on Saturdays.

Likud

Formed in 1973 by Menachem Begin, this right-of-center Israeli party struggled under Labor's decades-long near dominance of the political scene. When it won its first election, in 1977, the stunned news anchor on Israel's sole TV channel declared it a revolution. Strongly supporting Jewish settlement in Judea and Samaria and intent on replacing Labor's socialist bent with a more deregulated, free-market economy, Likud soon rose to power: in the last forty years, it's been in power for all but ten.

Lipstadt, Deborah (b. 1947)

American historian sued by Holocaust denier David Irving for calling him, well, a Holocaust denier. Lipstadt defended herself in an English court and won, inspiring a 2016 biopic in which she was played by Rachel Weisz.

Lispector, Clarice (1920–1977)

Brazilian Jewish novelist whose family escaped pogroms in Ukraine by moving to South America. She experienced a meteoric rise to fame early on in her career after the 1943 publication of her first novel, *Near to the Wild Heart*. A lot of her fiction isn't exactly experimental, but neither is it straightforward—it deals heavily in internal monologues and nonlinear plots. Her writing can feel at times very much like an Oulipian exercise. Lispector's stories meandered, and today, with the renaissance of interest in her work, more people than ever like meandering with her.

Long Island

The other Promised Land.

Lower East Side

Downtown Manhattan neighborhood where immigrant Jews once lived in tenement walkups and sold pickles out of pushcarts. Today, a place where hipster Jews live in overpriced walkups and buy artisanally brined pickles.

lox

Cured salmon. The first thing to disappear from the break-fast, bris, or shiva spread.

Lubavitch, Lubavitcher

See **Chabad-Lubavitch**.

lulav

A palm tree frond. Together with the etrog (citron), hadass (myrtle), and aravah (willow), it's one of the four species blessed daily during the holiday of Sukkot. The commandment comes to us from Leviticus, and later traditions instruct us to shake the lulav in six directions while saying a blessing, one of Judaism's all-time funnest rituals.

FROM

"Ma nishtana"

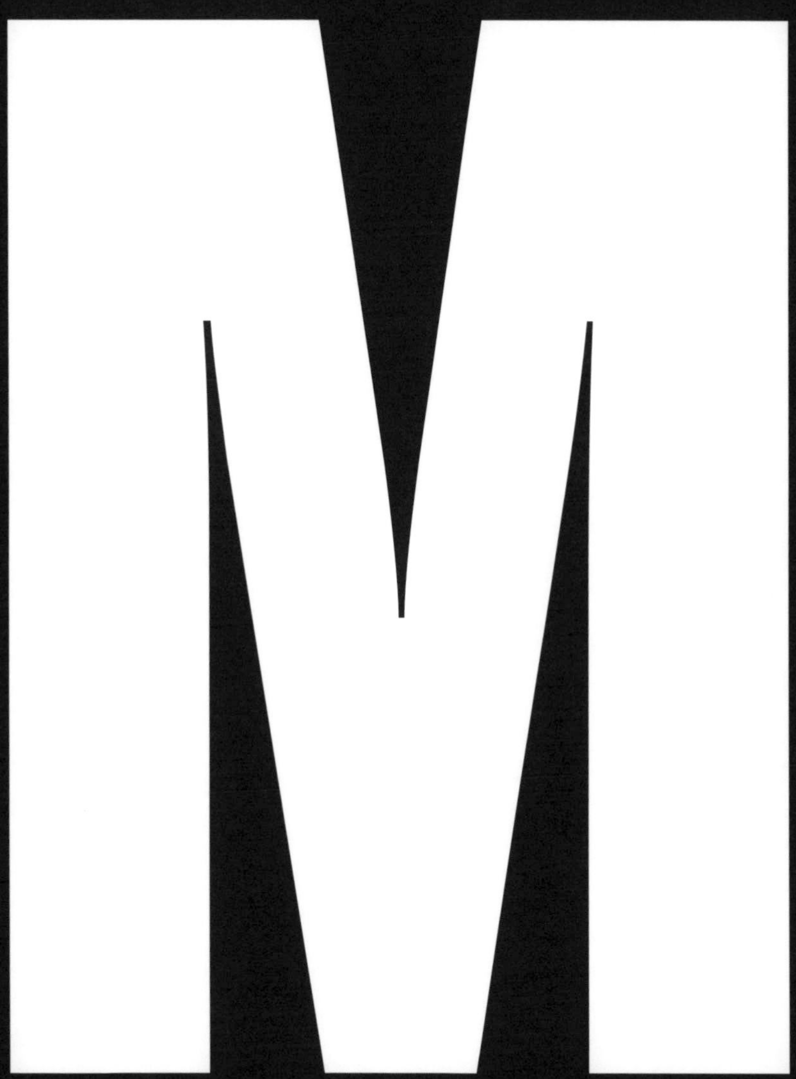

TO

Myerson, Bess

"Ma nishtana"

The phrase kicking off each of the Four Questions, asking, "Why is this night different?"

Maccabee, Judah

A kickass priest who led the Jews' revolt, from around 167 to 160 BCE, against the evil Antiochus, giving us the miraculous triumph we still celebrate each Hanukkah. The Talmud's sages never mentioned Judah, most likely because they feared the wrath of the Romans and didn't want to be seen as advocating any future rebellions. Interestingly, Judah became a Christian hero, beloved by everyone from the Crusaders to George Frideric Handel, who honored him in his oratorio *Judas Maccabaeus*. With Zionism's ascent, Judah Maccabee became a beloved action hero, and he is the guiding inspiration of the quadrennial Maccabiah Games.

Maccabees

See Hanukkah, page 122.

Maccabiah Games

The third largest sporting event in the world! (That is actually a fact: the 2017 games had ten thousand participants.) Held every four years in Israel, this international Jewish Olympics features athletes competing in everything from chess to golf to gymnastics to rugby.

machatunim

Yiddish term for what your parents are to your in-laws. That there is a word for this relationship tells you everything you need to know about our culture.

macher

Big shot. The kind of person who knows people, sits on boards, makes connections—you get it. You may not know exactly what the machers are doing, but you always want to keep on their friendly side, just in case.

machzor

The prayer book, or siddur, used specifically for the holidays of Rosh Hashanah and Yom Kippur.

Madoff, Bernard (b. 1938)

See Shonde, page 240.

mah-jongg

Tile game invented in China in the nineteenth century that has been part of the Jewish American experience since the 1920s. The introduction of mah-jongg to America is largely attributed to Joseph Babcock, a Standard Oil employee who encountered it while working in Suzhou, China. He added English numerals to the tiles, created a booklet that simplified the game's rules, and helped import thousands of sets. The game's popularity soared between 1923 and 1925, with its elaborately adorned tiles inspiring mah-jongg fashions, recipes, and other novelties. In the Jewish community, mah-jongg made regular appearances at synagogue functions and fundraisers, thanks to its portability and exoticism. In 1937, a group of Jewish women formed the National Mah Jongg League, which streamlined the rules and indirectly cemented the game's association with Jewish life and philanthropy. In the postwar years, it became a pastime at Jewish resorts, and a regular fixture of Jewish home life. Today, mah-jongg remains a tradition for established players, while enticing new players with its aesthetic, tactile, and nostalgic qualities.

Maimonides (c. 1135–1204)

Common moniker for Moses ben Maimon; he is also known in Hebrew as the Rambam, making him a man of many names. A Sephardi medieval philosopher, physician, and Jewish thinker, Maimonides was born in Córdoba, Spain. His *Guide for the Perplexed* (1190) is a masterwork explaining Judaism in rational terms, and the *Mishneh Torah* (compiled between 1170 and 1180), is a lucid and compelling catalog of most of halacha, the collective body of law. His "negative theology"—arguing that while we can't say for certain that God exists, we can say that he doesn't not-exist—was deeply influential for a host of Christian theologians, including Thomas Aquinas.

Malamud, Bernard (1914–1986)

Underappreciated today, the American literary genius may never again get his due, largely because his best works were short stories. Each century is allowed at most three canonical short-story writers, and in twentieth-century Anglophone literature, Flannery O'Connor, Raymond Carver, and Alice Munro got the slots. But go read the stories collected in *The Magic Barrel* (1958) and just *try* denying that they are unimprovable masterpieces. (Start with "The First Seven Years," "Angel Levine," and the title story.) Malamud's star has dimmed for many other reasons: he was overshadowed by the bigger personality of Saul Bellow and the bigger productivity of Philip Roth; he was a whimsical magical realist at a time, the 1950s through the 1970s, when sardonic realism was all the rage; the most popular movie made from his writing, *The Natural*, had Robert Redford but little else going for it; and his writing was apolitical and resistant to trends, with little attention to the Holocaust or Israel. But in the end, he was a victim of his own discretion and brevity. He said more in ten pages than most writers can in five hundred, but most readers respond better to a clobber than a whisper.

Malina, Joshua (b. 1966)

Actor beloved for his roles as Will Bailey on *The West Wing*, Jeremy Goodwin on *Sports Night*, and David Rosen on *Scandal* and, more recently, for his public displays of Judaism on social media.

Mamet, David (b. 1947)

The author of *Glengarry Glen Ross*, about a cutthroat office full of morally bankrupt real estate agents, and other mind-bending plays and screenplays, Mamet has later in life become an engaged Jew and a super-Zionist, perplexing many in the left-leaning theatrical community. His pugnacious 2006 book *The Wicked Son: Anti-Semitism, Jewish Self-Hatred, and the Jews* is a product of his Jewish turn. Even if you can't get with his religion or politics, you can have your mind blown by *Oleanna* or *The Spanish Prisoner.*

Mamet, Zosia (b. 1988)

Actress best known for portraying Shoshanna Shapiro, the simple yet complex JAP on *Girls*. Daughter of David Mamet.

Manilow, Barry (b. 1943)

"I write the songs that make the whole world sing," Barry Manilow sang in 1975. "I write the songs of love and special things / I write the songs that make the young girls cry / I write the songs, I write the songs." And write them he did, becoming one of the century's most beloved purveyors of saccharine, Vegas-worthy anthems. Born Barry Alan Pincus, raised in Brooklyn, the singer-songwriter is known for "Mandy," for "Can't Smile without You," and for inheriting Liberace's mantle as your grandmother's favorite showman. Although his third act has been marred by the unfortunate hairstyle choices so common to celebrated men of a certain age, it has also been a time of personal triumph: he proudly came out as gay in 2017, surprising nobody (except your grandmother).

Manischewitz

The kosher-food company responsible for the classic kosher wine, known for its purple hue and its sickly sweet taste. Without a bottle of Manischewitz, no Passover table is complete; with it, no Passover table is truly elegant. Classy Jews have traded up to any of the hundreds of "better" kosher wines, but anyone with a sense of history will proudly quaff Manischewitz, which because of its sweetness is also a terrific starter wine for little Jews. We're not the only ones who love the sweet stuff: it's the drink of choice, on ice, on San Andres and Providencia, a pair of Colombian-territory Caribbean islands off the coast of Nicaragua. The Manischewitz company, founded in Cincinnati in 1888 and now owned by a soulless private-equity firm, also introduced the popular crackers known as Tam-Tams and makes matzos, egg noodles, and more.

March of the Living

Annual gathering of students from around the world who march from Auschwitz to Birkenau to remember the evils of Nazism and honor the memory of its victims, then are whisked off to Israel, which some find deeply moving and others find problematic.

MARX BROTHERS

THE BROTHERS' BEST

Animal Crackers (1930)

A Night at the Opera (1935)

Duck Soup (1933)

A Day at the Races (1937)

Vaudeville stars who did groundbreaking work in film and television, Groucho (Julius, 1890–1977), Harpo (Adolf, 1888–1964), Chico (Leonard, 1887–1961), Zeppo (Herbert, 1901–1979), and Gummo (Milton, 1892–1977; don't worry, he never made any movies, so it's okay if you never heard of him) Marx created a comedy of chaos that went from erudite wordplay one minute to lowbrow slapstick the next. Groucho's quick-witted persona influenced everyone from Bugs Bunny to Woody Allen, and Harpo's near-Dadaist silent prop comedy was bizarre but strangely warm. Why Chico read as Italian we can't tell you. Zeppo couldn't act even in the straight roles, so he eventually took an office position with the Marx team. (Gummo was supposedly hilarious but didn't like performing.) In 1930, as talking pictures were still in their infancy, Groucho would slip esoteric Yiddish terms like *schnorrer* into his songs. Their anti-war masterpiece *Duck Soup* regularly ranks high on critics' lists of all-time favorites. But never mind that, pick a card.

margarine

This nondairy butter substitute is the original kosher hack: if you keep kosher and are serving meat, you can't use butter, but margarine will do the trick. An elderly person in your life may still refer to margarine as "oleo" or, even more old-school, "oleomargarine." It was originally made from beef tallow but now is made from vegetable oil.

marijuana

Is cannabis the kaneh bosem plant mentioned in the Bible? Will more rabbis declare medicinal marijuana kosher, as some have these last few years? Will making it legal become the next big project for the tikkun olam crowd? And if not now, when?

marit ayin

Hebrew for "appearance to the eye," this halachic concept reminds us that people are fond of jumping to conclusions, which is why you should think twice before doing something that may look shady, even if it isn't. Imagine, for example, a religious guy walking into a burger joint and ordering one of those delicious new vegan burgers that look *just like the real thing*, topped with a slice of cashew cheese and seitan bacon. It's totally kosher, but if the man's buddies were to walk by and take a look at his plate, they might think that their friend had abandoned his faith and now freely munched on bacon cheeseburgers.

Marjorie Morningstar

Bestselling 1955 Herman Wouk novel featuring, arguably, the first depiction of the Jewish American Princess, or JAP, in literature. It's also a 1958 movie starring the goyish but ethnically ambiguous actress Natalie Wood. "Marjorie Morningstar" is Marjorie Morgenstern's stage name—she wants to be an actress. She's gorgeous and vibrant and falls in love with a pretentious Jewish writer who mocks her for not eating bacon and refusing to have premarital sex. He calls her a "Shirley," his term for a boring Jewish wifey type who only cares about a giant diamond ring and a house in the 'burbs. The question of whether the book's ending is sexist or satisfying is one for your book club. *(Spoiler alert: it's sexist.)*

maror

You think you know this Passover staple? Think again: according to the Mishnah, the term *maror*, Hebrew for "bitter," applies to all sorts of vegetables, including, most famously, horseradish and lettuce, but also chicory, sweet clover, and dandelion. Unless you're foraging for everything on your Seder plate, however, you're likely using the traditional *chrain*, which is grated horseradish mixed with cooked beets. The symbolism's the same: reminding us of slavery's bitter afflictions.

marrano

See **converso**.

The Marvelous Mrs. Maisel

Television series that premiered in March 2017 on Amazon. Created, written, and produced by Amy Sherman-Palladino and Dan Palladino, the married team behind *Gilmore Girls*, the show follows Miriam "Midge" Maisel, a Jewish housewife in 1950s New York City, as her picture-perfect marriage falls apart and she seeks refuge onstage at comedy clubs. Played by Rachel Brosnahan, Midge is bold and assertive, with great comic timing and a sharp Joan Rivers–esque wit. Viewers, both Jewish and not, flocked to the series—which in its first season won the Emmy and Golden Globe awards for best comedy—even as some grumbled about the Jewish inconsistencies (who serves lamb at Yom Kippur break-fast?).

Marxism

A movement based on the economic and political theories of Karl Marx (1818–1883). The son of a middle-class, ethnically Jewish family that converted to Evangelical Christianity before his birth, Marx, along with Friedrich Engels, the scion of a family of wealthy German industrialists, cowrote *The Communist Manifesto*. Marxism holds that history is driven principally not by people or ideas but by the relationships between materialist forces and the struggle between economic classes. In 1844, Marx published "On the Jewish Question," in which he wrote, "What is the secular basis of Judaism? Practical need, self-interest. What is the worldly religion of the Jew? Huckstering." For some Marxism nearly as funny as that, see **Marx Brothers**.

Masada

Big rock in southern Israel that overlooks the Dead Sea; in ancient times, it was a fortified home for Herod the Great, who built palaces on the plateau at the top. In the years 73–74 CE, at the end of the Jewish-Roman war, Jewish warriors at Masada held off the Roman army—at least until they didn't, at which point 960 of them committed suicide. The story, or legend, is chronicled by Jewish historian Josephus, who had been captured by the Romans earlier in the war. The worthy resistance, and heroic suicide, of the Jewish zealots at Masada has become prime Zionist lore, annually drawing thousands of tourists—from bar and bat mitzvah babes to Birthrighters to bubbes—to climb the dusty path to the top at sunrise and take many pictures with their iPhones.

Masbia

A network of kosher soup kitchens in Brooklyn and Queens, feeding more than four hundred people daily. Started by two Hasidic activists, it's funded partially by New York City and largely by local philanthropists, and it takes pride in its upscale dining rooms, designed to give the needy a sense of dignity and comfort.

Mason, Jackie (b. 1931)

A critic once derided this genius comedian by saying that he spoke "with the Yiddish locutions of an immigrant who just completed a course in English. By mail." But Mason, born Yacov Moshe Maza in Sheboygan, Wisconsin, is a real trailblazer, easily one of the most underrated comics in history. He was doing insult humor years before Don Rickles showed up, and was a rising star until a run-in with Ed Sullivan derailed his career (see It Should Be a Holiday!, page 126). He recovered with a string of movie appearances and, later, several wildly successful one-man shows on Broadway, touching on politics, race, gender, and other sensitive subjects. He also voiced Rabbi Hyman Krustofski, Krusty the Clown's father, on *The Simpsons*, making him one of the most prominent Jewish characters on American TV.

Matisyahu (b. 1979)

The Orthodox rapper shocked fans when, in 2011, he shaved his beard and announced that he was no longer Hasidic. He had been something of a novelty, with his beatboxing and reggae-infused music and his long beard, peyot, and kippah. Born Matthew Paul Miller in a Reconstructionist Jewish family, he began identifying with the Chabad branch of Hasidism in 2001, and his early hits reflected his religious bent: on 2004's "King without a Crown," he rapped, "Sing to my God, songs of love and healing / I want Moshiach now, time it starts revealing." Post-beard, he struggled to find his sound—and look—but has since settled into an endearing dad-reggae vibe.

matkot

The official sport of every Israeli beach. It's kind of like paddleball, if the goal was to assassinate or maim the other player by hitting the hard rubber projectile as hard as you could with your paddle while directing it to your opponent's head, throat, or nether regions. Even if you're not fond of playing, you're still not safe: try to catch some rays, and all you'll hear is the menacing *thwok thwok* reminding you that there's a ball out there with your name on it.

matriarchs

See Matriarchs and Patriarchs, page 176.

matrilineal descent

According to traditional Jewish law, Jewish identity is passed down by the mother (who got it from her mother, who got it from her mother, and so on). If your mother is Jewish, so are you. According to legend, Jews used matrilineal descent because we always know who a baby's mother is but can't know for sure who the father is. However, in Torah, Joseph is married to a non-Jew, but his sons are considered Jewish. The same went for Moses and King Solomon. The rabbis of the Talmud wrote a new rule requiring matrilineal descent, possibly influenced by Roman law of the time. Anyway, in more liberal wings of Judaism, this rule is changing. The Reform movement, for example, now honors both patrilineal and matrilineal descent.

matzo

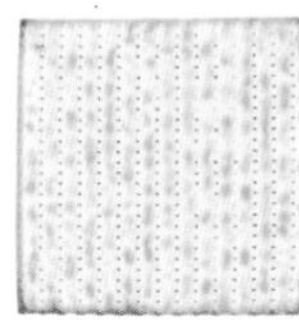

Unleavened bread, the bread of affliction, the dry cracker that we are commanded—not just asked, but *commanded*—to eat during the holiday of Passover. According to the Torah, the Jews fleeing the Egyptians in the desert did not have time to let their bread rise, so they ate their bread unleavened. And so do we. For as it is written in Exodus 12:18: "In the first month, from the fourteenth day of the month at evening, you shall eat unleavened bread until the twenty-first day of the month at evening." And if we are smart, we eat it with butter, or slathered in egg yolk, or fried with both in a tasty matzo brei. But not if you don't eat gebrokts! (Again, nothing's ever really simple with our people.)

MatzoBall

First held in Boston in 1986, this Christmas Eve get-together for young, single Jews has become legendary, spreading to numerous other cities and bringing about, according to its organizers, more than one thousand marriages. These days, a few MatzoBall babies, children born to parents who met at the annual shindig, are now attending the party to find their own bashert.

Maus

A graphic novel about the Holocaust, serialized from 1980 to 1991. In 1992, it became the first graphic novel to win a Pulitzer Prize. In cartoonist Art Spiegelman's telling, the Jews were the mice, the Germans the cats, and the Poles pigs. The book elevated graphic novels into a serious and respectable art form. It also made Holocaust literature more popular than ever before.

May, Elaine (b. 1932)

After starting out performing in her father's traveling Yiddish theater company, May (born Elaine Berlin) became famous for her improv comedy duo with Mike Nichols. She influenced the sensibilities of a generation of comics who copied her grasp of irony, and, later, as an actor, writer, and

Maus: Art Spiegelman's graphic series, first published in 1987, revolutionized both graphic novels and Holocaust literature.

MATRIARCHS & PATRIARCHS

Every Friday night, Jewish parents around the world bless their daughters with a prayer that they grow up and be like Sarah, Rachel, Rebecca, and Leah, the foremothers of Judaism, whose stories are told in Genesis. In non-Orthodox Judaism, their names have been added to prayers that used to mention only their husbands.

The Jewish forefathers—Abraham, Isaac, and Jacob—are also central figures in Jewish prayer and literature, and are frequently evoked in Jewish liturgy as a reminder to God to show the Jewish people mercy and compassion, for the sake of the patriarchs' deeds.

SARAH

Commended for her hospitality, Sarah is described as maintaining a tent that was open on four sides, to welcome travelers from any direction. The wife of Abraham is also remembered for her laughter upon learning that God intended for her to conceive Isaac at age ninety, and her command to send Hagar and Ishmael into the desert.

ABRAHAM

The founding father of Judaism is associated with hospitality, love, and faithfulness. He heeds the Lord and circumcises himself at ninety-nine (how's *that* for piety?). Most famously, he commits to binding and killing his son Isaac because God commands it (in the end, God stays his hand).

ISAAC

One moment he's about to be sacrificed by his father, the next he's elderly and blind and fooled by his wife and his son Jacob. But maybe Isaac, whose Hebrew name, Yitzchak, literally means "he will laugh," had the last laugh, enjoying a life free of the drama experienced by his father and son.

REBECCA

You know that bit of parenting advice that tells you never to pick favorites? Nobody told Isaac's wife, Rebecca, who helps her younger son, Jacob, deceive her firstborn, Esau, and then his father, Isaac.

JACOB

Abraham's grandson first manipulated his older brother, Esau, into selling his birthright for a bowl of lentil stew. Then he tricked his father into giving him the firstborn blessing intended for Esau. Later on, his name was changed to Israel—"one who wrestles with God"—giving the nation its name.

RACHEL

This matriarch was so beautiful that Jacob agreed to work for seven years for the right to marry her (and seven more after being tricked into marrying her sister). Like other famous women in the Torah, Rachel was infertile for a long time—when she finally did give birth, she gave us Joseph and Benjamin.

LEAH

Talk about getting no love: Leah was married to Jacob only after her father, Laban, tricked him into marrying her instead of her younger sister, Rachel. Still, Leah was rewarded with being, arguably, the real matriarch of the Jewish people: most of us today are likely descendants of her son Judah.

director, contributed to some of the best-loved movies in recent memory, including *Tootsie*, *Reds*, and *Heaven Can Wait*.

Maysles, Albert (1926–2015)

Groundbreaking documentarian and hipster eyewear icon, Maysles, with his brother David, gave us such classics of cinema verité as *Gimme Shelter* and *Grey Gardens,* pioneering the "fly on the wall" approach, devoid of narration or titles, that would ultimately become the standard of highbrow documentary filmmaking. He not only introduced us to the Beales of *Grey Gardens* but also convinced artsy Jewish boys everywhere that with the right pair of glasses, they too could look like a downtown auteur.

mazel tov

Or *mazaaal tov*, if you want to go Hebrew rather than Yiddish. Meaning something like "good fortune," it's the ultimate Jewish phrase of congratulations, fit for any occasion. It's so useful that it has entered, with some variation, into a host of other languages: *vermasseln*, for example, is German for screwing things up, as in having really bad massel, or mazel, or mazal.

Meara, Anne (1929–2015)

See **Stiller, Jerry, and Anne Meara.**

mechitza

A wall or barrier that separates women from men in an Orthodox synagogue. The mechitza can be high or it can be low; it can be entirely opaque or it can be a fabric scrim. The forcefulness of the mechitza says something about the Orthodox shul you are dealing with. A high, wooden mechitza, completely obscuring any view of the women's section from the men's, and vice versa, is a sign that a congregation is really, truly, *utterly* serious about keeping the sexes apart during prayer. A mechitza that is solid up to about chest level but then is topped off by smoky glass or a length of muslin says, "We're Orthodox, but we're not crazy. Our kids are allowed to go to Mets games and secular universities."

Meeropol, Abel (1903–1986)

American songwriter who wrote the 1937 classic "Strange Fruit," the song about lynching made famous by Billie Holiday. A Communist, Meeropol sympathized with Julius and Ethel Rosenberg, and when they were executed in 1953 for conspiracy to commit espionage, he adopted and raised their sons, Michael and Robert.

Meir, Golda (1898–1978)

Fourth prime minister of Israel; she served from 1969 to 1974. She was one of the first female heads of state ever, the only woman to lead Israel, and the most important human ever to grow up in Milwaukee.

Member of the Tribe (MOT)

A fellow Jew.

Mendes-Nasi, Doña Gracia (1510–1569)

One of the wealthiest Jewish women in Renaissance Europe, she used her power and influence to build an underground network that helped hundreds of Portuguese and Spanish conversos escape the Inquisition.

menorah

Not the thing you light on Hanukkah. That is a menorah, yes, but it's a specific kind, properly called a hanukkiah. In Exodus, God tells Moses to build a seven-branched lamp or candelabra, a menorah—but according to the Talmud, one may not use such a true menorah outside the Temple, which of course was destroyed in 70 CE. So that menorah now exists mainly as a motif in Jewish art (and as the official logo of the State of Israel).

mensch

The kind of person you ought to be.

meshuga

Yiddish (and Hebrew) word for a crazy person. Also known as a *meshugeneh*. And frequently known to engage in meshugas, or mishigas, which is the sort of tomfoolery a meshugeneh enjoys.

MILLER, ARTHUR

(1915–2005)

MILLER'S BEST

All My Sons
(1947)

The Crucible
(1953)

***Death of a Salesman* (1949)**

***A View from the Bridge* (1955)**

Along the course of your life you've likely had at least two encounters with Arthur Miller's canonical plays. Chances are you were assigned *The Crucible* as required reading in high school and have seen a filmed production of *Death of a Salesman.* Miller's plays are some of the most important works for the stage of the past one hundred years. In the great tradition of celebrated intellectual figures, he ended up before the House Un-American Activities Committee during the McCarthy era. Miller was also married to Marilyn Monroe, who converted to Judaism, leading Egypt to ban her movies.

Messiah, Moshiach

According to Jewish tradition, he'll only come when all Jews are pious and righteous and kind to each other. Also according to Jewish tradition, once all Jews are pious and righteous and kind to each other, they'll hardly have any need for the Messiah. Maimonides best captured the Jewish attitude toward the redeemer when he noted that when the Messiah finally comes, everything will be exactly the same, except that Jews would no longer have to live under foreign yoke—which is why some Jews saw the birth of the State of Israel as the fulfillment of the messianic promise.

Messianic Jews

"Messianic Jews," as they call themselves, are usually ethnic Jews who believe in the divinity of Jesus but still identify with their ancestral Judaism. In short, they see themselves as Jewish followers of Jesus—Jewish Christians, if you will. They are Jews who have been "saved" or "born again" but don't want to leave their Jewish identities behind. Often they call their houses of worship synagogues or temples; they use smatterings of Hebrew in their worship; and they may observe Jewish holidays, like Sukkot or Purim, that most Christians have abandoned. They say (accurately) that the early Christians, too, identified as Jews, and thus they believe there is nothing problematic about this identity. Which, from a Christian point of view, there isn't. But other Jews think Messianic Jews are trying to have it both ways. Culturally and religiously speaking, to accept Jesus as Messiah is to leave the Jewish community behind. And there is a perfectly good name for Jews who believe Jesus is the Messiah: Christians.

metzitzah b'peh

A custom in some Haredi communities—a sizable minority—in which the mohel places his mouth over the newly circumcised baby's penis during the bris and sucks out some blood. The tradition is not in Torah and has led to fatal cases of neonatal herpes.

Meyers, Seth

See **Alda, Alan**.

mezuzah

A piece of parchment, called a klaf, placed into a decorative casing and attached to the doorpost of a Jewish home. On the klaf, the Shema prayer has been handwritten by a *sofer*, or scribe. Affixing a mezuzah to one's door fulfills the commandment in Deuteronomy to write God's commandments "upon the posts of thy house, and on thy gates," and evokes the story of the Exodus, with the Jews avoiding the plague of the death of the firstborn by marking their doorposts with the blood of the paschal lamb. Some Jews believe every room, the bathroom excluded, ought to have a

mezuzah, while others think the front door's enough. It's customary to kiss the mezuzah on your way in and out of the house (by touching the mezuzah and then kissing your fingers). The mezuzah is also believed by many Jews to bring a home good luck and protect it from evil. And not just Jews, anymore, apparently: in 2010, the *New York Times* reported on the growing tradition of gentiles who have bought houses once owned by Jews and decided to keep the mezuzot up.

Miami Beach

The *other* other Promised Land.

Midler, Bette (b. 1945)

"The Divine Miss M" is an American chanteuse, actor, and redhead best known for her songs "The Rose" and "Wind Beneath My Wings." An icon to gay men of a certain generation, she got her start singing at the Continental Baths bathhouse in New York City in 1970; her accompanist for a time was Barry Manilow. Did you ever know that you're her hero? That you're everything she wishes she could be?

Midrash

A genre of biblical exegesis. Midrashim (the plural) can be legalistic, but they can also take the form of legends and fantastic stories addressing some difficult-to-understand passage in the Torah.

mikveh

The ancient Jewish practice of full-body immersion in a body of water, which historically was an ocean, lake, or river. Since most Jews don't have access in all weather to a naturally occurring mikveh, the term usually refers to a constructed mikveh: a bath, housed inside a small building, that holds a portion of natural, flowing water, which can be taken from, for instance, a melting glacier or rain-collecting cistern. The mikveh is central to the Orthodox Jewish lifestyle: women must immerse in the mikveh after their period and after childbirth, and observant men may immerse to purify before a wedding, before High Holidays, or even before morning prayer. But today, many groups have sought to make a mikveh of one's own: there are men's mikvaot (the plural), and innovative liturgists have written prayers for women to say when immersing after mastectomies, stillbirths, and divorces. The mikveh has become the place where spiritual Jews of all denominations mark milestones.

milchig

Yiddish for "milky," indicating that a meal contains dairy, which matters because Jews who keep kosher don't mix milk and meat. So after eating anything milchig, they wait for a period of time before eating meat again.

Milk, Harvey (1930–1978)

Jewish boy from Long Island who moved in 1972 to San Francisco, opened a camera shop that became an activist hub for the city's gay community, got elected to the city's Board of Supervisors, and was murdered by an angry former colleague on the board. Milk was the first openly gay elected official in California, and his outspokenness, charisma, and violent death made him famous as a queer pioneer. He has been memorialized in the 1984 documentary *The Times of Harvey Milk* and in the 2008 Gus Van Sant movie *Milk*, in which he was played by Sean Penn. (See **LGBT Jews**.)

minyan

The quorum of ten Jews—in Orthodox Judaism, ten Jewish males—required for certain Jewish rituals. For example, without a minyan, the Torah cannot be read aloud; a wedding can't be held; and certain prayers in the daily service, such as the Kaddish or the repetition of the Amidah, cannot be said. Typically, one is not counted in the minyan until after the age of bar or bat mitzvah, although in ancient times some sages said that any child who was sufficiently learned could be counted. If you're Jewish, and somebody ever asks you to come "help make the minyan," go: you might be the tenth man or woman, the one who makes it possible, say, for a mourner to recite the prayer for the dead. It's a mitzvah.

Miriam

The paragon of sisterly love, she watched over her baby brother, Moses, as he floated on the Nile and helped secure his adoption by Pharaoh's daughter. Later, as Moses led the Israelites through the parted Red Sea, Miriam played the timbrel and sang, inspiring the Israelites with her prophecies.

mishloach manot

Literally meaning "sending portions," this mitzvah, one of Judaism's most festive, involves sending your friends small gift baskets stuffed with delicious food on the holiday of Purim.

Miami Beach: Collins Avenue, the city's main thoroughfare, as seen from the iconic Fontainebleau hotel in 1957

Mishnah

Meaning "study by repetition," the Mishnah is, without doubt, the central work of rabbinic literature. It was compiled by a group of rabbis called the Tannaim, of whom we know about 120, over a period of about two hundred years during the first and second centuries CE. Yehuda HaNasi, who died in 217 CE and served as the leader of the Jewish community during the Roman occupation, was the final redactor of the Mishnah. The first generation of Tannaim lived through the destruction of the Second Temple in 70 CE, and their mission was a particularly daunting one: to save Judaism by turning it from a temple-based religion into one focused on textual study and analysis. The implications of this move are profound.

The Mishnah has six orders, or Sedarim, collectively referred to as the Shas (Shisha Sedarim in Hebrew), a term that is often used to refer to the Talmud as a whole (the Talmud being an extended commentary on the Mishnah). Each deals with a particular topic. The six are:

Zeraim, or seeds, dealing with agricultural law, tithing, etc.

Moed, or festival, covering the laws of Shabbat and the holidays

Nashim, or women, addressing marriages, divorces, and sex

Nezikin, or damages, dealing with civil law and the courts

Kodashim, or holy things, dealing with sacrificial rites and dietary laws

Tohorot, or purities, dealing with the purity or impurity of the dead, food, etc.

Each order contains between seven and twelve tractates, for a total of sixty-three. Some of the famous Tannaim who make frequent appearances include Hillel, Shammai, Yochanan Ben Zakai, Akiva, and Shimon Bar Yochai, who tradition believes also wrote Sefer HaZohar, the main text of Kabbalah.

mitzvah, mitzvot

There are 613 of these divine commandments, and 248 of them (the number of organs in the human body) identify things you should be doing, while 365 (the number of days in the year) represent things you should not. They cover every aspect of human existence, from prayers and blessings to animal husbandry. Some are obvious (no incest! yuck) while others are obscure (no consulting with . . . wizards? Uh, okay). And some are eternal, like always loving and fearing God.

Mizrahi Jews

Jews who hail from Middle Eastern countries like Iraq, Iran, Yemen, Egypt, Syria, or Lebanon. They are not to be confused with Sephardi Jews, who trace their lineage to Spain and Portugal, although most Mizrahi Jews follow Sephardi customs. According to the latest available statistics, 61 percent of Israeli Jews are fully or partially Mizrahi.

Modern Orthodox

See Branches of Judaism, page 44.

mohel, mohelet

A ritual circumciser, trained to perform the covenant of brit milah, or, in Yiddish, bris. The circumcision is technically the duty of the boy's father, so the mohel will ask the parents to verbally confirm the outsourcing of this sacred obligation. You'll still often hear the Yiddish pronunciation, *moyel*, but if you want to go full Hebrew, it's *moe-hell*. In non-Orthodox Judaism, you can hire—for this very important task—a female mohel, and she's called a mohelet. (It's hardly a new trend: In the Bible, Moses was circumcised by his mother.)

money

According to the anti-Semites, a thing Jews control all of. According to your bank statement, a thing you could use a lot more of.

monotheism

Belief in one god. Our gift to the world.

Montreal bagel

For those who think size matters, the Montreal bagel may compel you to raise an eyebrow. Compared to the girthier New York specimen, the Montreal bagel is small and skinny, roughly eleven centimeters in diameter with a gaping three-centimeter-round hole (yes, we're measuring in metric—this is Canada, after all). It's boiled in honey-sweetened water, often coated in sesame seeds, loaded up on long narrow peels, and baked in a wood-burning oven. Haters are gonna hate, but before you question the legitimacy of this bagel, you must try one hot out of the oven from St. Viateur or Fairmount Bagels, two institutions in the Mile End neighborhood of Montreal that are the standard-bearers of the tradition.

IN THE MID-1920S, SONGWRITER JEROME KERN WROTE A PITHY TRIBUTE TO HIS MOST FAMOUS COLLEAGUE: "IRVING BERLIN HAS NO PLACE IN AMERICAN MUSIC. HE *IS* AMERICAN MUSIC." IT MAY BE A STRETCH TO EXTEND KERN'S FORMULA FROM BERLIN TO THE JEWS AT LARGE—BUT IT'S NOT A HUGE LEAP. FOR NEARLY A CENTURY AND A HALF, JEWS HAVE BEEN PIVOTAL SHAPERS OF POP, LEAVING AN INDELIBLE MARK IN BOTH THE CREATIVE AND BUSINESS SPHERES OF VAUDEVILLE, TIN PAN ALLEY, BROADWAY, MOVIE MUSICALS, RAGTIME, JAZZ, ROCK AND ROLL, AND HIP-HOP. STRUCTURALLY, SONICALLY, SPIRITUALLY, AMERICAN MUSIC IS UNIMAGINABLE WITHOUT JEWS.

The story of the pop music business, like the Hollywood film industry, begins with scrappy Jewish entrepreneurs. In 1886, three teenage brothers, Isidore, Julius, and Jay Witmark, established the New York music publishing company M. Witmark and Sons. Soon dozens of song outfits, most of them Jewish owned, were clustered on and around Manhattan's West Twenty-eighth Street, an area that became known as Tin Pan Alley because of the clatter of ill-tuned pianos that poured from publishers' offices into the street. The new music firms brought energy and innovation—an emphasis on factory-style production, hard-sell promotion, and songs with broad populist appeal—to what had previously been a sleepy cottage industry. One of the first Jewish songwriter-moguls, Charles K. Harris, hung a sign on his office door that a shmatte salesman could be proud of: "Songs written to order."

Tin Pan Alley's music was jaunty and modern, with rhythms imported from black ragtime and lyrics that emphasized novelty and topicality. The songs reached audiences via sheet music sales and live performances, often by Jews. Vaudeville headliners like Al Jolson, Sophie Tucker, Fanny Brice, and Eddie Cantor gave American pop an unmistakably Jewish tinge—spicing performances with shtick derived from Yiddish theatrical traditions and dousing sentimental ballads with gallons of schmaltz.

In the 1920s, a new songwriting vanguard pioneered a more refined kind of song: melodically sumptuous, harmonically sophisticated, inflected with African American blues and jazz and European classical music, with lyrics that made wry poetry from the slangy American vernacular. The result was the so-called Great American Songbook, a body of enduring American standards that was largely the creation of Jews just a step or two removed from the Pale of Settlement: Berlin, Kern, George and Ira Gershwin, Richard Rodgers and Lorenz Hart, Oscar Hammerstein II, Harold Arlen, and Yip Harburg. The period's most celebrated gentile composer, Cole Porter, once announced that he had discovered the secret to songwriting greatness: "I'll write Jewish tunes."

Another wave of Jewish songwriters emerged in the rock and soul era. The new pop dream factory was the Brill Building in Midtown Manhattan, where Jerry Leiber and Mike Stoller, Gerry Goffin and Carole King, Burt Bacharach and Hal David, Phil Spector, and others crafted irresistable teen pop hits. Jewish singers like Barbra Streisand and Neil Diamond updated the brassy balladeering of the vaudeville stars. The singer-songwriter movement of the 1960s and '70s brought more Jewish voices: Paul Simon, Randy Newman, Laura Nyro, and the indomitable Bob Dylan, né Robert Zimmerman, whose poetic brilliance, lashing moral vision, and tricksterish persona-play all carried a distinctly Jewish flavor. Jews played leading roles in arty proto-punk (Lou Reed), punk (the Ramones), glam and metal (Kiss, David Lee Roth), and virtually every genre in between.

But the greatest Jewish influence was behind the scenes. As record producers, managers, and moguls, Jews dominated the record business for much of the twentieth century and continue to play an outsize role in the twenty-first.

Why, exactly, have Jews flourished in American music? The simplest answer: It's a good gig. Jewish immigrants brought an expressive music culture to the New World and gravitated to show business at a time when more respectable professions were closed to them. But the deeper reason may lie in the Jewish knack, as perennial outsiders, for the kind of cultural cross-pollination that is a hallmark of American pop. In particular, Jews played a crucial role as mediators of black music. To survey black-Jewish musical interactions—a saga that takes in Jolson's infamous blackface performances, Berlin's ragtime hits, the Gershwin brothers' *Porgy and Bess*, Benny Goodman's jazz stardom, and the relationship of Jewish musical impresarios and African American musicians—is to confront a history that is fruitful and fraught, defined by both collaboration and exploitation.

But Jewish musical ventriloquism is rich, varied, and woolly. Whether it's Arlen and Harburg channeling the voice of a Kansan schoolgirl in "Over the Rainbow," Dylan distilling centuries of folk tradition into his ironic-prophetic disquisitions, or the Beastie Boys crashing rap's party like mischievous hipster-badkhans, Jews have found inspired ways to transmute musical ideas and influences into something new—an ineffable Other Thing that we may as well call "Jewish."

Moses
You may know him largely from the Haggadah or that Charlton Heston movie, but the Jewish people's greatest leader—who led us out of slavery in Egypt and brought us the first five books of Torah—was a dark and complicated figure. Frequently exasperated with his stiff-necked people, he nonetheless persevered. Prone to tyranny, he nonetheless accepted his advisors' wise counsel and set up a representative system of government. Leading his people to the cusp of Canaan but not permitted to enter it, he became the embodiment of the sacrifices that leaders frequently must make. In an eerie turn of events, Martin Luther King Jr. delivered a speech on April 3, 1968, saying that he, like Moses, had been to the mountaintop and seen the Promised Land. He was assassinated the following day.

Mossad
Who's asking?

Mostel, Zero (1915–1977)
Broadway's first and still most iconic Tevye in *Fiddler on the Roof.*

BESS MYERSON

Mount Sinai
Mountain in Egypt where the Israelites received God's laws. Also, the hospital on the Upper East Side of Manhattan where your aunt Sylvia had her gallbladder removed.

Mourner's Kaddish
See **Kaddish**; **death**.

MS *St. Louis*
The MS *St. Louis* was an ocean liner that embarked from Hamburg, Germany, on May 13, 1939. On board were 937 men, women, and children, the majority of them Jews fleeing Hitler's advancing agenda. Refused entry by the authorities in Havana, Cuba, the ship's captain, Gustav Schröder, tried his luck in Canada and the United States, neither of which would open its gates. Despondent, Schröder headed back to Europe, where approximately a quarter of his passengers would eventually be murdered by the Nazis. Schröder was named one of the Righteous Among the Nations by Yad Vashem, and his ship's voyage inspired many artistic adaptations, most famously the 1974 novel turned into a 1976 film, *Voyage of the Damned.*

Munich Olympics
Midway into the 1972 Olympic Games, eight Palestinian terrorists broke into the Olympic village and took the Israeli delegation hostage. The Israeli athletes fought bitterly but were overpowered by the heavily armed terrorists, who brutally castrated at least one of them and shot others before demanding the release of hundreds of their colleagues held by Israel and West Germany. A failed rescue attempt led to the death of eleven Israeli athletes. In 2012, the German magazine *Der Spiegel* published an article claiming that German authorities knew about the attack weeks in advance and did nothing to prevent it.

music
See Pop Music and Jews, page 182.

Myerson, Bess (1924–2014)
Miss America 1945, Myerson was the first, and so far the only, Jewish woman to win the title. Myerson was crowned Miss America on September 8, 1945, soon after Japan announced its surrender to end World War II. Given the destruction of European Jewry in the Holocaust, Myerson's victory had tremendous symbolic importance. In 1988, she pled guilty to shoplifting $44.07 of merchandise, including cosmetics, in South Williamsport, Pennsylvania, making her the most famous shoplifting Jewess until Winona Ryder's conviction in 2002.

FROM

Nabokov, Vera

TO

Nuremberg

Nabokov, Vera (1902–1991)
The Russian Jewish wife, editor, translator, and business manager of Vladimir Nabokov. She didn't write his books, but she helped author his life.

Nachman of Breslov (1772–1810)
Since the passing of the sassy, saucy sages of the Talmud, most of the rabbinic greats have been, well, not so much fun. Too much yeshiva, not enough corner pub. Not so with Reb Nachman, as he was known. If you are looking for a good time with a soulful man, for a stiff drink with someone who will *really listen*, this is the Hasidic master for you. The great-grandson of the Baal Shem Tov, the founder of Hasidism, Reb Nachman believed that it's important to speak to God as you would to a good friend. Ever humble, he ordered his students to burn all his writings, not wanting to leave behind anything that might be misinterpreted—thank God, some of his stuff survived, mainly in the form of fables and tales—and took pleasure in speaking to sinners behind bars, arguing that they were the ones who most needed help. But more than anything, he enjoyed wandering the fields alone, talking to the Lord. His most memorable teaching is the rejection of despair and the insistence on perpetual happiness. He is buried in the Ukrainian town of Uman, where tens of thousands of people visit his grave every Rosh Hashanah and, as he did, ecstatically dance in the fields. His followers, Breslovers, are known for wearing large, white knit yarmulkes embroidered with the chant "Na Nach Nachma Nachman Me'Uman," and are famous for singing, dancing, and imbibing the occasional drink, a great aid to spiritual awakening. (It should be said that we are talking about Breslover men; their wives have considerably less fun, in public, anyway.) Unlike many of their pious brethren, the Breslovers can be known by the smiles on their faces. Look, we're not telling you to drop out of college, renounce your worldly possessions, and send Mom an e-mail telling her that she shouldn't worry, you'll write again when you have found bliss. But if you *do* decide to take that course, look up the Breslovers on your travels.

NER TAMID

***The Nanny* (1993–1999)**

She was working in a bridal shop in Flushing, Queens,
Till her boyfriend kicked her out in one of those crushing scenes.
What was she to do, where was she to go?
She was out on her fanny . . .

(See **Drescher, Fran**.)

Nathan, Joan (b. 1943)
Chances are, if your mother or grandmother didn't pass along her recipe for kugel or latkes, Joan Nathan is the one you turn to. She took the trouble to translate family recipes from a "bissell of this" and a "dash of that" to measurements that you can use. Nathan has spent her life chronicling, collecting, investigating, and preserving Jewish food traditions from around the globe. The author of eleven cookbooks and counting, she strives to unearth the details of every meal at which Jews have gathered, past and present, as well as what was in their pots and on their plates. She's unearthed recipes from China, India, Uzbekistan, Syria, and Strasbourg and continues to shed new light on the familiar. Always attuned to how Jewish food is evolving, she even has a recipe for cannabis-infused matzo ball soup.

Nazis
They were literally, *literally*, Nazis.

nebbish
Through the 1980s, most likely a puny, pitiful weakling in a teen comedy. From the 1990s onward, most likely a billionaire founder of a software company.

neo-Nazis
To judge by the Internet, a group that rules the planet and includes everyone outside your immediate friends and family. In reality, a small cadre made up almost entirely of broken, deformed miscreants, riven by infighting and prone to continuous, unintentional self-satire. The neo-Nazi believes that the Holocaust never happened, but if it did, the Jews had it coming.

Ner Tamid

The eternal flame that hangs above the ark, or *aron kodesh*, in a synagogue. It harkens back to an undying flame that the priests tended in Temple times.

neshama

The catchall Hebrew word for soul. What is it? And how does it work? That's a subject of much debate in Jewish theology. According to Kabbalah, which has most comprehensively addressed the subject, our souls are divided into five parts: the nefesh, which is the life force of the physical body; the ruach, which has to do with emotions and morals; the neshama, which controls our intellectual mind and our awareness of God; the yechida, which is one with God; and the chaya, which is essentially a part of God. Kabbalah also teaches that souls reincarnate, so if you're not happy with the way things are going, you'll soon have another chance at getting life right.

Netanyahu, Benjamin (b. 1949)

Israeli prime minister. The second son of historian Ben-Zion Netanyahu, "Bibi" grew up in Jerusalem and Pennsylvania and attended MIT. Like his brother, Yoni, who was killed commanding Israel's successful 1976 rescue of hijacked hostages at Entebbe, Netanyahu served in Israel's elite special forces. His American upbringing would serve him well when he turned to politics, as his flawless English made him a favorite on television and on the pro-Israel speaking circuit. In 1984, he was appointed Israel's ambassador to the United Nations. In 1988, Netanyahu returned to Israel and joined the hawkish Likud party, later assuming its leadership and ultimately defeating Shimon Peres in the 1996 election, shortly after the assassination of Yitzhak Rabin. Bibi soon came under heavy criticism from his right-wing base, however, after he conceded much of Hebron to Palestinian control at Bill Clinton's urging. His support in tatters, in 1999 Netanyahu was booted from office by Labor, led by the dovish general Ehud Barak. Ten years later, however, the peace negotiations championed by Barak had foundered, and Israel's withdrawals from Lebanon and Gaza had led to the shelling of Israeli cities by the terrorist groups Hamas and Hezbollah. Claiming vindication, and running on a security-first platform, Netanyahu returned to power in 2009 and has been prime minister ever since. In 2019, Israeli voters, undisturbed by numerous allegations of bribery and fraud against Netanyahu, elected him to an unprecedented fifth term in office, making him Israel's longest-serving prime minister, ahead of the nation's founding father, David Ben-Gurion.

New Testament

The teachings of Jesus Christ. It's fine to call the New Testament the New Testament, but just don't call the original book the "Old Testament." We prefer "Hebrew Bible."

New York bagel

One of the most controversial Ashkenazi American foods, this once Jewish, now global, pastry has the power to delight, disappoint, and enrage. When made properly, the New York bagel is a yeast-risen dough ring that's boiled and baked, yielding a twisted, chewy interior and a shiny crust. Once upon a time, New York bagels were supposedly small enough to palm. Though today's New York bagel is only an inch or so wider than the more diminutive Montreal bagel, the girth of the bloated, virtually holeless breadstuff makes it appear supersize. And a new round of furor over gimmicky flavors, like rainbow swirl, ensures that New York bagel obsession will never die.

The New York Times

According to some critics, a pro-Israel rag run by unrepentant Zionists. According to other critics, an anti-Israel rag run by self-loathing assimilated Jews. Both groups of critics are *this close* to canceling their subscriptions.

Nichols, Mike (1931–2014)

After redefining American comedy with Elaine May, this actor and writer decided that he liked the other side of the camera better and became a director. His first movie was *Who's Afraid of Virginia Woolf?* His second was *The Graduate*, which won him an Oscar. Working with Paul Simon on original music for the film, he liked one of the singer's tunes, but suggested that he change the lyrics from "Here's to you, Mrs. Roosevelt" to "Here's to you, Mrs. Robinson."

niddah

According to Leviticus, the state a woman is in while menstruating, as well as a term for a menstruating woman. The word essentially means "to separate," which is what Jewish law demands during that time of the month, forbidding physical contact until the woman has had a chance to dip in the mikveh and purify herself. There are many more laws pertaining to niddah, so if you're into that sort of thing, the Talmud has a whole tractate about it.

niggun

Wordless Hasidic melody.

Nimoy, Leonard (1931–2015)

See **Spock**.

1948 War

See **War of Independence**.

1967 borders

In the aftermath of the Six-Day War, Israel found itself in possession of new territories taken from the Jordanians, the Egyptians, and the Syrians, including Judea and Samaria, eastern Jerusalem, the Golan Heights, the Gaza Strip, and the Sinai Peninsula. It has since ceded control of some of these territories, unilaterally leaving the Gaza Strip in 2005, for example, and returning the Sinai to Egypt as part of the 1978 Camp David Accords. But critics of Israel's policies since the war, many of them on the Israeli left, are advocating for a return to the Green Line, the pre-1967-war borders, which would mean dismantling Israeli settlements and ending what some refer to as Israel's occupation of the West Bank.

1967 War

See **Six-Day War**.

Noah

The most righteous brother of his generation, selected by God to survive the Flood and repopulate the earth (as you can read in Genesis). As part of this covenant, Noah receives seven commandments, which, according to Jewish tradition, apply not only to Jews but to all human beings: don't worship idols; don't curse God; establish just courts; don't commit murder; don't commit adultery; don't steal; and don't tear the flesh off a living creature. Jews, we have 613 commandments—but gentiles, stick with those seven, and you're cool.

Noah's Ark

The world's first aircraft carrier. It's believed to have had three levels: the top one for Noah and his family, the middle one for the animals, and the bottom one for—how shall we put it?—refuse. How did the animals not eat one another? How could the ark contain enough food for everyone? How come we have trees and plants, if those not stored on the ark were supposedly destroyed by the Flood? Don't ask so many questions.

Nobel Prize

As your grandmother has probably mentioned, Jews win a lot of them. If there were a Nobel Prize for winning Nobel Prizes, we'd have won that one, too.

nu?

The most versatile Yiddish word—and the hardest to define—this tiny question can have dozens of English equivalents, depending on the context. Sometimes it's used on its own to prod a response, something along the lines of "Go on . . ." or "Well . . . ?" or "So . . . ?" Sometimes it's used as a response in itself, signaling agreement with what someone else said, along the lines of "of course" or "What did you expect?" or "So what can you do?" It can mean "What's going on?" or "How are things?" or "How did it go?" It can stand on its own or be used before or after almost any phrase. It may well be the ultimate Jewish expression: in *The Joys of Yiddish*, Leo Rosten called it "the one word which can identify a Jew." *Nu*, can you think of a better example?

Nuremberg

The second largest city in the German state of Bavaria, after Munich. In the late 1920s and early 1930s, the city was the site of massive Nazi rallies, the most famous of which was held in 1934 and captured by Leni Riefenstahl in her propaganda film *Triumph of the Will*. In 1935, Hitler convened the Reichstag in Nuremberg and passed the Nuremberg laws, which stripped Jews of German citizenship. After the Nazis' defeat, the city was symbolically chosen for the international tribunal trying Germans accused of war crimes and crimes against humanity.

FROM

off the derech

TO

Ozick, Cynthia

off the derech

Or "OTD," for short. It means "off the path" in Hebrew, and is used by Orthodox Jews to describe anyone who is no longer observant. These days, formerly observant Jews prefer the term *XO*, for "ex-Orthodox."

Old Testament

Jews don't say this. We say Hebrew Bible, or Torah, or Tanakh. It's Christians, who believe that Jesus came along to give (with help from Matthew, Mark, Luke, John, Paul, and other writers) a "New Testament," who call our original holy Scripture the "Old Testament."

olive

Because Judaism has so many food-related commandments, the Talmud's wise rabbis needed a unit of measurement to determine how much of something you have to eat to have really *eaten* it. They came up with *kezayit*, or "as an olive," which, to be specific, they then further qualified as being roughly the size of one-third or one-half of an egg. If you've consumed an olive's worth of something, you've consumed it.

oneg Shabbat

Sometimes referred to simply as an *oneg*, which is Hebrew for "pleasure." If you're invited to one, what you're in for is a lively Friday-night gathering, where Jews get together, eat, drink, and enjoy the gift of their holy day of rest. Used in such campus dialogue as, "After Shabbat dinner, let's meet up with Chava and Kevin and head to the Chabad house for the Jell-O-shot oneg." (Another way to fulfill the mitzvah of oneg Shabbat is to engage in sexual congress.)

120

In Genesis 6:3, God declares, "My spirit shall not abide in man forever, for he is flesh: his days shall be 120 years." Why 120? No one knows. We do know, however, that a few of history's most righteous Jews, from Moses to Hillel the Elder, made it to 120. Today, "may you live to 120" is a common Jewish birthday greeting, although it's recently been amended to "may you live to 100 as 20," indicating that life is about more than mere longevity.

Operation Magic Carpet

Following the United Nations vote to partition British Mandatory Palestine into a Jewish state and an Arab state, violent riots broke out in Yemen, targeting the local Jewish community. Between December 1948 and September 1950, the newly formed Jewish state airlifted forty-eight thousand Yemenite Jews to Israel, one of the most logistically complicated and successful operations in the country's history.

Operation Solomon

Responding to political instability in Ethiopia in 1991, Israel launched a covert military operation. In the course of thirty-six hours, thirty-five aircraft, making nonstop flights, carried 14,500 Ethiopian Jews to safety in Israel.

Orthodox Judaism

See Branches of Judaism, page 44.

Oslo Accords

The 1993 agreement between Israel and the Palestine Liberation Organization (PLO) was supposed to be the essential first step toward peace between Israelis and Palestinians—which, who knows, it may still turn out to be. Under the initial accords, Israel pulled its army from certain urban areas in the West Bank, while the PLO and its leadership, including Yasser Arafat, were allowed to transform themselves into the Palestinian Authority, an interim government that would serve while an end to the conflict was negotiated. In exchange, the Palestinians recognized Israel's right to exist and committed themselves to seeking a peaceful solution to their grievances with Israel. The agreement established a status quo, and a framework for peaceful conflict resolution, that's proven to be either remarkably durable or bafflingly impossible to kill off, depending on one's point of view. While a majority of Israelis consider the Oslo process a failure, the agreement ended some of Israel's diplomatic isolation over the Palestinian issue, established a land-for-peace formulation that's guided every subsequent talk between Israelis and Palestinians, and codified

Operation Solomon: Ethiopian Jews onboard an Israeli Air Force Boeing 707 heading from Addis Ababa to Tel Aviv in 1991

the eventual end of Israeli rule over most of Gaza and the West Bank as the conflict's ideal resolution. These are not insignificant accomplishments, even if that handshake between Arafat and Yitzhak Rabin on the White House lawn seems like it took place in an entirely different universe.

Oz, Amos (1939–2018)

The most prominent Israeli writer of the twenty-first century, Oz was one of the country's biggest intellectual exports. Starting with 1968's *My Michael*, his novels weave together personal and national anxieties, often as a way of exploring the major Jewish traumas of the past century. A passionate advocate for peace with the Palestinians, he was considered the chief spokesman of the Israeli left. He enjoyed a surge in popularity late in his career, brought about by his 2002 memoir, *A Tale of Love and Darkness*, which was adapted into a 2015 film by Natalie Portman.

OZICK, CYNTHIA

(B. 1928)

One of a trio of Jewish American literary greats whose reputations have suffered unfairly because their best works are not necessarily novels—the others would be Bernard Malamud and Grace Paley. Ozick got a relatively late start, but once she got started, she had no literary adolescence: her first story collection, *The Pagan Rabbi and Other Stories* (1971), remains among her finest works. Of her novels, *The Messiah of Stockholm* (1987) is the place to start. She is equally at home in nonfiction, and the finest essays in collections like *Art and Ardor* (1983) are as enjoyable to read as her best stories (like, say, "The Shawl")—not least because they are fearless, cantankerous, and brilliant, whether she is attacking Israel's attackers or putting an overrated writer in his place.

ODE TO OZICK

The Messiah of Stockholm (1987)

Heir to the Glimmering World (2004)

The Puttermesser Papers (1997)

Foreign Bodies (2010)

FROM

Page, Larry

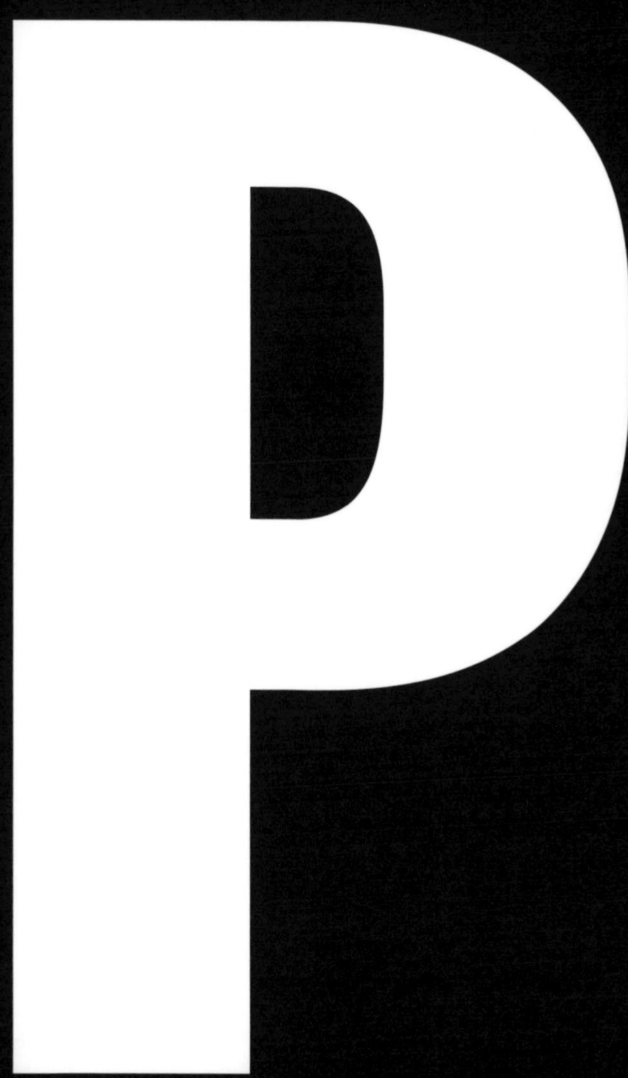

TO

Purim

Page, Larry
No, seriously—Google it.

Pale of Settlement
The Pale, a stretch of Imperial Russia that today would include parts of Belarus, Lithuania, Moldova, Ukraine, Latvia, Poland, and Russia, was where Jews were permitted permanent residence from about 1800 to 1917. *Pale* in this instance comes from the Latin *palus*, or "stake." Literally, then, the Pale is a series of stakes—fences or boundaries. A gigantic eruv, in other words. At its peak, the Pale was home to some 4.5 million Jews, or 40 percent of world Jewry.

Palestine
Since at least the time of the ancient Greeks, the name Palestine was used to describe most of the area currently known as the land of Israel. It was politicized early on: in 135 CE, the Romans, having just crushed the Bar Kochba rebellion, changed the region's name from Iudaea Province to Syria Palaestina, in an attempt to erase the Jewish connection to the land. It didn't work. It took a few millennia, but after a succession of conquering empires came and went, much of the region was once again known as Israel when the Jewish state declared its independence in 1948.

History being as fond as it is of plot twists, these days the name is used colloquially to refer to the future state of the Palestinian people. While such a state has yet to be politically realized on the ground, it is symbolically recognized by many world governments. Like Israel's borders, the exact future borders of Palestine remain the subject of controversy. Some advocates call for a Palestinian state alongside Israel, while others call for Palestine to replace Israel.

Paley, Grace (1922–2007)

Author of but three short-story collections, yet one of the most important authors of the twentieth century. Her stories "focused especially on single mothers, whose days were an exquisite mix of sexual yearning and pulverizing fatigue," her *New York Times* obituary read. "In a sense, her work was about what happened to the women that Roth and Bellow and Malamud's men had loved and left behind." Her stories feature terse bits of dialogue, women saying not much to neighbors and to fellow mothers on the playground—she had the courage and the clarity to write short. In the introduction to *The Collected Stories* (1994), she explains how she made the move from frustrated poet to successful short-story writer: "I became sick enough for the children to remain in Greenwich House After School until suppertime for several weeks, but not so sick that I couldn't sit at our living-room table to write or type all day." Paley was an activist, known for her feminism and antiwar politics and her willingness to do the unglamorous work of leafleting and envelope stuffing.

Paltrow, Gwyneth (b. 1972)

Hollywood royalty (the daughter of über-WASP actress Blythe Danner and producer-director Bruce Paltrow, descended of Polish rabbis), she won an Oscar at twenty-six for *Shakespeare in Love*, and named her children Rosh Hashanah–appropriate Apple and Passover-themed Moses. Later she started the Goop wellness empire, then married Brad Falchuk—son of Nancy, former president of Hadassah.

pareve
Neither milchig nor fleishig—that is, containing neither milk nor meat—pareve describes foods like fish, margarine, and pasta that can safely be combined in a meal with dairy or meat. The term is sometimes used metaphorically to describe something or someone blandly inoffensive.

Passover
See opposite page.

Patinkin, Mandy (b. 1952)
Juilliard-trained actor and singer who has made his mark on almost every artistic medium. Musical theater buffs will remember him as Che in the original production of *Evita* or as the lead in *Sunday in the Park with George*. TV fans will recognize him from *Homeland* or *Chicago Hope*. Moviegoers remember his turn as Inigo Montoya in *The Princess Bride*, while music aficionados will recall his album of Yiddish songs, *Mamaloshen*. (As well as singing iconic tunes like "Oyfn Pripetshik" and "Belz," he offers a memorable Yiddish medley of "Take Me Out to the Ball Game" and "God Bless America.") All that aside, Patinkin is an essential Jewish performer because of his role in *Yentl* as Barbra Streisand's love interest Avigdor, the sexiest yeshiva boy ever to appear on the big screen—or anywhere else, for that matter.

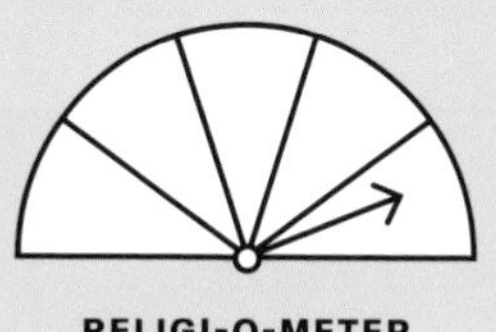

RELIGI-O-METER

PASSOVER

Passover marks the liberation of the Israelites, who were slaves in ancient Egypt, and recounts the story of their exodus to the Promised Land. Key things to remember: Moses, Ten Plagues, matzo, the parting of the Red Sea.

WHAT'S IT ALL ABOUT?

The Hebrew name is Pesach, which comes from the word *pasach*, commonly translated as "pass over"—a reference to the Exodus passage that tells of God passing over the doors of Jewish homes, slaying the firstborn sons of the Egyptians. When the ancient Israelites left Egypt, they didn't have enough time to let their dough rise before fleeing. That's why we eat matzo instead of bread during the holiday.

In the diaspora, Passover is observed for eight days with two Seders, while in Israel it lasts for seven with a single Seder.

ANY DOS AND DON'TS?

Passover's two major observations have to do with chametz, or unleavened bread, and the celebration of a Seder. The avoidance of chametz, referring to all grain products that have either already been fermented (bread, cake, some alcoholic beverages) or can cause fermentation (yeast), is at the heart of numerous rituals. Before Passover, Jews embark on a serious spring cleaning. Although the halacha states no obligation to rid the home of any bit of chametz smaller than an olive, it is customary to clean out every nook, and tradition calls for a candlelight search of the premises on the morning of the first Seder, a ritual called *bidekat chametz*, using a feather to inspect and sweep out even the hardest-to-reach corners. Alternatively, chametz can be symbolically sold to a non-Jewish neighbor for the duration of the holiday, either by an individual or by a rabbi acting on behalf of an entire community.

The Seder, which means "order," is rich in meaning. Through Torah readings, Midrashim, songs, and discussion, Seder participants relive, as commanded, the events of Exodus.

The Seder is also a culinary celebration with foods symbolizing elements of the Israelites' story. It originally revolved around the paschal lamb, which was delivered to the Temple, sacrificed, roasted whole, and eaten. In the absence of a Temple, Jews are prohibited from animal sacrifice, removing from the Seder its most prominent offering—though it endures on the Seder plate symbolically in the form of a shank bone. There are plenty of other meaningful dishes: maror, bitter herbs that symbolize the hardship of slavery in Egypt; karpas, a raw vegetable dipped in salt water to symbolize spring and the Israelites' tears; charoset, a sweet paste made of fruits and nuts, symbolizing the mortar with which our ancestors built the houses of Egypt; and, of course, the matzo. In addition to the fact that it harkens to the haste with which the Israelites fled their oppressors—so fast that they didn't have time to wait for their bread to rise—it also is known as *lechem oni*, the "bread of affliction," a reminder of humility.

The Seder's other greatest hits include the recitation of the Four Questions, asked by children to encourage a discussion of the meal's symbolism, and the search for the afikoman, a hidden piece of matzo that children look for after the meal. Children often trade in their afikoman findings for a prize from their parents.

Mandy Patinkin: The legendary actor of stage and screen is perhaps best known for uttering the following twelve words in the 1987 cult classic *The Princess Bride*: "My name is Inigo Montoya. You killed my father. Prepare to die."

patriarchs

See Matriarchs and Patriarchs, page 176.

Pearl, Daniel (1963–2002)

Israeli-American *Wall Street Journal* reporter who in 2002 was kidnapped and beheaded by Islamist terrorists in Pakistan. In a video made by his captors just before his death, Pearl famously stated, "My father is Jewish, my mother is Jewish, I am Jewish." (Those words are now etched on the grave of former New York City mayor Ed Koch.)

Peet, Amanda (b. 1972)

Television and film Jewess, popular since the early 2000s. She also wrote *Dear Santa, Love, Rachel Rosenstein*, a 2015 children's Christmas book about a Jewish girl. She is married to *Game of Thrones* producer/writer David Benioff. Oh, and she is a provaccination activist, countering the anti-vaxxer nonsense that some other celebrities spew.

Peres, Shimon (1923–2016)

Israeli prime minister, president, and Nobel Peace Prize laureate. You'd think this impressive bio would be enough to earn him some respect, but in Israel he was widely known as the Loser, mainly because he was frequently overshadowed by his more handsome and popular frenemy Yitzhak Rabin. Despite his reputation as the ultimate dove and the architect of the Oslo Accords, Peres was often a security-minded hawk and is largely credited with being one of the driving forces behind Israel's top-secret nuclear program.

Persian Jews

As the Book of Esther tells us, Jews have lived in Iran for a very long time. That more or less ended with the Islamic Revolution of 1979: out of a community of 80,000 to 100,000, more than 60,000 fled, mostly to America or Israel. About 9,000 live in Iran today, facing discrimination from the reigning mullahs. In the United States, lots of Persian Jews can be found in Great Neck, New York, and in Los Angeles.

peyos

"You shall not round off the corners of your head," Leviticus commanded us, and many Orthodox Jewish men obey, keeping their sidelocks untrimmed. Most likely, the original commandment was put in place to make sure guys didn't get too fixated on their hair, which is why it's funny that peyos are often used as a mark of distinction between various sects in the Orthodox world, with some letting those curly sideburns lie low and others elegantly coiling them around the ear.

Pharaoh

Why did the Egyptian meanie deserve all those plagues? Because, the Torah tells us, God Himself hardened the Pharaoh's heart, which means he watched all of God's miracles and, out of his own free will, still refused to do the right thing and let the enslaved Israelites go. Let that be a lesson to us all to keep our eyes, our minds, and our hearts always open. On an unrelated note, the word in Hebrew is pronounced "parr-o," with a *p* rather than an *f* sound at the beginning. If you're hanging with observant or Jewishly literate folks and drop a *parr-o* into the convo, you're in like Flynn.

Phish

The academic explanation goes a little something like this: whereas the Grateful Dead were an improvisational rock band founded by bluegrass obsessives, Phish is the creation of four guys whose musical imaginations were steeped in New Wave and prog. The Dead covered Chuck Berry and Woody Guthrie; Phish covered XTC and Zappa. Phish conjoins musical exuberance—jams too giant for even a sober mind to process; palaces made of keyboard and bass; guitar licks so towering that they seem like they've been launched at passing satellites or distant solar systems—with the forward-thinking ethos of '70s and '80s art rock. The academic explanation is, of course, useless: like 'em or hate 'em, a Phish concert is unlike any other experience in music, one that a true fan hasn't exhausted even after ten or one hundred shows. Because New York is Phish's traditional stomping ground, the band boasts a significant Jewish following. Two of the band's four members (the rhythm section, for what it's worth) come from a Jewish background; as of late 2018, the group had performed "Avinu Malkeinu" some eighty times (always after "The Man Who Stepped into Yesterday") and "Yerushalayim Shel Zahav" twelve times, most recently on New Year's Eve in 1994.

pickles

What started off as a preserving technique has become a cornerstone of the Jewish American flavor profile—tangy, salty, garlicky, maybe even a little sweet. It's the sour analog to the meaty sandwich, the last flavor we want in our mouth at the end of the meal, and the most lasting. We can get into the half-sour-versus-full-sour argument, but can't we all agree that a sandwich wouldn't be a sandwich without a pickle spear next to it?

Picon, Molly (1898–1992)

"Queen of Second Avenue" and star of Yiddish theater and early Yiddish cinema. Her career lasted from the 1910s through the late 1980s, and her popularity was such that she drew crowds even from non-Yiddish-speaking audiences. Picon hosted radio shows starting in the 1930s and transitioned into English-speaking roles, notably with the 1961 musical *Milk and Honey* (about a group of American widows traveling in Israel) and the 1963 film *Come Blow Your Horn* with Frank Sinatra. Her most famous film role was as Yente the Matchmaker in *Fiddler on the Roof.* "People are still buying what I'm selling," she told a *New York Times* reporter in 1976, and she continued to work in the theater and take small roles in TV and film (she played Roger Moore's mother in *The Cannonball Run*) into her nineties. She was also a noted philanthropist who worked with displaced Jewish Holocaust survivors and sold Israel bonds.

PICKLES

Pidyon Haben

Firstborn sons are a big deal in the Bible—just ask Pharaoh. Because God spared the Israelites the terrible plague of the death of the firstborn, Jewish law says every Jewish father must, thirty days after the birth of his first male child, pay a *kohen*—a direct descendant of Aaron, Moses's brother and the first Israelite priest—a few silver coins in order to redeem the child and secure for him a long and happy life. Naturally, a festive meal follows this ceremony.

Pirkei Avot

Translated as "Chapters of the Fathers," another name for the Mishnah's tractate Avot, which is unique for containing no mention of halacha and focusing instead exclusively on ethics. Because of the staggering amount of insightful aphorisms it contains—like Hillel the Elder's "If I am not for myself, who is for me? And if I am only for myself, what am I? And if not now, when?"—it is frequently bound and read as a stand-alone volume. It is customary to read a chapter every Shabbat between the holidays of Passover and Shavuot.

pizza bagel

An American semi-Semite, or half-Jew, whose non-Jewish side of the family is Italian. Famous pizza bagels include radio personality Mike Pesca and New York City mayor Fiorello La Guardia. "Pizza bagel" should not be used to describe an Italian Jew from Italy, where Jews have lived for millennia. Not only does this confuse matters, as Italian Jewishness is very much its own thing, but the term makes no sense in that context, as Italians tend not to eat bagels, and in many regions of Italy they don't eat anything resembling what Americans think of as pizza.

pogroms

Anti-Semitic attacks that claimed the lives of thousands of Jews in the Russian empire from the seventeenth to the early twentieth centuries.

Poland

See opposite page.

POLIN Museum of the History of Polish Jews

Warsaw museum commemorating a thousand years of Jewish life in Poland, built on the grounds of the former Warsaw Ghetto.

politics

See Politics and Jews, page 200.

Portman, Natalie (b. 1981)

Opinions may differ on whether Portman is one of the great movie talents of her generation, but she is certainly one of the great movie stars. Born in Jerusalem—the family name was Hershlag—and raised on Long Island, Portman got her breakout role in the 1994 cult classic *Léon: The Professional*, where she played the child companion of a trained assassin, and cemented her status as one of

POLAND

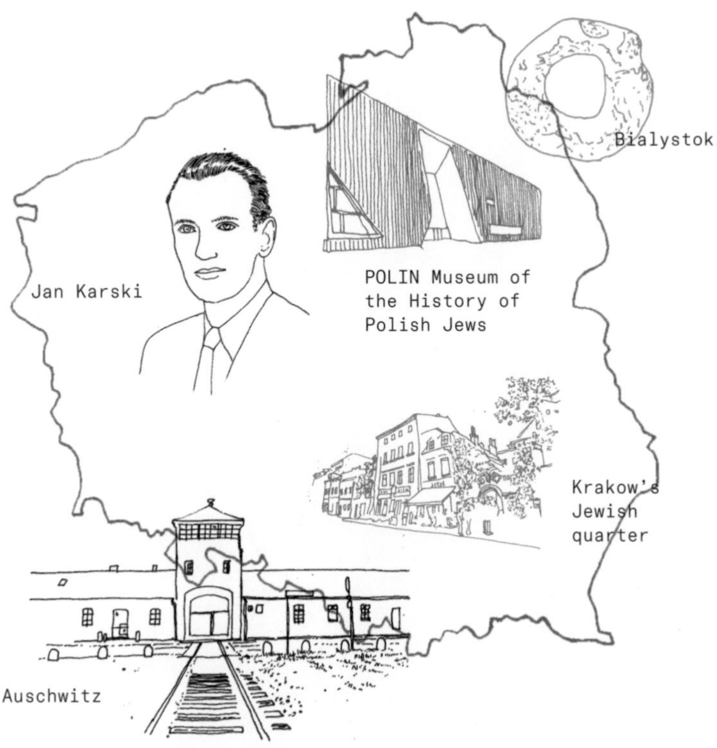

In 2018, Poland's government passed a controversial (and since partially rescinded) law that basically made it illegal to attribute the Holocaust to the Poles. It was a misguided step, but it revealed the central tension at the heart of Jewish-Polish relations: a thousand years of complicated and, often, thriving Jewish life in Poland, and then the Holocaust.

A well-known rabbinic quip asserts that the country's Hebrew name, Polin, was made up of the words *po* and *lin*, or "here you can sleep," indicating that it was a safe haven for Jews. A series of Polish kings proved this idiom true during the Crusades, welcoming throngs of Jewish refugees fleeing violent persecution.

Over the centuries, Poland's Jews were largely accepted and integrated into the society far more thoroughly than they were nearly anywhere else in Europe. While Germany's Jews, for example, were restricted to finance alone, Poland's Jews worked as traders and merchants. Numerous pogroms did occur, both sporadically and in organized waves, and some members of the Polish royalty were less kind to the Jews. But it tells you everything you need to know about the relationships between Jews and non-Jews in Poland that once the Nazis occupied the country, they decreed that any Pole aiding or hiding Jews would be executed. Poland was the only country where such a law was passed, suggesting that the SS believed that Poles would attempt to help their Jewish neighbors. Many did: even though the percentage of the Polish population that risked its life to save Jews is small, 6,863 Poles have been recognized by Yad Vashem as Righteous Among the Nations, more than from any other country. It's essential to remember these sacrifices alongside the atrocities, and to commemorate not only the death of so many Jews on Polish soil but also centuries of creative and productive lives led there.

POLITICS

"Yeah," Yogi Berra is said to have said, after Dublin had elected its first Jewish mayor, "only in America can a thing like this happen."

America has had its share of Jewish politicians at every level of government—beginning even before the nation's founding with double-first Francis Salvador, a Sephardic immigrant from London and plantation owner in South Carolina who became the first Jew elected to public office in the colonies, when he joined the aspiring state's Revolutionary Provincial Congress in 1774, and then became the first Jew killed in the Revolutionary War two years later.

After independence, things slowed down some for Semite statesmen, and it wasn't until 1845 that the House elected its first Jewish member, Know-Nothing Lewis Charles Levin, a brilliant orator and virulent anti-Catholic who served three terms representing Pennsylvania's first district. The first Jewish senator, depending on how you count, was either "Florida Fire Eater" David Levy Yulee, also elected in 1845, or Louisiana's Judah Philip Benjamin, first elected in 1852, who later served in the Confederacy first as attorney general and then as secretary of war—which, again depending on how you count, may make him the first Jewish cabinet member.

If you don't count Benjamin, it's more than a half century until we get a Jew in the US cabinet: German-born Oscar Straus, in between three stints over three decades as the US ambassador to the Ottoman Empire, served as Teddy Roosevelt's secretary of commerce and labor from 1906 to 1909, a role that also placed him in charge of the Bureau of Immigration.

As for the first Jewish governor, that was Washington Montgomery Bartlett, a nonobservant Californian (nonobservant as a Jew, that is; very observant as a Californian). He died months after taking office in 1887, and his funeral was held at an Episcopal church in San Francisco. The second Jewish governor, Bavarian immigrant Moses Alexander, served nearly a half century later in Idaho, from 1915 to 1919. Just before launching his political career by getting elected mayor of Boise in the 1890s, Alexander had led the effort to build Ahavath Beth Israel, the state's first synagogue, now the oldest continuously used synagogue in America west of the Mississippi.

The first Jewish woman in Congress was Florence Prag Kahn, who in 1925 won a special election to fill her husband's seat after his death. Just the fifth woman ever to serve in the House, Kahn ended up winning five terms of her own and becoming the first woman to sit on the House Committee on Military Affairs. Jump ahead to the 1970s, and the remaining firsts start stacking up. Dianne Feinstein became the first elected Jewish female mayor of a big city, San Francisco, in 1978, launching a political career that would see her join Barbara Boxer in 1993—the same year Ruth Bader Ginsburg would become the first Jewish woman on the Supreme Court—as the first Jewish women to serve in the US Senate.

In 2000, of course, Joe Lieberman became the first Jewish vice presidential nominee on a major-party ticket, running with Democrat Al Gore. In 2006, he became an independent after losing the Democratic primary, then won the general election and a third term in the Senate. And in 2008, Republican John McCain came *this close* to adding Lieberman to the ticket, which would have made Lieberman the first Jewish vice presidential candidate for both parties.

Eight years and two elections later, we came to 2016, the year that a faithless elector made Bernie Sanders the first Jewish candidate to win a presidential primary, in New Hampshire, and then the first Jewish candidate to receive an electoral vote for president.

In 2017, Brooklyn's own Charles Schumer became the first Jewish floor leader in the Senate, and Ivanka Trump the first Jewish member of a first family.

her generation's most radiant stars in 1996's *Beautiful Girls*. By 1999, she had earned her way into both Harvard, where she served as Alan Dershowitz's research assistant, and the *Star Wars* franchise, where she served as Queen Padmé Amidala. Jews who can name zero Portman movies know that her son is named Aleph, she opposes Israeli prime minister Benjamin Netanyahu, and she is one of the best-looking Jews, and people, alive.

Portnoy's Complaint

Philip Roth's 1969 primal scream from the analyst's couch is the funniest dirty novel and the dirtiest funny novel in American literary history. It's a central text for anyone wishing to understand shiksappeal or the onanistic temptations of organ meat. Its depiction of an overbearing Jewish mother is offensive yet canonical, and it is profound on the subject of Jews and therapy. You'll read it, hate yourself for loving it, and then read it again.

Potok, Chaim (1929–2002)

The oldest son of Jewish immigrants from Poland, Potok and his siblings all became or married rabbis. Always wanting to be a writer, however, he finally released his first novel at age thirty-eight. It was *The Chosen*, a smart and soulful tale of two friends who struggle with their faith, their fathers, and the temptations of secular life. It became a major hit, establishing Potok as a new voice in Jewish American letters. His influence on the younger generations of writers that tackled similar themes and sensibilities was immense.

prayer

See **daven**.

prep

Fashion sensibility invented by Jewish designers to help middle-class WASPs feel like wealthy WASPs. It reached its apotheosis in the styles of the great Ralph Lauren.

Prinz, Joachim (1902–1988)

German American rabbi who ardently supported Zionism and passionately advocated for civil rights.

The Producers (1967)

The outrageous movie that dared to poke fun at Hitler (while lampooning Jewish entertainment business shysters), this film secured Mel Brooks's position as one of the trailblazers of comedy. Zero Mostel and Gene Wilder, the titular producers, realize that they will make more money if their play is a flop instead of a hit. In search of the worst possible script, they find a deranged Nazi sympathizer whose musical, *Springtime for Hitler*, is subtitled *A Gay Romp with Adolf and Eva at Berchtesgaden*. They cast the show with maniacs and find a looney director, and the show is laughed off the stage. Unfortunately, the laughter continues—the audience thinks it's a comedy. "Where did we go right?" Mostel asks, in one of a hundred classic lines. The film was adapted into an enormously successful Broadway musical (for which Brooks wrote the music and lyrics) starring Nathan Lane and Matthew Broderick, which was then turned back into a 2005 film. An arc of *Curb Your Enthusiasm* saw Larry David acting in the show opposite David Schwimmer.

Promised Land

What's so promised about the Promised Land, anyway? When Moses first sends spies to check it out, most of them come back with reports of angry giants and warlike peoples who would not take kindly to the Israelites just traipsing in. But the spies were missing the point. The promise wasn't then and isn't now inherent to the land itself. The promise was and is all about the people: only by observing the commandments and building a just society in a real country could the Jews become that proverbial light unto the nations. Without mindful people passing laws that protect the weak, the poor, and the needy, Canaan becomes just another Egypt, the Promised Land just another house of bondage. But live according to the merciful commandments, and you'll see the promise come true. In that sense, really, every land is potentially promised, waiting just for us to make it so.

proselytizing

Something Jews used to do! Jews in the Greco-Roman world proselytized, and successfully. They stopped when the people who ruled them—the Roman empire in its Christian phase, then Islam, then numerous emperors and kings of Christendom—told them to stop. They stopped because they didn't want to get killed. But while many contemporary Jews cherish the myth that we never proselytized, believing that it makes Judaism a tolerant, universalistic tradition, there is no actual Jewish prohibition on trying to convert others.

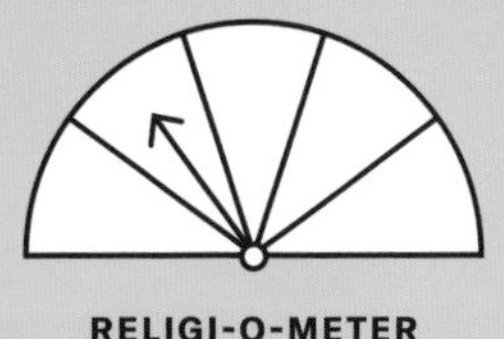

RELIGI-O-METER

PURIM

Purim celebrates the foiling of a plan to destroy the Jews of Persia in the fourth century BCE. We celebrate by dressing in costume, eating hamantaschen, and making merry.

Purim is the Hebrew word for "lots," and the lots in question were drawn by Haman, an evil advisor to the Persian king Ahasuerus, in order to decide on which day the kingdom's Jews would be put to death. The plan was foiled thanks to Esther, the king's Jewish wife; the Jews, saved from the gallows Haman had constructed, used those same gallows to execute him, his descendants, and thousands of other enemies. To commemorate this story of slyness and survival, we get rowdy each year on the fourteenth day of Adar.

Esther herself spends much of the story concealing her Jewish identity, and Mordechai, her uncle, learns of Haman's plot when he secretly eavesdrops on two royal guards. These days Jewish children dress up for Purim, either as the story's characters or their favorite Marvel superheroes.

The Producers: Gene Wilder as Leo Bloom, Zero Mostel as Max Bialystock, and Lee Meredith as the Swedish secretary Ulla in the 1967 film

Protocols of the Elders of Zion

The book you're made to read when you are inducted into the international cabal that controls the media, banking, and Hollywood.*

Proust, Marcel (1871–1922)

How might we summarize the life and work of an author whose masterful novel, *In Search of Lost Time*, runs more than 4,200 pages? The task is so preposterous that it inspired a Monty Python sketch. But if you haven't read him, do: it'll change your life. No modern author has been more insightful on art, love, friendship, loss, grief, joy, pastries, and all the other things that make human life worth living. That the novel also captures France in the throes of the Dreyfus Affair is an added bonus for anyone who wants to understand how hatred of Jews can drive a civilized society insane.

pru urvu

Appearing in the first chapter of the first book of the Bible, the very first commandment urges us to be fruitful and multiply. Copy that.

*Just kidding: It's a hoax created by the czarist Russian police to slander the Jews. That so many people have since believed it to be true, and that so many believe it still, tells you just how dumb anti-Semites truly are.

Psalms

In Hebrew, this biblical book is called Tehilim, the plural form of *tehila*, or "glorious praise." It consists of 150 poems believed to have been largely composed by King David and touching on everything from the glory of God to communal and individual lamentations. Reading Psalms is believed to bring good luck and is frequently done at the bedside of a sick person or at a time of personal or collective danger. Many psalms have been set to classical or pop music, including the beloved classic "On the Rivers of Babylon."

Purim

See page 203.

FROM

questioning

TO

Qumran

questioning

? Something Jews like to think we are unusually good at. It's not uncommon to hear a secular or nonobservant Jew say something like, "To me, the essence of Judaism is not any sort of blind faith but endless questioning. We question everything!" While there is a certain basic truth in this sort of claim—at the center of Jewish Scripture lies the Talmud, which is a record of rabbis arguing vociferously, and yeshiva education uses a pedagogy of one-on-one disputation—it's often a thin mask for callow, self-serving chauvinism. What the speaker really means is, "Those other, lesser religions make you believe or do stuff, but I don't have to believe or do anything to be Jewish, I just have to ask questions." Or, "Even though I don't believe in anything Jewish or celebrate Jewish holidays or learn anything Jewish or feel a special connection to the Jewish people, I like to argue a lot, so I am as Jewish as anybody." To be sure, questioning *is* a positive Jewish value. But questioning is also a positive NPR value and a positive eighth-grade-chemistry-lab value. The Jews didn't invent questioning, and we haven't cornered the market on it.

Qumran

Archaeological site located a mile from the Dead Sea where, tucked away in caves dug into the rock, the Dead Sea Scrolls were discovered in 1947.

FROM

rabbi

TO

rye bread

RADNER, GILDA

(1946–1989)

GOLDEN GILDA

Beloved comedian and original *Saturday Night Live* cast member, Radner immortalized such characters as obnoxious personal advice expert Roseanne Roseannadanna, malaprop-prone Emily Litella (based on Radner's nanny from her childhood in Grosse Pointe, Michigan), demonstrative Girl Scout Judy Miller, and of course the snickering nerd Lisa Loopner. We'll never forget her iconic ad for Jewess Jeans, either. Her untimely death at forty-two from ovarian cancer left behind a bereft comedy world (Steve Martin wept openly on air while hosting *Saturday Night Live*) and a grieving widower, actor Gene Wilder, whom Radner married in 1984, but brought new awareness of the genetic Ashkenazi predisposition to certain cancers (see BRCA). Wilder endowed the Gilda Radner Hereditary Cancer Program at Los Angeles's Cedars-Sinai Medical Center.

Emily Litella
(character, 1975)

Baba Wawa
(character, 1976)

Roseanne Roseannadanna
(character, 1977)

Judy Miller
(character, 1978)

rabbi

"My master" or "my teacher." These days, we assume that anyone called rabbi has been ordained; historically, however, any learned, upright man could be greeted with a hearty "Good morning, Rabbi!" or "*Vos makhst du, Reb Mordechai?*"

Rabin, Yitzhak (1922–1995)

A decorated soldier in Israel's War of Independence, Rabin went on to command the IDF during the Six-Day War before retiring and going into politics. He followed Golda Meir as prime minister but was forced to resign three years after his election when it was revealed that he and his wife kept a foreign bank account, which was illegal at the time. He served as minister of defense during the first Intifada, and was known for advocating a hard-line approach against the Palestinian rioters. In 1992, he was again elected prime minister, campaigning on a platform of peace. A year later, he surprised Israel and the world when, together with his longtime political frenemy Shimon Peres, he announced the Oslo Accords. The move won him international acclaim and the Nobel Peace Prize, but many at home considered setting up an armed Palestinian Authority headed by a former terrorist like Yasser Arafat to be a grievous mistake. On November 4, 1995, making his way from a pro-peace rally in Tel Aviv's main square, he was shot at close range by a young right-wing religious Israeli. He died a short while later in a nearby hospital.

Rachel

See Matriarchs and Patriarchs, page 176.

radical Jews

See page 212.

Raisman, Aly (b. 1994)

American gymnast and three-time Olympic gold medalist. The Massachusetts native captained the US women's gymnastics team at the 2016 Rio Games and the 2012 London Games, where she performed her floor routine to "Hava Nagila" and later dedicated her performance to the eleven Israeli Olympians killed at the 1972 Munich Olympics.

Rambam
See **Maimonides**.

Ramon, Ilan (1954–2003)
The first—and, to date, the only—Israeli astronaut, Ramon was a decorated F-16 fighter pilot in the Israel Air Force and the youngest participant in 1981's Operation Opera, the airstrike against Saddam Hussein's nuclear reactor in Osiraq. In 1997, he was selected by NASA as a payload specialist and, six years later, took off on board the space shuttle *Columbia*. The son and grandson of Auschwitz survivors, Ramon took with him a drawing of a moonscape sketched by a sixteen-year-old who died in the concentration camp, and was the first man to request kosher food in space. He was killed with the other crew members as the shuttle disintegrated upon reentering orbit, and was posthumously awarded the Congressional Space Medal of Honor, the only foreign national ever to receive this honor. Tragedy continued to haunt the Ramon family: his son, Assaf, also an F-16 pilot, died in a 2009 training accident, and his widow, Rona, died of pancreatic cancer in 2018 at age fifty-four.

ARCHIE RAND

Rand, Archie (b. 1949)
Brooklyn-born artist who in 2015 published the very cool *613*, a book featuring an illustration for each of the 613 commandments.

Rand, Ayn (1905–1982)
Born Alissa Zinovievna Rosenbaum in Russia, she's best remembered for her two massive novels *Atlas Shrugged* and *The Fountainhead*, beloved of brainy adolescent girls and libertarian middle-aged men.

Rashi (1040–1105)
Acronym by which Rabbi Shlomo Yitzchaki is known. The medieval French scholar is known for his comprehensive commentaries on the Bible and Talmud. His commentary has been published in every edition of the Talmud (with extremely rare exceptions) since the 1500s, and is now seen as a crucial part of the text.

Rebbe, the Rebbe
This is a term that any Hasid might use to refer to his or her spiritual leader, but in popular discourse it almost always refers to the late Lubavitcher leader Menachem Mendel Schneerson (1902–1994), one of the most influential rabbis of our time. As a young man, he moved with his father around the Soviet Union, and in 1928 he married the daughter of Yosef Yitzchak Schneersohn (note the father-in-law's different spelling), the sixth Lubavitcher Rebbe (see **Schneerson, Chaya Mushka**). Together, they moved from Warsaw to Berlin, where Menachem Mendel learned mathematics, physics, and philosophy, and then to Paris, where he studied at the Sorbonne. The couple fled to New York, where, in 1950, Schneerson inherited his father-in-law's mantle and became the seventh Lubavitcher Rebbe. He turned his movement, Chabad, into an empire. He also stressed the importance of putting on tefillin as a way to get closer to God. Every Sunday, he would receive the public in his study in Crown Heights, Brooklyn, giving each person who came to see him a dollar and his blessing. After his death in 1994, some of his followers proclaimed him the Messiah, although the opinion is not widely held. His burial place—the *Ohel*, "tent," in Queens—is frequented by tens of thousands of believers every year, who leave him written notes and ask him to pray for their well-being and for their loved ones.

Rebecca
See Matriarchs and Patriarchs, page 176.

Reconstructionism
See Branches of Judaism, page 44.

Reed, Lou (1942–2013)

As leader of the incalculably influential Velvet Underground in the late 1960s, and as a solo artist whose discography stretched from the 1970s until his death in 2013, Lou Reed epitomized the rock-and-roller as hard-bitten poet. Raised in

RADICAL JEWS

Are Jews really more prone to radical politics than other peoples, and if so, why? Although one can always look further back for sources—to Spinoza, to Torah—a useful history of Jewish political radicalism might start in the late nineteenth and early twentieth centuries, when Jews, fleeing poverty, persecution, and conscription, immigrated in great waves to the United States and other Western countries. Many brought with them traditions of radical politics developed in the old country. In Russia and across the Pale of Settlement, there were Bundists, secular, Yiddish Marxist Social Democrats; Mensheviks, whom we might equate to Democratic socialists; Bolsheviks, who became Leninist communists; and anarchists of various stripes.

The finer distinctions between Old World radical factions were largely lost in America, and what remained were two broad groups: There was a large working-class labor movement—in 1914, the United Hebrew Trades had 104 affiliated unions and 250,000 members out of a total Jewish population in New York of roughly 1.5 million—that was radical for its time but harder to classify by today's standards. Overlapping with that broad labor movement was a more middle-class and intelligentsia-driven revolutionary group committed to communist internationalism.

After peaking between the 1920s and '30s, both the radical communists and the labor movement lost support. This happened as Jews moved out of the needle trades and other union jobs, and due to the Molotov-Ribbentrop Pact, in which the Soviet Union formed an alliance with Nazi Germany. Radicalism ebbed and flowed in the postwar years. Jewish liberals and radicals alike were active in the civil rights movement. But revolutionary politics reemerged in the late 1960s with the Vietnam War, the rise of the New Left and radical groups like the Black Panthers and SDS creating rifts between generations and between liberals and the left.

That is to say nothing of the radicalism among some of the early socialist Zionists like Dov Ber Borochov and Nachman Syrkin that their followers brought to Mandatory Palestine. But before getting to that, there is still the fundamental question of why. Why are Jews so overrepresented in radical politics? Or, on the flip side, if we're not overrepresented, why does it sure seem that way?

The Talmudic tradition of challenging authority and arguing one's way to the truth is one possible source. "The Jewish heretic who transcends Jewry belongs to a Jewish tradition," wrote Isaac Deutscher in his essay "The Non Jewish Jew," on the roots of Jewish radicalism. The historian Walter Laqueur offers a more straightforward reason for Jews' attraction to radicalism: "Despite its occasional manifestations of anti-Semitism, the Left offered the Jews an opportunity to be politically active, whereas the parties favoring the established order by and large excluded Jews altogether from their ranks." Some radicals have shed their religious heritage as an encumbrance to political commitments, while others have tried to ground their ideology in Jewish tradition.

There are three groups most interested in the question of Jewish radicalism: Jewish radicals, Jewish conservatives, and anti-Semites. From them we get three archetypal responses to the question of "why?" The anti-Semite responds with some version of the rootless cosmopolitan—Jews are the devils of history, always disrupting harmony and creating disorder. The radical says that the Jews' historical experience of persecution has made them unwilling to tolerate any oppression and determined to create a more just world—the liberal tolerance we now take for granted, they say, was only made possible by the radicals. Jewish conservatives argue that the radicals have misread their own history and may, along the way, have internalized a self-hatred that leads them to reject the self-interest and self-determination they champion in other groups while embracing the naive premises of utopian politics.

"Jewish radicalism" is a badge of honor, a form of secular religion, a lament, an accusation, a sneer. It can have no final or definitive meaning because it's rooted in that mysterious noun, *Jew*, that always carries beneath it the meaning a speaker wishes to express, the one they would rather conceal.

a Jewish family on Long Island, Reed was a bridge-and-tunnel suburbanite who immigrated to the big city and became more definitively a New Yorker than any native. Reed's songs were blunt and acerbic, casting a withering eye on sex, drugs, and the downtown demimonde he inhabited as a member of Andy Warhol's inner circle. The landmark glam-rock album *Transformer* (1972) yielded his most famous song, "Walk on the Wild Side"; *Berlin* (1973) was a morbid and beautiful rock opera; *Metal Machine Music* (1975) was a pure sonic assault; and *The Blue Mask* (1982) was one of the rock era's great contemplations of marriage.

Refaeli, Bar (b. 1985)
Israeli supermodel. Leonardo DiCaprio's ex. How much is she loved back home? When she got married in 2015, the government agreed to shut down the airspace above her home to keep the paparazzi from using drones to snap pictures.

Reform movement
See Branches of Judaism, page 44.

refusenik
Imagine you've made a decision to leave the hated country of your birth, a place where you couldn't practice your religion or even claim your cultural identity. You must inform everyone, from your boss to all the people who live in your apartment building. You have to tell your friends that you no longer wish to be fellow citizens with them. And then your request for an exit visa—the necessary document to step foot outside the country—is rejected, refused. This was the experience for tens of thousands of Jews living in the Soviet Union from the late 1960s until the late 1980s, when the gates were finally opened. They became pariahs simply for stating their desire to emigrate. By creating this underclass of refuseniks (*otkazniki* in Russian), the Soviet Union also seeded a dedicated group of underground activists. Condemned to waiting (sometimes for months, often years, or even decades) for permission to leave and thrown out of Soviet society, the refuseniks in their liminal state had little left to lose and kept agitating to get out. The most high profile of them—names like Sharansky and Slepak and Nudel—became causes célèbres in the West. It was only when they were refused no longer that it was clear the Soviet Union was changing.

Reiner, Carl (b. 1922)

Writer, director, comedian, and actor who has been part of some of the most important and influential comedy of the twentieth century. Reiner was born in the Bronx to immigrant parents. He joined the army during World War II, eventually working as a French interpreter. His big break came in 1950 when he was cast in Sid Caesar's *Your Show of Shows*. He also worked in Caesar's fabled writers' room, where he met Mel Brooks. At private parties, Reiner and Brooks would do a bit of shtick called the "2000 Year Old Man," which somehow became a series of bestselling albums. He drew on his time with Sid Caesar for *The Dick Van Dyke Show*, which he created in 1961, and mined his early career a second time with the film *Enter Laughing* in 1967. Reiner directed several comedy classics, including Steve Martin's 1979 *The Jerk*, and he continued to act (*Ocean's 11* and its sequels, in the 2000s) and do voice-over for animation. His son Rob Reiner directed *When Harry Met Sally* and *A Few Good Men* but will forever be known as Meathead on *All in the Family*.

Renewal movement
See Branches of Judaism, page 44.

repentance
See **teshuva**.

Rhoda (1974–1978)
Mary Tyler Moore spinoff sitcom about Rhoda Morgenstern, a Jewish woman who grew up in the Bronx, moved cross-country to Minneapolis ("where it's cold, and I figured I'd keep better," she explains in each episode's introduction), and ultimately returned to her hometown ("New York, this is your last chance!" she announces over the opening credits). Portrayed by Valerie Harper—who isn't Jewish, but once said she was "Jewish in my heart"—Rhoda was the most enduring Jewish character on television since Gertrude Berg's Molly Goldberg on *The Goldbergs* decades earlier.

Ringelblum Archive
A collection of documents detailing life in the Warsaw Ghetto. Compiled by a team of writers, rabbis, and scholars in the ghetto and led by historian Emanuel Ringelblum, the archive included essays, diaries, testimonies, drawings, and any other documentation capturing the hardships of life under Nazi rule.

It was concealed in large milk cans and unearthed after World War II by one of the group's few survivors. Today the collection is housed in the Jewish Historical Institute in Warsaw.

Rivers, Joan (1933–2014)

Iconic stand-up comedian and plastic surgery aficionado, the comedian and actor born Joan Molinsky pioneered so many aspects of American humor that it's hard to remember a time when they didn't exist. A master of self-deprecation, she constantly turned her acidic wit on herself—her looks, her love life, her hypocrisies—and anyone else who caught her eye. Her career took off in 1965 on *The Tonight Show* with Johnny Carson, where she became a frequent guest; in 1986, she left her gig as Carson's regular fill-in to become the first woman to host her own late show, the ill-fated *The Late Show Starring Joan Rivers*—an accomplishment for which Carson never forgave her. In the late 1990s and early 2000s, she had a third (or fourth) act as a red carpet commentator and host of E!'s *Fashion Police*. An influence on talents as disparate as Sarah Silverman, Kathy Griffin, Whoopi Goldberg, and David Letterman, she was one of only four Americans invited to Prince Charles's 2005 wedding to Camilla Parker Bowles.

rootless cosmopolitan

See **dog whistles**.

Rosenberg, Julius (1918–1953) and Ethel (1915–1953)

Jewish American members of the Communist Party accused of divulging atomic-weapons secrets to the Soviet Union; they were convicted of conspiracy to commit espionage and executed in 1953. Ethel's brother, David Greenglass, worked at the nuclear laboratory at Los Alamos, New Mexico, and passed information to Ethel. The Rosenbergs' trial and conviction came at the height of McCarthyite anticommunist fervor in the United States, and their supporters were convinced that the couple had been framed or railroaded (indeed, there were irregularities in the trial). Given the Rosenbergs' obvious Jewishness, the case always had undertones of anti-Semitism, and many remain convinced that it was no accident that the only Americans ever executed for treason were a couple of working-class New York Jews. Despite international attention to the case and substantial pressure to commute their sentences, they went to the electric chair

RICH, ADRIENNE

(1929–2012)

This pioneering feminist poet and essayist became increasingly rabble-rousing over the course of her seven-decade career. She also became increasingly Jewish. Her early poetry was applauded for its elegance and formal restraint, but later she dove into race, gender, sexuality, religion, and free verse, all of which freaked people out. By 1970, she was engaged in the civil rights movement and in protesting the Vietnam War; she left her husband (who killed himself later that year) and came out as a lesbian. Her 1973 collection *Diving into the Wreck: Poems 1971–1972* won the National Book Award; she accepted the honor with Audre Lorde and Alice Walker "on behalf of all women." Her 1976 work of nonfiction, *Of Woman Born: Motherhood as Experience and Institution*, wrestled with motherhood and the patriarchy. Though her mother was not Jewish and Rich was baptized as a child, she asserted and explored her Jewish identity more and more in her later work. In all, she wrote thirty-two books of poetry and prose, and won both a Guggenheim Fellowship and a MacArthur "genius grant." The *New York Times* eulogized her as "a poet of towering reputation and towering rage," which seems about right. We should all be reading more Adrienne Rich.

THE ESSENTIAL ADRIENNE RICH

"Diving into the Wreck" (1973)

"Phenomenology of Anger" (1973)

"Power" (1974)

"Yom Kippur 1984" (1986)

"What Kind of Times Are These" (1995)

ROIPHE, ANNE

(B. 1935)

Although identified with Second Wave Feminism, Roiphe's voluminous oeuvre of novels, memoirs, and essays cannot be reduced to any political point of view. She is a woman of letters, a New York intellectual, a vocal Jew, and the author, most famously, of the novel *Up the Sandbox!* (1970), a book about women's sexual liberation that was turned into a not-terrible movie with Barbra Streisand. This passage from her 2014 essay "My Jewish Feminism" captures her virtues as a writer, how she mixes mordant wit with poignant warmth and never flinches: "My mother told me that I had a good nose but bad hair. I translate now: I had a gentile nose and frizzy, curly black Jewish hair. When I reached my late teens, I learned that many lovely Jewish girls were gifted as a graduation present a visit to the plastic surgeon, so we could reduce our inherited noses, wiping out centuries-old familial connections and leaving faces looking stunned and somehow empty, as if an eraser had passed over their features."

THE BEST OF ANNE ROIPHE

Up the Sandbox!
(1970)

Generation Without Memory: A Jewish Journey in Christian America
(1981)

1185 Park Avenue
(1999)

Epilogue: A Memoir
(2008)

at Sing Sing. In the years since, new information has reinforced the prosecution's case, and most scholars now agree that both husband and wife were spies, with Julius playing a greater part than his wife. Fun historical fact: One member of the prosecution team was Roy Cohn, later a mentor to Donald Trump.

Rosh Hashanah

See page 218.

Ross, Barney (1909–1967)

In an era of boxing when Jews were the toughest contenders and the greatest athletes, Barney Ross was one of the toughest and the greatest. He grew up in a rough Chicago Jewish ghetto and at a young age fell in with Chicago mobsters. Soon he stepped into the ring to support his family, and as the Nazi party rose to prominence in Germany, American Jews saw Ross as one of their greatest icons, tough enough to stand up to Hitler. He did just that when he signed up to join the Marines. As a boxer, he won over seventy fights and lost only four, without ever being knocked out. The fact that he stayed on his feet even during his few losses was of great symbolic importance for the Jewish community. He's considered one of the greatest fighters in the history of the sport and helped pioneer the tradition of moving weight classes.

Rosten, Leo (1908–1997)

Polish American writer best known for his indispensable lexicon, *The Joys of Yiddish*, published in 1968. But he also wrote wrote screenplays (including the one for the Humphrey Bogart thriller *All Through the Night*) and penned comic short stories for the *New Yorker.* His recurring protagonist was Hyman Kaplan, a charming, antic night-school student with an idiosyncratic command of English. At a time when much of America's Jewish population were immigrants from Eastern Europe, Rosten's readers had inevitably all encountered a Kaplan in their lives, either in the form of an uncle or a classmate, or even in themselves. The rest of us have encountered Rosten on our bookshelves or in Yiddish words that he brought from obscurity into mainstream English.

Roth, Henry (1906–1995)

Henry Roth belonged to one of the greatest Jewish American literary traditions: he came from Eastern Europe and attended City College. Roth's experimental 1930s novel *Call It Sleep,* a meandering account of life in a New York Jewish ghetto, has become a sort of historical record of Jewish life in early 1900s New York City. Although *Call It Sleep* has fallen out of print off and on, it was championed by critics like Irving Howe—even as Roth became sort of a Jewish Harper Lee, in that after his wildly celebrated first book he mostly went silent for more than half a century. His long silence became less mysterious in 1998, when a 1994 letter written by his sister, Rose, was discovered: the letter seemed to confirm that the two had had an incestuous relationship as children, which critics inferred had made it difficult for him to finish his long-planned quartet of highly autobiographical novels. In 1995, it was learned, the two had signed a contract in which Roth agreed to pay his sister $10,000, she promised not to sue him, and he made certain concessions about how he'd portray his young protagonist's sex life with relatives in the final two novels of his quartet.

Roth, Hyman

Character in *The Godfather: Part II* based on Meyer Lansky, one of the most notorious Jewish gangsters during the 1920s and '30s, and a good friend of Lucky Luciano (the father of the modern Mafia). See Jewish Gangsters, page 106.

Rothschilds

Crack open a history book and you'll find that the Rothschilds are a rather humdrum family of Jewish bankers and businesspeople who hail from a financial dynasty that began back in eighteenth-century Europe. Load up the Internet, however, and things get a lot more . . . interesting. That's because in today's fever swamps, the name "Rothschild" has become a stand-in for the Jewish conspiracy that secretly controls the world—which means that the family is held responsible for a whole lot more than just a few business transactions. According to everyone from neo-Nazis to Louis Farrakhan, "the Rothschilds" control your media, government, and the global economy. A local elected official in Washington, DC, even claimed that the Rothschilds were behind climate change, in order "to create natural disasters they can pay for to own the cities," he helpfully explained. (See **dog whistles**.)

Rothstein, Arnold (1882–1928)

See Jewish Gangsters, page 106.

Rubin, Rebecca

Little Jewish girls (to be fair, it was really their moms and bubbes) kvelled when the American Girl company created its first Jewish historical doll in 2009. Born in

ROTH, PHILIP

(1933–2018)

The most famous of American novelists had his admirers as well as his haters, as any great artist should. When the haters say that they "hate Philip Roth," the only sensible question is "*Which* Philip Roth?" For he had at least four careers. He was the prodigy who sent up second-generation neurosis and Jewish materialism in works like *Goodbye, Columbus* (1959), published when he was twenty-six, and *Portnoy's Complaint* (1969); the postmodern experimentalist, investigating sex and mortality at midlife in such works as *The Counterlife* (1986); the author of Big American Novels, in the realist tradition, like *American Pastoral* (1997); and the elegiac writer who pondered death in such late works as *Everyman* (2006). One of these novelists might strike you as callow. Another might strike you as obscene. And yet . . . another will be compassionate and poignant, and still another will be spiritually profound. Chances are that at least one of them will change your life. You'll have to read to find out which one.

THE RANGE OF ROTH

Goodbye, Columbus (1959)

Portnoy's Complaint (1969)

The Ghost Writer (1979)

The Counterlife (1986)

Operation Shylock (1993)

Sabbath's Theater (1995)

American Pastoral (1997)

The Plot Against America (2004)

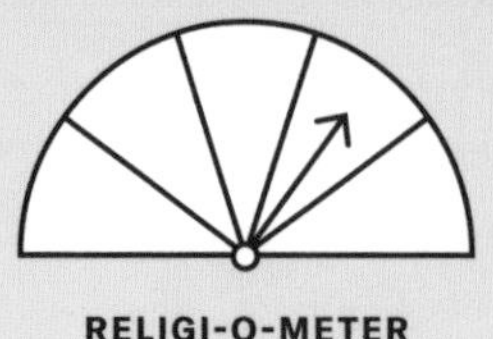

RELIGI-O-METER

ROSH HASHANAH

The holiday that marks the start of the new Jewish year. Rosh Hashanah is two days in the diaspora, one day in Israel.

WHAT'S IT ALL ABOUT?

Since the holiday is commonly known as the Jewish New Year, one would think Rosh Hashanah would mark the first day of the first month of the Hebrew calendar. It doesn't: Tishrei, on the first day of which we celebrate this major holiday, is the calendar's seventh month. Why, then, is it given the distinction of marking the new year?

Seven has always had special meaning in Judaism; although Rosh Hashanah itself isn't mentioned by name in the Bible, God, speaking to Moses in Leviticus 23:24, imagines the holiday as a sort of Sabbath for the soul: "On the first day of the seventh month," says the Almighty, "you are to have a day of rest, a sacred assembly commemorated with trumpet blasts."

These blasts come courtesy of the *shofar*, or ram's horn, which is blown to awaken the congregation from its spiritual slumber and drive worshippers to repent. In the Mishnah, the holiday is also referred to as "the day of judgment." The world, the rabbis tell us, is assessed four times a year: on Passover, God passes judgment on the earth's fertility for the coming year; on Shavuot, he judges the fruit of the trees, and on Sukkot, the rain. But on Rosh Hashanah, it's man's turn to stand trial, in the hopes of making it into the Book of Life.

Casting away sin, however, is serious business, so the custom of Tashlich was created, most likely in thirteenth-century Germany. The practice has its roots in the Book of Micah, which commands us, in the penultimate verse of its last chapter, to cast all our sins "into the depths of the sea." On the afternoon of the first day of Rosh Hashanah, Jews congregate by bodies of flowing water—usually rivers, seas, or, when necessary, faucets—toss in bits of bread while reciting portions of Micah, and emerge cleansed and ready to repent.

WHAT DO WE EAT?

You know all about the apples dipped in honey, which we eat to symbolize our wishes for a sweet new year. But did you know about the Rosh Hashanah Seder? Though not celebrated as universally as the meal on Passover, it is nonetheless customary in many Jewish communities to hold a culinary ceremony on the first evening of Rosh Hashanah, chomping on myriad foods—from the head of a fish to leeks and gourds and black-eyed peas and pomegranates—and expounding on the symbolism of each one. The fish's head, for example, represents our desire to be in the lead, and the pomegranate our wish to see our rights and good deeds become as plentiful as that fruit's seeds. Some foods, however, are eaten because their names make for convenient puns in Hebrew or Aramaic: the carrot, for example, or *gezer* in Hebrew, is eaten to ward off *gzerot*, evil decrees, against the Jews. Then, too, there is the challah. On Rosh Hashanah, the bread that appears year-round in its braided form is made on this holiday into a round, swirled shape, often enhanced with raisins. There are different explanations, among them that the circular shape has, like the world, no beginning and no end, or that the swirl looks like a crown, alluding to the head—or *rosh*—of the year.

WHAT DO WE DO?

During services, we recite two special prayers. The first is the Unetaneh Tokef, a beautiful medieval poem about the solemnity of the day. "On Rosh Hashanah," it reads, "will be inscribed and on Yom Kippur will be sealed how many will pass from the earth and how many will be created; who will live and who will die . . . But repentance, prayer, and charity can remove the evil of the decree." The other prayer, the El Maleh Rachamim, is read frequently in the Days of Awe (the ten days from Rosh Hashanah to Yom Kippur), and is a prayer for the souls of the departed, believed to be watching over those of the living in these crucial times.

And then there's the shofar. Although it is traditionally blasted (that's the technical term for what one does with a shofar, and the one who does it is called the blaster) every day during Elul, the month preceding Tishrei, it is on Rosh Hashanah that awakening is expected to begin in earnest. The horn makes three sounds: *tekiah*, one long blast; *teruah*, a series of nine staccato blasts; and *shevarim*, a series of three broken sounds. Saadia Gaon, the great tenth-century rabbi, wrote extensively about the spiritual importance of the shofar, seeing in the instrument everything from an allusion to the ram Abraham sacrificed instead of Isaac to a reference to Sinai, where a shofar was blasted as God delivered his divine covenant to the Israelites. Whatever the meaning, it is considered a great mitzvah to hear the shofar on Rosh Hashanah.

RUSSIA

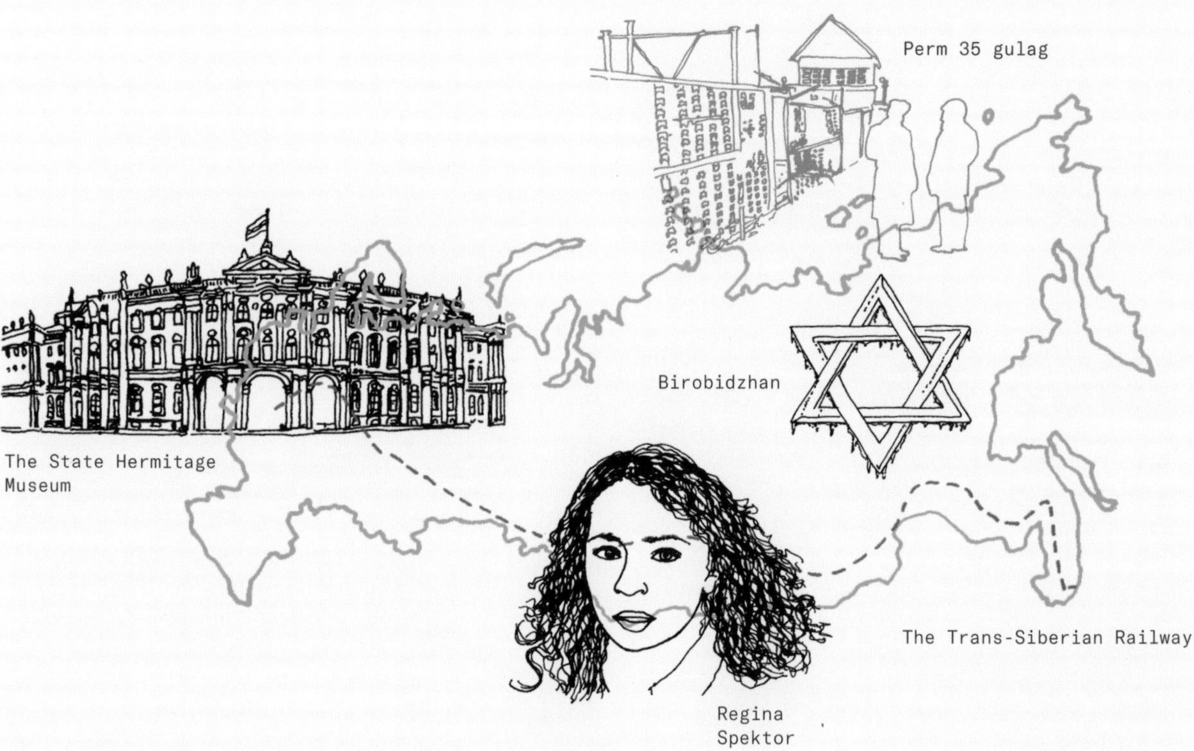

Throughout most of its history, Russia veered between barely tolerating its Jews and actively persecuting them. No Jews were allowed in czarist Russia, making the country Jew-free for centuries. In the eighteenth century, when the Russians took over much of Poland and, with it, many of Poland's Jews, they set up the Pale of Settlement and continued to torment Jews in every way imaginable, including actively instigating two waves of murderous pogroms. Life under the Soviets wasn't much better, and those brave enough to try and leave were punished and harassed (see **Soviet Jewry movement; refuseniks**). It's no wonder that nearly all of the most celebrated Jews born in Russia, from Ze'ev Jabotinsky to MGM's Louis B. Mayer, made a name for themselves only after they escaped Russia's pernicious grip.

1905 in New York City, Rebecca Rubin loves Coney Island, accompanying her Yiddish-speaking dad to work in his shoe store, dreaming of being a movie star, and noodging her mom to let her light Shabbat candles. She is bossy and loves to read. The Rebecca doll comes with a book about Rebecca and costs $115 plus tax. Her bed, which costs $125, is made of metal scrollwork adorned with gold medallions, with a lace bedspread lined in purple fabric and trimmed in sheer ruffles, plus an embroidered white bolster with tassels. Truth to tell, it's a little ungapatchka.

Rubin, Rick (b. 1963)

Possessor of the coolest beard in Malibu, Rubin is also one of the greatest producers in the history of American popular music, able to extrapolate song-ness from the conjectural noise that artists produce while playing around in a studio. He is meticulous in his attention to how even minute passages and effects can make the difference between a great song and one that is barely memorable. His genius for hearing the music that musicians meant to play, or almost played but didn't, has made him a sonic guru to the Beastie Boys, LL Cool J, Run-DMC, Slayer, Johnny Cash, the Red Hot Chili Peppers, Sheryl Crow, Tom Petty, Jay-Z, Kanye West, and the Avett Brothers.

Rubin's original act of culture-shaping came at the age of nineteen, when he captured on tape the hip-hop music that he was hearing in the parks and nightclubs of New York City, then reshaped that sound in a way that was true to itself and at the same time appealed to a predominantly white-skinned, suburban record-buying audience. The records Rubin put out under the Def Jam label, which he created in his dorm room at NYU, were nothing like the music on Sylvia Robinson's Sugar Hill label, which sounded like disco. They were records that a kid in an inner-city housing project *and* a suburban kid out in Lido Beach, Long Island, where Rick grew up, could both agree were cool. Rick's music became LL Cool J's music, which became Run-DMC's music and the Beastie Boys' music, which begat Public Enemy's music, which—with an assist from the West Coast—begat Biggie Smalls, which begat Jay-Z and Eminem, which begat Kanye West and his many rivals, acolytes, and heirs. DJ Kool Herc and Afrika Bambaataa invented hip-hop, but Rubin deserves some credit for making hip-hop great.

But Rubin's greatest genius has never been strictly for hip-hop, nor for any particular genre of music. It's for making records that convey the brilliance and originality of the American imagination, as expressed by artists of every race, gender, and creed, who made lasting American art and also made money. In that sense, his work is an expression of a particular American Jewish genius that George Gershwin, Louis B. Mayer, Billy Wilder, Leo Castelli, and Calvin Klein would all recognize.

RYE BREAD

Rubinstein, Helena (~1872–1965)

Born in Krakow, Poland, the eldest of seven girls, Rubinstein was taught from a young age that beauty was paramount. That maxim was proved when she moved to Australia at age twenty-four and was approached by women wondering how she had achieved her clear complexion. She sold women the jars of face cream she had brought with her in her suitcase, and from there her skincare empire was born. (Helena Rubinstein Inc. was later bought by L'Oréal in 1988 for "several hundred million francs.") She was the original Goop (see **Paltrow, Gwyneth**), offering women advice on diet and lifestyle from her salons in Paris, London, and New York City. She seemed to really know what she was talking about: Rubinstein died at ninety-two years old, with a multimillion-dollar business to her name.

Rumkowski, Chaim (1877–1944)

The head of the Jewish Council in the Lodz ghetto, Rumkowski was a brazen megalomaniac who printed his own face on the ghetto's currency and believed that he could outwit the Nazi death machine by making "his" ghetto indispensable to the Nazi war effort. Perhaps his most infamous and defining moment came when he implored the ghetto's tortured Jews to hand over their children and parents for deportation to death camps, as the price of keeping his workshops open. His speech on that occasion is by turns grotesquely self-pitying and chilling, and biblical in its force: "I was unworthy of having a child of my own, so I gave the best years of my life to children," the emperor of the ghetto implored. "I've lived and breathed with children. I never imagined I would be forced to deliver this sacrifice to the altar with my own hands. In my old age, I must stretch out my hands and beg: Brothers and sisters! Hand them over to me! Fathers and mothers: Give me your children!"

Chaim Rumkowski was a monster, born of a monstrous set of circumstances. And yet, at the same time, some historians have estimated that as many as three thousand Jews from Lodz may have survived the Holocaust in part because of Rumkowski's appetite for bargaining with death in favor of life. Leslie Epstein's *The King of the Jews*, perhaps the greatest novel to deal with the Holocaust, is a retelling of Rumkowski's story.

Russ & Daughters

Joel Russ arrived in Manhattan from Poland in 1907 and eked out a living selling schmaltz herring out of a barrel on the Lower East Side. When he saved a bit of money, he bought a pushcart. By 1914, he had earned enough to open a small store, and in 1920 he managed to move to a slightly bigger location on nearby East Houston Street. It stands there still: bucking the tradition of the time, he made his three daughters partners in 1935, renaming the store Russ & Daughters and turning it into an appetizing empire.

PEOPLE AT RUSS & DAUGHTERS ON HOUSTON

Russell, Anthony Mordechai Tzvi (b. 1979)

A black, gay Jew married to a rabbi, and an opera singer who has become a leading interpreter of Yiddish art songs.

Russia

See page 220.

Ruth

"Whither thou goest, I will go; and where thou lodgest, I will lodge: thy people *shall be* my people, and thy God my God." So said Ruth the Moabite to her mother-in-law, Naomi, in the Torah's Book of Ruth, becoming not only the mother of all converts but also the progenitor, according to tradition, of King David himself. We read the Book of Ruth on the holiday of Shavuot.

rye bread

The stuff that keeps your hands from getting dirty when you're eating deli.

FROM

Sabbath

TO

synagogue

Sabbath

See **Shabbat**.

Sabin, Albert (1906–1993)

Although far less known than his peer Jonas Salk, whose polio vaccine came to market first, Sabin's oral polio vaccine was easier to take; it came into widespread use a few years after Salk's, and together, the vaccines, with subsequent refinements, have nearly eradicated polio. Sabin, born in Bialystok, Poland, also developed vaccines for encephalitis and dengue. Yeah, he mattered.

sable

A type of fur for people who think mink isn't expensive enough. Also a type of sliced fish for people who think lox isn't expensive enough.

Salk, Jonas (1914–1955)

Medical researcher and virologist who invented the first widely released polio vaccine, which came into use for the public in 1955 after several years of testing. Before Salk—and his contemporary Albert Sabin, who invented a more easily taken oral vaccine—hundreds of thousands were still crippled, or killed, by polio annually; after Salk, the disease was nearly eradicated (according to the World Health Organization, there were twenty-two cases of polio on earth in 2017). Salk deserved, and got, worldwide fame. He was one of the few humans ever to noticeably improve the world during his own lifetime.

JONAS SALK

Samson

The original Avenger. When he found out the woman he loved was promised to another, he captured three hundred foxes, tied torches to their tails, and set them loose to burn down the fields of his enemies. Those enemies, in turn, demanded that Samson be extradited so that they might avenge their losses, and when he was delivered to them, he grabbed the cheekbone of a donkey and used it to slaughter a thousand Philistines. But not being quite so strong with women as he was with men, he let Delilah learn the secret of his luscious locks, rob him of his might, and drive him to spectacular suicide: he destroyed the Philistines' temple, killing himself and everyone in it. He remains the closest thing the Bible has to a mythological hero, a Jewish Hercules for the ages.

sandek

The sandek holds the baby on his lap or is the one to hand the baby over to the mohel during the bris. While the honor of being asked to be a sandek is traditionally restricted to men (often a beloved family member, like a grandfather, or a respected member of the community, like a rabbi), in more progressive Jewish circles today, a woman may get the nod. Choose someone with a steady hand.

Sandler, Adam (b. 1966)

You can learn everything you need to know about Adam Sandler just by looking at the names he chose to give the characters he played in his mega-popular comedies: Danny Maccabbee. Sonny Koufax. Henry Roth. Chuck Levine. While other actors often treat their Jewishness as something between a punchline and an inconvenience, Sandler wears his with great pride and joy. It is, oddly, the key to his comedy as well: think what you will about Billy Madison or Happy Gilmore—it's hard to deny the appeal of Sandler's infectious enthusiasm, the simple and silly warmth of a man comfortable in his skin. Oh, yeah, and there's also "The Hanukkah Song."

Sanhedrin

An assembly of rabbis sitting in judgment in every city in the ancient land of Israel. The name comes from Greek—*synedrion* means "sitting together"—but the concept is a Jewish innovation. Like Ruth Bader Ginsburgs of old, these wise men opined on every conceivable subject, from land disputes to death penalties. Each local Sanhedrin consisted of twenty-three rabbis, but the Great Sanhedrin, the Supreme Court of the day, convened in the Temple in Jerusalem and consisted of seventy-one of the wisest, chaired by the *nasi*, or president. After the Second Temple's destruction, the Great Sanhedrin moved to the Galilee, where it struggled to remain relevant under Roman occupation for a few hundred years. It was finally disbanded in 425 CE, although Napoleon, never one to shy away from grandiose plans, tried to revive it in 1806. The same spirit that made the Sanhedrins such vibrant places of disputation now moves countless law schools the world over.

Sarah

See Matriarchs and Patriarchs, page 176.

Sassoon, Vidal (1928–2012)

High-living, four-times-married British Jewish hairdresser and hair-product entrepreneur. As a poor child—he lived for a time in a Jewish orphanage—he joined a gang that fought Mosleyites, British fascist followers of Oswald Mosley, in the streets. In 1948, he went to Israel and fought in its War of Independence. But he was best known for his line of shampoos and other products and for his devilishly stylish TV ads, in which he famously intoned, "If you don't look good, we don't look good."

savta and saba

Think Bubbe and Zayde sound too shtetl-chic? Not a fan of the all-American Nana and Poppop? Find Grandma and Grandpa just too bland? Hebrew has just what you need: they're your savta and saba now, bub.

scallions

What Persian Jews whip each other with while singing "Dayenu" during the Passover Seder. Yes, this tradition is awesome.

scapegoat

Colloquially, of course, a scapegoat is one who is wrongly blamed for the sins of another. To learned Jews, however, a scapegoat is, literally, a goat. In Leviticus 16, Aaron, Moses's brother, rounds up two goats to bear the sins of the community; one is sacrificed, while the other is sent into the wilderness "to make expiation."

Schechter, Solomon (1847–1915)

In many ways, the Romanian-born Schechter, who in 1902 became one of the early leaders of the Jewish Theological Seminary, was the founding rabbi of Conservative Judaism. In 1913, he convened the United Synagogue of America (today, the United Synagogue of Conservative Judaism) as a network of congregations too observant for the growing Reform movement but more open to change, and more willing to engage in biblical criticism, than Orthodoxy. To this day, Conservative-movement day schools are known as Solomon Schechter schools.

Schindler's List (1993)

Maudlin but irresistible film, directed by Steven Spielberg and based on a novel by Thomas Keneally, which in turn was based on the true story of Oskar Schindler, a German industrialist who saved more than one thousand Jews, most Polish, during the Holocaust by employing them in his factories. For a time, the movie became one of those unfortunate works of art whose supporters want it treated as a religious artifact rather than a product of human sensibility. Thus, controversy arose in Germany when it was to be shown on television with several commercial breaks, which Jewish activists felt would dilute its message. In the United States, the television show *Seinfeld* gently satirized this reverence in a 1994 episode in which Newman spots his nemesis, Jerry, making out with his latest girlfriend in a movie theater during *Schindler's List*. Newman rats Jerry out to his visiting parents, who are suitably ashamed. (See Holocaust Movies: A Guide, page 137.)

schlemiel vs. schlimazel

What's the difference? An old joke explains it: The schlemiel is the moron who orders hot coffee on an airplane and then carelessly spills it all over the guy sitting next to him. The schlimazel? He's the guy sitting next to him. For those who wish to go deeper on this topic, see the title sequence to the old ABC half-hour comedy *Laverne & Shirley,* which begins with the unforgettable chant, "1, 2, 3, 4, 5, 6, 7, 8! Schlemiel! Schlimazel! Hasenpfeffer Incorporated."

schlep

Like so many fine Yiddish words, this one is both a verb and a noun. As the former, it describes the hauling of cumbersome packages—after you buy your four pounds of lox at Russ & Daughters, you have to schlep it back home. As the latter, it refers to a long and annoying commute—getting from the Lower East Side back home to the Upper West Side is a schlep.

schmaltz

The nectar of the gods: rendered chicken fat. You can spread it on bread, use it to roast potatoes, or, in keeping with tradition, use it to fry meat, since the more goyish butter is prohibited from that usage by the laws of kashrut. While some art-world twits use it to mean that which is "overwrought" and "maudlin," others

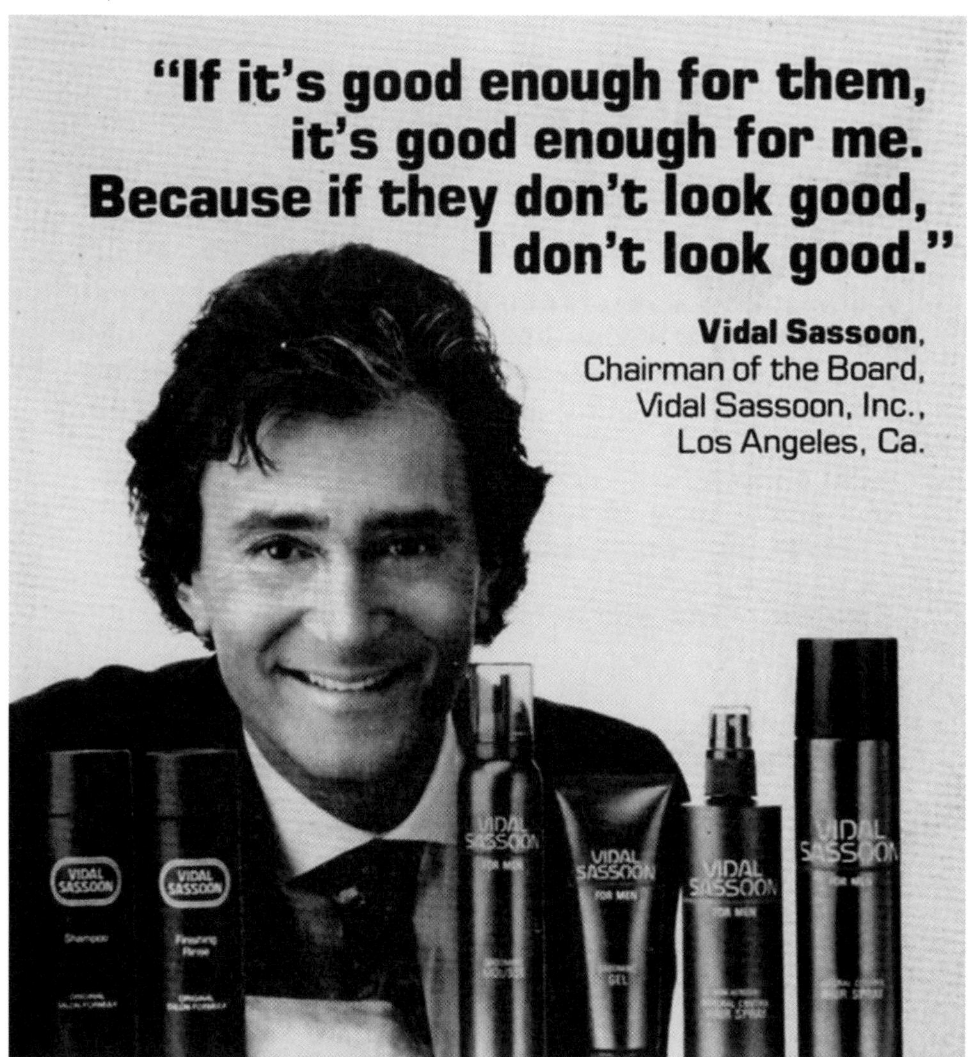

Vidal Sassoon: The British Jewish hairdresser took his clients' locks very seriously, as seen in this 1980s ad.

still hear the word and think warmly of Jewish cooking. Hence the expression "to fall into the schmaltz pot," meaning to catch a very lucky break.

schmear

Schmear, the noun, is the stuff you schmear on a bagel. *Schmear*, the verb, is what you do to a schmear. Got it?

schmuck

A crass Yiddish word for "dick," best used to describe a person. There is some controversy about its origins. In 2011, the Yiddishist Michael Wex explained it this way in a magazine interview: "Basically, the Yiddish word comes out of baby talk. A little boy's penis is a *shtekl*, a 'little stick.' *Shtekl* became *shmeckle*, in a kind of baby-rhyming thing, and *shmeckle* became *shmuck*. *Shmeckle* is prepubescent and not a dirty word, but *shmuck*, the non-diminutive, became obscene."

schmutz

Yiddish for "dirt." Was there ever a word that sounded more like the thing it was describing?

Schneerson, Chaya Mushka (1901–1988)

The daughter of the sixth Lubavitcher Rebbe, Yosef Yitzchak Schneersohn, and the wife of the seventh and last Lubavitcher Rebbe, Menachem Mendel Schneerson. Childless herself, she considered all of the Chabad Hasidim her children, and after her death in 1988 at age eighty-six, they repaid the affection by naming a generation of Lubavitcher girls "Chaya Mushka." There are thousands of them, all around the same age. "During the 1990s in Crown Heights, Brooklyn, where the Lubavitch movement has its world headquarters, schools were flooded with Chaya Mushkas," the Jewish newspaper *Forward* reported in a 2011 story. "[Mushky] Duchman said that at her Beth Rivkah school in Brooklyn, about 75 of the 120 girls in her grade were called Chaya Mushka."

Schneerson, Menachem Mendel

See **Rebbe**.

schnorrer

Yiddish for one who schnorrs: a sponger, leech, moocher, layabout. A schnorrer is one (thin) cut above a common beggar. The schnorrer is active; he does not just rattle some change in a cup and see what comes. He uses his wits, or at least his chutzpah, to get something out of you. He knows just how little he has to spend to get free Wi-Fi in the café, just how long he can crash on your sofa, and which happy hours have the best free wings.

Schoenberg, Arnold (1874–1951)

Austrian Jewish composer who immigrated to the United States after the rise of the Nazi party. Schoenberg is most famous for his experimental work in atonality, while his grandson Randol is most famous for helping people recover art looted by the Nazis (and was portrayed by Ryan Reynolds in the 2015 movie *Woman in Gold*).

Scholem, Gershom (1897–1982)

German-born Israeli philosopher and the first modern academic to seriously study Kabbalah. His voluminous writings remain deeply influential today.

schvitz

Yiddish noun *and* verb: you schvitz while taking a schvitz in the schvitz (see **banya**).

2nd Ave Deli

See Delicatessen, page 74.

Second Temple, aka the Temple

The First Temple, built by King Solomon in Jerusalem, was destroyed by the Babylonians in 586 BCE when the city was captured and the Jews sent into exile. The exile was mercifully short lived, and the Jews returning home got busy rebuilding their spiritual center anew atop Mount Moriah, on the exact spot where Abraham was said to have tied Isaac to the altar, ready to sacrifice his only child to God. Around 20 BCE, Herod, the Roman-appointed king of Judea, began an extravagant renovation of the Temple, and was said to have employed one thousand priests as carpenters and masons to make sure the Temple was thoroughly holy. His grand masterpiece, however, wasn't long for the world: In 66 CE, the Jews rebelled against the Romans, and four years later the Roman general Titus marched in with his legions and burned much of Jerusalem—the Temple included—to the ground. Jews the world over mark this tragedy on the ninth day of the Hebrew month of Av, a day of mourning known as Tisha B'Av. On that day, Jews lament not just the destruction of the Second Temple but all the catastrophes that ever befell the Jewish people. The only remnant of the Second Temple is a segment of the external fortifying wall, known as the Western Wall, or the Kotel.

Seder

Any dinner that requires us to drink four cups of wine is fine with us. If there's a text to read and argue about, even better. And if the text is about liberations—personal, spiritual, national—dayenu. (See Passover, page 195; **Four Questions**.)

Seinfeld

Wildly successful 1990s sitcom that presented New York as it truly is: a city of Jews airing their mishegas with one another at coffee shops and in apartments.

SEINFELD

Seinfeld, Jerry (b. 1954)

Comic, television star, and teen kibbutznik who made a fortune complaining about minor inconveniences. Born in Brooklyn but raised on Long Island, the seemingly Ashkenormative comedian's maternal grandparents were from Aleppo, Syria.

self-hating

If you are a Jew who has ever wanted to change your name, your hair, your nose, or your accent, you might be a little self-hating. Join the club, the club known as the human race. It's impossible, especially as a member of a historically stigmatized people, not to have moments of self-hating. With some Jews, the self-hatred becomes a big problem, and these Jews will get visibly uncomfortable around other Jews, or when somebody outs them as a fellow Jew (see **bageling**) or when too much Yiddish is dropped in a conversation. They are also the first to make it clear that *they* don't bargain-hunt, or approve of the Israeli government, or take off work for Yom Kippur (it's not *that* they say these things, it's *how* they say them). You don't want to be a Jew like that. Most of us are, sometimes. Fight it.

seltzer

Equal parts aperitif and digestif, fizzy seltzer primes the Jewish belly for gastronomic excess and settles it once the damage has been done. With the addition of milk and chocolate syrup, it's an egg cream, but on its own, seltzer is Jewish champagne.

semi-Semite

A half-Jew, somebody with one Jewish parent (or, one supposes, one Jewish grandparent on each side). If you are a semi-Semite whose non-Jewish side of the family is Italian, then you may also call yourself a pizza bagel. If the non-Jewish side of your family is Hindu, then you are a Hinjew.

Sephardi Jews, Sephardim

Expelled from Spain and Portugal in the 1490s, Sephardi Jews—the word is from "Sepharad," meaning Spain—sought refuge around the world, mainly in parts of North Africa and the Middle East (and, later, the Americas). Bringing with them a rich tradition of liturgy and customs, they deeply influenced the local Jewish communities into which they blended. As a result, the term "Sephardi Jews" is used interchangeably today to describe both those Jews who originally hailed from Spain and Portugal and Mizrahi Jews who come from Middle Eastern countries like Egypt, Syria, and Iraq.

settlements

What's a settlement? The question isn't as easy as it may seem. Tel Aviv University, for example, the alma mater of more or less the entire Israeli left, was built on top of Al-Shaykh Muwannis, a Palestinian village abandoned in 1948, about a month before Israel's War of Independence. To some Palestinians, every Israeli community built since the first Jews in the modern era returned to their ancient land in the 1880s qualifies as a settlement. To some Israelis, there's no such thing as a settlement, because the towns most commonly referred to as settlements happen to be smack in the middle of the biblical cradle of the Jewish people. To all but political philosophers and partisans, however, the term describes the Jewish communities built in Judea and Samaria—also known as the West Bank—after Israel took these territories in the Six-Day War. As of 2017, there are slightly more than four hundred thousand Jews living east of the Green Line, the border as it stood prior to the 1967 war, not including the Jews living in East Jerusalem, which some Palestinians consider occupied territory but which Israel officially annexed

SENDAK, MAURICE

(1928–2012)

One of the most important children's books writers and illustrators of the twentieth century. *Where the Wild Things Are* made him a star, propelling generations of bores to argue whether it's meant as a Freudian allegory or a postcolonialist takedown, but inspiring millions of kids to put on a little crown and roar. He also illustrated the Little Bear book series, written by Else Holmelund Minarik. A committed atheist, Sendak remained deeply attached to his Jewish roots. One of his last major works was an illustration of Tony Kushner's *Brundibár*, based on a children's opera most famously performed in the Theresienstadt concentration camp.

WILD THING

Nutshell Library (*Chicken Soup with Rice, Pierre, Alligators All Around,* and *One Was Johnny*; 1962)

***Where the Wild Things Are* (1963)**

***In the Night Kitchen* (1970)**

***Outside Over There* (1981)**

in 1980. Did we say this stuff is complicated? It is, even more so because of the fierce dispute over the legality of the settlements: Israel claims they're legal according to international law and stresses the right of Jews to once again dwell in their historical homeland. Many in the international community disagree. Still, the vitriol that is often applied to discussions of "settlers" obscures the point that this large population of people is incredibly diverse, from ideological, religious true believers to the family of four that just wanted a nicer house with a better view. Any future arrangement achieved in any future peace treaty will have to take all these nuances into account.

seven

The holiest number in Judaism. It took God seven days to create the world. We sit shiva for seven days. On Sukkot, there are seven mitzvot we are called to fulfill. The ancient Temple had a menorah with seven lamps, and the priests serving there would sprinkle the blood of the sacrificial animal seven times. At a Jewish wedding, the bride circles the groom seven times. We celebrate a bride and groom for seven days. You get the picture. For a good time, get a Kabbalist really stoned and listen to him or her go on and on about seven's mystical properties.

Seventeenth of Tammuz

See Fast Days, page 94.

sex

Despite what you might have heard, Judaism is not exactly "sex positive," although certain schools of thought have been. Nor is Judaism "anti-sex," although certain communities and thought leaders have been. "Judaism's approach to sex" is not a simplistic, one-note narrative.

In the Bible, sex appears prominently. There is an assumption that sex is a normal, positive, ongoing activity between husband and wife. Procreation is a fundamental value of the Bible; as a result, sex often (but certainly not always) appears in that context. (See **pru urvu**.) The Bible is astonishingly honest when it recounts any number of cases of sexual deceit, subversion, and coercion. Sex between men is condemned, and there is an almost obsessive focus on menstrual purity, from which today's Orthodox Jews get their rules of niddah.

The medieval mystical traditions, and the Hasidim who followed them, introduced the strongest note of asceticism into the Jewish view of sex. While waxing poetic about the beauty of sexuality as the ultimate unifier of the internal parts of God, sex between humans was more suspect. Masturbation took a heavy hit; texts equated it to murder.

Today, secular, liberal Jews are as liberal as anyone about sexuality: surveys show that Jews are at the forefront of LGBT acceptance, for example. (See **LGBT Jews**.) But in more observant, Orthodox communities, sex has been treated more conservatively—so Jews are among the most liberal of the liberal *and* among the most conservative of the conservative. Among Orthodox Jews, sex is highly regulated, perhaps more so than in any other religious community. For the Haredi, there is total physical separation of

Seder: A very 1970 Passover Seder celebrating the Exodus from Egypt

the sexes prior to marriage, and for Modern Orthodox Jews, too, sex in marriage is regulated by a woman's menstrual period. Upon the first sight of blood, she becomes a niddah, and husband and wife separate for approximately twelve days; the woman then immerses in a mikveh, after which husband and wife may touch again. There are hugely disparate opinions as to what sexual activities are allowed between a husband and wife. Additionally, most Orthodox communities today still do not approve of gay sex or of trans people. Sex education is another area where more traditional Jews lag behind their secular counterparts. And given the state of general sex education today, that's a very low bar.

SHABBOS GOY

Shabbat

Saturday, the last day of the Jewish week, is the day of rest. It's a weekly holiday, and Jewish holidays begin in the evening, so Shabbat goes from Friday at sundown to Saturday at nightfall. Shabbat is as old as Torah, being described in Genesis, where after God has created the heavens and earth, the sea and sky, and all the animals, he rests: "On the seventh day God finished the work that He had been doing, and He ceased on the seventh day from all the work that He had done. And God blessed the seventh day and declared it holy, because on it God ceased from all the work of creation that He had done." Jews are commanded to refrain from working on Shabbat. (See Shabbat in Seven Easy Steps, page 234.)

"Shabbat shalom"

Hebrew greeting used on Shabbat (see Jewish Greetings, page 114).

Shabbos goy

Observing the Sabbath and need someone to turn on the stove, turn off the lights, or perform other small tasks forbidden by *halacha*, or Jewish law? That's what a Shabbos goy is for. Just ask Elvis, Jackie Robinson, Colin Powell, Martin Scorsese, and Harry S. Truman, all of whom reportedly did their Jewish neighbors a solid by occasionally helping out on Shabbat. As with any Jewish loophole, this one isn't without contention: many religious Jews frown upon outsourcing these Shabbat-prohibited tasks, even in a pinch. (Also, some people believe Elvis is actually Jewish, but that's for another day . . .)

shadchan

The original dating app, the matchmaker's job was to make good setups. In ultra-Orthodox communities, this is still a job. Anyone who has ever swiped left probably wishes she or he could pay a knowledgeable and experienced person to take care of her or his love connections (see **shidduch**).

shalom

Did you know it means "hello," "good-bye," *and* "peace"?

Shalom Sesame

Paying no attention to what usually happens when Israelis and American Jews get together, this attempt to introduce *Sesame Street*'s iconic characters to their Israeli counterparts was mercifully short lived. The series, an attempt to teach American kids Hebrew and basic Jewish concepts, had five iterations, beginning in 1986, each featuring anywhere from two to ten episodes. By the time Mahboub, the Arab Israeli Muppet, showed up, even the gentlest of children had tuned out: there are conflicts out there that even Big Bird can't resolve.

Sharansky, Natan (b. 1948)

Seldom has there been a more unlikely leader than Natan Sharansky (born Anatoly Borisovich Shcharansky), the impish, balding, wisecracking chess champion from Ukraine who found himself the embodied symbol of the movement to free Jews from the Soviet Union. Sharansky began his activism in the 1970s when he became friendly with Andrei Sakharov, the nuclear physicist turned dissident and human rights defender, acting as his translator and liaison to Western correspondents in Moscow. Though always an effervescent presence among the refusenik activists, the spotlight truly turned on him in 1977 when he was arrested for treason and accused of spying for the Americans. His subsequent trial and sentencing to thirteen years of forced labor was covered with great attention in the West. He was on the cover of *Time* magazine, and his

Natan Sharansky: December 1982 demonstration calling for the dissident's release

SHABBAT IN SEVEN EASY STEPS

You look tired. It's been a hard week. You deserve a break. Luckily, Shabbat is here, and you don't have to be observant to enjoy the magical gift of relaxation and restoration. Just follow these easy steps.

① **Bless the people you love.** Nothing gets you in a better mood than feeling grateful for the people who make your life so rich. You can look up the specific blessing online or in a prayer book called a siddur, or just speak from the heart and let them know how you really feel.

② **Light some candles.** There's a blessing for this one, too, but the point is to enjoy the warmth and the light and the special atmosphere that lets you know tonight's going to be different.

③ **Enjoy a cup of wine.** Thanking the Lord is optional.

④ **Invest in a really good meal.** You don't have to be at work in the morning, so why not put in a little extra time and plan a fun meal? Also, remember: A challah makes every meal special.

⑤ **Rest.** You may not be one to observe Shabbat hard-core. You may want to turn on your TV, or hop in a car and drive somewhere nice. But why not capture at least some of the day's glory by, say, deciding not to check your work e-mail, or putting down your cell phone for twenty-five hours? You'd be surprised how far a little digital detox can go.

⑥ **Learn something.** If you're curious, read some Torah or another Jewish text. But even if you simply pick up a book about birds or Thai cooking or anything else you're into and spend a little time learning something that makes you happier, you're on the right track.

⑦ **Say good-bye.** As Shabbat ends, we do a Havdalah, a special ceremony to celebrate the end of our holy day and the beginning of the week. Try it: it kicks things off to a nice start.

wife, Avital, embarked on a decade-long campaign to bring attention to his cause. Sharansky became shorthand for the plight of all Soviet Jews.

His release as part of a prisoner exchange in 1986 was covered live, as the little man, whose pants were so oversize he had to hold them up, crossed the Glienicke Bridge from East to West Germany. It was the first major sign that many more Jews would soon follow—nearly a million and a half. Sharansky had a reputation as a man of extreme principle, unbreakable in prison, and an absolutist in his commitment to human rights. After moving to Israel, he quickly entered politics, eventually forming the Yisrael BaAliyah party and serving in two ministerial posts in right-wing governments, becoming a much more divisive figure than he had been during his long imprisonment. But in recent years, he has still been called on to help heal the growing divide between Israel and American Jews, for whom Sharansky still retains mythic status as the brave freedom fighter on whose behalf they struggled mightily for so long.

Sharon, Ariel (1928–2014)

The legendary Israeli general and prime minister Ariel Sharon was revered by many and reviled by more. Seriously wounded as a young officer during Israel's War of Independence, he miraculously recovered and went on to found Unit 101, the IDF's first commando outfit. Known for its legendary fighters and unconventional methods, the unit spent much of its time retaliating for Arab terrorist attacks. In October 1953, for example, after Palestinians sneaked into the Israeli town of Yehud and murdered a mother and her two children, the 101 decided to respond by striking the terrorists' village, Qibya. Sharon and his men attacked the village, blowing up forty-five homes and killing dozens of civilians. Many, including senior Israeli politicians, were shocked by the attack, accusing Sharon of war crimes. Others argued that the attack and others like it proved extremely effective in curbing terrorism. Sharon remained controversial throughout his military service, and he was never appointed chief of staff, even though he performed brilliantly during the Yom Kippur War.

Those who didn't want him as the army's commander, however, were soon forced to accept him in an even more influential role: in 1981, Prime Minister Menachem Begin appointed Sharon minister of defense. A year later, Sharon initiated a massive military operation to destroy Palestinian terrorist infrastructure in southern Lebanon, which quickly escalated into a full-blown war, with the IDF taking vast swaths of Lebanon, including Beirut. In September, Lebanese Christian militia, enraged by the murder of their leader, entered two Palestinian refugee camps in Beirut (Sabra and Shatila) and massacred hundreds of people. An official Israeli investigatory committee found Sharon guilty of ignoring the possibility of the militias' attacking civilians, and he was promptly fired from his post. But when *Time* magazine published a piece accusing Sharon of having encouraged the attack, he sued for libel and, after a widely covered trial, settled out of court. He spent decades holding a host of high-level positions, including member of Knesset and foreign minister, until running for prime minister in 2001 and winning. Israelis, wary of the collapse of peace talks with the Palestinians and renewed Palestinian violence, gave Sharon their trust. He surprised many, however, when he orchestrated Israel's unilateral withdrawal from Gaza, which many of his former colleagues and admirers on the right saw as a betrayal. On January 4, 2006, he suffered a severe stroke that sent him into a coma. He remained in that condition for eight years, and died January 11, 2014.

shatnez

Two Biblical verses prohibit the combination of wool and linen fibers, a blend known as shatnez. Although many reasons have been assigned to it, it's a law that ultimately falls into the category of *hukim*, laws with reasons beyond human comprehension; compliance is an act of faith. Observant Jews avoid the blend completely, and people make a practice of checking clothing labels. If someone forgets to check the label and later realizes he or she is wearing shatnez, the garment should be removed as soon as possible, which can be dramatic and exciting. For harder cases, shatnez laboratories exist, where specialists examine fabrics to determine their contents.

Shavuot

See page 236.

Shebrew

Slang term for a Jewish woman. It should be used only jokingly, only by a woman, and only in reference to herself or a close friend. If you have to ask if you can call someone a Shebrew, you can't (see **Jewess**).

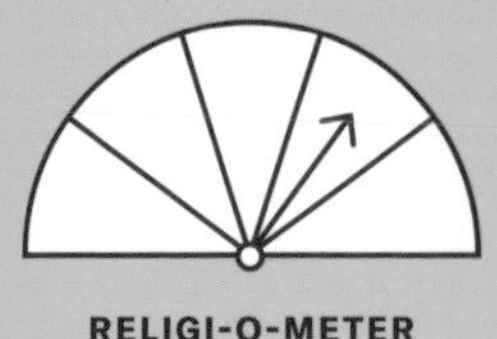

SHAVUOT

The day the Israelites got the Torah. To celebrate, we eat cheese and other dairy products. And stay up all night to study.

WHAT'S IT ALL ABOUT?

As you may recall, the Israelites left Egypt in a bit of a hurry, and it took some weeks until they were ready to attend to the business of receiving the word of God and become the official Chosen People. How many weeks? Seven, the Hebrew word for which, *sheva*, shares a root with the word *shavuot*, which means "weeks."

WHAT DO WE DO?

Traditionally, we read the Book of Ruth on Shavuot. It's like *Desperate Housewives* of Canaan—Dead husbands! Levirate marriages! Sexy harvest scenes!—whose heroine is a Moabite who converts to Judaism and becomes the great-grandmother of King David (symbolism alert: just as the Israelites accept the Torah and become Jews, Ruth embraces the Torah and becomes a Jew herself).

And then, of course, there's the matter of all-night learning. We weren't kidding about that: it's called a *tikkun*, and tradition has it that since the Jews didn't rise early enough to receive the Torah in Sinai—some accounts have God himself nudging them from their sleep, in what must have been the most terrifying wake-up call ever—they have resolved to stay up all night and study the Torah, commemorate the day it was given, and make up for the drowsiness of their ancestors. While religious Jews still adhere to Torah study, many less observant ones choose to spend the night studying anything from Jewish history, poetry, and art to contemporary Israeli television shows.

WHAT DO WE EAT?

Delicious dairy products. Cheesecakes are big. If your ancestors hail from the tri-state area—Poland, Russia, Ukraine—so are blintzes. The rational explanation for this particular culinary choice is that the Torah was given on the Sabbath, and as no animals could be slaughtered to celebrate the happy occasion, the Israelites likely shrugged their shoulders and collectively agreed to nosh on some Brie. More mystical Jews believe that the numbers speak for themselves: the word *dairy* in Hebrew is *chalav*, and if you add the numerical value of the three Hebrew letters that make up that word, you get the number forty. Which is a number you'd remember if you had to wander in the desert for as many years.

Shehecheyanu

A brief and charming prayer thanking God for giving us life and sustaining us and bringing us forth to this occasion. It's recited any time we have new and exciting experiences, from buying a snazzy outfit to having a child. It's also recited on the first night of major Jewish holidays like Passover, Rosh Hashanah, and Sukkot, and is a common song in Jewish preschools.

sheitel

In many Orthodox communities, married women cover their hair. Some do so with a *sheitel*, or wig. The fancy ones, which can cost thousands of dollars, are made of real human hair. (The religious world was roiled in 2004 to learn that a popular brand of sheitel used hair taken from a service conducted in a Hindu temple, making it nonkosher on account of idolatry.)

shekels

The ancient and modern currency of the land of Israel. May your wallet burst with 'em.

Shema

The most widely known prayer in Judaism. It's recited during both morning and evening prayer services. Its words are Judaism condensed to a single, simple sentence: "Hear, O Israel, the Lord is our God, the Lord is one." Many recite this prayer every night before going to bed, and some say it on their deathbeds, a final testament of faith.

Sheraton, Mimi (b. 1926)

A highly prolific food writer and reporter, born in Flatbush, Brooklyn, Mimi Sheraton is as famous for her biting opinions as she is for her deep culinary knowledge. Sheraton was the first full-time female restaurant critic for the *New York Times* (1976–1983). On the job, she became famous for her rigor, for donning disguises, and for not mincing words. Sheraton is the Statler *and* the Waldorf of the food world, and can deliver a burn better than a cast-iron skillet. She has continued to raise heckling to an art form in her later career, with a rapt Twitter following that waits to see what gastronomic darling she'll kill next (kale, for instance, is best prepared "farm-to-garbage pail," while eating Montreal bagels is like "chewing broken glass"). But Sheraton is as much a champion as she is a naysayer and has a special touch with the Jewish foods she grew up with.

Sherman, Allan (1924–1973)

Weird Al Yankovic's spiritual grandfather, Sherman was best known for his comic songs of the 1960s, especially "Hello Muddah, Hello Fadduh! (A Letter from Camp)," which peaked at number-two on the pop charts in 1963. But he was hardly a one-hit wonder; he released three number one albums in a row. He had a knack for turning then well-known songs into Borscht Belt–style (see **Catskills**) comedy bits, often with Jewish content: "Winchester Cathedral" became "Westchester Hadassah," and the calypso hit "Matilda" became "My Zelda" ("Why did she go and fall in love? / I haven't seen her since Tisha B'Av. / My Zelda, she took the money and ran with the tailor"), while the French nursery rhyme "Frère Jacques" turned into "Sarah Jackman," in which Sherman asks after his friend's extended family, from her brother Bernie ("he's a big attorney") to her uncle Sidney ("they took out a kidney").

Sheva Brachot

See Wedding, page 283.

sheygetz

The male equivalent of shiksa, and just as offensive—referring to a gentile man, it comes from the Hebrew *sheketz*, or "abomination."

shidduch

In Yiddish or Hebrew, a romantic match. In the old days, and still in very traditional communities, a shidduch was arranged by the families or by a shadchan, a matchmaker. The couple might have no choice, or they might—in some communities, the meeting was arranged, but the couple could refuse the match. Today, we still make shidduchim (the plural). At least, your grandmother does, and your mother's best friend tries to. But don't sneer at the idea of the shidduch: even in the age of JDate and JSwipe, it's often those who know you in real life who know what you need.

Shifra and Puah

In Exodus, Shifra and Puah were the midwives commanded by Pharaoh to drown every Jewish boy. They refused, telling the mad Egyptian king that even if they were to comply, Jewish women would still find a way to subvert his evil decree. As a result, little boy Moses escapes death and finds his way to greatness. For their courage and their faith, they were rewarded with being the mothers of Judaism's priestly class.

shiksa

Derogatory term for a non-Jewish woman; you'll often hear this word said about a woman who has married (or is dating) a nice Jewish boy. While some such women have embraced the term (see **shiksappeal**), it remains, for the most part, a degrading thing to call someone.

shiksappeal

The magnetic Death-Star-tractor-beam pull that non-Jewish women have on some Jewish men (see ***Seinfeld***).

shiva

Seven-day period of mourning following a funeral (see **death**).

shmatte

An old Yiddish joke: Surele is having coffee with her friend Rivkele. Rivkele accidentally spills coffee on Surele's dress. "Oy vey!" cries Rivkele, trying to wipe it off. "Where is your shmatte?" "Oy vey!" replies Surele sadly. "He's already at work." *Shmatte* can mean "wimp" or a person unworthy of respect, as referenced in the joke above. It can also mean shoddy or junk merchandise. Literally, a *shmatte* is a rag or tatter. For such a humble little word, shmatte holds within itself an outsize piece of Yiddish American history. According to Adam D. Mendelsohn's *The Rag Race: How Jews Sewed Their Way to Success in America and the British Empire*, in 1910, more than 50 percent of Russian-born and 44 percent of American-born Jewish men were employed in the shmatte trade. So central was the garment shop to Jewish life that it was the subject (and often location) of countless pieces of Yiddish literature, including a play by H. Leivick called *Shmates*. From the street-level ragpickers to the middleman sorters and bundlers to the David Levinskyesque garmento kings (see **Cahan, Abraham**), the shmatte trade was an entire ecosystem unto itself, one in which American Jews flourished like no other.

shmita

Judaism, at its core, is an agricultural religion, and just as humans must rest, so must the land: The Jewish calendar is divided into seven-year cycles, the seventh of which is a *shnat shmita*, or year of release, during which we do not plow, plant, or harvest the land. The main reason for this commandment, still observed by many in contemporary Israel, is to remind us that the land does not belong to any of us but to its creator.

Shoah

Hebrew word for the Holocaust.

Shoah (1985)

In 1973, the Israeli government commissioned French filmmaker Claude Lanzmann to direct what they hoped would be a two-hour film about the Holocaust "from the viewpoint of the Jews." Instead, Lanzmann recorded more than 350 hours of footage, interviewing survivors, perpetrators, and bystanders, and cut a 566-minute film, released twelve years later, that remains a deeply moving masterwork. The film, Roger Ebert wrote after its release, "is not a documentary, not journalism, not propaganda, not political. It is an act of witness."

shochet

The person performing the *shechita*, or kosher ritual slaughtering, of an animal.

shofar

The real reason you go to shul on the High Holidays. In ancient times, this musical instrument, made of a ram's horn, was used for anything from announcing the first day of each month to freaking out the enemy on the battlefield, as Joshua did when he had his men blast (blow) the shofar while laying siege to Jericho. These days, we hear the shofar mostly on Rosh Hashanah and Yom Kippur, but its ability to awaken the soul hasn't diminished a bit.

shomer negiah

According to Jewish law, a man and a woman who are not married are prohibited to touch each other in any manner, as it may lead to lustful activities (or mixed dancing). Still, some rabbis believe that if someone of the opposite sex holds out his or her hand, you should always shake it, because being shomer negiah doesn't mean you should make other people feel awkward. Like so many things about Jewish law, this one, too, is complicated. Oh, and it's also the reason why you're likely to see some male Orthodox passengers holding up El Al flights by insisting they can't sit next to female passengers. You know, because nothing is more lustful than accidentally touching the person sitting next to you in coach on an eleven-hour flight.

shomer Shabbos

To "be shomer Shabbos," as they say in Yiddish (the Hebrew is *shomer Shabbat*), is to "guard the Sabbath" or "observe the Sabbath"—that is, to follow the rules specific to behavior on the Sabbath. In Torah, the Sabbath, Saturday, is a day of rest, the day on which God rested after six busy days of creating everything in the world. A shomer Shabbos person honors that day by refraining from work from sundown Friday until nightfall Saturday (because the rabbinic principle is the more Shabbos, the better, you are always free to start before sundown on Friday, and you're not free to end early on Saturday). The rabbis made a list of thirty-nine *melachot*, or behaviors that are forbidden on the Sabbath, including sowing, plowing, reaping, tying a knot, tanning, writing, erasing, and kindling a fire. Those rules have been extended as prohibitions on other activities: if one may not kindle a fire, then, the thinking goes, one may not use a combustion engine, turn on electricity, and so forth. And that's why religious Jews don't drive or turn on lights on Shabbat. But Shabbat observance need not be 100 percent all or nothing. Lately, for example, some tech-addled iPhone junkies are attempting to observe "secular Sabbaths," not checking e-mail one day a week, not texting, turning off the TV—that sort of thing. (See ***The Big Lebowski***.)

shonde

See page 240.

shpilkes

Yiddish word for what nervous Jews feel the night before a big test, a long flight, or any other anxiety-inducing occasion.

shtetl

When thinking about the shtetl, the kind of small Eastern European town—bigger than a village, not as large as a *shtot*, or city—in which three-quarters of Eastern European Jews resided, we think of the fiddler on the roof as painted by Marc Chagall, or put to music by Bock and Harnick, all poverty and piety and tradition. But as recent scholarship shows, the shtetls were much more diverse than that, real places where people led rich and layered lives: not every shtetl dweller was poor, the poor weren't all pious, and the mix of mopey and merry probably approximated human civilizations everywhere.

shtick

Yiddish for "bit" or "piece," it refers to a comic's, or a character's, recurring theme or motif. Groucho Marx's cigar was his shtick. Gilbert Gottfried's yelling is his shtick. If someone's being totally sincere, it's insulting to talk about shtick—Bernie Sanders's populism is not "shtick," although many argue, including admirers, that Donald Trump's populism is.

shul

See **synagogue**.

shvach

Even with all the fabulous Yiddish words that have made their way into English, there are still thousands more that should have. (Basically, Yiddish is so lexically rich that we should all just learn it now.) Chief among the Yiddish words that should make the leap is *shvach*, which in the original German means "weak" but in Yiddish is far more insulting. Anything can be described as shvach, but when applied to a person, it means not just physically weak but spineless, flimsy, pathetic.

Shylock

The moneylender at the heart of *The Merchant of Venice* is Shakespeare's lone Jewish character and one of the most variable and versatile of all the bard's creations. The Nazis staged versions of the play in which Shylock was a walking caricature. But then there are those who've argued that the character—utterer of the famous lines "If you prick us, do we not bleed? If you tickle us, do we not laugh?"—represents a call for tolerance and understanding. Still others, like the literary critic Kenneth Gross, have argued that Shylock is nothing less than a stand-in for Shakespeare himself. Still, if someone calls a Jew a "Shylock," chances are they aren't looking to make nice.

Shyne (b. 1979)

Born Jamal Michael Barrow, the P. Diddy protégé embraced Judaism while in prison for his role in a 1999 club shooting with Diddy (then called Sean Combs) and Diddy's then girlfriend Jennifer Lopez. He changed his name to Moses Michael Levi Barrow, converted to Orthodox Judaism, and moved to Israel, where he told the *New York Times*, "My entire life screams that I have a Jewish neshama."

The concept of shonde (from the Yiddish *shonde far di goyim*, "a scandal before the gentiles") has haunted me all my life. The fear of creating a scandal, of causing embarrassment or shame within the Jewish community, kept me from publishing a sexually graphic novel I wrote and sold to a publisher over twenty years ago. The young female protagonist is involved in a heated, somewhat sadomasochistic relationship with a lout of a lawyer, and on page 210, to be exact, is commanded to crawl toward him wearing nothing but her birthday suit. On page 212, I called it quits and withdrew the book, unable to stare down the inner censor that accompanied my every other word, which in this case took the form of the women's section in my parents' shul, the Fifth Avenue Synagogue. I imagined Mrs. Finkel and Mrs. Hirsch reading along with growing horror as my fictional character's breasts scraped the floor and making absolutely no distinction between said character and me. The novel was written in the first person, which is generally enough to persuade unsophisticated readers who don't understand the fine-tunings of the creative process that the heroine and the author are one and the same.

SPORTS • FINAL
Friday, March 13, 2009
DAILY NEWS
50¢
2.5 MILLION READERS EVERY DAY
61727-054
BERNIE MADOFF IN SLAMMER AT LAST - PAGES 4-8
Why take a chance? Play both!
MEGA MILLIONS $26 Million! $23 Million! LOTTO

The history of shunning, whereby an individual malefactor is collectively indicted, would undoubtedly make for an interesting study. Meanwhile there can be no doubt that before social media and cell phone videos hijacked the arts of tarring and feathering a putative offender—of excommunicating him or her—there was the shonde. The word is Yiddish in origin, as many juicy terms are, and although it was originally employed only in connection to Jews who were avoided by other Jews for some egregious, shame-inducing behavior, these days it has passed into non-Jewish usage. But no matter the speaker, "It's a shonde," in the very casualness of its locution, is more likely to be whispered among a group of women at a fund-raising luncheon than thundered from the pulpit.

Shondes can be fictional characters like Shylock as well as real-life specimens like Bernie Madoff. For years, Julius Rosenberg reigned as the ultimate shonde. Religious heretics, like Shabbtai Zvi, can be shondes, but so can political visionaries, like Theodor Herzl, to those who disagree with them. In his depictions of smothering Jewish mothers and pervy Jewish sons, Philip Roth was a definite shonde far di goyim until he became a full-fledged literary icon, immune to such accusations. Eliot Spitzer and Anthony Weiner are definitely shondes. Then there are the men and women who walk perilously close to shonde territory without directly crossing over into it. I am thinking of Jared Kushner, a source of pride among some Jews and a laughingstock among others. Monica Lewinsky was portrayed as a shonde—although, looking back, perhaps the people who should be ashamed were the ones trying to ruin her life for the sin of wearing a thong.

There remains for me the question of whether, in these fragmented times, when the rate of Jewish intermarriage climbs inexorably upward and a dazzlingly high percentage of Jews don't identify as Jewish at all, the optics of shonde still apply as anything other than a cultural meme or stereotype, like the macher. Does anyone care what the community thinks, outside of a tiny group of deeply affiliated Jews? For a method of social control to work, there has to be an intact, viable context for it to work in, and I'm not sure that one still exists. Whether that's a good development or a bad one is not entirely clear to me, but you can be sure the old-fashioned brunch- or mah-jongg-table tut-tutting of shonde policing beats the character-smearing tactics of Internet shaming hands down.

And just so you know, I've picked up that abandoned novel again all these years later. Keep your eye out for it.

—Daphne Merkin

Big Shonde: Barry Freundel

On October 14, 2014, ten days after Yom Kippur, Rabbi Bernard "Barry" Freundel, one of the most influential rabbis in America, was arrested by the DC Metropolitan Police on suspicion of voyeurism. His alleged crime was unthinkable: placing secret cameras in a mikveh to capture nude videos of women in the mikveh bathrooms prior to immersion in the sacred ritual bath. The computers and digital storage devices seized confirmed authorities' suspicions. He was charged with six counts, with the final count of filmed women growing to over 150. Most of them were either students in his classes or women studying, under his direction, for conversion to Judaism. He pled guilty to fifty-two counts of voyeurism and was sentenced to six and a half years in prison.

A conversion candidate under Freundel, I was one of his victims. Many of us feared that the sentencing judge wouldn't take Freundel's crimes seriously, so a dozen affected women came forward at the sentencing to give testimony to the impact of his crimes. I told the judge and Freundel himself, "This case doesn't just affect one hundred fifty-two victims. It affects the entire Jewish community and future victims of sex crimes at the hands of rabbis. Will they think it's worth it to come forward? Will they feel safe? If you get off lightly today, I fear what will happen the next time a rabbi is exposed as a deviant."

The prison sentence, and the $14.5 million settlement reached three years after the rabbi was sent to prison, sent the right message. But the case exposed a deep and pervasive problem in the Orthodox Jewish community: the power rabbis have over women in their communities, especially in the realm of conversion.

The Freundel case came several years before #MeToo, but it now should be seen as an important, early first step toward justice for victims of misogyny, abuse, and assault in Jewish spaces.

—Bethany Mandel

siddur

Hebrew word for a traditional prayer book. Make sure to open it from the back, then read the Hebrew right to left. And don't hold it upside down.

Siegel, Bugsy (1906–1947)

See Jewish Gangsters, page 106.

Silverman, Sarah (b. 1970)

Her sister is a famous rabbi, she is a brilliant comedian. One of her most Jewish moments is her Christmas song "Give the Jew Girl Toys," in which she taunts Santa: "You have a list, well, Schindler did, too / Liam Neeson played him, Tim Allen played you."

SARAH SILVERMAN

Silverstone, Alicia (b. 1976)

If you weren't a teenager in the 1990s, you may never understand just what a revelation Silverstone was for Jewish pop culture obsessives. After breaking out in three Aerosmith music videos, she was cast as the spoiled but sweet Cher Horowitz in Amy Heckerling's *Clueless*. The role won her an MTV Movie Award, a Blockbuster award, and the undying loyalty of Jewish boys everywhere.

simcha

Hebrew for "happiness" or "joy," the word is most often used to mean a party, celebration, or any happy occasion. It also inspired the famous rabbi Nachman of Breslov to say that "it is a great mitzvah to always be in a consistent state of simcha." Amen to that.

Simchat Torah, Shemini Atzeret

See opposite page.

Simmons, Gail (b. 1976)

This food writer, proud Canadian, and most relatable judge on the long-running competitive cooking show *Top Chef* has gone on the record as saying that a "schmaltz and pickle juice diet is the elixir of life." She really gets us.

PAUL SIMON

Simon, Paul (b. 1941)

Paul Simon met his future singing partner, Art Garfunkel—of the stupendous last name and sublime Jewfro—when they were sixth graders in Queens. Together they gave us a bridge over troubled waters, gave future presidential candidate Bernie Sanders his finest TV spot (based on their song "America"), and gave *The Graduate* the soundtrack it deserved (people remember "Mrs. Robinson," but "The Sound of Silence" and "Scarborough Fair/Canticle" are there, too). After they split, Simon the solo artist made breezy, catchy background music for New Yorkers' post-'60s, pre-punk late-morning hangover, including "Kodachrome," "Me and Julio Down by the Schoolyard," and "50 Ways to Leave Your Lover." In 1986, he helped open Western ears to world music, collaborating with South African musicians on *Graceland* (1986). Like his now ex-partner, Garfunkel, Simon had a minor acting career, playing Tony Lacey in Woody Allen's *Annie Hall* (1977).

Six-Day War

Also known as the 1967 War. For two decades following Israel's founding in 1948, the Jewish state's relationship with its Arab neighbors remained tense, with military skirmishes breaking out regularly. Tensions flared up in May 1967, when Egypt's leader Gamel Abdel Nasser announced that he was closing the Straits of Tiran to Israeli shipping. A week later, he signed a pact with the Jordanians, who promptly invited the Iraqi army to deploy soldiers and armed units close to the Israeli border. Fearing an imminent attack, Israel formed a National Unity Government in early June and decided on a preemptive attack. At 7:45 a.m. on June 5, the Israeli Air Force launched Operation Focus, which destroyed most of Egypt's bombers and fighter jets. War immediately

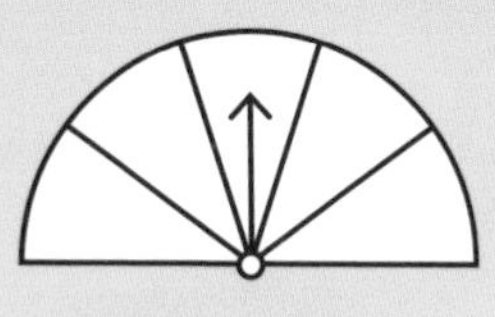

RELIGI-O-METER

SIMCHAT TORAH, SHEMINI ATZERET

Simchat Torah is the holiday that celebrates the conclusion of the yearly cycle of reading the Torah, after which we begin anew reading the Five Books of Moses, starting from the first chapter of Genesis. Falling at the end of Sukkot, Shemini Atzeret is the holiday on which Jews start praying for rain.

In Israel, Shemini Atzeret is celebrated on the same day as Simchat Torah. In the diaspora, Simchat Torah falls the day after Shemini Atzeret.

WHAT'S IT ALL ABOUT?

The Book of Numbers explains Shemini Atzeret simply: "On the eighth day you should hold a solemn gathering; you shall not work at your occupation." That's about it. The "eighth day"—*shemini*—concept suggests the holiday is part of Sukkot, a final eighth day of the holiday; it is, however, not part of Sukkot, though the two holidays share a focus on agriculture and Shemini Atzeret follows directly after the holiday of Sukkot. The focus of Simchat Torah is the Five Books of Moses—finishing reading them, that is. On Simchat Torah, minyan congregants read the Torah's last portion and then jump right back to the beginning and read the first, creating a never-ending cycle of book reading.

SINGER, ISAAC BASHEVIS

(1904–1991)

The winner of the 1978 Nobel Prize in literature is one of America's most beloved Yiddish writers. From his stories and novels emerged a Jewish life to which the clever and assimilated Jews born stateside to comfortable parents have all but lost their access, a world of piety, spirits, demons, betrayals, and great, unbridled passions. Several of his works were turned into major motion pictures, most famously *Yentl*, originally published in his 1963 collection, *Short Friday and Other Stories*.

SINGER'S SHORTLIST

Satan in Goray (1935)

Gimpel the Fool and Other Stories (1957)

The Slave (1962)

Short Friday and Other Stories (1963)

Enemies, A Love Story (1972)

A Crown of Feathers and Other Stories (1974)

Shosha (1978)

broke out, with Egypt, Jordan, and Iraq, joined by Syria, fighting Israel. Despite having fewer than half as many soldiers as their opponents, the IDF prevailed, with the overwhelmed Arab armies agreeing to a ceasefire six days later on June 10. By the end of the war, Israel had seized the West Bank and East Jerusalem from Jordan, the Golan Heights from Syria, and the Gaza Strip and Sinai Peninsula from Egypt. Of these, only East Jerusalem was officially annexed to Israel. Photographs of Israeli paratroopers praying at the Western Wall, Judaism's holiest spot, which for decades had been inaccessible to Jews, became instantly iconic, with many in Israel and around the world seeing the victory as a divine miracle. The war's outcome, however, soon spawned many earthly challenges, with Israel now governing millions of Palestinians living in the West Bank and Gaza, a conflict that simmers still.

The sixties
See The Jewish Sixties, page 246.

613
According to tradition, 613 is the number of mitzvot, or commandments, in the Torah. The medieval sage Maimonides famously made a count of all of them, but he wasn't the first to do so.

Smirnoff, Yakov (b. 1951)

Odessa-born comedian, now American citizen, Smirnoff (né Yakov Naumovich Pokhis) was a pre-Internet pop culture fixture of a certain phase of the Cold War. He peaked in 1988, when he was invited to entertain President Ronald Reagan at the White House Correspondents Association dinner (an honor he shared with such eighties luminaries as Rich Little and Sinbad). For better or worse, his hugely popular naive-émigré persona probably did more to shape American attitudes toward the Soviet Jewish refugees arriving in the late 1970s and through the 1980s than any bracing speech by Natan Sharansky. Because under his now eye-roll-inducing refrain of "What a country!" was a heartfelt embrace of newfound freedom.

snowbirds
Jews who have had it with frigid Northeastern winters and decamp to Florida for half the year. They have been known to eat dinner at five o'clock and call the grandchildren at seven, just before bedtime (theirs, not the grandchildren's).

socialism, socialists
From Marx to Trotsky to Rosa Luxemburg, Jews were the authors of much of socialist history, and if Bernie Sanders is any indication, our revolutionary game is still strong. See Radical Jews, page 212; Politics and Jews, page 200.

SodaStream
Israel-based manufacturer of home seltzer-making devices. The company had a factory in the West Bank, which made it a target of pro-Palestinian activists and

BDS supporters. Facing pressure, they ultimately moved the factory, ironically losing five hundred Palestinians their jobs in a very public scuffle that also involved the company's celebrity endorser, Scarlett Johansson. In 2018, SodaStream was bought by PepsiCo for $3.2 billion.

SUSAN SONTAG

Soloveitchik, Joseph (1903–1993)

When they call you simply "the Rav" (the Rabbi), you know you have some clout. A scholar, teacher, and philosopher who headed Yeshiva University's theological seminary, Soloveitchik trained more than two thousand Orthodox rabbis in the course of his career and taught and influenced tens of thousands of students. Considered the spiritual father of Modern Orthodoxy, Soloveitchik advocated a synthesis between religious and secular teachings, and wrote, in *The Lonely Man of Faith* (1965), about man's dual nature as a reverential creature yearning for God on one hand and a social animal seeking the approval of peers on the other.

Sondheim, Stephen (b. 1930)

Brilliant composer and lyricist who made the Broadway musical grow up. *Company* (1970), *Follies* (1971), *A Little Night Music* (1973), *Sweeney Todd* (1979), *Merrily We Roll Along* (1981), *Sunday in the Park with George* (1984), *Into the Woods* (1987), *Assassins* (1990)—with these and other shows, Sondheim asserted that the musical could accommodate the same range of subject matter, the same breadth of ideas and emotions, as any other art form. He collaborated with Leonard Bernstein on *West Side Story* and with Jule Styne on *Gypsy*. Sondheim's philosophical, often dark sensibility can be traced back to a childhood he has described as emotionally isolated. He was born and raised in Manhattan, in a large Central Park West apartment that he shared, following his parents' divorce, with an emotionally abusive mother. His childhood, Sondheim told his biographer, was "luxurious . . . an environment that supplies you with everything but human contact."

Song of Songs

Attributed to King Solomon, this moving poem is part of the Ketuvim, or writings, that make up the final part of the Hebrew Bible. It's about love and yearning and sex and jealousy and all that other good stuff that makes us human. With lines like "Set me as a seal upon thine heart, as a seal upon thine arm: for love is strong as death; jealousy is cruel as the grave," it's as steamy today as it was back in the days of good ol' Solomon.

Sontag, Susan (1933–2004)

Influential essayist, novelist, director, and activist. Her early essays included "Notes on Camp" and "Against Interpretation" (both 1964); in the latter, she famously wrote, "In place of a hermeneutics we need an erotics of art." In her last notable work, an essay in the *New Yorker* published two weeks after September 11, 2001, she all but blamed America for the attacks, calling them "a monstrous dose of reality." In the last years of her life, her partner was the photographer Annie Leibovitz.

Soros, George (b. 1930)

Holocaust survivor, billionaire, and supporter of many progressive causes and organizations around the world. Frequently cited by anti-Semites as proof that the Jews really do control everything (see **dog whistles**). Just as frequently defended by supporters as a one-man bulwark against global illiberalism. In reality, thankfully, neither of those things.

Soup Nazi

Fictional chef whose stringent rules made him a beloved *Seinfeld* character. The *real* Soup Nazi, who didn't like the nickname but certainly liked the publicity, is Ali "Al" Yeganeh, an Iranian immigrant whose storefront in Midtown Manhattan was extremely popular for its high-quality soups. During lunchtime, a line would form around the block, and in an effort to keep things moving, a fairly strict ordering process was instated. After it was lampooned on *Seinfeld,* Yeganeh's shop went from crowded to insane. Yeganeh turned his shop into a franchise—The Original Soup

The Jewish Sixties

For four centuries, European Jews have loomed so large in movements of the Enlightenment (Baruch Spinoza, Moses Mendelssohn) and the left (socialists, communists, Old Left, New Left) that a believer might be forgiven for thinking the Jews had been divinely recruited to speak up for human equality and sweet reason. For their part, lamebrained exponents of the canard that Elders of Zion conspire in conclaves to poison the innocent and rule the world brandished the fact that Karl Marx was the grandson of two rabbis (though Karl's father converted to Christianity before he was born) and that Leon Trotsky, among other eminent Bolsheviks, was born Jewish. So were the influential European Social-ist Democrats Eduard Bernstein and Léon Blum, along with some rulers of Soviet satellite states. (Of course, any generalization that "the Jews" always lean left ignores Benjamin Disraeli, Vladimir Jabotinsky, Milton Friedman, and Stephen Miller.)

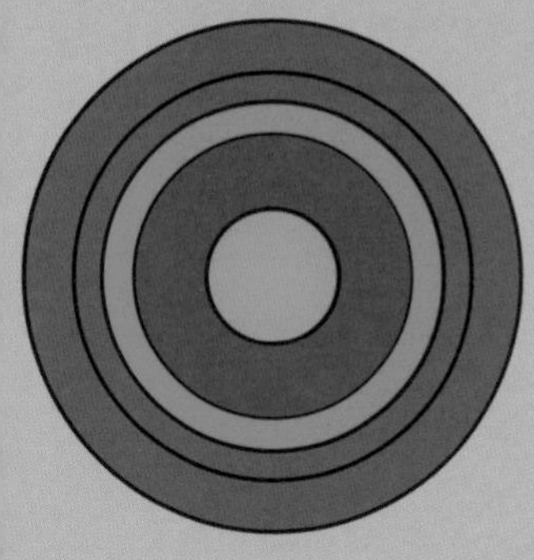

Still, it is obvious that the 1960s' American left and the counterculture of the 1960s would be unrecognizable without Jews, most of them not practitioners of Judaism but culturally Jewish in some fashion. On the countercultural side, Allen Ginsberg was the iconic bard, familiar not only for poetic jeremiads and psalms but for his hirsute presence in the thick of antiwar demonstrations. Yippies Abbie Hoffman, Jerry Rubin, and Paul Krassner were unimaginable without Ginsberg. If one cocked an ear for the theme songs that accompanied the movements, what would protest have sounded like without Bob Dylan and Phil Ochs? Dull.

Jews were crucial in starting many radical and liberal groups, including the leading organization of the student New Left, Students for a Democratic Society (SDS). The founding father, and first president, was Al Haber. Among Haber's earliest recruits were Dick and Mickey Flacks and Bob Ross, in Ann Arbor; another was Paul Booth, head of the Swarthmore SDS chapter; another was Steve Max of New York City. All went on to play crucial roles in the radicalism of the following decade, as did Carol (Cohen) McEldowney, Richard Rothstein, and the half-Jewish Paul Potter. In the final inferno that destroyed SDS, the terrorist Weather Underground numbered among its leaders Mark Rudd, Kathy Boudin, and the half-Jewish Bernardine Dohrn, while other factions were led by Michael Klonsky and Jared Israel of the Maoist Progressive Labor Party (which had been founded by the breakaway communist Milt Rosen). Jewish academics such as William Gamson and Barry Commoner led antiwar teach-ins. Noam Chomsky became a leading intellectual light on the left, and rabbis Joachim Prinz and Abraham Heschel were prominent religious voices in civil rights.

Contemporary feminism (see Feminism and Jews, page 96) was launched in no small measure by Betty Friedan and personified by Gloria Steinem; prominent feminist activists of the younger, New Left generation were Heather (Tobis) Booth, Shulamith Firestone, Ellen Willis, Robin Morgan, Alix Kates Shulman, Susan Brownmiller, Marilyn (Salzman) Webb, and Naomi Weisstein.

Why the left-wing tilt? A bedrock assumption of those years was that Jews had a particular and urgent stake in resisting political evil (in the name of universalist principles, paradoxically). During the civil rights era, Jews identified with African Americans, just as African Americans identified with the Jewish liberation from Pharaonic Egypt. Many civil rights workers were "red diaper babies," children of earlier radicals. Jews and blacks cooperated closely until the rise of Black Power and the brutal collision between Jewish teachers and black parents in New York City in 1968–69. In a word, Jews were welcome on the left.

And, surely, a powerful influence was the continuing shock of the Holocaust. "Never Again" was interpreted as "Never again consign any people to wholesale slaughter." Jews were ourselves not at risk, and were by and large comfortable, in an America with declining anti-Semitism. And until the Six-Day War, the State of Israel was not unpopular with the New Left, many of whose members held romantic views of Israel's socialistic, kibbutznik spirit—just as anticolonial sentimentalists would later lionize the Palestinian national movement. But no matter the cause, the passion to fulfill the biblical commandment and pursue justice still burns bright.

Man—and the Soup Nazi shouting "No soup for you!" lives on in reruns.

Soutine, Chaim (1893–1943)

Perhaps the most underrated of modernist painters. Born in Belarus, he was the tenth of eleven children. At twenty, he moved to Paris to study art and was quickly hailed as an original. He once kept an animal carcass in his studio so he could observe and paint it. The stench drove his neighbors to call the police, but Soutine was unmoved, telling the officers that art was more important than hygiene. But when his friend and neighbor Marc Chagall came over and saw the animal's blood leaking into the corridor, he ran out of the building, screaming, "Someone has killed Soutine." In 2015, the resulting painting, *Le Bœuf*, was sold in a Christie's auction in New York for more than $28 million.

Soviet Jewry movement

To be a Jew in the Soviet Union in the decades following World War II was to experience a sort of schizophrenia. On one hand, Jews were denied any ability to have a Jewish identity. All but a handful of synagogues were closed. Jewish cultural and social institutions were outlawed. There were known quotas on what schools or jobs were open to Jews. On the other hand, Jews could not assimilate even if they wanted to because they were administratively categorized as Jews and kept apart as a separate minority. On top of all this, though Israel and America beckoned, it was impossible to leave. Out of the frustration of this situation was born a 1960s dissident movement that soon echoed in the West among what was at first dismissed as "students and housewives." The movement soon became personalized through the story of refuseniks and even, in 1970, a high-stakes attempt by a small group of Jews in Leningrad to hijack a plane and fly it out of the country. The greatest legislative achievement of the movement came in the mid-1970s with the Jackson-Vanik Amendment, which made improved trade relations between the two superpowers contingent on the Soviet Union changing its emigration policy.

The plight of Soviet Jews held a central place in the public consciousness in an era when the problem of human rights became a driver of American foreign policy and its greatest cudgel against the communist foe. The movement's concerns were so central that when Mikhail Gorbachev finally attempted to reform his society in the 1980s, he knew he had to loosen emigration restrictions if he was to find any common ground with the Americans. It was a move that eventually led to a flood of a million and a half Soviet Jews leaving for Israel and the United States, and presaged the end of the Soviet Union, undone finally by the number of people who simply didn't like their lives there anymore. The movement's lasting achievement, beyond the sheer numbers of people who found freedom through it, was the unity it created, bringing under one banner a cause that appealed to Jews to help other Jews as well as a human rights principle that all people should be allowed to vote with their feet. This convergence, particular and universal, has been rare in Jewish history and is in large part the reason for the movement's great success. (See **Sharansky, Natan**.)

Spanish and Portuguese Synagogue

Also known as Congregation Shearith Israel, this shul on the Upper West Side of Manhattan is the oldest Jewish congregation in the United States, a fact its members are likely to slip into conversation early and often. Established in 1654, it was, until 1825, the only synagogue in New York City. During the Revolutionary War, when hundreds of prominent New Yorkers greeted King George III's soldiers with a "Declaration of Dependence," Shearith Israel stood out for its support of George Washington, an allegiance that eventually compelled them to pack up their Torah scrolls and flee to Philadelphia for a time. Although its Sephardi membership has diminished and the congregation is more Ashkenazi than ever, the prayer minhag is still Sephardi, and the clergy still dress in some really dapper duds, "canonicals" of ministerial gowns, lace collars, and clergy caps.

Spelling, Aaron (1923–2006)

Born to Polish and Russian immigrants in Dallas, Texas, Spelling became the single most prolific writer and producer in US television history. He was responsible for the often-imitated and award-winning dramas *Charlie's Angels*, *Fantasy Island*, *The Love Boat*, *Dynasty*, and *Beverly Hills, 90210* (which starred his daughter, Tori), as well as *Sunset Beach* and other hits.

Spider-Man

Perhaps the world's most beloved comic book character. He started life as Peter Parker, a nebbishy and neurotic high school nerd from Queens, and if he hadn't been bitten by that radioactive spider, he might have ended up as a character in a Philip Roth novel. (See **comic books**.)

Spiegelman, Art (b. 1948)

Contrary to popular belief, Art Spiegelman is not a movement like art nouveau or art deco but the name of an actual artist, like Art Garfunkel. But he is kind of a movement, in that he made graphic novels respectable. By far his most famous work is the seminal piece of Holocaust art, *Maus*—a graphic novel about his father's experience in the Holocaust.

SPIELBERG, STEVEN

(B. 1946)

Film director and Hollywood macher whose artistic talent is matched only by his industry clout. Approval from Mr. Spielberg is the Tinseltown version of a voice echoing from atop Mount Sinai. His skills emerged early, first on television, with an innate understanding of how to use visual language to enthrall audiences. *Jaws* (1975) radically changed the movie business, effectively inventing the notion of the summer blockbuster. (While a tremendous success, *Jaws* was a difficult shoot; for decades Spielberg would visit the set of the *Orca* on the Universal lot to brood, as if revisiting a battlefield.)

THE REAL SPIEL

Jaws (1975)

Close Encounters of the Third Kind (1977)

Raiders of the Lost Ark (1981)

E.T. the Extra-Terrestrial (1982)

Schindler's List (1993)

Saving Private Ryan (1998)

Other big early Spielberg hits include 1977's *Close Encounters of the Third Kind* and 1982's *E.T. the Extra-Terrestrial*, followed by *Jurassic Park*, which cemented his style of mixing thrills and wonderment. With his chum George Lucas, he created the Indiana Jones character. Heading into the 1990s, he made more serious work, culminating in the Oscar-winning *Schindler's List* (1993). Working on it led the secular Spielberg to move closer to his Jewish heritage, and revenue from the project helped set up the USC Shoah Foundation, which has recorded more than fifty thousand survivor testimonies.

spinagogue

The twenty-first-century practice of attending SoulCycle on Jewish holidays as a way to reflect, recharge, and tap it back.

Spinoza, Baruch (1632–1677)

A Jewish philosopher born in Holland to a family of Portuguese Jews. His philosophy, rejecting the notion of a transcendental God and seeing the divine instead in nature and all its facets, made him one of the forefathers of the Enlightenment. It also made him an enemy of his own Jewish community, which found his rejection of divinely inspired morals intolerable. He was formally shunned, but remains one of the most widely read and discussed thinkers in the world to this day (see Are We All Actually Related?, page 19).

"spiritual, not religious"

What you say you are when you have no idea what either of these terms actually means.

Spock

Half-human, half-Vulcan science officer aboard the USS *Enterprise* and voice of logic to Captain James T. Kirk (William Shatner) as they zoom across the

galaxy in the twenty-third century (or on television's *Star Trek*, 1966–1969). Played by Leonard Nimoy, who was raised Orthodox in Boston, Spock (or Mr. Spock, if you want to get formal) was one of the late 1960s' unlikely sex symbols. His unusual look, with pointy ears and eyebrows, never let the viewer forget his outsider status as a Vulcan. The Vulcans' complex belief system, ancient wisdom, harsh dogma, and preoccupation with study and knowledge could easily be read as Jewish. The planet of Vulcan is hot, like Israel, and if you pay attention you'll see that Spock is quite often zinging his colleagues and making great jokes—it's just that those around him are seldom up to his level of intelligence. The famous Vulcan salute, devised on set by Nimoy himself, is based on the Kohanim's priestly blessing. The hand gesture and the optimism associated with the accompanying phrase "live long and prosper" has become a reference not just to *Star Trek* but to space exploration in general. There's even a Vulcan salute emoji. Spock was famously eulogized by his friend Kirk, who said: "Of all the souls I have encountered in my travels, his was the most human."

sports

See Sports and Jews, opposite page.

Star of David

The six-pointed star (also known as the Shield of David, or Magen David) that can be found on the flag of Israel, on your uncle's tallit, on the kippot you gave out at your bat mitzvah, and on the lintel above the door to your synagogue. But as the great scholar Gershom Scholem wrote in 1949, "Actually the six-pointed star is not a Jewish symbol . . . It has none of the criteria that mark the nature and development of the true symbol. It does not express any 'idea,' it does not arouse ancient associations rooted in our experiences, and it is not a shorthand representation of an entire spiritual reality, understood immediately by the observer. It does not remind us of anything in biblical or in rabbinic Judaism." The six-pointed star was a magical symbol popular in many traditions in the Middle Ages, and only in the nineteenth century did its rising popularity among Jews, who used it on the seals of their local communities and to decorate their synagogues, lead to its specific association with one community. Thus did a symbol that had been associated with many practices Jews would have considered heretical become adopted as something supposedly sacred to Jews.

Stein, Gertrude (1874–1946)

Impenetrable writer, she ran a salon in Paris where almost every single important jazz era and modernist artist convened: Picasso, Hemingway, Fitzgerald, Ezra Pound, Matisse, and others. With her partner, Alice B. Toklas, somehow remained publicly Jewish in France during the Nazi occupation; how is still a great mystery to this day.

SPORTS AND JEWS

You know the joke about sports and Jews. You may even know the exact form it takes in the 1980 film *Airplane!*, in which a passenger requests "light" reading material and the stewardess replies: "How about this leaflet, 'Famous Jewish Sports Legends'?" Ha ha. But is it true?

Mark Spitz

American swimmer who captured a then record seven Olympic gold medals in 1972

Red Auerbach

Coached the Boston Celtics to nine championships, guided them to seven more as an executive

Al Davis

Iconic, innovative impresario of the NFL's Oakland, then Los Angeles, and then again Oakland Raiders

Benny Leonard

Lightweight champion in the 1910s and '20s, a time when Jews dominated boxing's ranks

Sandy Koufax

Three-time Cy Young Award winner for the Brooklyn/LA Dodgers

Renee Richards

Trailblazing transgender tennis player who won the right to play in women's tournaments in (legal) court

Since ancient times, all the way back to Hellenic gymnasiums, sports were a means of defining in-groups and out-groups—not shocking given their literal connection to biology and the body. And Jews' status as the out-group was perhaps the one thing even Jews were not blamed for. Over the millennia, Jews internalized those distinctions and embraced them, defining ourselves by our lack of physicality.

But then something surprising began to happen: with modernity came assimilation, vesting Jews with an uneasy agency over our growing athletic prowess. In America, especially, Jews started . . . getting good at sports. Jews proceeded to adopt and excel at mainstream athletics the same way they converged with societies generally: fitfully and never totally—with some important exceptions, such as the greatest of all left-handed pitchers. Yet while everyone who went to Hebrew school can tell you that Sandy Koufax sat out a World Series game on Yom Kippur, how many of them who aren't baseball fans can tell you what team he played for, or if they ended up winning the series?

You can trace Jews' evolving status in America by looking at their success in different sports. Jewish engagement with sports journeyed alongside Jewish prosperity. In the twentieth century's early decades, Jews excelled at the urban mass entertainments of boxing and baseball. The NBA debuted right after World War II, just early enough that the scorer of the league's first points was Ossie Schectman (this was back when the Knicks scored points) and just late enough that the league's first commissioner was Maurice Podoloff. Follow the Jews into the suburbs and you'll find Mark Spitz lapping everyone in the pool, then Kerri Strug vaulting above the competition, then Sarah Hughes skating to gold.

NOTABLE JEWS IN SPORTS

Hank Greenberg

Detroit Tigers star who slugged fifty-eight home runs in 1938

But it's not just the athletes themselves. As in Hollywood and the pop-music industry (see Pop Music and Jews, page 182), Jews got involved behind the scenes and in the front offices and started calling the shots. From basketball's sixth man to football's vertical passing attack, from players' unions to fantasy baseball, Jews were involved with most of the innovations that made modern sports fun and exciting.

Jewish Jocks, a volume of original essays, highlights not only Koufax and Spitz but also Red Auerbach and his fellow Jewish coach Red, the Knicks' Red Holzman; the iconic broadcaster Howard Cosell; and Marvin Miller, who practically invented the modern players' union, irrevocably changing baseball for the better. While not "jocks" in the traditional sense, their restless and pioneering intellectual achievements were indispensable to the shape of sports today. They made sports their own. It just took a little longer.

The story of, say, general manager Theo Epstein's precocious mastering of "moneyball" to help bring Boston its first World Series title in eighty-six years is a story that meshes much more cleanly with those characteristics Jews don't mind telling jokes about: the things we are good at. But maybe it is time to be okay admitting that, all in all, playing sports is not something at which Jews are particularly superb. After all, the gentiles deserve to be good at something.

Sid Luckman

Quarterback for NFL-champion Chicago Bears who helped revolutionize the position

Sarah Hughes

American figure skater who won Olympic gold in 2002

Dolph Schayes

Syracuse Nationals power forward who was one of the NBA's biggest stars in the league's first decade

STREISAND, BARBRA

(B. 1942)

BABS ON THE BIG SCREEN

Funny Girl **(1968)**

A Star Is Born **(1976)**

The Way We Were **(1973)**

Yentl **(1983)**

The most famous, powerful, and influential Jewish woman to have ever lived, including every woman mentioned in the Bible. If you need an encyclopedia entry to explain the importance of this legendary singer, actress, director, EGOT winner, home design guru, and coton de Tulear cloning pioneer, you're probably reading the wrong encyclopedia.

The voice? Like butter. The nails? To die for. The nose? Real.

Steinem, Gloria (b. 1934)

Feminist powerhouse. Her father, a traveling salesman in Toledo, Ohio, was Jewish; her mother, who battled severe mental illness, was Scotch Presbyterian. Steinem wasn't raised Jewish, but she has fought anti-Semitism and is perceived by everyone with eyes as more Jewish than goyish. A Smith grad, Steinem came to public prominence as a journalist, infiltrating the Playboy Club in 1963 in a bustier and cottontail to write about the dismaying work conditions for Bunnies. In 1971, she cofounded *Ms.* magazine and the National Women's Political Caucus. In 1978, she wrote the snarky, hilarious *Ms.* essay "If Men Could Menstruate," containing such gems as: "Men would brag about how long and how much . . . Generals, right-wing politicians, and religious fundamentalists would cite menstruation ('*men*-struation') as proof that only men could serve in the Army." In 2013, President Obama awarded Steinem the Presidential Medal of Freedom.

Steinsaltz, Adin (b. 1937)

Israeli rabbi and scholar best known for his accessible, annotated version of the entire Talmud in Hebrew and English.

Stern, Howard (b. 1954)

The King of All Media. Starting out as a funny and lewd radio provocateur, the greatest of his generation of "shock jocks," Stern emerged as the best interviewer of his generation, holding soulful and uncommonly candid conversations that bring out the very private sides of his very public guests. He is a strong advocate of therapy and meditation, a fierce defender of Israel, and a passionate animal-rights activist. For all that, he's earned our heartfelt "Baba Booey."

Stern, Isaac (1920–2001)

American violinist born in Poland, who will always be better than every Jewish kid who now has to learn the violin.

Stewart, Jon (b. 1962)

Né Jonathan Stuart Leibowitz, this comedian, actor (the classic *Half Baked*), and director was the finest purveyor of Fake News ever on television.

Stiller, Jerry (b. 1927), and Anne Meara (1929–2015)

Comedy team known for their nightclub act, albums, and appearances on *The Ed Sullivan Show*, which frequently dealt with their intermarriage: Stiller is Jewish, Meara was Irish Catholic. They ended their joint act in 1970, at the peak of their popularity, because the onstage sparring, played for laughs, was affecting their relationship. Stiller starred opposite Walter Matthau in one of the greatest New York City movies ever, *The Taking of Pelham One Two Three*. He had a resurgence in the 1990s as George Costanza's ranting, loose-screw father on *Seinfeld*, and reprised the shtick on Kevin James's show *The King of Queens*. Meara appeared in television shows throughout the 1980s (*Archie Bunker's Place*, *ALF*) and had a recurring role on *Sex and the City*. She showed up toward the end of *The King of Queens*'s run, and her character married Stiller's on the series finale. The pair had two children, actors Amy Stiller and Ben Stiller.

Stine, R. L. (b. 1943)

Robert Lawrence Stine has been terrifying you for as long as you can remember. Often called the "Stephen King of children's literature," the brilliantly spooky Stine is responsible for the 1990s young adult horror fiction series Goosebumps, which became the TV series that scared you every day after school, and the long-running teen book series Fear Street. In the 2015 *Goosebumps* film and the 2018 sequel, Israeli actress Odeya Rush plays the daughter of the fictionalized R. L. Stine (played by Jack Black). Stine makes a cameo in both films.

Stoudemire, Amar'e (b. 1982)

The most Jewish player in the NBA. After discovering Jewish roots on his mother's side, the six-foot-ten power forward began the process of converting and moved his family to Israel, where he played for Hapoel Jerusalem. Not the first Jewish millionaire to buy a professional basketball team, but definitely the first to *play* for that team.

stranger in a strange land

What our ancestors have so frequently been, from Abraham onward, and the reason why so many Jews gravitate toward helping the displaced, the marginalized, and the afflicted. Before it was the title of a 1961 sci-fi novel by Robert Heinlein and of a bitching 1986 tune by Iron Maiden, you could find the phrase in the King James translation of Exodus, wherein Zipporah gives birth to a son whom the father, Moses, names Gershom, which means "a stranger there" in Hebrew, "for he said, 'I have been a stranger in a strange land.'"

Strauss, Levi (1829–1902)

German Jew who came to America and founded Levi Strauss & Co., effectively inventing blue jeans. While working as an importer of dry goods in San Francisco during the gold rush, Strauss realized the potential for manufacturing durable pants with rivets on the pockets. The first pair of blue jeans was named the model XX, and would eventually be renamed the 501, still in production today.

sukkah

Hebrew for "booth" or "tabernacle," the *sukkah* is the hut that Jews are commanded to build, eat in, and, if possible, dwell in during the fall harvest holiday known as Sukkot. Because the holiday typically falls during October, with its cooler nights even in warmer climes, only the hardiest Jews sleep in the sukkah. But it's a pretty cool thing to do. For a sukkah to be kosher, it must have three walls, tied so tight that they do not sway in the wind. The roof must be made of organic material, like branches, arranged so that the interior has more shade than sun. The sukkah gives rise to one of the most interesting discussions in the Talmud, in which it's debated whether a sukkah built on a boat is kosher—to which some rabbis say yes, unless, of course, it's built on top of another sukkah. You can build your sukkah on top of a camel, and you may use an elephant as one of the walls of your sukkah—but only if the elephant is tied up, because otherwise it might wander off, and then your sukkah is treyf. Even in the absence of elephants, it's fun to build a sukkah, and the tradition has seen a renaissance in recent years—in the 1950s, only Orthodox and more observant Conservative Jews would ever have built a sukkah, whereas today even secular Jews get in on the fun.

Sukkot

See opposite page.

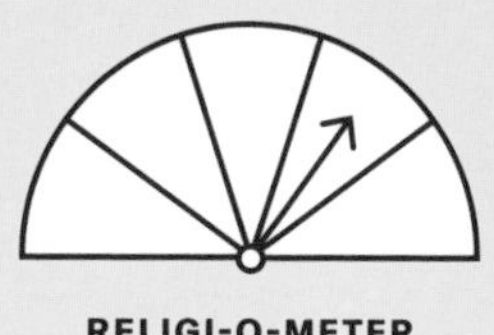

RELIGI-O-METER

SUKKOT

A fall harvest holiday—lasting seven days in Israel, eight in the diaspora—that begins on the fifteenth of Tishrei, which falls between late September and late October. Sukkot celebrates the pilgrimage Jews made to the Temple in Jerusalem, bearing fruits and sacrifices. Traditionally, people build temporary dwellings called sukkahs, in which they eat and sleep during the holiday.

WHAT'S IT ALL ABOUT?

Sukkot is without a doubt the most action-packed of all Jewish holidays. We're commanded to build a temporary dwelling, take our meals al fresco, shake special tree branches, and so on.

While the first two days of Sukkot are considered the holiday proper, the following five are referred to as Hol Hamoed, or the weekdays of the festival. During these days, none of the holiday's religious restrictions apply, but Jews are forbidden from strenuous work and are commanded to use that time for enjoyment.

ANY DOS AND DON'TS?

Perhaps the best known Sukkot custom involves the Four Species, or *arba minim*, as they're known in Hebrew: a palm frond (*lulav*), myrtle tree boughs (*hadass*), willow tree branches (*aravah*), and a citron (*etrog*). Throughout the holiday, the four are held together and waved around daily with an accompanying prayer, a commemoration of a similar ceremony practiced by the Temple's priests in the ancient days.

The Four Species, tradition has it, symbolize both nature's offerings and humanity's diversity: the lulav has taste but no smell, symbolizing those Jews who read the Torah but don't bother with good deeds; the hadass is fragrant but tasteless, symbolizing those Jews who do good deeds but don't read the Torah; the aravah has neither taste nor smell, just like those Jews who care for neither good deeds nor the good book; and the etrog has both, symbolizing one perfect Jew.

Sukkot: In celebration of Sukkot, Israeli prime minister Golda Meir visits a sukkah in Brooklyn in October 1969 with New York City mayor John Lindsay. Rabbi Emanuel Rackman of the Fifth Avenue Synagogue says a blessing over the challah.

"Sunrise, Sunset"

Song expertly crafted, as if by scientists, to make Jewish mothers cry. Written by composer Jerry Bock and lyricist Sheldon Harnick for the musical *Fiddler on the Roof*, based on Sholem Aleichem's stories about Tevye the Dairyman. The Old World melody, sung by Tevye and Golde at their daughter's wedding, is drenched in melancholy, and the nostalgic lyrics are basically, "Oy, our children are all grown up!" (It's a little more eloquent than that.) The song is a staple at Jewish weddings. In 2011, Harnick released a version of the lyrics appropriate for same-sex weddings.

superstition

The palm-shaped hamsa will protect you against the evil eye. So will spitting three times. When you're sewing, chew on thread: it indicates that you're still alive, because, you know, the deceased have their shrouds sewn around them. When you sneeze, tug on your ears, and repeat the pleasing Yiddish phrase *tzu langehmazaldikker yohrn*, or "here's to long, lucky ears." Always close an open book—not doing so invites demons to steal the knowledge that's inside and use it against you. Put some salt in your pockets and in the corners of the room, because demons hate it. Those are some Jewish superstitions; your bubbe knows more.

survivor

Jewish shorthand for Holocaust survivor. The potential for semantic confusion is the basis of a *Curb Your Enthusiasm* subplot in which Larry David brings a Holocaust survivor to a dinner party only to find out the other survivor in attendance is a former contestant on the reality show *Survivor*.

swastika

Ancient symbol of auspiciousness popular in Hindu, Buddhist, and Jain culture that the Nazis co-opted as their logo, tilting it forty-five degrees and flipping it to face right, and ensuring much confusion and horror for Jews visiting India and East Asia today.

sweater

Did you bring one?

Sweet'N Low

While running a cafeteria in the Brooklyn Navy Yard, Benjamin Eisenstadt invented the sugar packet, but neglected to patent it. Then, in 1957, together with his son, Marvin, he invented the pink-packaged artificial sweetener that we still love and use today.

synagogue

What's in a name? Generally speaking, "temple" only if you're Reform, because, per early Reform thinking, Judaism now exists in the diaspora, for good, and there's no sense hoping for a rebuilding of *that* Temple, the ancient one in Jerusalem. (Today, Reform Jews are more diverse, and many are comfortable aspiring to a return to the land of Israel, however far off in the future.) *Synagogue* is just the Greek translation for *beit knesset*, Hebrew for "house of assembly," which is what it's still called in Israel. And *shul* comes from the Yiddish for "school," suggesting its role as a place of study as well as of worship. You'll also hear *beit tefillah*, "house of worship," and *beit midrash*, "house of study." A tiny, haimish one is sometimes called a shtiebel. Whatever you call it, it remains a place barely a third of American Jews still bother visiting.

FROM

Tabernacle

TO

Tzom Gedalia

Tabernacle

Also known as the Mishkan, or "residence," this was God's earthly dwelling place in the 440-year period between the Exodus and the building of Solomon's Temple. It was made of wood, gold, jewels, and anything else that the Israelites could smuggle out of Egypt. The word comes from the Greek *tabernaculum*, "tent." Twice a day, a priest would enter the Tabernacle, stand before the solid-gold altar, and burn incense, reminding the desert-dwelling folks outside that even a forty-year journey through the wilderness doesn't mean you should worship like slobs.

Tablet

Technically, a Jewish magazine founded in 2009. Metaphysically, the shtetl home base for many of your favorite writers, reporters, Tweeters, podcasters, and artists commenting on Jewish life in the new century. The broader machine that produced the book you're holding.

tallit

The fringed prayer shawl that men, and some women, wear during morning services in synagogue. It derives from the biblical commandment to attach fringes to the corners of our clothes. Some Sephardi Jews like theirs all white, and some Ashkenazi Jews prefer white with black stripes. Some give it to boys or girls to celebrate their bar or bat mitzvah, some receive it as a wedding gift, and some choose to be buried in it. If you hear it called a "tallis," you're hearing the Yiddish pronunciation.

Talmud, Talmudic

Technically, we have two Talmuds: the Babylonian, completed around the year 500 CE in Iran (then known as Babylonia), and the Yerushalmi, also known as the Jerusalem or Palestinian Talmud, which was completed around one hundred years earlier in the land of Israel. But when people talk about the Talmud, they're usually referring to the Babylonian. It is the central compendium of Jewish law, theology, rituals, and customs, serving as the guide for daily life for all Jews for millennia. The Talmud, or Gemara, is a text that is a commentary on the Mishnah.

TALMUD

מגילה

Tanakh

Hebrew acronym for Torah, Nevi'im, and Ketuvim. Which are:

Torah: The Five Books of Moses, also called the Pentateuch, which is Greek for "five books." Believed to have been delivered by God on Mount Sinai, which puts the date of its delivery roughly at 1312 BCE. We read a portion of Torah in shul every week, a total of fifty-four portions.

Nevi'im: The part of the Bible that deals with the prophets. Divided into two parts—Nevi'im Rishonim, which includes action figures like Joshua and King David, and Nevi'im Aharonim, which includes fiery pontificators like Isaiah, Jeremiah, and Ezekiel. Joshua, the hero of the first book of Nevi'im, lived between 1355 and 1245 BCE, whereas Malachi, the hero of the last book of Nevi'im, probably knocked about around 445 BCE. After we're done reading a Torah portion in shul, we read a corresponding selection from Nevi'im, a custom whose origins were lost to time.

Ketuvim: Literally meaning "writings," the final part of the Bible is the most poetic, with books like Lamentations, Proverbs, Psalms, and Job living side by side with scrolls like Esther's. These books are not part of the weekly liturgical reading in shul, though selections are chanted as part of the haftarah, which is read each Shabbat at the conclusion of the Torah reading.

Tanya

See **Alter Rebbe**.

Tashlich

The ritual, typically performed on the afternoon of the first day of Rosh Hashanah, of tossing pieces of bread into a body of water, symbolically casting away the sins of the year that's ending. Even if you are not a synagogue-goer, even if you aren't sure what you believe, Tashlich is worth doing: it's outdoors, you can bring your dog, the accompanying prayers are short and lovely, and you will likely make new Jewish friends down by the riverside. Have some lunch, grab some stale bread, and go to the East River in Manhattan, or Venice Beach in Los Angeles, or Lake Washington or the Quinnipiac River or Pomps Pond or Valley Green, and you may find an Orthodox father with his young daughter, standing beside a secular woman and her grandson, standing beside two men and their new baby, all silently dribbling hunks of last week's bagel into the sleepy water, whispering apologies to each other for old wrongs, promising a better year to come. This is Judaism.

ELIZABETH TAYLOR

tattoos

The source of one of the biggest Jewish urban legends. The fuss over Jews and tattoos comes from Leviticus 19:28, which reads: "You shall not make cuts in your flesh for a person [who died]. You shall not etch a tattoo on yourselves. I am the Lord." This commandment follows one about not cutting your beard, but to our knowledge, no one has been kept out of a cemetery for improper beard length and you won't be for having a tattoo, either. Some suggest that the reason behind these prohibitions was to separate the Jews from pagans, who frequently were tattooed and clean-shaven. The taboo on tattoos was complicated after the Holocaust, during which Auschwitz prisoners had numbers permanently inked onto their forearms.

Tay-Sachs

A rare, fatal genetic disorder that disproportionately affects Ashkenazi Jews. Jewish couples should get tested for Tay-Sachs, among various other genetic disorders, before having children.

Taylor, Elizabeth (1932–2011)

The last of the great Golden Age of Hollywood movie stars, Elizabeth Taylor is famous for her violet eyes, her stunning jewelry collection, and her fiery, unconventional love life (she got married eight times, twice to Welsh acting legend Richard Burton, with whom she shared one of the most passionate and commented-on love affairs of the twentieth century). As for her films, many (like *Giant*, *Cat on a Hot Tin Roof*, *Who's Afraid of Virginia Woolf*, and *Father of the Bride*) are undisputed classics. She converted to Judaism in 1959, a year after the death of her Jewish third husband, Mike Todd, in a tragic plane crash, and conveniently right before she married Jewish singer Eddie Fisher. In later years, battling addiction and ill health, Taylor devoted much of her time to helping AIDS sufferers, at a time when the disease was barely mentionable in polite society (see **AIDS activism**). They truly don't make 'em like her anymore.

tefillah

One of the many words in Torah translated as "prayer." It means prayer in general, not a specific entreaty.

tefillin

Little black boxes containing pieces of parchment on which are written Jewish prayers, including the Shema. In traditional Judaism, a Jewish man wears two tefillin during the morning prayer service; they're attached to leather straps, which are used to bind one box, the shel yad, to the arm, and one, the shel rosh, to the head. The tradition dates back to the Torah, where several times God tells the Jewish people to remember His words by wearing them, as in Deuteronomy 6:8: "Bind them as a sign on your hand and let them serve as a symbol on your forehead." For most of Jewish history, only post-bar mitzvah men wore tefillin, but the tradition has spread to women in liberal Judaism and is embraced by some Orthodox feminists, too.

television

See TV and Jews, page 264.

temple

See **synagogue**.

Ten Commandments

The first 10 of the 613 commandments given by God (see **mitzvot**).

Yoo-hoo, Mrs. Goldberg! It all began with Gertrude Berg, who, like so many of the early stars of television, had become famous on the radio. Alongside the likes of radio stars like Lucille Ball, Berg transported her hit series *The Goldbergs*, about the travails of a working-class Jewish family in the Bronx, to TV in 1949. In those first years of television, when early adopters would have to pay $900 just to own a set, television broadcasts were available mostly in East Coast cities like New York, Baltimore, Boston, and Philadelphia.

The audience was overwhelmingly urban, sophisticated, and intellectual (to quote Liz Lemon from *30 Rock*, "Jack, just say 'Jewish.' This is taking forever!"). Jewish performers like Berg and Ernie Kovacs were ascendant in the 1950s, as was Sid Caesar and his sketch comedy series *Your Show of Shows*, whose legendary writers' room included Neil Simon, Mel Brooks, and Carl Reiner. These comedians were translating the antic, restless humor of Catskills tummlers and vaudevillians for a new audience luxuriating in the pleasure of being entertained at home. Television was a domestic medium—families gathered in their living rooms to watch stories about other families in living rooms of their own—and the presence of Jews in these stories was a bold claim to belonging. These were American stories, too.

By the early 1960s, television had gone nationwide and become far less urbane. National audiences preferred *The Beverly Hillbillies* to Phil Silvers, whose legendary scam artist Sgt. Bilko sometimes seemed to have stepped onto an American army base straight from the pages of Sholem Aleichem. But this was only a temporary setback, as the early 1970s abandoned white bread for something a bit more flavorful. The movement was led by Member of the Tribe Norman Lear, who wanted to tell a story about his own ornery, irrepressible father, and was inspired by a British TV series to create Archie Bunker and *All in the Family*. Flip the dial, and you could see Valerie Harper as Mary Richards's world-weary New York–expat friend Rhoda Morgenstern on *The Mary Tyler Moore Show*; she later got her own show, *Rhoda*. Meanwhile, in 1972, former Sid Caesar writer Larry Gelbart created the legendary *M*A*S*H*, based on the 1970 movie of the same name.

There was often a desire to mask television's Jewishness, to recast it in a gentler, gentile mode—a strategy perfected by the most legendary of Jewish television shows. In the 1990s, *Seinfeld* exposed genuine contemporary Jewish ritual—the fighting over flavors of babka and the back talk about converts' rights to tell Jewish jokes—while also perversely camouflaging its most Jewish characters as something else. (Who actually believed Jason Alexander's George Costanza was Italian?) Jerry visited Florida, attended brises, and got in trouble with his parents for making out with his girlfriend during *Schindler's List*—as close to a Jewish mortal sin as possible. *Friends*, too, was in part about being young and Jewish in Manhattan, but Ross and Monica left most of the ritualized Jewishness to the older generation.

Its lips loosened by *Seinfeld*, television today has grown increasingly comfortable with displaying its Jewishness unabashedly, whether it is the Pfeffermans' Yom Kippur break-fast spread on *Transparent*, Abbi and Ilana going on Birthright (pardon me, "Birthmark") on *Broad City*, or Midge's untrammeled delight at spending the summer in the Catskills on *The Marvelous Mrs. Maisel*. We are not only seeing more Jews on television; we are seeing more *of* Jews on television. The progression of television history has been from the general to the particular, from Cliff Huxtable to Paper Boi, and a heavily Jewish industry has grown steadily more comfortable (or at least less uncomfortable) with the thought of telling their own stories.

And so *Seinfeld* creator Larry David—or his fictional doppelganger of the same name on *Curb Your Enthusiasm*—could be roped into joining a shiva minyan accompanied by former Red Sox first baseman Bill Buckner, only to be lavishly cursed out by a Red Sox fan still furious about Buckner screwing up the 1986 World Series, booted from the premises, and made to bear witness to Buckner, catching a baby tossed out of a burning building and borne off on the shoulders of celebrating onlookers. The Jewish story and the American story were one and the same, just as Mrs. Goldberg could have told you from the start. Yoo-hoo!

THE TEN COMMANDMENTS

I.

I am the Lord, your God, Who took you out of the land of Egypt, out of the house of bondage.

II.

You shall not have the gods of others in My presence. You shall not make for yourself a graven image or any likeness, which is in the heavens above, which is on the earth below, or which is in the water beneath the earth. You shall neither prostrate yourself before them nor worship them, for I, the Lord, your God, am a zealous God, Who visits the iniquity of the fathers upon the sons, upon the third and the fourth generation of those who hate Me, and [I] perform loving kindness to thousands [of generations], to those who love Me and to those who keep My commandments.

V.

Honor your father and your mother, in order that your days be lengthened on the land that the Lord, your God, is giving you.

VI.

You shall not murder.

VII.

You shall not commit adultery.

III.

You shall not take the name of the Lord, your God, in vain, for the Lord will not hold blameless anyone who takes His name in vain.

IV.

Remember the Sabbath day to sanctify it. Six days may you work and perform all your labor, but the seventh day is a Sabbath to the Lord, your God; you shall perform no labor, neither you, your son, your daughter, your manservant, your maidservant, your beast, nor your stranger who is in your cities. For [in] six days the Lord made the heaven and the earth, the sea and all that is in them, and He rested on the seventh day. Therefore, the Lord blessed the Sabbath day and sanctified it.

VIII.

You shall not steal.

IX.

You shall not bear false witness against your neighbor.

X.

You shall not covet your neighbor's house. You shall not covet your neighbor's wife, his manservant, his ox, his donkey, or whatever belongs to your neighbor.

Ten Plagues

See opposite page.

Tenth of Tevet

See Fast Days, page 94.

teshuva

Literally meaning "return," *teshuva* is among the central tenets of Jewish theology. The return in question is, of course, to God, a path that is open to everyone at any time, no matter how grave their sins. The Talmud captured the essence of teshuva neatly when it stated that "in the place where those who have repented stand, even the utterly righteous cannot stand," meaning that there's no spiritual achievement greater than working hard, learning from mistakes, and doing better.

Thanksgivukkah

When the first day of Hanukkah overlapped with Thanksgiving in 2012, creating the greatest holiday mashup since Chrismukkah. Don't throw out your Menurkey just yet: this super-rare calendrical convergence will occur again in 2070 and 2165 (see **Hebrew calendar**).

therapy

What Jews do. Okay, other people do it, too. But not like Jews. First off, we started it all. Love him or hate him, that big old Jewish atheist Sigmund Freud was the godfather of modern therapy in all its guises, from traditional, five-day-a-week, reclining-on-the-sofa analysis to cognitive behavioral therapy, from primal scream to family systems to rebirthing to whatever Dr. Phil had on his afternoon talk show yesterday. Although his disciple and then rival Carl Jung was a gentile, most of the other great pioneers, like Alfred Adler, Erich Fromm, Anna Freud, and Karen Horney, were Jews. The practitioners of old-fashioned analysis and talk therapy continue to be disproportionately Jewish, although as therapy has come to include ever more subfields, its Jew quotient has gone down. But what's particularly Jewish about therapy is less its practitioner corps than the patients: from the advent of modern therapy with Freud until, approximately, the big-screen debut of *Annie Hall*, Jews were ridiculously more likely than gentiles to seek out therapy. Was it because we were more neurotic? More likely to admit to being neurotic? Less inhibited talking about ourselves? More trusting in the medical profession (many analysts and therapists being psychiatrists, after all)? It's hard to say. And Jews were hardly the only analysands, as Betty Draper in television's *Mad Men* can tell you. But for bookish, collegiate, or intellectual Jews, or those who aspired to be seen as such, a stint in therapy was long a rite of passage.

"They tried to kill us, we survived, let's eat"

A tired, oft-told, jokey summation of what all Jewish holidays are about. The phrase is variously attributed to Catskills humor, assorted songs, and your uncle Myron. Although it describes the story of Passover (sort of), it really doesn't work for any other holiday. And it's not that funny. Somebody is going to keep recycling the joke, but don't let it be you.

Third Reich

Hitler bragged it would last a thousand years. It lasted twelve, while the Jewish state established three years after the Reich's calamitous demise is still going strong.

Thomashefsky, Boris (1868–1939)

As a teenager, Thomashefsky moved with his family from Ukraine to New York City, where he almost immediately mounted the first Yiddish play performed in America. A singer and an actor, he performed in Yiddish plays and operas, eventually becoming a star on a thriving national circuit. Thomashefsky adapted many classic plays, like *Hamlet*, for the Yiddish stage, and he and his wife, Bessie, formed what would become one of the premier Yiddish theater troupes. His son changed the family name, meaning that his grandson, the great classical conductor Michael Tilson Thomas, has a shvach Anglo-sounding name instead of a Yiddish name with real yichus.

tikkun olam

Jewish concept meaning "to repair the world." In sixteenth-century Kabbalah, it referred to the way that prayer could help stitch back together the shattered shards of God's divine light, returning the world to spiritual perfection. In the late twentieth century, "tikkun olam" was adopted by liberal Jews to refer to works of social justice. That interpretation has become definitive for the vast majority of liberal and Reform Jews, many of whom will now say that tikkun olam is the central tenet of their Judaism: "As a Jew, I believe in tikkun olam, which is why I stand with Planned Parenthood and am doing my best to only buy free-range

TEN PLAGUES

Like any great horror film, the story of the Ten Plagues begins with the mildly creepy and ends with the intolerably macabre. It's no wonder we're commanded to drink four cups during the Passover Seder: the story is much too grim to take sober.

I.
Blood

II.
Frogs

III.
Lice

IV.
Wild animals

V.
Pestilence

VI.
Boils

VII.
Hail

VIII.
Locusts

IX.
Darkness

X.
Killing of the firstborn

ham." That interpretation, while no less valid than any other, drives many more traditional or conservative Jews to distraction. They find it ahistorical (which is true) but also idolatrous in its own way, turning Judaism into a convenient accessory to the politics that one prefers to hold. While that's an unfair charge—for we all have the tendency to remake Judaism into what we'd like it to be—it is true that "tikkun olam" has become a cliché, and for that reason alone should be retired to the island where we sent "it takes a village."

Tisha B'Av

According to Jewish tradition, the Ninth of Av is the day when both the First and the Second Temples were destroyed. Falling in July or August, it's a day of fasting and mourning, and its observance begins by congregating in shul, sitting on the floor, and reading the Book of Lamentations (often by candlelight), composed after and describing the destruction of Jerusalem and the subsequent exile. Tisha B'Av concludes the Three Weeks, a period of mourning and contemplation that begins on the Seventeenth of Tammuz, the day Jerusalem's walls were breached (see Fast Days, page 94).

tkhines

Hebrew for "supplications," these prayers for the ladies, written mostly in Yiddish, were first compiled and published in seventeenth-century Amsterdam, eventually allowing observant Jewish women throughout Europe a way to partake in religious life. While the men read Hebrew and had command of the sacred texts, women increasingly took to writing and reading this genre of personal devotionals. Each prayer began with a heading that captured its spirit, such as "A confession to say with devotion, but not too quickly." Some Yiddish-speaking Hasidic women still recite tkhines today, as well as members of the Jewish Renewal communities, which incorporated tkhines into their religious worship and prayer.

Tofutti

Founded in New Jersey by David Mintz in 1981, Tofutti produces popular soy-based dairy-free foods, most famously ice cream. Tofutti products are kosher, pareve, lactose-free, and vegan, and as a result, the company enjoys an especially diverse customer base: Orthodox Jews, vegans, the lactose intolerant, and any combination of the three. An Orthodox Jew, Mintz was famously encouraged in his pursuit to create a quality pareve dessert by the Lubavitcher Rebbe, who understood that such a product would make it easier for people to keep kosher.

Topol, Chaim (b. 1935)

Known simply as Topol, the Tel Aviv–born actor had already gained an international reputation for his roles in several notable Israeli films when Norman Jewison, helming the film adaptation of *Fiddler on the Roof*, approached him to play Tevye. Topol, who was then thirty-six and in top shape, had to be made to look twenty years older and thirty pounds heavier, and his radiant performance won him an Oscar nomination and lifelong fame.

Torah

Literally "instruction" or "teaching" or "law," Torah means all that and so much more. Here's a partial list: Torah is the first five books of the Hebrew Bible, the ones dictated by Moses (Genesis, Exodus, Leviticus, Numbers, and Deuteronomy); but it can also refer to the whole Hebrew Bible (including prophetic books like Jeremiah and Isaiah, and literary-historical writings like the books of Esther and Jonah); but it can also refer to the whole of Jewish sacred texts (so the Hebrew Bible, plus the commentary on it known as the Mishnah, plus the commentary on that known as Talmud, and later works, like those of Maimonides); but it can also include the body of legends and lore that have grown up around the written works. Oh, and the Torah is also a physical document: the parchment scroll, read in synagogue, on which the first five books of the Hebrew Bible are written.

So it's all context. If people say, "This Shabbat, I am reading Torah in shul," they mean that in synagogue they'll read, from the Torah scroll, a passage from, say, Genesis or Exodus. If they say, "After college, I am going to Israel for a year to learn Torah," they are going to learn something in Jewish scriptural studies, but they could just as easily be learning medieval commentary as the original biblical stories.

Basically, Torah is the teaching. All of it.

tradition

See ***Fiddler on the Roof***.

Tree of Life

In Hebrew, *etz chaim*, this is a common metaphor for the Torah, derived from the Torah itself, as in Proverbs 3:18, where the Lord's wisdom is referred to as "a tree of life to them that grasp her."

Triangle Shirtwaist Factory: The 1911 fire at this women's blouse factory in New York City, which killed 146 people, precipitated a major change in labor laws.

Tree of Life is also a common name for Jewish congregations, including the one in Pittsburgh, Pennsylvania, where on October 27, 2018, a gunman killed eleven Jews in the deadliest anti-Semitic attack in American history. Although the attack occurred inside the building owned by the Tree of Life/Or L'Simcha Congregation, among the murdered were members of two other smaller congregations that rented space there, New Light Congregation and Congregation Dor Hadash. The victims, ranging in age from fifty-four to ninety-seven, were Joyce Fienberg, Richard Gottfried, Rose Mallinger, Jerry Rabinowitz, Cecil Rosenthal, David Rosenthal, Bernice Simon, Sylvan Simon, Daniel Stein, Melvin Wax, and Irving Younger.

treyf

Not kosher. A ham and cheese sandwich is treyf. Shrimp cocktail—treyf. But like all the best Yiddish words, this one means more than it means. Anything that's really out of bounds, subversive, especially in a non-Jewish way, is treyf. A communion wafer might technically be kosher, but it's, you know, *super* treyf.

Triangle Shirtwaist Factory

On March 25, 1911, against the backdrop of contentious strikes for workers' rights and workplace safety, a women's blouse factory in Greenwich Village caught fire. The workers, mostly young Jewish and Italian immigrant girls, had been locked inside to prevent theft. Somehow a scrap of fabric on the eighth floor caught fire, and within minutes, the building was ablaze. The fire department's ladders and hoses couldn't reach the eighth floor. Hallways were impassable; exits were too few; fire escapes collapsed under the weight of too many bodies. Girls leapt to their deaths, died of smoke inhalation, were burned alive. The final death count was 146, making the Triangle fire the greatest workplace disaster in New York history until 9/11. Factory owners Max Blanck and Isaac Harris got off, as rich folks do, thanks in large part to defense attorney Max Steuer's devastating work discrediting a young survivor, Kate Alterman (his cross-examination technique is still taught in law schools today). But the fire had a huge impact on child-labor laws, workplace regulations, union representation, building codes, fire safety, and firefighting equipment.

tsuris

Yiddish for troubles or problems, usually of the minor but deeply vexing kind.

Tu B'Av

Jewish Valentine's Day! Instead of splurging on overpriced roses and tacky boxes of chocolate, the unmarried daughters of Jerusalem, back in the days of the Second Temple, would dress in white and go dancing in the vineyards on that day, celebrating the beginning of grape harvest season. The guys, taking advantage of the full moon, would swing by and watch them, and amorousness ensued. Traditionally, this was one day in which all the ancient tribes of Israel, usually keeping to themselves, were encouraged to intermingle. Because we don't do the whole tribal thing anymore, Tu B'Av, which falls in July or August, is celebrated these days with concerts, parties, and other gatherings designed to make the heart grow fonder.

Tu B'Shevat

See opposite page.

Tucker, Sophie (~1886–1966)

Born Sonya Kalish in what's now Ukraine, Sophie Tucker came to these shores as an infant and conquered them as a grown woman. Her career lasted decades, during which she was a singer, vaudevillian, and radio star. In 1938, she was elected president of the American Federation of Actors, a trade union. She had fans in Europe and throughout the United States, but she only sang her signature song, "My Yiddishe Momme," when she was confident that the audience knew some Yiddish.

Twelve Tribes

Jacob, renamed Israel after his all-night wrestling match with an angel, had twelve sons, each of whom became the patriarch of a tribe of his own: Reuben, Simeon, Levi, Judah, Issachar, Zebulun, Asher, Gad, Dan, Naphtali, Joseph, and Benjamin. (He also had a daughter, the unlucky Dinah, and at the end of his life, he elevated two grandchildren, Menashe and Ephraim, sons of Joseph, to the level of sons.) Even though each tribe had its own territory (except Levi's), they were all still Jews and therefore found plenty of reasons for infighting. Several groups around the world, from the Bene Israel in India to the Igbo Jews of Nigeria (see World Jewry, page 288), have claimed to be descendants of the lost tribes, dispersed around the world after being exiled from the land of Israel by the Romans.

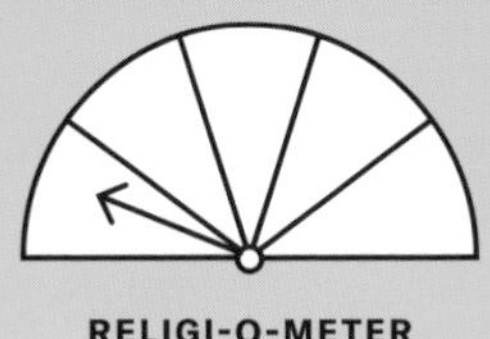

TU B'SHEVAT

A relatively obscure Jewish holiday, known in English as "the New Year of the Trees." The holiday's name refers to its date on the Hebrew calendar, the fifteenth day of the month of Shevat. Some Jews hold environmentally themed Seders, and many others gorge themselves on fruit mentioned in the Torah. Take that, Arbor Day.

A few years before Greenpeace was founded, the Mishnah had a thing or two to say about how we should conserve our natural resources. To that end, it gave us a celebration related to the agricultural cycle for the tithing of fruits. Today, Tu B'Shevat has had a bit of a renaissance among even nonobservant Jews, in Israel and in the diaspora, as a day of ecological awareness, a day for planting trees and having earnest discussions about environmentalism. The Hasidic custom of holding a Tu B'Shevat Seder has taken hold more widely; if you are invited to such a meal, bring a dish featuring one of the "seven species" mentioned in the Torah: wheat, barley, grapes, figs, pomegranates, olive oil, and dates.

Twitty, Michael (b. 1977)

African American Jewish writer and historian who won a 2018 James Beard Foundation award for his book *The Cooking Gene: A Journey Through African American Culinary History in the Old South.*

two-state solution

The resolution to the Israeli-Palestinian conflict long favored by pluralities of Israelis and Palestinians, and by the international community. The plan envisions two sovereign states, one Jewish and one Palestinian, living in close quarters but at peace. Attempts to broker a mutually satisfactory two-state solution have bedeviled policymakers and American presidents for decades, with each side of the dispute blaming the other for the impasse. At the same time, militant minorities in both populations have remained adamantly opposed to any division of what they see as "greater Israel" or "historic Palestine."

"2000 Year Old Man"

Comedy routine brought out at parties by Carl Reiner and Mel Brooks that begat numerous hit records, television appearances, and even a cartoon. The quasi-improvised bit had Reiner as a straight-laced interviewer (who regularly broke character by laughing) talking with a two-thousand-year-old "man from the East," which was just Brooks sounding like an old immigrant Jew. Brooks offered sage wisdom, like his secret to longevity: Will Tolive. "Not the will to live! Dr. Tolive. Dr. Will Tolive! A genius." Also, never run for a bus—there'll always be another. The shtick was so great that only some kind of jerk writing an encyclopedia would point out that two thousand years wasn't long enough for Brooks to have lived like a caveman. But why worry? His confused observations on world history seemed legit. Jesus Christ was likely a "nice boy, but thin," and maybe Paul Revere *was* shouting, "The Yiddish are coming!"

tzedakah

Hebrew for "justice," "righteousness," and "charity." The meanings are all connected. The tzedakah one gives as money—in many Jewish homes, there is a tzedakah box for spare coins, to be donated at the end of the month—is seen as an obligation, as something that a *tzadik,* a righteous person, simply does. Giving tzedakah is also connected to Jewish holidays. At Purim, for example, Jews have four obligations: to feast and make merry, to give gifts of food known as mishloach manot to one another, to hear the megillah read, and to give "presents to the poor," tzedakah.

Tzfat

Hilltop city in northern Israel known for its history of mysticism; its bazaar of artists' stalls where tourists load up on menorahs, kippot, candlesticks, and other Judaica, ideally after some haggling; and its magnetic appeal for backpackers looking to get high—on Judaism, that is. Confusingly, it is also spelled "Safed," "Safad," or "Zafat," presumably because the *tzf* consonant cluster is difficult for Americans.

tzitzit

Hebrew word—*tzitzis* is the Yiddish—for the knotted tassels or fringes worn by observant Jewish males and growing numbers of Jewish females. They are found at the four corners of the tallit, which is worn during morning prayer and goes over the clothes, and at the corners of the *tallit katan* (little tallit), an undergarment worn all day. Torah twice tells Jews to wear tzitzit; for example, in Deuteronomy 22:12, God tells Moses, "You shall make tassels on the four corners of the garment with which you cover yourself."

tznius

Literally "modesty," but in practice, usually a list of rules concerning what girls and women can wear and do. Don't be too naked. Don't wear clothing associated with the "opposite gender." Don't be too loud, verbally or visually. Watch the hemlines. As a song popular in Jewish day schools (sung to the tune of the "Colonel Bogey March," aka "Hitler Has Only One Big Ball") put it: "Tznius, it is our battle cry! / Tznius, you'd better do or die! / Tznius, cover your knee-us! / Cover your elbows, and shoulders, and thighs!" Of course, different communities have different standards of modesty (How thick must a woman's stockings be? Must married women wear wigs? Is it a sin for men to even hear *kol isha,* a woman's singing voice?) and different opinions about whether "modesty" oppresses or liberates women. Modern Orthodox Jews view Talmudic statements about tznius as open to interpretation, and Reform Jews have dismissed male/female binary dictates about clothing and public participation in Jewish ritual life. But if anyone wants to cover their knee-us, they should feel free-us to make that choice.

Tzom Gedalia

See Fast Days, page 94.

FROM

Uganda

TO

Uzi

Uganda

The almost-home of modern Israel, from 1903 to 1905, based on a proposal by the father of Zionism, Theodor Herzl. Shortly before the Sixth Zionist Congress in 1903 in Basel, Switzerland, the British government, which ran Uganda as a colonial protectorate, entertained the idea of allocating a "Jewish territory" in East Africa "on conditions which will enable members to observe their national customs." Had Herzl's idea for a temporary refuge for Russian Jews in immediate danger panned out, what would Judaism and Israel have looked like today?

Also, the home of the Abayudaya. (See World Jewry, page 288.)

ultra-Orthodox

See Branches of Judaism, page 44.

Unetaneh Tokef

A deeply moving *piyyut*, or Jewish liturgical poem, chanted on Rosh Hashanah and Yom Kippur. Its main theme is God's judgment—a preoccupation at that particular time of year—and its heart is a list of all the sordid ways the Almighty may choose to end our short lives. It was memorably adapted by Leonard Cohen in his song "Who by Fire." According to legend, the poem was written by the eleventh-century rabbi Amnon of Mainz, who was asked to convert to Catholicism but refused. Irate, the Archbishop of Mainz ordered his men to cut off Amnon's hands and feet, and had him delivered, bleeding badly, back to his synagogue on top of a knight's shield. It was just before Rosh Hashanah, and, dying, Amnon cried out the poem in its entirety, composing it as he went along. The story may be apocryphal, but it's a good reminder that as we are mortals, humility becomes us all.

ungapatchka

Yiddish for garish, overdone, overly busy, in poor taste.

unions

Workers' organizations developed in the nineteenth century in the wake of the mass urbanization and brutal working conditions produced by the Industrial Revolution. Unions assert labor's collective bargaining power in the face of the otherwise overwhelming dominance of owners and bosses. The prominent role of Jews in labor unions started in Europe and carried over into America after great waves of immigration in the early twentieth century brought to American cities Jewish Bundists, anarchists, Social Democrats, socialists, and communists, each with their own ideas about how to syndicalize, collectivize, and unionize labor. Jewish labor leaders like David Dubinsky, Benjamin Stolberg, and Alex Rose were especially prominent in the garment and fur trades, where Jews clustered. The Jewish role in unions gradually declined as the garment trades either moved to the southern United States or out of the country altogether, and as Jews moved into white-collar professions.

United States Holocaust Memorial Museum

Sure, Yad Vashem remains the world's premier Holocaust museum and research center, but since it was established in Washington, DC, in 1993, the USHMM has become a major destination for education and scholarship, receiving more than 40 million visitors and housing more than 105.2 million pages of archival documents and 191.1 million digital images.

Unorthodox

The world's most popular Jewish podcast, with millions of downloads since its debut in the summer of 2015. Listeners from across the world tune in weekly to hear the News of the Jews, plus discussions about circumcisions and conversions and debates about weighty questions like which is more Jewish, aluminum foil or Saran wrap. Also, the occasional Holocaust joke. Guests of the show have included everyone from actor David Duchovny and comedians Judy Gold and Nick Kroll to handbag designer Rebecca Minkoff, Monty Python's John Cleese, and superstar Jesuit priest Father James Martin. In other words, it's everything we believe the Jewish community ought to be: Open to everyone, curious about everything. Sort of like this book.

Upper East Side

Ah, Manhattan's Upper East Side, where Ivanka Trump once frequented Congregation Kehilath Jeshurun, where the moneyed sons and daughters of Modern Orthodoxy still attend Ramaz, where the Jewish Museum shines, where the nannies of lawyers and hedge fund managers gently push strollers through Central Park, and where Woody Allen still plays the clarinet at the Carlyle.

Upper West Side

Ah, Manhattan's Upper West Side, where the line at the fish counter at Zabar's is three people deep, where

Ungapatchka: Building a huge tower on Fifth Avenue and putting your name on it in giant gold letters you can find four top-notch kosher burger joints in a half-mile stretch, where Jews rushing to shul with their tallit bags brush past Jews rushing to Barney Greengrass with their NPR totes, and where grumpy old men still enjoy the afternoon sun on a bench on a median on Broadway, arguing about Marxism.

Upsherin

Ceremony in which a three-year-old Jewish boy receives his first haircut. Its origins are obscure, but it probably dates to the sixteenth century, and for much of its history was practiced mainly by Sephardim. In observant communities, the boy's *peyos*, or sidelocks, are left intact, and henceforth he will begin to wear a kippah and the fringes known as tzitzit. In other words, his life of looking like an Orthodox Jew has begun! And his life of learning like one has begun, too: the upsherin is said to mark the beginning of learning prayers and Torah. Once only popular with Hasidim and other very observant Jews, the practice has caught on among non-Orthodox Jews, too—especially hippie-ish and Renewal Jews, but also just some people who like offbeat rituals.

urim and thummim

Parts of the *hoshen*, the holy breastplate worn by the high priest in the Mishkan and the First Temple in Jerusalem. They were used to divine God's will, a function that lent them a place on Yale University's crest (see **Aaron**; **kohanim**).

Uzi

After Israel's War of Independence, the country's generals realized they needed a new and better weapon. They summoned Uzi Gal, a real-life Tony Stark, and asked him to invent a submachine gun small enough to carry, cheap to manufacture, and reliable enough to hit its targets every time. He came back with the iconic stubby gun, which—much to Gal's dismay—was promptly named after him. After being introduced to the public at the 1955 Israeli Independence Day parade, it was picked up by more than ninety armies around the world, not to mention a whole battalion of '80s action-film stars.

URIS, LEON

(1924–2003)

The author of numerous critically ignored but unputdownable bestselling beach reads, including the 1958 Zionist classic *Exodus*, a rousing book turned into an even more rousing movie, with hunky young Paul Newman as the hero, Ari Ben Canaan. You won't find Uris on any college syllabi, but his historical novels will stay with you: if you want the basic facts of early Irish nationalism, turn to *Trinity* (1976), just as if you want an uncomplicated, highly memorable version of the founding of the state of Israel, nothing will top *Exodus*. Like Herman Wouk and James Jones and James Clavell, he wrote capable, luscious, intensely researched historical novels, and in the process gave the twentieth century its mental furniture, even as he may be forgotten in the twenty-first.

THE GOOD BOOK

Exodus
(1958)

Mila 18
(1961)

FROM

Vashti

TO

von Fürstenberg, Diane

Vashti

King Ahasuerus's first wife. As the Book of Esther begins, she's famously summoned by her husband to dance in the nude in front of his guests; she refuses, and is promptly executed for her insolence. This act of resistance would win her the love of Jewish feminists, who frequently hail her as a progenitor of the women's liberation movement. But some rabbis of the Talmud disagree: Vashti, they remind us, had a nasty habit of abusing her female Jewish maids by—you guessed it—making them dance around naked. On Shabbat. So the punishment, said the rabbis, fits the crime, and Vashti's glory is unmerited.

verklempt

Derived from Yiddish. Meaning overcome with emotion, tearful. Perhaps no American word demonstrates the power of pop culture on the Jewish vernacular like this word. In the original Yiddish—for which the proper rendering would be more like *farklemt*—the word is "sad," akin to "depressed" or "grieving"; in English, to be "verklempt" is to be choked up in a good or poignant way. Linda Richman, the character played by (gentile) comedian Mike Myers in the great nineties *Saturday Night Live* "Coffee Talk" sketches—he based the character on his Jewish then mother-in-law—did more than any actual Jew to make the word popular in English.

DIANE VON FÜRSTENBERG

Vilna Gaon (1720–1797)

Rabbi Elijah of Vilna was better known as the Genius, or Gaon, of Vilna. Lauded for his command of the Torah and Talmud, on which he wrote extensively, the Vilna Gaon was also well versed in secular matters, writing on subjects like grammar and math. His insistence on the importance of the secular alongside the sacred put him at odds with the burgeoning Hasidic movement, which eschewed the secular world.

Vishniac, Roman (1897–1990)

Russian-born photographer best known for his iconic photographs of Eastern European Jews in the years before the Holocaust. Vishniac's photos show religious Jews living in shtetl poverty and were for a long time the primary images Americans had of prewar Jewish life in Europe: pious and poor. However, when the International Center of Photography acquired Vishniac's archive in 2010, research revealed that Vishniac had been commissioned by the American Jewish Joint Distribution Committee to document daily life in the shtetls as part of the organization's fund-raising effort—suggesting that his photos were not meant to be a perfect representation of prewar Jewish life but a selective window into one slice of it, caught for posterity in nostalgia's amber.

von Fürstenberg, Diane (b. 1946)

Born Diane Simone Michelle Halfin in Brussels to a mother recently liberated from Auschwitz, DVF (as she is known) would go on to revolutionize women's fashion. She married Prince Egon of the German House of Fürstenberg in 1969, despite his family's objections to her Jewishness, and soon after began designing clothing for women. (She separated from the prince in 1973, divorcing him in 1983, but she kept his name, because wouldn't you?) In 1974, she debuted the wrap dress, an easy-to-wear knit frock that was equally flattering and comfortable. It liberated women from zippers and hooks and latches, and allowed working women to look professional yet stylish.

FROM

Walters, Barbara

TO

Wouk, Herman

Walters, Barbara (b. 1929)

Groundbreaking television journalist and the first female coanchor of an evening news program. For years, she also hosted occasional nighttime celebrity interview specials, in which the subjects would cry (it was almost a prerequisite), and she created the morning show *The View*. Gilda Radner famously parodied Walters as "Baba Wawa." She ceased appearing on *The View* in 2014 (its seventeenth season), but the show remains a springboard for women journalists and commentators of varying political persuasions.

Wandering Jew

Sometime around the thirteenth century, a legend emerged of a Jew who taunted Jesus on his way to the crucifixion and was cursed for his wickedness to roam the earth until Christ's Second Coming. The myth of the Wandering Jew has inspired everyone from the Nazis to Mark Twain, the latter riffing on it humorously in his travelogue and the former using it as one more bit of murderous anti-Semitic propaganda.

War of Independence

On May 14, 1948, the day Israel declared its independence, the nascent Jewish state was invaded by the armies of five Arab countries, bolstered by armed volunteers from still other Arab countries. Despite being vastly underarmed—the Arabs had tanks, fighter jets, and cannons, far more than the newly minted Israel Defense Forces—the IDF managed to subdue its attackers and prevail. More than six thousand Israelis died in the war, about 1 percent of the country's population at the time. By the time the final agreement was signed, in July 1949, the Jewish state had expanded to 77 percent of what had been Mandatory Palestine. The war also displaced hundreds of thousands of Arab residents of Palestine, who became refugees as a result. Israelis refer to the war as Milchemet Ha'Shichrur, the War of Liberation, while Palestinians call it the Nakba, the Catastrophe.

Warsaw

See Warsaw Ghetto Uprising, page 284.

WASP

The gin-sipping, sailing, preppy aristocrat some Jews aspire to be and others hope their daughters won't marry.

Wasserstein, Wendy (1950–2006)

American playwright best known for *The Heidi Chronicles*, which debuted on Broadway in 1988. Much of her work focuses on the struggle of women in modern America, and like so many great Jewish artists, she used humor to express these poignant ideas. Another one of Wasserstein's major works is *The Sisters Rosensweig*, in which three middle-aged sisters come together to celebrate one of their birthdays before chaos ensues—when it opened, casting three middle-aged women in a play was seen as unconventional. She was the first woman to win a Tony for Best Play.

Waze

The best GPS-enabled navigation app, invented by Israelis, the worst people in the world at asking for directions.

wedding

See opposite page.

Weiner, Matthew (b. 1965)

A writer for *The Sopranos* (1999–2007) and creator of the 2018 television series *The Romanoffs*, he is perhaps best known as the creator of *Mad Men* (2007–2015)—a show that brims with Jewish history, allusions, and references, none more important than the caricature-shattering role of Rachel Menken (played by Maggie Siff). With one storyline, Menken—the gorgeous, shrewd, psychologically brilliant head of a midcentury American department store, inherited from her father—became one of the most intriguing female characters on TV.

Weiss, Avi (b. 1944)

Famous Modern Orthodox rabbi, longtime rabbi of a big synagogue in the Bronx. He is known for his controversial "Open Orthodoxy," which includes relatively liberal views on women's roles. In the 1970s, Weiss was a leading advocate for the liberation of Soviet Jewry. In 1999, he founded Yeshivat Chovevei Torah, a rabbinical seminary for men, and in 2009 cofounded Yeshivat Maharat to train female Orthodox clergy. Mention his name to a Modern Orthodox person, and you'll get either a big grin or a sour grimace.

West Bank

As in, of the Jordan River. Many Israelis, especially those who are religious and on the right, call the region

WEDDING

The Jewish wedding, a beautiful and beloved tradition, is quite a simple affair. All it requires are a ketubah, witnesses, and a chuppah. Everything else—the flowers, the hora, the food trucks—that's all up to you.

KETUBAH

The Jewish marriage contract. In rabbinic times, the ketubah was a prenuptial agreement protecting the bride from abandonment by specifying the money she would receive in the event that her husband left her; its text was read out loud under the chuppah, a tradition still in practice at Orthodox weddings. Today, the text is often altered to suit the political, cultural, and artistic preferences of the couple. There are ketubot (the plural) for interfaith couples, for same-sex couples, and, probably, somewhere, for throuples. The ketubah is beautifully calligraphed and features the signatures of the required two Jewish witnesses not related to the couple, and is often framed and displayed in the couple's home after the wedding.

SHEVA BRACHOT

According to Jewish tradition, there are seven blessings known as the Sheva Brachot, recited by an officiant. The bride and the groom are then to be fêted for seven days after their wedding with a series of seven feasts, *also* known as the Sheva Brachot. According to Jewish tradition, each feast must include the recitation of seven blessings, thanking the Lord for bringing joy to the happy couple.

CHUPPAH

The canopy in a Jewish wedding. It is often formed by tying the groom's *tallit*, or prayer shawl, to four posts, held by close relatives of the bride and groom (or bride and bride, or groom and groom). It can also be formed by hiring an overpriced Jewish-wedding planner to hire a florist to braid dyed roses around artisanally hewn poles of cedar, on top of which is stretched a length of silk organza. The constant is that the couple and the officiant stand under the chuppah with a few family members or friends. It symbolizes the home that the couple will build together. More broadly, *chuppah* refers to marriage, as in the Jewish blessing at a baby-naming or bris that wishes for the child to grow up "to Torah, to chuppah, and to *ma'asim tovim*"—to learn Torah, to get married, and to do good deeds.

AUFRUF

Yiddish for "calling up," this ceremony involves honoring a groom-to-be by inviting him to have an aliyah on the Shabbat before his wedding. Upon completion of his duties, he may be pelted with candy and praised in song. In more recent years and more liberal communities, the bride is called up to the Torah as well.

WARSAW GHETTO UPRISING

Starting in the mid- to late nineteenth century, Warsaw became a major center of Jewish life, owing to people displaced from smaller shtetls by pogroms. The city was home to a thriving Jewish cultural and artistic scene. On the eve of the Holocaust, the city was home to nearly four hundred thousand Jews.

That soon changed as anti-Jewish measures were implemented, chief among them the construction of a ghetto, which began in 1940. Jews from Warsaw were forced to move into the ghetto, and were soon joined by displaced Jews from across Europe. The population of the Warsaw Ghetto would swell to more than half a million people.

WARSAW GHETTO UPRISING

In the summer of 1942, the Nazis conducted mass deportations from the Warsaw Ghetto to Treblinka, sending more than 250,000 Jews to near certain death. In April 1943, facing the liquidation of the ghetto, resistance fighters sprang into action. The Warsaw Ghetto Uprising was a monthlong Maccabean battle, ending with the ghetto burned to the ground and most of its inhabitants dead.

HEROES OF THE WARSAW GHETTO UPRISING

The commander of the Warsaw Ghetto Uprising, Mordecai Anielewicz (1919–1943), was twenty-four when he died. He had returned to the ghetto by choice in order to fight. For three weeks, he and his compatriots in the Jewish Fighting Organization (ZOB) held off two brigades of well-trained SS men commanded by the German general Jürgen Stroop. The ZOB was a band of perhaps 225 starving teenagers, armed with a collection of mostly homemade weapons. The two thousand German troops who sought to send them to Treblinka were armed with heavy weapons, armored cars, and flamethrowers. Anielewicz and over 120 other Jewish fighters, including his girlfriend, Mira Fuchrer, would realize their wish by dying together in a bunker beneath 18 Mila Street.

On May 16, after systematically blowing up and burning every house in the ghetto, killing more than seven thousand Jews, and deporting over forty thousand more, Jürgen Stroop personally dynamited the Grand Synagogue of Warsaw to celebrate his great triumph. But for weeks afterward, Jews continued to kill German soldiers in the rubble of the Warsaw Ghetto, holding out longer than the French Army resisted Hitler.

Four days after the uprising began, Anielewicz wrote his last known letter, addressed to his ZOB comrade Yitzhak (Antek) Zukerman, who was in hiding outside the ghetto:

It is impossible to describe the conditions under which the Jews of the ghetto are now living. Only a few will be able to hold out. The remainder will die sooner or later. Their fate is decided. In almost all the hiding places in which thousands are concealing themselves it is not possible to light a candle for lack of air. With the aid of our transmitter we heard the marvelous report on our fighting by the "Shavit" radio station. The fact that we are remembered beyond the ghetto walls encourages us in our struggle. Peace go with you, my friend! Perhaps we may still meet again! The dream of my life has risen to become fact. Self-defense in the ghetto will have been a reality. Jewish armed resistance and revenge are facts. I have been a witness to the magnificent, heroic fighting of Jewish men in battle.

Marek Edelman (1919–2009) was the only battle commander of the Jewish fighting groups who kindled the Warsaw Ghetto Uprising to survive the fighting. When the war was over, he wrote a spare, documentary account titled *The Ghetto Fights*. The greatness of Edelman's book is that there are no superfluous words. Every word feels like it was cleansed in fire.

After writing his searing account of how the Jews of Warsaw died, Edelman disappeared into obscurity as a cardiologist in communist Poland. He was rediscovered by a young Polish Jewish journalist named Hanna Krall, who interviewed him over many months in the early 1970s and used his stories of life and death in the ghetto as the subject of one of the greatest works of twentieth-century literary nonfiction, *Shielding the Flame*.

Edelman was a lifelong Bundist, a secular Jewish socialist who refused to embrace the Communist Party. As such, he became one of the early heroes and moral leaders of the Solidarity movement. In his later years, he wrote several autobiographies, which included their fair share of attacks on personal rivals and ideological foes, ensuring that none of his readers would ever confuse the word "Bundist" with "Buddhist."

The great book that Marek Edelman wrote about the uprising, and the even greater book that Edelman inspired, by Hanna Krall, are truly one book, about the life and death of the Warsaw Ghetto. There is no greater story of Jewish heroism in the face of crushing adversity; there is no more horrifying, migraine-inducing account of the moral calculus involved in determining whether it is better to kill small children with an injection to the heart than to let them suffer in locked cattle cars before being gassed to death; there is no more stark account of shameful Jewish excuse-making and inaction while millions of fellow Jews were starved, beaten, gassed, shot, and burned alive.

Chayka Grossman (1919–1996) was a badass female ghetto fighter who survived the Holocaust, immigrated to Israel, became a member of the Knesset, helped pass laws protecting the welfare of children, and sponsored the law allowing Israeli women to obtain abortions. A leader of the youth wing of Hashomer Hatzair in Poland, she became a key courier between the ghetto resistance movements, which largely consisted of teenagers with guns. Renowned for her bravery and calmness under pressure, she obtained precious weapons, as well as some of the first reports about the Nazi extermination program, and brought the leaders of the Warsaw Ghetto Uprising to Warsaw. She then returned to Bialystok, where she helped organize and lead the Bialystok Ghetto uprising. Her only illusion was that her fellow Jews, who were also marked for death, would join her at the decisive moment and fight.

After the war ended, Grossman emigrated from Poland to Palestine, where it was her fate to inform the Zionist leadership, and those who had left Poland before the Holocaust, of the wholesale slaughter of their families and friends. She also published *The Underground Army*, a gripping and richly detailed account of her life as a ghetto courier, organizer, and fighter.

Western Wall: Worshippers at the Western Wall of what was once the Temple in Jerusalem, Judaism's holiest site by its biblical name, Judea and Samaria. Others, particularly on the left, call it the Occupied Territories, or the Territories for short. Elsewhere in the world, West Bank is the term of art.

Western Wall

Judaism's holiest spot. Originally a retaining wall built to support Herod's massive extension of the Second Temple, it alone remained standing after the Romans destroyed the Temple in 70 CE. Also known as the Wailing Wall or the Kotel, millions of people visit it each year, writing their prayers on slips of paper and placing them in the wall's cracks.

Westheimer, Dr. Ruth (b. 1928)

Born Karola Ruth Siegel in Germany, the future Dr. Ruth was, as a ten-year-old, one of nearly ten thousand Jewish children saved from the Nazis by the Kindertransport, ending up in Switzerland. After both her parents died in the Holocaust, the orphaned Siegel moved to Palestine and joined the Haganah as a sniper, later immigrating to the United States, where, taking the last name of her third husband, she became Dr. Ruth Westheimer and revolutionized public discussion of sexual matters with her radio show, *Sexually Speaking*. In the 1980s and '90s, she was a frequent guest of talk show hosts including Johnny Carson and David Letterman, and was even parodied on *Saturday Night Live*. Dan Savage, Candace Bushnell, and other sex writers can throw metaphorical grenades, but only Dr. Ruth has thrown literal ones, too.

Wiesel, Elie (1928–2016)

Romanian-born survivor of Auschwitz and Buchenwald who became a journalist, novelist, playwright, and living symbol. His great achievement was *Night* (1960), which was translated into thirty languages and reminded an already-forgetting world that it should never forget. If you've read one Holocaust book, it's Anne Frank's diary; if you've read two, the other is *Night*. "To read it is to lose one's own innocence about the Holocaust all over again," critic Ruth Franklin wrote in 2006. The book is "almost unbearably painful, and certainly beyond criticism," A. Alvarez wrote in *Commentary*. Indeed, Wiesel was, in the eyes of many, beyond criticism. During his last five and a half decades, he wrote dozens more books but remained more influential as a teacher, lecturer, activist, and survivor—he was, indeed, the world's most famous survivor. In 1986, he won the Nobel Peace Prize, but more important was his 1980 appointment to President Jimmy Carter's Holocaust Memorial Council, which eventually got the United States Holocaust Memorial Museum built.

Wiesenthal, Simon (1908–2005)

After surviving several concentration camps and a death march from Poland to Austria, this Ukranian Jew devoted his life to tracking down Nazi war criminals. Wiesenthal helped discover that Adolf Eichmann was living in Buenos Aires, and he helped identify several other high-profile Nazis. Today the Simon Wiesenthal Center in Los Angeles bears his name.

Willis, Ellen (1941–2006)

Feminist writer and activist, a cofounder of the radical feminist group Redstockings in the late 1960s, she is best known as a cultural reporter and rock critic. She wrote for the *New Yorker*, *Village Voice*, *Rolling Stone*, *Ms.*, and elsewhere and published several books. Start with her essay collection *No More Nice Girls*.

Wine

See Passover, page 195; **Shabbat**; Purim, page 203; **Kiddush**; **l'chaim**; **Manischewitz**.

Winehouse, Amy (1983–2011)

Tremendously talented pop, jazz, and R&B singer-songwriter thrown to the wolves of fame. Born in North London, she released her first album, *Frank*, when she was just nineteen. With *Back to Black* (2006), she became an international sensation. But her life was soon a media circus, with the tabloid machine pushing her toward ever more damaging behavior. Her hummable, upbeat "Rehab" is painful to listen to now, as it lightly brushes aside her early addiction problems (and states that her father urged her to keep working instead of taking care of herself). Winehouse died at age twenty-seven from alcohol abuse.

Wolf, Dick (b. 1946)

Creator of television programs that, despite their graphic nature, work as a soothing balm as one half watches one of their nine billion reruns on basic cable. His career began in advertising, after which he

World Jewry

Like "World Music" at Tower Records, World Jewry is a highly inadequate catchall term for a number of eccentric flowerings of Judaism not describable as Ashkenazi, Sephardi, and Mizrahi. These groups often claim descent from one of the Lost Tribes or have roots in evangelical Christianity. They are increasingly the focus of conversion and repatriation efforts in Israel and the United States. Economic as well as religious factors may motivate some members of these groups to attempt to immigrate to Israel, a trend that has tested the Jewish State's laws of return and citizenship and its willingness to absorb economic migrants.

These groups include but are not limited to:

BEIT ISRAEL OF IVORY COAST

Since the early 2000s, a largely middle-class Jewish community in Abidjan, an outgrowth of a local Kabbalist center, now practicing conventional Orthodox Judaism.

HOUSE OF ISRAEL OF GHANA

Small group of Jews founded in Sefwi Wiawso in the mid-1970s after a community leader's vision. A synagogue was built in 1998.

BENE MENASHE

Group of self-described Jews living in today's northeast India claiming descent from one of the Ten Lost Tribes of Israel, who were sent into exile by the Assyrian empire. Legend holds that their ancestors wandered through Central Asia and the Far East for centuries, before settling along the border with Burma (now Myanmar) and Bangladesh.

IGBO

Members of the Igbo people of Nigeria who practice a form of Judaism. Some claim descent from Jewish communities in the West African and Saharan Songhai empire, while others are recent converts.

ABAYUDAYA

This tribe of approximately three thousand people is descended from Ugandans who converted to Judaism in 1919. They currently run a yeshiva, an Orthodox shul, and a Jewish hospital, and keep Shabbat and kashrut.

BENE EPHRAIM

Also called Telugu Jews for the language of the community located in modern India, near the delta of the Krishna River, the Bene Ephraim claim descent from the Tribe of Ephraim.

KASUKU JEWS OF KENYA

Isolated, rural community of Jews in the western highlands, often associated with the Abayudaya, with whom they share traits.

JEWISH COMMUNITY OF MADAGASCAR

Some reports describe a majority of Malagasies believing they are of Jewish ancestry, from seafaring members of the Lost Tribes. Recent Orthodox conversions have solidified a tiny group of Jews on the island. (Madagascar, as it happens, was also the object of a Nazi proposal for Jewish relocation that was scrapped.)

LEMBA

Bantu ethnic group of Zimbabwe and South Africa with religious practices and beliefs that resemble Judaism.

became a writer for *Hill Street Blues* and *Miami Vice*. In 1990, he created the first *Law & Order*. It ran for twenty seasons, and the spinoff *Special Victims Unit* is still going. There were other spinoffs, as well as video games and foreign-language adaptations. Notable Jews Jerry Orbach, Steven Hill (Solomon Krakovsky), George Dzundza, Richard Belzer, and Jeff Goldblum have had starring roles as either police (Law) or attorneys (Order). And if you ever meet someone claiming to be a New York actor who doesn't have a *Law & Order* appearance under his or her belt, someone is telling you a fib.

World Jewry

See page 288.

worrying

What we do.

Wouk, Herman (1915–2019)

Wouk may not get the critical laurels heaped on his contemporaries Saul Bellow and Bernard Malamud, but the author of *The Caine Mutiny* (1951), *Marjorie Morningstar* (1955), and *The Winds of War* (1971) outsold his more highbrow confrères, and he sure as heck outlived them, too.

X-Men

X-Men

The popular comic book series, created by Stan Lee and Jack Kirby, revolves around the relationship between Charles Xavier, or Professor X, and Max Eisenhardt, or Magneto, two powerful mutants with very different views on how to treat poor, ordinary humans. They meet in a Haifa clinic for traumatized Holocaust survivors—Magneto is a survivor himself, having discovered his powers in Auschwitz—and strike up a fraught friendship sustained by conversations about revenge versus forgiveness, faith versus disbelief, and other issues that animated Jewish emotional and intellectual life in the second half of the twentieth century. Forget the mostly schlocky blockbuster movies: the comic books remain as profound a meditation on otherness, prejudice, and genocide as any American work produced before or since. (See **comic books**.)

FROM

yachting

TO

You Don't Mess with the Zohan

yachting
No clue.

Yad Vashem
Israel's official Holocaust memorial and museum is the country's second most popular tourist site (see **Western Wall**). Established in 1953 and built on Mount Herzl in Jerusalem, Yad Vashem focuses on research and education and is unique in that it pays tribute to the Righteous Among the Nations, honoring gentiles who saved Jews during the Holocaust.

yahrzeit
The anniversary of someone's death, especially that of a parent. Traditionally commemorated by lighting a yahrzeit candle.

yahrzeit candle
A small candle, designed to burn for twenty-six hours, that Jews light on the anniversary of a loved one's death, as well as on Yom Kippur and Yom Hashoah. The Hebrew name for it, *ner neshama*, or soul candle, captures its essence neatly.

yarmulke
See **kippah**.

yellow star
The Nazis may have made the yellow star an indelible image, forcing Jews to affix the symbol to their clothes between 1939 and 1945, but Jews had been forced to wear some kind of identifying badge as far back as the Middle Ages (by papal order) and, before that, under Muslim rule in the eighth century CE. Still, the yellow star "Jude" badge, on view at Holocaust museums the world over, remains the most haunting reminder of this practice.

Yemenite Jews
According to some scholars, Yemenite Jews should be considered a distinct community of Jews, like Ashkenazi or Sephardi Jews. Archaeological evidence suggests Jews may have lived in Yemen starting as early as the third century BCE, with many involved in the spice trade. Kept in relative isolation inside their mountainous nation, they developed their own customs and traditions and are known for their erudition in Torah and Talmud. Facing persecution, many Yemenite Jews immigrated to Israel in 1949 and 1950. In the 1980s, the Yemenite Israeli singer Ofra Haza became an international pop sensation when she chanted a few of the community's traditional prayers set to dance music.

yenta
Yiddish for a gossip or busybody. Some people think a yenta is a matchmaker, but that's incorrect; the mix-up is likely due to *Fiddler on the Roof*, in which the matchmaker happens to be named Yente.

Yentl
Hollywood's first Jewish feminist musical, starring and directed by Barbra Streisand. The culmination of years of work, this 1983 adaptation of an Isaac Bashevis Singer story is a remarkable look at shtetl history and chauvinism, and doesn't lack for laughs, either. The headstrong Yentl secretly studies Torah and, after the death of her father, cuts her hair, pretends to be a boy, and attends a yeshiva. Trouble comes when she falls in love with her classmate, played by Mandy Patinkin, and ends up in an arranged marriage with the girl Mandy loves (Amy Irving). It gets complicated! "What kind of a creature are you?" "I'm just a woman!" is just one of the timeless lines of dialogue in this extraordinary film.

yeshiva
A catchall name for Orthodox schools. A yeshiva for the elementary school set is called a *cheder*, which literally means "a room," while post-bar mitzvah boys attend a *yeshiva ketana*, or small yeshiva, and college-age young men go to a *yeshiva gedola*, or large yeshiva. And yes, it's almost always men, although the last few decades have seen the spread of yeshivas for women (like, for instance, Yeshivat Maharat and the redoubtable Drisha).

yeshiva bocher
A *bocher* is a lad in Yiddish, but also a full-time yeshiva student.

Yeshiva University
YU is the flagship of Modern Orthodox Judaism in America. Founded in 1886, the Manhattan university has sought to fuse high-level religious learning with secular instruction. In the words of supporter Albert Einstein, who raised money in Hollywood on the school's behalf, it was "destined to be" of "great significance" for the "continuance of Jewish spirit and for spiritual balance of our youth." Famous alumni include author Chaim Potok, Vermont governor Howard Dean (medical school), labor leader Randi Weingarten, and US ambassador to Egypt and Israel Daniel Kurtzer.

Yentl: Barbra Streisand directed, cowrote, coproduced, and starred in this 1983 film about a woman who disguises herself as a man in order to study Talmudic law.

Yeshivat Maharat

Cofounded in 2009 by Avi Weiss, this is the only Orthodox-identifying school in the United States to ordain women as rabbis—although in deference to tradition, many of the school's twenty-six or so ordinands (and counting) use other titles, like maharat, rabba, or rabbanit. Many Orthodox Jews believe that the movement represented by Yeshivat Maharat will cause, or has already caused, another major split in Orthodoxy, akin to the divide that already exists between Modern Orthodoxy and Haredi Judaism. Only a minority of even Orthodox Jews actively care about this issue, but those who care *really* care. To some, the ordination of women is an unforgivable heresy; to others, it's an innovation whose time has come.

Yezierska, Anzia (1880–1970)

Immigrant author of the 1925 coming-of-age novel *Bread Givers*. Yezierska was born in Poland and moved to the United States in 1890. She was a major fictional chronicler of the Lower East Side. Her work, too little read for decades, has seen a renaissance as she's been reclaimed by historians of women and immigration.

yichud room

An Ashkenazi wedding custom of leaving the bride and groom alone for a few minutes after their *chuppah*, or wedding ceremony. Yichud is the halachic prohibition against persons of opposite genders who aren't married to each other being alone in seclusion; the yichud room is the first such time a religious couple, theoretically, would be alone together. Still, many newlyweds continue the custom. They go to a room, the door guarded by a couple of friends to ensure their privacy, and talk or . . . whatever. Rumors of marriages being consummated in the yichud room are probably exaggerated, but it is customary to provide food and drink for the bride and groom to enjoy in their first moments alone as a married couple.

yichus

Good family tree, august lineage. What you have if you come from a long line of successful rabbis—or orthodontists, for that matter.

Yiddish

Yiddish literally means "Jewish," whether as an adjective or in the nominative, pointing to the language spoken by Ashkenazi Yidn (Jews). The generally agreed-upon statistic is that in 1939 there were something like 13 million Yiddish speakers. Today the number is a fraction of that, more like 1.5 million (although this is likely a dramatic undercount). Given that Yiddish-speaking Haredi populations in Israel and the United States (and elsewhere, to a lesser extent) are exploding, it's unlikely that Yiddish will become extinct in the near future, as was once presumed—indeed, the average age of the Yiddish speaker will actually drop.

Yiddish and modern German share a common linguistic ancestor in Middle High German but are now separated by about a thousand intervening years, as well as the global diasporic dispersion of Yiddish speakers. Linguist Yudel Mark wrote that among European languages, Yiddish has a relatively large number of words due in part to its status as a fusion language. Yiddish contains Germanic, Slavic, Latin, Romance, and *loshn koydesh* (Hebrew-Aramaic) elements.

Yiddish contains within itself the whole of European Jewish history, as well as expressing the genius of that experience, one of dynamic creativity of a cohesive cultural minority within a sometimes welcoming, sometimes hostile, ethnopolitical majority.

Yiddish Book Center

As a graduate student in Montreal, Aaron Lansky discovered that younger Jews, unable to read Yiddish, were throwing out their grandparents' old books. So he decided to do something about it, and in 1980 he founded the Yiddish Book Center, which has since rescued over one million volumes of Yiddish literature. Located in Amherst, Massachusetts, this museum, library, educational organization, conference center, and now oral-history repository is not just conceptually cool but actually very fun to visit. Its gorgeous building, set on an apple orchard right next to Hampshire College, is delightful for children and a great stop for foliage-mad adults.

Yiddish Press

See page 298.

Yiddishkeit

Yiddish for "Jewishness." It can refer to Judaism the religion, or to Jews' folk practices or pop culture. To some, it's prayer or Torah study; to others, socialism; to others, Chinese food on Christmas Eve. Whatever Jews do when we're being our Jewy selves, that is Yiddishkeit.

YIDDISH WORDS FOR MODERN TERMS

BINGE-WATCH שלינגען עפּיזאָדן (פֿון)
shlíngen epizódn (fun)

CLIMATE CHANGE דער קלימאַטן־בײַט
der klimátn-bayt

COWORKING SPACE דער שותּפֿות־ביורא
der shútfes-byuró

E-MAIL (LETTER) דער בליצבריוו; דאָס בליצבריוול, ־עך
der blítsbriv; dos blítsbrivl, –ekh

E-MAIL (SYSTEM) די בליצפּאָסט
di blítspost

ENERGY CONSERVATION די ענערגיע־אײַנהיטונג
di enérgye-áynhitung

FACEBOOK (דער) פֿייסבוק
(der) féysbuk

FLASH DRIVE דער שליסלדיסק, ־ן
der shlísldisk, -n

FRENEMY דער חבֿר־שונא, חבֿרים־שונאים
der kháver-sóyne, khavéyrim-sónim

GO VIRAL (ווילד) אָנרײַסן; אָנכאַפּן זיך
(vild) ónraysn; ónkhapn zikh

LOCAVORE דער לאָקאַל־פֿרעסער, ־ס
der lokál-fréser, –s

SELFIE דאָס זיכעלע, ־ך
dos zíkhele, –kh

The *Comprehensive English-Yiddish Dictionary*, an 850-page volume, adapts the Eastern European language for the modern world. Editor in chief Gitl Schaechter-Viswanath offers twelve ways to bring the *mamaloshen* (mother tongue) into your daily life.

Extra!

Yiddish Press

Extra!

SINCE 1860 | PRESENTED BY NEWISH JEWISH | $$$

When the modern Yiddish press got its start in the Pale of Settlement during the 1860s, even its editors thought it was a joke. "We're not going to wait until the pranksters mock us. We're going to state right here that Yiddish isn't a real language," is what the editors of the newspaper *Kol mevaser* wrote in their second issue. Suffering from the self-hatred of German-speaking leaders of the Haskalah, or enlightenment movement, Jewish intellectuals thought that Jews would never be able to become modern if they continued to speak Yiddish, a language that, according to them, was not suitable for intelligent thought.

But because they hoped to educate the poor masses of Eastern European Jews—the largest Jewish population in the world—they had no choice but to do it in the language they understood: Yiddish. As a result, newspapers in Yiddish began to appear, feeding a hungry population of readers with news about the world around them, history, literature, art, science, theater—everything.

The Yiddish press became a venue in which every aspect of Jewish life was described, discussed, and furiously disputed. From the 1860s through the 1940s and beyond, thousands of Yiddish publications appeared all over the world. As Eastern Europe bled Yiddish-speaking migrants, Yiddish newspapers and magazines began to appear wherever immigrants landed, popping up all over the United States, Canada, and South America and throughout Europe and in settlements in Australia, South Africa, and China. Jews liked to stay informed, and the Yiddish press was their main source.

Places like New York and Warsaw produced dozens of daily, weekly, and monthly publications. New York in the 1920s had five daily Yiddish newspapers, ranging in orientation from traditionally religious to communist, with everything in between. The Yiddish press taught its readers about politics, history, art, and science and served as a guide for them in new and unfamiliar places. More than anything, it eased their way into modernity in a language they understood.

MAJOR YIDDISH NEWSPAPERS

AN INCOMPLETE LIST

New York

YIDISHES TAGEBLAT

Founded in 1885 as an outgrowth of the weekly *Yidishe gazetn*. Was well known for buying out competitors. A somewhat sensationalistic and conservative daily, it was subsumed by the *Morgn zhurnal* in 1928.

FRAYE ARBETER SHTIME

Anarchist weekly founded in 1890. Home for anarchist politics and experimental literature. Closed in 1977.

FORVERTS

Socialist daily founded in 1897. Most successful and important Yiddish paper in history. Had sensationalistic aspects, but also published high-quality literature and informational pieces. Became a weekly in 1983 and a monthly in 2017, and went online-only in 2019.

MORGN ZHURNAL

Daily founded in 1901—it was both Orthodox and Zionist in orientation. Ceased publication in 1971.

DI VARHAYT

Founded as a socialist-Zionist breakaway from the *Forverts* in 1904, it was subsumed by *Der tog* in 1919.

DER TOG

Founded in 1914, it was conceived of as a left-centrist intellectual paper, which attracted excellent writers. It joined forces with the *Morgn zhurnal* in 1953. Ceased publication in 1971.

MORGN FRAYHAYT

A communist daily founded in 1922, this paper attracted high-quality writers but lost many of them after its steadfast support of Soviet policies reduced its appeal, especially in 1929, 1939, and 1956.

ODESSA

KOL MEVASER

Founded in 1862, this weekly was the first Yiddish newspaper permitted in the Russian Empire. With frequent contributions by writers like Mendele Moykher-Sforim and Y. Y. Linetski, it became the cradle for modern Yiddish literature. Ceased publication in 1872.

WARSAW

DER YID

Zionist weekly founded in 1899. Written mostly in Warsaw but published in Krakow in order to avoid the censor, it had excellent writers, among them Y. L. Peretz.

HAYNT

A Zionist daily founded in 1908, it was the most popular and successful Yiddish paper in Poland. Ceased publication in 1939.

DER MOMENT

Founded in 1910 by writers who were dissatisfied with *Haynt*, its initial political home was the Folkist party, which held that Yiddish culture espoused values worth promoting through a program of cultural autonomy. During the second half of the 1930s, it became a vehicle for Vladimir Jabotinsky, leader of the Zionist-Revisionists. Ceased publication in 1939.

UNDZER EKSPRES

Sensationalistic daily founded in 1926. In spite of its sensationalistic nature, it had excellent writers on staff who produced high-quality journalism. Ceased publication in 1939.

FOLKSTSAYTUNG

Bundist, social-democratic daily published in Warsaw from 1921 to 1939. High-quality reportage with anticommunist, antireligious, and anti-Zionist leanings.

Moscow

DER EMES

Founded as the Yiddish variant of *Pravda* in 1918, it functioned initially as the mouthpiece of the Yevsektsia, or the Jewish section of the Communist Party. It continued publication after the Yevsektsia was liquidated in 1930, but itself was closed in 1938 during a Soviet campaign against Jewish culture.

ST. PETERSBURG

YIDISHE FOLKSBLAT

Founded in 1881 by the former editor of *Kol mevaser*, this was a literary-oriented weekly in which the work of the leading Yiddish authors of the day, among them Sholem Aleichem, could be found.

DER FRAYND

Founded in 1903, it was the first Yiddish daily newspaper permitted in the Russian Empire. Nominally Zionist, it moved to Warsaw in 1909. Ceased publication in 1914.

YIVO

Acronym for the Yidisher Visnshaftlekher Institut, or Yiddish Scientific Institute, this research organization was formed in Poland in 1925. With big names like Sigmund Freud and Albert Einstein on its board of trustees, its goal was to study, preserve, and teach about Yiddish culture and European Jewish life. As the Nazis advanced, a group of scholars calling itself the Paper Brigade rescued and hid many of YIVO's archival treasures. The organization moved to New York, where it's located today.

Yizkor

Because Judaism believes the soul is eternal, it also believes the soul benefits from the good deeds of loved ones even after an individual passes away. To that end, many say the Yizkor prayer—the word is Hebrew for "He shall remember"—which asks God to remember the departed and keep his or her soul. Synagogues offer the Yizkor prayer four times a year: on Yom Kippur, and on the last days of Sukkot (see Simchat Torah, Shemini Atzeret, page 243), Passover, and Shavuot.

Yom Haatzmaut

Israel's day of independence. Celebrated each year on the fifth of Iyar, the day begins with a moving ceremony commemorating the transition from Yom Hazikaron, Israel's memorial day, reminding Israelis that their liberty was made possible by considerable sacrifice. The day is then observed by grilling copious amounts of meat, hitting each other on the head with tiny plastic hammers, and watching the International Bible Quiz, broadcast live from Jerusalem.

Yom Hashoah

On December 28, 1949, Israel's Chief Rabbinate brought the remains of thousands of Jewish victims of the Nazis to burial in Jerusalem, marking the first impromptu Holocaust Memorial Day. Several years later, the Knesset designated the twenty-seventh of Nisan as the official day of remembrance. The date was chosen because it comes a week after Passover and eight days before Yom Ha'atzmaut. Its official name is Yom Hazikaron laShoah ve-laG'vurah, or the Day of Remembrance for the Holocaust and for Heroism, commemorating those who fought the Nazis. Outside of Israel, Yom Hashoah is observed on various dates, with some Jewish communities keeping with the Israeli tradition, some commemorating April 19—the anniversary of the Warsaw Ghetto Uprising—and some observing International Holocaust Remembrance Day on January 27, the day Auschwitz was liberated in 1945.

Yom Hazikaron

Israel's memorial day. As of 2018, 23,646 Israelis have died in military or security service, which means that there is hardly an Israeli alive who has no personal connection to someone who fell in the line of duty. On Yom Hazikaron, a special TV channel broadcasts the names of the dead; even with only a few seconds allotted to each person, it takes the entire day.

Yom Kippur

See opposite page.

Yom Kippur War

At 1:55 p.m. on October 6, 1973, Syria and Egypt launched a massive joint attack on Israel. It came as a shock for two reasons: First of all, it was Yom Kippur, and many Israelis were fasting and praying in synagogue. Second of all, Israeli intelligence, badly misreading ample warning signs, had issued a report the day before assessing that the probability of war was low. For the first five days, things seemed dire for Israel, with the IDF scrambling to recruit and mobilize its reservists. Then, however, the tide turned, with the IDF defeating the Syrians and forging deep into Egypt, stopping sixty-two miles from Cairo. The war quickly sparked conflict between the Soviet Union, which supported and armed Egypt, and the United States—President Richard Nixon sent Israel massive military aid, helping it overpower its enemies. Wishing to avoid a major Cold War conflagration, however, the Americans pressured Israel not to proceed any farther into Egypt, which brought the war to its end. The bitter defeat shocked the Arab world and contributed to Egyptian president Anwar Sadat's willingness to make peace with Israel four years later.

yontif

Yiddish, from the Hebrew *yom tov,* meaning "good day," the term refers to biblically mandated days of celebration and commemoration, including the first and last days of Passover, Shavuot, both days of Rosh Hashanah, Yom Kippur, the first day of Sukkot, and Shemini Atzeret. As on Shabbat, all work is prohibited on a yontif, and special customs and rituals are frequently observed. Traditionally, Jews have greeted each other on these holidays by saying "gut yontif," although in recent years the Hebrew "chag sameach" has overtaken it (see Jewish Greetings, page 114).

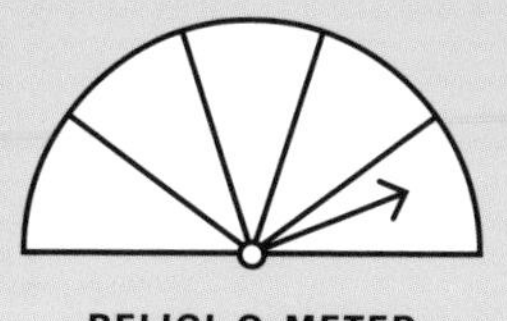

RELIGI-O-METER

YOM KIPPUR

The Day of Atonement, when Jews fast and ask forgiveness for the sins they committed in the past year and for ones they'll inadvertently commit in the new year to come.

WHAT'S IT ALL ABOUT?

Yom Kippur is the most awesome of all Jewish holidays. We mean that literally: the very last of the Days of Awe, the ten-day period beginning with Rosh Hashanah, Yom Kippur marks the sealing of the Book of Life, and with it our fates for the coming year. Jews—even some who cheerfully ignore other holidays—fast, repent, confess, and do their best to unload themselves of their sins and get on the Almighty's merciful side.

ANY DOS AND DON'TS?

The Mishnah, in tractate Yoma 8:1, is very clear on the don'ts: No eating or drinking on Yom Kippur. No wearing leather shoes. No bathing. No anointing oneself with perfumes or lotions. And no sex. The Bible itself, interestingly, mentions nothing about these prohibitions. Leviticus 23 only forbids us from doing work and tells us to afflict our souls, not our bodies. It's customary to wear white to symbolize one's purity. After the destruction of the Temple, the exile from Zion, and the writing of the Talmud, the holiday's focus shifted from the high priest and his purification rituals to the responsibility of each Jew to atone for his or her own sins. And while the connection between a gurgling stomach and a reflective mind may be lost on some, it is worth noticing that Yom Kippur is the only fast day on the Jewish calendar not observed in commemoration of some historical tragedy, but rather designed purely to allow us to take leave of earthly distractions and focus on our sinful souls.

York, Charlotte

Television's most famous convert to Judaism. Charlotte was one of the four main characters—the least vulgar, and usually the most romantic—on HBO's *Sex and the City* (1998–2004) and in the subsequent movies. Played by Kristin Davis, Charlotte underwent a dramatic transformation over the course of the series. Her first husband was the uptight (and impotent) WASP Trey MacDougal (Kyle MacLachlan), but her real bashert was to be Harry Goldenblatt (Evan Handler). Even though he was bald and sweaty and a bit rough around the edges, she fell for him. Before they could get married, Charlotte converted to Judaism. Viewers watched the whole thing, from her Shabbat dinners to her meetings with the rabbi to her visit to the mikveh. The most memorable line comes when her next-door neighbor emerges as Charlotte is nailing a mezuzah to her door and asks, "What on earth is all that banging?" Charlotte replies, without missing a beat: "Oh, good morning, Mrs. Collier. I'm a Jew now. How are you?"

CHARLOTTE YORK

You Don't Mess with the Zohan

A moving Adam Sandler documentary about the life of a retired Israeli Mossad operative. All right, it isn't a documentary. But this hilarious 2008 comedy nonetheless captures certain aspects of Israeli life uncannily well. If you've never been to a Tel Aviv beach, you can watch the movie's first five minutes to know exactly what it's like.

FROM

Zabar's

TO

Zyklon B

Zabar's
See **appetizing**.

zaftig
Pleasantly plump.

zayde
Yiddish for "grandpa." He's married to your bubbe.

Zingerman's
See Delicatessen, page 74.

Zion
See **Promised Land**.

Zionism (and anti-Zionism)
Zionism is the political movement to establish Jewish self-rule in the historic Jewish homeland, Israel. The Jewish religious and cultural attachment to the land of Israel runs deep: references to Zion and Jerusalem—home of Judaism's Temples and holiest sites—are rife in Jewish liturgy and literature, with countless Jewish writers expressing a longing to return to them. Though Jews maintained a presence in the land for centuries, and repeatedly returned, the majority was ultimately exiled. Thus, the Passover Seder, the world's most-observed Jewish ritual, ends with the exhortation, "Next year in Jerusalem!" Building upon this ancient bedrock, modern Zionism first took shape as a national movement in nineteenth-century Europe. After centuries of being murdered in pogroms, forced into ghettos, and barred from full participation in civic and cultural life, many European Jews came to the conclusion that true Jewish flourishing could only be achieved under Jewish self-rule. As a minority, they believed, Jews would be forever persecuted by hostile gentile majorities; Jews would only be able to defend and actualize themselves by governing themselves in their own nation state. Led by Austro-Hungarian journalist Theodor Herzl, who convened the First Zionist Congress in 1897, the Zionist movement began sending waves of pioneers to settle the land of Israel, and ultimately proclaimed a Jewish state in 1948. Today, Israel is home to half of the world's Jewish population.

Even as it succeeded as a political movement, Zionism had its dissenters. Ultra-Orthodox religious leaders opposed it on the grounds that the movement was led by secular Jews like Herzl and preempted the Messiah, who was traditionally believed to be the one to lead Jews back to Israel. Others in the more liberal American Jewish establishment worried that the existence of a Jewish state would cause their countrymen to question their loyalties.

Much of this sentiment was tempered or died away in the decades after Israel's successful founding, but in recent years, new forms of anti-Zionism have arisen in their place. Today, ardently antinationalist Jews oppose the very existence of a Jewish state, seeing it as an ethnocentric anachronism and an affront to universalism. Some pro-Palestinian advocates and their allies call for replacing the Jewish state with a non-Jewish one.

Thus, while contemporary debates over Zionism may seem like mere debates over this-or-that policy of this-or-that Israeli administration, at their core, these arguments are often also fundamentally about how Jews should exist in the world. Do Jews need a homeland where they are not governed by gentiles, and where they can foster their own majority culture and protect themselves with their own army? Or should Jews simply live as dispersed minorities in non-Jewish nations?

Zuckerberg, Mark (b. 1984)

Nice Jewish boy from White Plains, New York, whose invention of Facebook probably made his Jewish mother kvell, until her boy's social network managed to break our electoral process, make our media irrelevant, and turn us into a bunch of argumentative jerks.

Zyklon B
Gas used by the Nazis to kill approximately one million people in concentration camp gas chambers. An unfortunate entry to end this book. Damn you, Hitler!

Zayde: Gene Hackman as Royal Tenenbaum in the 2004 film *The Royal Tenenbaums*, proof that not all zaydes are warm and fuzzy

Acknowledgments

This book, like our podcast, is the product of many brilliant, hardworking, slightly crazy people, to whom we are extremely grateful.

We couldn't have created this book, or our podcast, or really anything, without the unwavering support and ambitious vision of Alana Newhouse, founder and editor in chief of *Tablet*.

Thank you to our *Unorthodox* family: producer Josh Kross and associate producers Sara Fredman-Aeder and Noah Levinson, who have spent way too many hours listening to us, editing us, and helping make our podcast all that it is. We quite literally couldn't do it without you.

Wayne Hoffman, *Tablet*'s executive editor, has been our North Star on this and all *Unorthodox* projects, lending an ear (or a couch) and refereeing the occasional drama. In publisher Morton Landowne, we have a tireless champion and avid listener. And we are indebted to the board of Nextbook, *Tablet*'s parent organization, for their invaluable support.

We are deeply grateful to our colleagues at *Tablet*, all of whom contributed to this book as writers, readers, and sounding boards: Matthew Fishbane, Marjorie Ingall, Armin Rosen, Yair Rosenberg, David Samuels, Gabriel Sanders, Jacob Siegel, and Esther Werdiger. Menachem Butler provided our hechsher, schooling us on biblical facts and making the arcane accessible.

Our team at Artisan, our publishing bashert, brought this book to life and imbued it with the perfect visual sensibility: Lia Ronnen, Michelle Ishay-Cohen, Jane Treuhaft, Zach Greenwald, Bella Lemos, Nancy Murray, and Hanh Le. Paula Brisco and Sara Vigneri crossed our *t*'s and dotted our *oys*.

Jin Auh and Alexandra Christie at the Wylie Agency guided us through the publishing wilderness, and in less than forty years.

Our contributors made this book a rich and idiosyncratic compendium, lending their particular expertise and obsession and helping to capture the vast range of the Jewish experience: Alexander Aciman, Sarah Aroeste, Saul Austerlitz, Gal Beckerman, Ben Cohen, Gabriella Gershenson, Todd Gitlin, Jordan Hoffman, A.J. Jacobs, Rokhl Kafrissen, Leah Koenig, Bethany Mandel, Bat Sheva Marcus, Adam Mendelsohn, Daphne Merkin, Eddy Portnoy, Robert Rockaway, Jody Rosen, Lisa Ann Sandell, Gitl Schaechter-Viswanath, Esther Schor, Rachel Shukert, Harry Siegel, Adam Teeter, Shira Telushkin, Marc Tracy, Melissa Martens Yaverbaum, Molly Yeh, Matthew Zeitlin, and David A. Zuckerman.

We're also thankful to Elazar Abrahams, Jillian Forstadt, Elissa Goldstein, Larry Greenberg, Sara Ivry, Sue Kaufman, Sophia Steinert-Evoy, Julie Subrin, and Shira Telushkin, who have helped shape our podcast in so many ways over the years.

Thank you to Paul Ruest, Noriko Okabe, and Ivan Kuraev, for giving us a home at Argot Studios, and listening to more Jewish jokes than anyone should have to.

And finally, we are forever indebted to our families for allowing us to spend most of our time on this book, and the rest on the podcast.

Contributors

Alexander Aciman is a writer living in New York. His work has appeared in the *Wall Street Journal*, the *New York Times*, the *Paris Review*, and elsewhere.

Sarah Aroeste is a Ladino singer-songwriter and author. She draws upon her Sephardic family roots, from Greece and Macedonia via medieval Spain, to bring Judeo-Spanish culture to a new generation.

Saul Austerlitz is the author of *Sitcom: A History in 24 Episodes from* I Love Lucy *to* Community and *Generation Friends: An Inside Look at the Show That Defined a Television Era.*

Gal Beckerman is an editor at the *New York Times Book Review* and the author of *When They Come for Us, We'll Be Gone: The Epic Struggle to Save Soviet Jewry.*

Ben Cohen is a sports reporter for the *Wall Street Journal.*

Matthew Fishbane is a senior editor at *Tablet.*

Gabriella Gershenson is a food writer and editor based in New York. She writes the Bits and Bites column for the *Wall Street Journal.*

Todd Gitlin is a professor of journalism and sociology and chair of the PhD program in communications at Columbia University, and the author of sixteen books, including *The Sixties: Years of Hope* and *Days of Rage.*

Jordan Hoffman is a writer and film critic living in New York City and a member of the New York Film Critics Circle. His work has been published in the *Guardian*, *Vanity Fair*, the *New York Daily News*, and the *Times of Israel.*

Wayne Hoffman is *Tablet*'s executive editor.

Marjorie Ingall is a *Tablet* columnist and the author of *Mamaleh Knows Best: What Jewish Mothers Do to Raise Successful, Creative, Empathetic, Independent Children.*

A. J. Jacobs is the author of *The Year of Living Biblically: One Man's Humble Quest to Follow the Bible as Literally as Possible* and *It's All Relative: Adventures Up and Down the World's Family Tree.*

Rokhl Kafrissen is a journalist and playwright in New York City whose work focuses on new Yiddish culture, feminism, and contemporary Jewish life. She writes about the world of Yiddish and Ashkenazi life in all its incarnations in her *Tablet* column, Rokhl's Golden City.

Leah Koenig is the author of *Modern Jewish Cooking: Recipes & Customs for Today's Kitchen* and *Little Book of Jewish Appetizers.*

Josh Kross is a producer of *Unorthodox* and several other podcasts, as well as an exhausted father of three.

Morton Landowne is the publisher of *Tablet* and the executive director of Nextbook.

Bethany Mandel is a stay-at-home mother and a writer. She is an editor at Ricochet and a columnist at the *Forward.*

Bat Sheva Marcus was dubbed "the Orthodox Sex Guru" by the *New York Times Magazine*. She is the clinical director of Maze Women's Sexual Health, and has been an active part of the Orthodox feminist scene for too many years for her to admit.

Adam Mendelsohn is director of the Kaplan Centre for Jewish Studies at the University of Cape Town in South Africa. He is the author of the National Jewish Book Award–winning *The Rag Race: How Jews Sewed Their Way to Success in America and the British Empire* and is working on a book about Jewish soldiers during the Civil War.

Daphne Merkin is a cultural critic and novelist. She contributes regularly to the *New York Times Book Review* and the *Wall Street Journal* Arts section. Her latest book is a memoir, *This Close to Happy: A Reckoning with Depression*.

Alana Newhouse is the founder and editor in chief of *Tablet*.

Eddy Portnoy is the academic advisor and exhibitions curator at the YIVO Institute of Jewish Research and author of *Bad Rabbi: And Other Strange but True Stories from the Yiddish Press*.

Robert Rockaway is professor emeritus at Tel Aviv University and the author of *But He Was Good to His Mother: The Lives and Crimes of Jewish Gangsters*.

Armin Rosen is a New York–based reporter at large for *Tablet*.

Jody Rosen is a *Tablet* columnist and contributing writer for the *New York Times Magazine*.

Yair Rosenberg is a senior writer at *Tablet*.

David Samuels is a writer. He lives with his wife and children in New York.

Lisa Ann Sandell is a book editor and author in New York City.

Gabriel Sanders is *Tablet*'s director of business development.

Gitl Schaechter-Viswanath is a Yiddish editor and poet. She coedited, with Paul Glasser, the *Comprehensive English-Yiddish Dictionary*, the first new English-Yiddish dictionary in nearly fifty years.

Esther Schor is a poet and professor of English at Princeton University. Her most recent book is *Bridge of Words: Esperanto and the Dream of a Universal Language*, a cultural history of the language movement and a memoir of her seven years among Esperantists in the United States, Vietnam, Turkey, Cuba, Holland, Brazil, and Uzbekistan.

Rachel Shukert is a writer and producer on the Emmy-nominated Netflix series *GLOW*. She is also the author of four books, including the bestselling memoir *Everything Is Going to Be Great: An Underfunded and Overexposed European Grand Tour*, and is also a contributing editor to *Tablet*.

Harry Siegel is a senior editor at The Daily Beast, a columnist for the *New York Daily News*, and a host of the podcast *FAQ NYC*.

Jacob Siegel is the news editor at *Tablet*.

Adam Teeter is the founder of VinePair.

Shira Telushkin is a writer in New York and a former producer of *Unorthodox*.

Marc Tracy, a *Tablet* staff writer from 2009 to 2012, covers college sports for the *New York Times*.

Esther Werdiger is *Tablet*'s art director.

Melissa Martens Yaverbaum is executive director of the Council of American Jewish Museums and has worked with museums for twenty-five years. Previously, she served as curator at the Museum of Jewish Heritage, the Jewish Museum of Maryland, and the Jane Addams Hull-House Museum, and she continues to curate exhibitions on Jewish history and culture.

Molly Yeh is the author of *Molly on the Range: Recipes and Stories from an Unlikely Life on a Farm* and the host of Food Network's *Girl Meets Farm*.

Matthew Zeitlin is a journalist in Brooklyn. He's written for BuzzFeed and Slate.

David A. Zuckerman, a lifelong New Yorker, has a background in fine arts and graphic design and currently works in IT.

Credits

Are We All Actually Related? (page 19) by A.J. Jacobs and David Zuckerman

Banking and Jews (page 26) by Matthew Zeitlin

Booze and Jews: Perfect Pairings (page 40) by Adam Teeter

Brooklyn (page 49) by Jacob Siegel

Chinese Food and Jews: A Christmas Love Story (page 63) by Josh Kross

Is "Rudolph the Red-Nosed Reindeer" a Jewish Song? (page 64) by Jody Rosen

How to Curse in Jewish (page 69) by Sarah Aroeste (Ladino), Esther Schor (Esperanto)

Delicatessen (page 74) by Leah Koenig

Egypt (page 86) by Armin Rosen

Fast Days (page 94) by Shira Telushkin

Feminism and Jews (page 96) by Marjorie Ingall

Food and Jews (page 100) by Alana Newhouse

Jewish Gangsters (page 106) by Robert Rockaway

The Garment Industry (page 110) by Adam Mendelsohn

Jewish Greetings (page 114) by Shira Telushkin

Hollywood and Jews (page 132) by Jordan Hoffman

Jewish Stars (page 134) by Jordan Hoffman

Holocaust Movies: A Guide (page 137) by Jordan Hoffman

Matriarchs and Patriarchs (page 176) by Shira Telushkin

Pop Music and Jews: An American Love Story (page 182) by Jody Rosen

Politics and Jews (page 200) by Harry Siegel

The Jewish Sixties (page 246) by Todd Gitlin

Sports and Jews (page 251) by Marc Tracy

TV and Jews (page 264) by Saul Austerlitz

Warsaw Ghetto Uprising (page 284) by David Samuels

Yiddish Words for Modern Terms (page 297) by Gitl Schaechter-Viswanath

Yiddish Press (page 298) by Eddy Portnoy

Index

S

T

PHOTO CREDITS **5:** bsd/Shutterstock; **12:** CSU Archives/Everett Collection/Alamy Stock Photo (Abzug, Bella), Stsvirkun/Shutterstock (Adam and Eve); **13:** stockcam/Getty Images (AEPi); **14:** Pictorial Parade/Archive Photos/Getty Images (Aleichem, Sholem), Michael Nitzschke/imageBROKER/Alamy Stock Photo (Al-Aqsa), Allstar Picture Library/Alamy Stock Photo (Alda, Alan), Godong/robertharding/Alamy Stock Photo (aliyah, left), GALI TIBBON/AFP/Getty Images (aliyah, right); **15:** United Archives GmbH/Alamy Stock Photo (Allen, Woody), Everett Collection (Allen, *Bananas*), AF archive/Alamy Stock Photo (Allen, *Manhattan*), Mary Evans/United Artists/Ronald Grant/Everett Collection (Allen, *Annie Hall*), Everett Collection (Allen, *Hannah and Her Sisters*), Image Source/Vetta/Getty Images (alter cockers); **16:** John Gaps III/AP Photo (Ann Landers and Dear Abby); **17:** "New Dread" by Roz Chast, originally published in The New Yorker. Copyright © 2013 by Roz Chast, used by permission of The Wylie Agency LLC (anxiety); **18:** Dionisvera/Shutterstock (apples and honey), Aaron Wood/Shutterstock (Arbeit Macht Frei), Heritage Image Partnership Ltd/Alamy Stock Photo (Arendt, Hannah); **19:** AF archive/Alamy Stock Photo (Groucho Marx), Hi-Story/Alamy Stock Photo (Karl Marx), Keystone Press/Alamy Stock Photo (Zsa Zsa Gabor), World History Archive / Alamy Stock Photo (Lauren Bacall), imageBROKER / Alamy Stock Photo (Shimon Peres), Allstar Picture Library / Alamy Stock Photo (Maggie Gyllenhaal), Pictorial Press Ltd / Alamy Stock Photo (Irving Berlin), Chronicle / Alamy Stock Photo (Sigmund Freud), The Picture Art Collection / Alamy Stock Photo (Baal Shem Tov), GL Archive / Alamy Stock Photo (Baruch Spinoza); **20:** Adam Scull / Alamy Stock Photo (Arthur, Bea), Dorling Kindersley/Getty Images (ass); **21:** Laurent Viteur/FilmMagic/Getty Images (Bar Rafaeli); **22:** akg-images/Alamy Stock Photo (Auschwitz); **24:** Credit Noah Fecks (babka); **25:** Carolyn Jenkins/Alamy Stock Photo (Bamba); **29:** Susan Le, Evi-O.Studio (Ponzi scheme); **30:** Frederic Lewis/Archive Photos/Getty Images (bar mitzvah), Glasshouse Images/Alamy Stock Photo (Bara, Theda), Chris Willson/Alamy Stock Photo (Barbie, left) Beepstock/Alamy Stock Photo (Barbie, right), jtyler/iStock (bark mitzvah); **31:** Trinity Mirror/Mirrorpix/Alamy Stock Photo (Beastie Boys); **32:** Ulf Andersen/Getty Images (Bellow, Saul), Courtesy Penguin Books (Bellow, *Herzog*); **33:** BerniesYearning/Splash/Newscom (Ben & Jerry's), Pictorial Press Ltd/Alamy Stock Photo (Ben-Gurion, David); **34:** Courtesy BENCHERS.COM (bentscher), Pictorial Press Ltd/Alamy Stock Photo (Berlin, Irving); **35:** Historic Collection/Alamy Stock Photo (Berg, Gertrude), Pictorial Press Ltd/Alamy Stock Photo (Bernstein, Leonard), dcphoto/Alamy Stock Photo (Bernstein, *West Side Story*); **36–37:** Sportsphoto / Alamy Stock Photo (*The Big Lebowski*); **38:** Credit Noah Fecks (birthright), Ziv Koren/Polaris/Newscom (Birthright Israel); **39:** Ilya S. Savenok/Getty Images (Blume, Judy); **40–41:** 4X5 Collection / SuperStock (Booze and Jews); **43:** Everett Collection Historical/Alamy Stock Photo (Louis Brandeis); **48:** Collection Christophel/Alamy Stock Photo (Brooks, Mel), Pictorial Press Ltd/Alamy Stock Photo (Brooks, *The Producers*), Everett Collection, Inc./Alamy Stock Photo (Brooks, *History of the World*), Moviestore Collection Ltd/ Alamy Stock Photo (Brooks, *Blazing Saddles*), Everett Collection, Inc./Alamy Stock Photo (Brooks, *Spaceballs*), Album/Alamy Stock Photo (Brooks, *Young Frankenstein*); **50:** Archives du 7e Art/Paramount Pictures/ Photo 12/Alamy Stock Photo (Broflovski, Kyle); **51:** MGM/AF Archive/Alamy Stock Photo (Fanny Brice); **52:** Everett Collection (Bugs Bunny); **54:** Bob Daugherty/AP Photo (Camp David Accords); **55:** Courtesy National Ramah Commission (Camp Ramah), Keystone Press / Alamy Stock Photo (Cantor, Eddie); **56:** Cal Sport Media / Alamy Stock Photo (Omri Casspi); **57:** Eric Bard/Corbis via Getty Images (Catskills); **58:** Peter Horree/ Alamy Stock Photo (Chabad-Lubavitch Mitzvah Tank); **59:** Sueddeutsche Zeitung Photo/Alamy Stock Photo (Chagall, Marc), World History Archive / Alamy Stock Photo (Chagall, *I and the Village*); **60:** Album/Alamy Stock Photo (Charlie Chaplin); **61:** Paramount/Courtesy Everett Collection (*Clueless*); **62:** Danussa/Shutterstock (Jews and Christmas); **63:** Bettman/Getty Images (Chinese Food & Jews); **65:** Jeffrey Mayer/ WireImage/Getty Images (Coen Brothers), Courtesy Everett Collection (Coen, *Barton Fink*), Gramercy Pictures/courtesy Everett Collection (Coen, *The Big Lebowski*), Everett Collection (Coen, *Fargo*), Focus Features/ Courtesy Everett Collection (Coen, *A Serious Man*); **66:** dpa picture alliance archive / Alamy Stock Photo (Cohen, Leonard), Mim Friday / Alamy Stock Photo (comic books); **67:** Tina Fineberg/AP Photo (Congregation Beit Simchat Torah); **68:** Pictorial Press Ltd/Alamy Stock Photo (Copland, Aaron); **72:** Pictorial Press Ltd / Alamy Stock Photo (Davis Jr., Sammy), Album / Alamy Stock Photo (Dayan, Moshe); **74:** pimlena/Shutterstock (sandwich); **75:** Ei Katsumata/Alamy Stock Photo (top), Danita Delimont / Alamy Stock Photo (middle left), Euskera Photography/Alamy Stock Photo (middle right), Rachel Lewis/Getty Images (bottom); **76:** Keystone Press/Alamy Stock Photo (*Der Stürmer*), Pictorial Press Ltd/Alamy Stock Photo (Neil Diamond); **77:** Terry Disney/Express/Getty Images (Department store); **78:** Cosmo Condina Middle East/Alamy Stock Photo (Dome of the Rock), WENN Rights Ltd / Alamy Stock Photo (Drake); **79:** Pictorial Press Ltd / Alamy Stock Photo (*Dirty Dancing*); **80:** Album/Alamy Stock Photo (Fran Drescher); **81:** Pictorial Press Ltd / Alamy Stock Photo (Dylan, Bob), Kirn Vintage Stock/Corbis via Getty Images (dry goods); **84:** Archive PL / Alamy Stock Photo (Eban, Abba), Everett Collection Inc / Alamy Stock Photo (Eichmann, Adolf); **85:** PictureLux / The Hollywood Archive / Alamy Stock Photo (Einstein, Albert); **87:** Timothy Greenfield-Sanders/Corbis via Getty Images (Emanuel brothers), Munawar Hosain/Fotos International/Getty Images (Ephron, Nora), Paramount/courtesy Everett Collection (Ephron, *Heartburn*),TriStar Pictures/courtesy Everett Collection (Ephron, *Sleepless in Seattle*), Mary Evans/Ronald Grant/Everett Collection (Ephron, *When Harry Met Sally*), Album / Alamy Stock Photo (Ephron, *You've Got Mail*); **88:** David Rubinger/CORBIS/Corbis via Getty Images (Entebbe); **90:** Allstar Picture Library / Alamy Stock Photo (*Exodus*); **92:** WENN Rights Ltd / Alamy Stock Photo (Tovah Feldshuh); **93:** Mary Evans/MIRISCH CORPORATION/CARTIER PRODUCTIONS/Ronald Grant/Everett Collection (*Fiddler on the Roof*); **97:** Everett Collection Inc / Alamy Stock Photo (Steinem, top), Michael Abramson/The LIFE Images Collection/Getty Images (Brownmiller, middle), Stephen Parker / Alamy Stock Photo (Dworkin, bottom); **98:** WENN Rights Ltd / Alamy Stock Photo (Carrie Fisher), Hi-Story / Alamy Stock Photo (Freud, Sigmund); **99:** Q-Images / Alamy Stock Photo (Florida); **100–101:** Credit Noah Fecks; **102:** Stacy Walsh Rosenstock / Alamy Stock Photo (Friedan, Betty); **104:** ZUMA Press, Inc. / Alamy Stock Photo (Gal Gadot), Trinity Mirror / Mirrorpix / Alamy Stock Photo (Garfunkel, Art), Robert Clare / Alamy Stock Photo (gelt); **105:** Lebrecht Music & Arts / Alamy Stock Photo (Gershwin, George); **106:** Science History Images / Alamy Stock Photo (Benjamin Siegel); **107:** New York Daily News Archive via Getty Images (top), New York Daily News Archive via Getty Images (bottom); **108:** CTK / Alamy Stock Photo (Ginsberg, Allen), TCD/Prod.DB / Alamy Stock Photo (Ginsburg, Ruth Bader); **109:** Archive PL / Alamy Stock Photo (Goldberg, Rube), Phillip Faraone/Getty Images (Goldblum, Jeff); **113:** Ewing Galloway / Alamy Stock Photo (goyish); **119:** Los Angeles Examiner/USC Libraries/Corbis via Getty Images (Hadassah); **120–121:** IPPA/Camera Press/Redux (Haganah); **123:** tomertu/Shutterstock (hamantaschen), Wolkenengel565/Shutterstock (hanukkiah, left), Zee/Alamy Photos (hanukkiah, right); **125:** emyerson/iStock (Havdalah), akg-images/Newscom (Hebrew calendar), Ed Endicott/Alamy Stock Photo (Hebrew National); **127:** Historic Collection/Alamy Stock Photo (Herzl, Theodor); **129:** Bettmann/Getty Images (Abraham Joshua Heschel); **130:** Michael Tighe/Donaldson Collection/Getty Images (Al Hirschfeld); **131:** John Shearer/The LIFE Picture Collection/Getty Images (Hoffman, Abbie), SPUTNIK/ Alamy Stock Photo (hora); **136:** IanDagnall Computing/Alamy Stock Photo (Harry Houdini); **138:** PaulVImages/Getty Images (Hydrox); **140:** Vladimir Pesyna/Sputnik/AP Images (IDF); **144:** The Advertising Archives/ Alamy Stock Photo (Al Jaffee); **145:** ReligiousStock/Alamy Stock Photo (Jesus Christ); **147:** Pictorial Press Ltd / Alamy Stock Photo (Jewfro, top left), ZUMA Press, Inc. / Alamy Stock Photo (Jewfro, top right), Trinity Mirror / Mirrorpix / Alamy Stock Photo (Jewfro, bottom left), ZUMA Press, Inc. / Alamy Stock Photo (Jewfro, bottom right), The Jewish Publication Society (*The Jewish Catalog*); **148:** Lebrecht Music & Arts / Alamy Stock Photo (Billy Joel); **149:** Dan MacMedan/Getty Images (Johansson, Scarlett), Richard Ellis/Getty Images (Jonah); **152:** Pictorial Press Ltd / Alamy Stock Photo (Kafka, Franz); **153:** Jason Mendez/Everett Collection/Alamy Live News (Karan, Donna), Steven May / Alamy Stock Photo (Karski, Jan); **154:** WENN Rights Ltd / Alamy Stock Photo (King, Carole), AF Archive/Alamy Stock Photo (Kindertransport); **155:** George Pickow/Three Lions/Hulton Archive/Getty Images (kibbutz); **156:** Hartmut Pöstges/imageBROKER/Alamy Stock Photo (kippah); **157:** Helmut Meyer zur Capellen/imageBROKER/Alamy Stock Photo (kohanim), Historic Collection/Alamy Stock Photo (Abraham Isaac Kook); **158:** Archive PL/Alamy Stock Photo (Sandy Koufax); **159:** Everett Collection (Krusty the Clown); **162:** Creativ Studio Heinemann, Red Chopsticks Images/Getty Images (latkes); **163**: cineclassico/Alamy Stock Photo (Hedy Lamarr); **164:** Globe Photos/ZUMA Press, Inc./Alamy Stock Photo (Lee, Stan); **165:** Courtesy Touchstone (Levi, Primo), Stephane Cardinale - Corbis/Getty Images (Lévy, Bernard-Henri), Robert Clay / Alamy Stock Photo (LGBT Jews, top), Album / Alamy Stock Photo (LGBT Jews, middle), Beth Dubber/© Amazon Studios/Courtesy: Everett Collection (LGBT Jews, bottom); **166–167:** Allan Tannenbaum/Getty Images (Lower East Side); **168:** iStock (lulav); **170:** GALI TIBBON/AFP/Getty Images (Maccabiah Games), Zev Radovan/BibleLandPictures/Alamy Stock Photo (Maimonides); **171:** Francis Specker/Alamy Stock Photo (Malina, Joshua), MediaPunch Inc/Alamy Stock Photo (Manilow, Barry), Keith Homan/Shutterstock (Manischewitz); **172:** Photo 12/Alamy Stock Photo (Marx Brothers), Pictorial Press Ltd/Alamy Stock Photo (Marx, *Animal* Crackers), Moviestore collection Ltd/Alamy Stock Photo (Marx, *A Night at the Opera*), Pictorial Press Ltd/Alamy Stock Photo (Marx, *Duck* Soup), Everett Collection, Inc. / Alamy Stock Photo (Marx, *A Day at the Races*), AF archive/Alamy Stock Photo (*Marjorie Morningstar*); **173:** Sarah Shatz/©Amazon/Courtesy: Everett Collection (*The Marvelous Mrs. Maisel*), PhotoStock-Israel/Getty Images (Masada); **174:** Francis Specker / Alamy Stock Photo (Matisyahu), Brent Hofacker / Alamy Stock Photo (matzo), Photo 12 / Alamy Stock Photo (May, Elaine); **175:** sjbooks / Alamy Stock Photo (*Maus*); **177:** Michele LAURENT/Gamma-Rapho via Getty Images (Meir, Golda), Wolkenengel565/Shutterstock (menorah, left), Zee/Alamy Stock Photo (menorah, right); **178:** Ronald Grant Archive / Alamy Stock Photo (Miller, Arthur), Playbill, Inc. (Miller, *All My Sons*) Mary Evans/Ronald Grant/Everett Collection (Miller, *The Crucible*), Playbill, Inc. (Miller, *Death of a Salesman*), Playbill, Inc. (Miller, *A View from the Bridge*), Terryfic3D/Getty Images (mezuzah); **179:** Keystone Press/Alamy Stock Photo (Midler, Bette), iStock (milchig); **180:** PhotoQuest/Getty Images (Miami Beach); **181:** Elena Elisseeva/Shutterstock (Montreal bagel); **184:** Alfred Eisenstaedt/The LIFE Premium Collection/Getty Images (Bess Myerson); **186:** Godong/Alamy Stock Photo (Ner Tamid); **187:** chris brignell/Alamy Stock Photo (New York bagel); **188:** Joe Vogan/Alamy Stock Photo (Noah's Ark); **190:** age fotostock/Alamy Stock Photo (olive), Gary Hershorn/Reuters (Oslo Accords); **191:** PATRICK BAZ/AFP/Getty Images (Operation Solomon); **192:** ©Basso Cannarsa/Agence Opale/Alamy Stock Photo (Ozick, Cynthia); **194:** Basso Cannarsa/Opale/Alamy Stock Photo (Paley, Grace), Photo by J. Merritt/Getty Images for Sun Valley Film Festival (Paltrow, Gwyneth); **196:** Moviestore collection Ltd / Alamy Stock Photo (Mandy Patinkin); **198:** Paramount Pictures/Courtesy of Getty Images (Picon, Molly), Fred W. McDarrah/Getty Images (pickles), Manny Carabel/Getty Images (Portman, Natalie); **202:** Cultura RM / Alamy Stock Photo (prep); **203:** Mr. Rashad/Shutterstock (Purim hamantaschen); **204–205:** Michael Ochs Archives/Getty Images (*The Producers*); **210:** ©Warner Brothers/courtesy Everett Collection (Radner, Gilda), PCN Photography/Alamy Stock Photo (Raisman, Aly); **211:** Todd Maisel/NY Daily News Archive via Getty Images (Archie Rand), Gijsbert Hanekroot/Redferns/Getty Images (Reed, Lou); **214:** Everett Collection (Reiner, Carl); **215:** CBS Photo Archive/Getty Images (Rivers, Joan), Richard Lautens/Toronto Star via Getty Images (Rich, Adrienne); **216:** Alan Chin/The New York Times/Redux (Roiphe, Anne), Julian Hibbard/Getty Images (Roth, Philip); **221:** The Advertising Archives/Alamy Stock Photo (rye bread); **222:** Credit Jason Polan (Russ & Daughters); **224:** ITAR-TASS News Agency/Alamy Stock Photo (Jonas Salk); **226:** The Advertising Archives/Alamy Stock Photo (Vidal Sassoon); **228:** Columbia TriStar Television/ Courtesy Everett Collection (*Seinfeld*); **229:** Mike McGregor/Contour by Getty Images (Sendak, Maurice); **230–231:** Ted Spiegel/CORBIS/Getty Images (Seder); **232:** John Springer Collection/CORBIS/Corbis via Getty Images (Shabbos goy); **233:** Keystone Press / Alamy Stock Photo (Nathan Sharansky); **235:** Photo by Ron Ilan/GPO via Getty Images (Sharon, Ariel); **237:** Iakov Filimonov/Shutterstock (sheitel), CBS/Getty Images (Sherman, Allan); **238**: ungvar/Shutterstock (shofar); **239:** ©Sony Pictures Classics/courtesy Everett Collection (Shylock); **240:** New York Daily News Archive via Getty Images (Shonde, Daily News); **241:** Evelyn Hockstein/For The Washington Post via Getty Images (Big Shonde, Barry Freundel); **242:** Jared Milgrim/The Photo Access/Alamy Stock Photo (Sarah Silverman), Michael Brito/Alamy Stock Photo (Paul Simon); **244:** Heritage Image Partnership Ltd/Alamy Stock Photo (Singer, Isaac Bashevis), Lisa O'Connor/ZUMA Press, Inc./Alamy Stock Photo (Smirnoff, Yakov); **245:** Jean-Regis Rouston/Roger Viollet/Getty Images (Susan Sontag); **248:** Barbara Alper/Getty Images (Soviet Jewry movement), Harry Langdon/Getty Images (Spelling, Aaron); **249:** Sportsphoto / Alamy Stock Photo (Spielberg, Steven), Pictorial Press Ltd / Alamy Stock Photo (Spielberg, *Jaws*), Pictorial Press Ltd / Alamy Stock Photo (Spielberg, *E.T.*), Photo 12 / Alamy Stock Photo (Spielberg, *Close Encounters*), Everett Collection, Inc. / Alamy Stock Photo (Spielberg, *Schindler's List*), PictureLux / The Hollywood Archive / Alamy Stock Photo (Spielberg, *Raiders of the Lost Ark*), Photo 12 / Alamy Stock Photo (Spielberg, *Saving Private Ryan*); **250:** CBS via Getty Images (Spock); **254:** GAB Archive/Redferns/Getty Images (Streisand, Barbra), PictureLux / The Hollywood Archive / Alamy Stock Photo (Streisand, *Funny Girl*), PictureLux / The Hollywood Archive / Alamy Stock Photo (Streisand, *A Star is Born*), Allstar Picture Library / Alamy Stock Photo (Streisand, *The Way We Were*), PictureLux / The Hollywood Archive / Alamy Stock Photo (Streisand, *Yentl*); **256:** Pictorial Press Ltd/Alamy Stock Photo (Strauss, Levi); **258–259:** Jerry Engel/New York Post Archives /(c) NYP Holdings, Inc. via Getty Images (Sukkot); **260:** PhotoStock-Israel / Alamy Stock Photo (superstition, top), ismail atalar / Alamy Stock Photo (superstition, bottom), Thomas J. Peterson / Alamy Stock Photo (Sweet'N Low); **262:** FALKENSTEINFOTO/Alamy Stock Photo (Talmud, Talmudic), illustratioz/Shutterstock (tallit); **263:** ScreenProd/ Photononstop/Alamy Stock Photo (Elizabeth Taylor), David Cohen 156/Shutterstock (tefillin); **264:** PitukTV/Shutterstock (T.V. and Jews); **268:** dpa picture alliance/Alamy Stock Photo (Thanksgivukkah); **269:** Ste studio/Shutterstock (Blood), Bahruz Rzayev/Shutterstock (Frogs), Dn Br/Shutterstock (Lice), Shuttertock (Wild Animals), Hein Nouwens/Shutterstock (Pestilence), ekler/Shutterstock (Hail), artsterdam design studio/Shutterstock (locusts), ekler/Shutterstock (Darkness), Martial Red/Shutterstock (Killing); **270:** Credit Noah Fecks (Tofutti); **271:** Science History Images / Alamy Stock Photo (Triangle Shirtwaist Factory); **272:** Pictorial Press Ltd / Alamy Stock Photo (Tucker, Sophie); **273:** Reinekke/Shutterstock (Tu B'Shevat tree); **276:** bsd/Shutterstock (*Unorthodox*); **277:** Teodoro Ortiz Tarrascusa / Alamy Stock Photo (Ungapatcha); **278:** Everett Collection Inc / Alamy Stock Photo (Uris, Leon), TCD/Prod.DB / Alamy Stock Photo (Uris, *Exodus*); **280:** Roy Rochlin/Getty Images (Diane von Fürstenberg); **282:** PictureLux / The Hollywood Archive / Alamy Stock Photo (Walters, Barbara); **283:** Rosie Whelan, Evi-O.Studio (Wedding art); **285:** Heritage Image Partnership Ltd / Alamy Stock Photo (Warsaw Ghetto Uprising, top), Photo 12 / Alamy Stock Photo (Warsaw Ghetto Uprising, bottom); **286:** AHMAD GHARABLI/AFP/Getty Images (Western Wall); **287:** Francois LOCHON/Gamma-Rapho via Getty Images (Wiesenthal, Simon), Kevin Mazur/WireImage (Winehouse, Amy); **288–289:** Andrei Minsk/Shutterstock (map); **295:** Ronald Grant Archive/Alamy Stock Photo (*Yentl*); **296:** Pictorial Press Ltd/Alamy Stock Photo (Yezierska, Anzia); **302:** AF Archive/Alamy Stock Photo (Charlotte York); **304:** umarazak/Shutterstock (Zuckerberg, Mark); **305:** Touchstone Pictures/Photo 12/Alamy Stock Photo (zayde)

Stephanie Butnick, Liel Leibovitz, and Mark Oppenheimer are the hosts of *Unorthodox*, the most popular Jewish podcast on iTunes with more than 4 million downloads.

STEPHANIE BUTNICK
is the deputy editor of *Tablet* and has written for the *Wall Street Journal*. She lives in New York City with her husband and their cat, Cat Stevens.

LIEL LEIBOVITZ
is a senior writer for *Tablet* and the author of several books, including *A Broken Hallelujah*, a spiritual biography of Leonard Cohen. He lives in New York City with his wife and their two children.

MARK OPPENHEIMER
is the former Beliefs columnist for the *New York Times* and author of *The Bar Mitzvah Crasher: Road-tripping Through Jewish America*. He lives with his family in New Haven, Connecticut.